ıch a

ı words

oman, her

letteı wonder y revealing. Had
ıtingale ıt been a reıormer she might
e been a writer; with a sure style and acer-
ıc wit, she fully exploits her ability to turn
memorable phrase. One gets here a vivid
sense of the urgencies and strains in the
Crimea as Florence Nightingale played the
role of "savior of the British soldier"; her
relentless campaign to improve housing,
food, and sanitation for the armed forces
throughout the empire, especially in India;
and the tenacity with which she worked for
hospital reforms and professional nursing.
Her letters bring to light conflicting views on
women: on the one hand she strove to expand
employment opportunities for women; on the
other, she had little respect for the female
intellect and women's ability to undertake
public responsibility. One sees also her own
personal relations and conflicts, including a
painful relationship with her mother and sister. Through it all there emerges a woman of
great brilliance and contradiction—stubborn
and inspiring, witty and impatient, dedicated
and meddling. Hers is a compelling life story.

Ever Yours,
Florence Nightingale

Ever Yours, Florence Nightingale

Selected Letters

Edited by
Martha Vicinus & Bea Nergaard

Harvard University Press
Cambridge, Massachusetts
1990

Copyright © 1989 by Martha Vicinus and Bea Nergaard
All rights reserved
Printed in the United States of America
10 9 8 7 6 5 4 3 2 1

This book is printed on acid-free paper, and its binding materials
have been chosen for strength and durability.

Library of Congress Cataloging in Publication Data

Nightingale, Florence, 1820–1910.
Ever yours, Florence Nightingale: selected letters / edited by
Martha Vicinus & Bea Nergaard.
p.   cm.
Includes bibliographical references (p.   ).
ISBN 0-674-27020-7
1. Nightingale, Florence, 1820–1910—Correspondence. 2. Nurses-
England—Correspondence.   I. Vicinus, Martha.   II. Nergaard, Bea.
III. Title
RT37.N5A4   1990
610.73′092—dc20
[B] 89-28443
CIP

To our sisters:
Patricia Coté, Registered nurse and teacher
Carolyn Miller, Science librarian
Bernice Nyhus, Registered nurse

Acknowledgements

Copyright of the Florence Nightingale letters is owned by the surviving trustees of the Henry Bonham Carter Will Trust. We wish to thank Radcliffes & Co., administrators on behalf of the trust, for permission to publish this selection of her letters. Permission to publish those letters held by the Greater London Record Office (GLRO) has been granted by the Chief Nursing Officer, St Thomas' Hospital. Our thanks to the Director of Special Collections, Boston University Library (BUL) and the librarian of the Woodward Biomedical Library, University of British Columbia (Woodward), for permission to publish letters in their nursing archives. We are grateful to the Earl of Harewood for permission to publish five Nightingale letters to Lady Canning; these are part of the Lord Canning Papers held by the West Yorkshire Archive Service/Leeds District Archives (LDA). The Wellcome Institute for the History of Medicine holds a collection of photocopied letters by Nightingale, donated by Sue Goldie. Sir Ralph Verney, Bt, who owns the originals of these letters, has given permission to publish transcriptions made from the photocopies.

In selecting, transcribing and checking these letters we were greatly aided by the patience and knowledge of librarians. The librarians in the Students' Room of the British Library were unfailingly helpful. Both for this project and past work we have relied upon the expertise of Mrs Bridget Howlett of the Greater London Record Office, Margaret R. Goostray of the Boston University Library Special Collections and R. J. Palmer of the Wellcome Institute for the History of Medicine. The prompt and accurate assistance of the Leeds District Archives, under W. J. Connor, District Archivist, saved us both time and effort.

The engraving of Florence Nightingale (1856) is reproduced by permission of the Director of Special Collections, Boston University Library. The map of the Crimea and the Black Sea is reproduced with the kind permission of Elspeth Huxley and George Weidenfeld and Nicolson, Ltd from Elspeth Huxley, *Florence Nightingale* (1975), p. 98. The photograph of W. E. Nightingale and his daughter Parthenope is courtesy of John M. Virgoe. The illustration of a ward, Barrack Hospital, Scutari, the illustration of Mrs Wardroper and her nurses, of Sir John McNeill, of Parthenope, Florence and Sir Harry Verney, and the example of her handwriting are all courtesy of the St Thomas' Archives. The picture of Sidney Herbert, Lord Herbert of Lea, and the photograph of Sir Robert Rawlinson and Dr John Sutherland are courtesy of the National Portrait Gallery, London. The illustration of the military barracks in India, drawn by Hilary Bonham Carter, is courtesy of the British Library.

Friends and fellow scholars have provided support, references and readings. Warren Olin-Ammentorp transcribed letters from microfilm with great accuracy; Kathy Hodgkins was an ever-useful assistant in London. Peg Lourie read portions of an early version of the manuscript; her helpful editorial and stylistic suggestions were most welcome. Sue Goldie [Moriarty] and Gail Malmgreen read the final manuscript with a keen eye for contradictions, possible errors and a lack of clarity; their suggestions have been invaluable. Anne Summers lent us her unpublished doctoral dissertation, and made numerous suggestions in regard to primary and secondary sources. Her knowledge of military nursing was an inspiration to us. Tijtske Akkerman, Ann Casperson, Cathy Hutchinson, the late Janet James, Marsha Richmond, Charles Rosenberg, Agnes Sommer, Domna Stanton and Randolph Vigne generously gave of their expertise and time. Barbara Caine, Leonore Davidoff, Anna Davin, Midge Mackenzie, Barbara Sicherman, and Thea Thompson listened and encouraged. Jonathan Hill deserves a special mention for his unfailing enthusiasm. He tracked down books for us, offered suggestions about military policy, discussed Victorian foreign affairs, and when we were most discouraged about the enormity of our project, he offered us good food and warm friendship.

Martha Vicinus thanks the University of Michigan for a Rackham Fellowship for an initial summer of research in London (1983) and a Rackham grant-in-aid of research to purchase microfilms and photocopies (1984). Two other timely grants from the University of Michigan College of Literature, Science and the Arts (1984) for typing and from the Office of the Vice-President for Research (1987) for a research assistant in London expedited our work. She is especially grateful for the support of John Knott, chair of the Department of English, University of Michigan (1982–87).

Contents

List of Illustrations

(following page 112)

Abbreviations

C.B.   Companion of the Bath
C. in C.   Commander-in-Chief
Commg.   Commanding
Commn.   Commission
De., Dep'y., D'y.   Deputy
Gds.   Guards
G. G.   Governor-General of India
H. of C., Ho. of C.   House of Commons
H. M., H. M'y.   Her Majesty
Hosp., Hosp'l.   Hospital
I.O.   India Office
Inf'y   Infirmary
Insp'r   Inspector
K. C. B.   Knight Commander of Bath
Ld.   Lord
Lt.   Lieutenant
L. T. C.   Land Transport Corps
Mem'a, Mem'm   Memoranda, memorandum
M. O.   Medical Office
Obed't   Obedient
N. A. Soc'y   National Society for Aid to the Sick and
                            Wounded
N.F.   Nightingale Fund
Parl., Parl't.   Parliament
P. M. O.   Principal Medical Officer
P. O.   Post Office
Pr., Prs., Pss.   Princess
Purv'r   Purveyor
R. C.   Roman Catholic
R.   Royal
Sec'y   Secretary
S. S.   Staff Surgeon or Secretary of State
S. of S.   Secretary of State
Sup't   Superintendent
W. O.   War Office

Abbreviations of Manuscript Sources

All references to secondary works cited are given in the Bibliography.

BL Add: British Library Additional manuscript number
BUL: Boston University Library
GLRO: Greater London Record Office manuscript number
LDA: Leeds District Archives
Mitchell: Mitchell Library of New South Wales, Australia
Wellcome: Collection of photocopied letters at the Wellcome Institute for the History of Medicine (the Sir Ralph Verney, Claydon, collection, unless otherwise indicated).

Woodward: Woodward Biomedical Library, University of British Columbia.

Ever Yours,
Florence Nightingale

Introduction

I have taken effectual means that all my papers shall be destroyed after my death. (25 June 1864 BL Add 45798: f243)

'Destroy', 'Return', 'Burn', or 'Most Private – Burn', underlined several times, were often scrawled across the upper left-hand corner of Florence Nightingale's letters. They were not destroyed in the end. Instead she left her papers, including around 10,000 letters, manuscripts of many of her major works, and drafts of others, to the discretion of her executor. The collection forms one of the largest manuscript collections at the British Library. An additional 3,000 to 4,000 letters are held in private hands and other libraries. Nightingale appreciated Sir George Lewis's quip, 'The indiscretion of biographers gives an added terror to death' (Woodham-Smith, pp. 388–89), but she took great pains to leave her biographers a veritable mountain of evidence.

Nightingale's renown, combined with her numerous letters, as well as the memorabilia, diaries and autobiographies of those she knew, ensures that we can see her only through the lens of conflicting opinions. Nightingale's own letters reveal more sides of her than she might have cared to admit; her very inconsistencies ensure different interpretations of her and her actions. Anyone with the temerity to prepare a one-volume edition of her letters and private notes must perforce present only a brief sketch of this complex, contradictory and brilliant woman. Although we have included letters representative of the full range of Nightingale's interests, our selection emphasizes the relationship between Nightingale's private conflicts and her enormously varied public responsibilities. Her personal notes form only a small percentage of the total collection of letters; we have published a large number in order to show the more intimate side of this very public figure. We have also emphasized her ongoing family conflicts, tracing her always difficult and often painful relationships with her mother and sister. Finally, Nightingale's attitude towards the feminist movement was at best lukewarm, but her vigorous and often angry letters reflect her struggling with possible new roles for women. We have included a cross-section of letters which discuss the role of women in society and the workplace, as well as numerous letters to men, discussing and defining their responsibilities.

Our selection is a part of the continuing reconsideration of Florence Nightingale (1820–1910) as a person who influenced not only her own age, but also subsequent generations. She is best remembered as the saviour of the common soldier in the Crimea and the founder of modern nursing. But her work in the Crimean War hospitals (1854–56) was only the preliminary stage to her major achievement; working unofficially behind the scenes, Nightingale spurred army sanitary reform. Improved housing, food and sanitation for the British soldier throughout the Empire, but most especially in India – where her interest in sanitation extended to the civilian population – was her life's work. Nursing assumed priority only after 1872, when her work with government officials had come to an end; by then many of her ideas about health and hospitals were outmoded, although her influence remained enormous. For example, she never accepted the germ theory of disease, but 'the system of accounting which she devised for the Army Medical Services in 1860–61 was commended by the Select Committee of Estimates in 1947, who learned, to their astonishment, how long ago it had been introduced and by whom' (Pickering, p. 144). The nursing reforms for which Nightingale has been remembered have been labelled 'female' and appropriate for a Victorian woman, while her major contribution as a sanitarian and unofficial government adviser, work in the 'male' sphere, has been denigrated or forgotten.

Throughout her life Nightingale struggled against the constraints placed upon women, but she also extolled the virtues of hard work, female modesty and anonymous service. Although she recognized her exceptional privileges, she had no sympathy for women who were less dedicated. She looked to a few close women friends for emotional support, and to men for active assistance. She trusted only those who were unquestioningly loyal. As with all great historical figures, time and circumstance conspired to provide her with the opportunities and challenges which she sought and never failed to accept. Nightingale became the heroine of the Crimea at least partially because an angry public, roused by the failure of the military to provide adequate medical supplies, hospital personnel and minimal comfort, needed one. Her work there, however controversial, assured her a place in history, but for a woman of action this was only the beginning. Her decision to concentrate on the difficult task of working with politicians, bureaucrats and army officials to reform the most hidebound and traditional of all male institutions may be hard to understand. Nursing, for all its problems, was certainly an easier field; the general public recognized the need for hospital reform, and existing nurses were unorganized and powerless. But Nightingale's emotional commitments lay with the army, to whom she remained a loyal taskmaster from her Crimean days until her death. The roots of this passion were embedded in the psyche of the individual; a brief survey of her life may reveal some of the complexities of this reformer.

Before Nightingale went to the Crimea, her life was typical of an unmarried upper-class lady. She visited her many relatives, travelled abroad for extended periods, and was expected to be at the call of her parents. But unlike her sister and cousins, Nightingale was not content. As often as she could, she would sneak away to visit hospitals and to work in village schools; she spent long hours studying government documents and statistics; she wrote letters to confidantes about God's purposes, particularly for her. The young Florence came to be known in the cultured upper-class milieu of early-Victorian England as a remarkable woman of unusual if undefined talent.

Few friends were aware of the inner turmoil between the pleasure of shining intellectually in social circles and the desire to do something practical that would fulfil a deeper need. She did not have a crisis of faith as did so many of her contemporaries, but she was never an easy believer. Although she was attracted to the Roman Catholic religious orders as an outlet for her ambitions, she always distrusted dogma. Throughout her life Nightingale remained a critical member of the Church of England, continually seeking to adapt its tenets to her emotional and religious needs. She debated endlessly with herself and others how best to combine public duty, family obligations and God's will. She never swerved from the theme that work was an intrinsic aspect of God's design. 'It is not knowing doctrine but bearing fruit that He desires for us', she declared (17 Apr 1889 BL Add 47746: f 10). In the end, Nightingale concluded that God's will and public duty were one, and could take priority over family demands.

As we know from her private notes and letters, Nightingale was locked in a love-hate relationship with her mother and sister, Parthenope. Convinced that they did not understand her, in her teens and twenties she formed intense friendships with women who sympathized with her plight. Unfortunately the letters to her favourite cousin, Marianne Nicholson Galton, appear to have been destroyed. All her life Nightingale depended upon the loyalty and sympathy of a few close friends. Until the age of thirty-two she seemed unable to break away from her mother and sister without their blessing, yet she abhorred life with them. Finally the rounds of quarrelling and illness, real or imagined, forced Florence's father to concede freedom. In 1852 William Nightingale gave his daughter an income of £500 per annum, and permission to work at a small hospital for sick ladies. Except for her brief training of about three months at Kaiserswerth in Germany, this was Nightingale's only direct nursing experience. In less than two years she was called to the Crimea, where she became an administrator not only of the nurses, but also unofficially of army purveying and the hospital orderlies. Her time there, as chapter 2 documents, was highly controversial, and she never gained complete control of all the nurses sent to care for the sick and wounded. But she became a national heroine, and was able to use her fame to further sanitary reform for the next forty years.

After Nightingale returned from the Crimea, she was very ill and thought death was imminent. From the time of her arrival at the military hospitals in October 1854 until her departure in July 1856, she had driven herself as one possessed. That enormous effort ought to have earned her a rest, but she was haunted by the spectres of those who had died from preventable diseases rather than from war wounds. Yet her official work for the War Office had ended. At home the painful, claustrophobic life of past years with her mother and Parthe threatened to swamp her again. They enjoyed helping her with such tasks as answering her innumerable letters, but their unsystematic ways and cloying sympathy only maddened someone obsessed with saving future generations of soldiers.

Nightingale took to her bed, isolated except for her Aunt Mai. She was an invalid for the rest of her life, admitting people – including her family – only by appointment, one at a time. The doctors urged rest, but she worked in a frenzy for five years as the key, though unofficial, member of two royal commissions to investigate the sanitary conditions of the army at home and in India. At the same time she was being consulted on the Poor Law, legislation on the contagious (venereal) diseases, hospital architecture, workhouse and voluntary hospital nursing, and the use of statistics. On the side she finished a treatise on modern religious belief. As George Pickering notes, Nightingale was psychoneurotic, using her illness to shield herself from family, friends and strangers so that she could focus solely on her work (Pickering, p. 10).

Nightingale's passion for sanitary reform coincided with wide-ranging medical, scientific and engineering advances. At a time when formal training was becoming essential, she relied upon her Crimea experience and information gained from her omnivorous reading and hospital touring. Like many self-educated reformers, Nightingale was often reluctant to change her mind in the face of new evidence. But she made a particular effort to consult the foremost figures in the various relevant fields – sanitation, engineering, architecture, Poor Law and contagious diseases legislation. She

4

made many mistakes, the most obvious of which was to rely exclusively upon cleanliness and fresh air as a cure for contagious diseases (see Rosenberg). Her contribution was not to the theory of sanitation but to its implementation, for she was an inspiring and stubborn leader. Where others stopped, daunted by what needed doing, she acted as a catalyst, bringing reformers together, learning from the experts, teaching the unconvinced and urging the reluctant. Those who laboured the hardest for her, often with little reward, remained loyal workers, committed to the larger cause that she led. She summarized her own role well in the comment, 'I believe it the rarest, tho' by no means the highest talent, to be able to gather all the threads of a *new* subject and put the knot on' (Sunday 14 {14? July 1864} Wellcome).

The public honoured the heroine of the Crimea by donating £45,000 to be used as she wished. After some delays, in 1861 a portion of the fund was used to underwrite the Nightingale School of Nursing at St Thomas' Hospital, the first training school without specific religious affiliation. Funds were also used to launch a short-lived experiment in midwifery training at King's College Hospital and to help underwrite the training and staffing of work-house hospitals and district nursing. All Nightingale's nursing work was done from her bed through letters and interviews with the secretary of the Nightingale Fund, fellow reformers, and the matrons and nurses of St Thomas' and other hospitals. Her lack of medical training and absence from the increasingly sophisticated world of hospital medicine meant that her views became progressively obsolete. Nevertheless, she still retained her influence over many nursing leaders and protégées. As friends from her political world died or retired, they were replaced by these nurses and matrons; their loyalty was psychologically important to the lonely and aging reformer.

As an invalid Nightingale was freed from the stresses of the working world to which her collaborators were subject. This self-enforced isolation not only narrowed her views over the years, but also aggravated her propensity to exaggerate, to criticize others' weaknesses, and to adopt a self-dramatizing pose. In a letter to a friend about her work problems, she wrote, 'Did it ever strike you how, if Christ had had to work *through* Pilate, how would he have done?' (25 June 1864 BL Add 45798: ff 245–46). A lack of generosity often characterized her assessment of others, although a few favourites could do no wrong. To her friend Mary Clarke Mohl she claimed, 'My people never made any sacrifice for me at all' (Lesser, p. 183). 'Clarkey', however, astutely observed to Florence's cousin Hilary, 'Flo's . . . imagination is so great a part of her life that if a crack is come to some of the images she has stored up there, all of fine china, she sees the crack for ever and can't look at anything else' (Lesser, p. 169).

Brilliant, impatient, confident, angry, obsessed, lonely, self-righteous and always searching, Nightingale's personality leaps off the pages of her letters, personal notes, jottings, drafts of letters and corrections of drafts. The child who wrote to her mother primly measuring her acts of kindness and naughtiness became the dutiful daughter who wrote long epistles to her family, elegantly describing the sights of Rome, Egypt and Greece. The young woman who discussed religious questions and philosophy with her father continued her quest for truth in her exchanges with Benjamin Jowett, the Oxford don. Cousin Hilary and Aunt Hannah Nicholson became sympathetic confidantes to the troubled young woman seaching for meaning in her life. Personal notes throughout her life traced her angry and troubled efforts to reconcile her needs with those of her mother and sister. The novice reformer penned page after page to the patient Sidney Herbert, Secretary at War, about how best to rationalize the army's purveying system, to improve conditions for soldiers and to ensure the future of women nurses in the military.

So important were letters to her that when she was ill in the Crimea, she insisted that pen and paper be given to her. Her incoherent jottings testify to her delirium – and to an overwhelming need to commit all her thoughts, ideas and commands to writing. Even when near death she needed to communicate – and memorialize – through the intermediary of paper. Experience appears to have taken on a reality only when it had been ordered and fixed in writing. Liz Herbert ruefully noted that Nightingale even made copies of personal letters to her closest friends (O'Malley, p. 273). Not surprisingly, drafts and revisions form a large percentage of her collected letters. No matter how much she might insist that she wanted no letters to survive, she did everything she could to ensure that they did. Like George Bernard Shaw, Nightingale was a highly self-conscious creator of her public and private personae.

After she became an invalid, letters became even more important for Nightingale. Both her collaborators and those who wished to influence her were kept waiting downstairs in the living room, while she exchanged notes with them from her bedroom. Anyone who seriously wished to capture her attention quickly realized that the most effective mode was via paper. Her chief assistant, Dr John Sutherland, sometimes exchanged half a dozen notes with her in a day. For many years Henry Bonham Carter, a cousin who became Secretary of the Nightingale [Nursing] Fund, received a letter from her almost every morning at breakfast. Her messenger then waited for his response (V. Bonham Carter, p. 111). Only after communicating in this manner for fourteen years did he persuade Nightingale that they could more efficiently settle some problems if she would admit him to her room. Her brother-in-law, Sir Harry Verney, who lived only a few doors away when Parliament was in session, looked forward to a daily letter on the breakfast tray from Nightingale.

Reformers are often isolated individuals. This was particularly true for someone like Nightingale who had to write letters that would ensure not only that her instructions were carried out but also that the recipients would continue to write to her, to inform her truthfully of the progress being made. She developed a variety of approaches for different correspondents, depending upon what she wanted, how powerful they were, and how important they were in her life. To each Nightingale showed a different, though characteristic, self.

Nightingale wrote from her bed giving as well as requesting advice from Mary Jones, matron at King's College Hospital, Mother Bermondsey, a friend from her Crimea days, and Mrs Wardroper, matron of St Thomas' Hospital. Assuming an air of confidentiality, she would draw one of these friends into her orbit by creating a shared world of the committed versus benighted outsiders. Many of her letters begin with a comment on her heavy workload, their shared belief in reform, and how God had given them both important work to complete. Then Nightingale would flatter by saying how much more worthy the recipient was than she herself to do God's work, but that alas, God had commanded her to lead. A letter to the philanthropist Catherine Marsh about the nurses, probationers and sisters at St Thomas' who came to have tea with her is typical:

> I am always strongly impressed with the feeling that there are but few of them who might not more properly be my head, than I theirs: (perhaps may be in another world): & that it is only the 'accident' or the incident of God's providence that has made me, – as it were, incidentally – *their* head in this world. (7 Feb 1877 BUL N62: Box 1, Folder 6)

Finally, she would urge her friend to undertake a specific task that she herself was unable to execute, lest God's will be frustrated, and Nightingale have to 'suffer the worst days of her life'. The format of shared work, flattery and outright command characterized those letters designed to gain obedience.

To those whom she admired, such as the philosopher John Stuart

Mill or the Governor-General of India, Sir John Lawrence, she was humble and circumspect in expressing her opinions. She complimented them and mentioned their influence on her before bombarding them with her suggestions or requests. She rarely missed an opportunity to remind her numerous military correspondents that they had an obligation to fulfil the terms of the Royal Commission reports that had been, she claimed, Sidney Herbert's greatest legacy following his premature death. As she aged Nightingale spent more time in drafting her letters to men in power, for she acknowledged them to be essential actors in her overall sanitary reform strategy. Indeed, from the beginning of her public career she had always started at the top, with the best-known expert or most powerful politician, hoping to influence him first.

These letters contrast markedly with those to friends and allies whom she trusted. Honest to the point of bluntness, Nightingale assumed that they would share her evaluations of a particular opponent or situation. With them she shared her barbed caricatures and humorous assessments of situations. She labelled the Reverend Mother Bridgeman, head of a group of Irish nuns in the Crimea, 'Rev. Brickbat', and she tartly refuted Charles Kingsley's romantic suggestion that women enter nursing sisterhoods only if they had been rejected in marriage: 'You would not expect a man to accept or value a woman's love very highly on the *rejected* plan. Yet it is thought such a good reason for God to accept it' (23 May 1862 BL Add 45790: f 281). On another occasion she told her father, 'I always feel there is hardly any one but me to defend the poor Creator' (6 Jan 1862 BL Add 45790: f 244). Had Nightingale not become a reformer she might have become a writer, as she herself once said; certainly she exploited to the fullest her ability to coin the memorable, if often damning, phrase.

Benjamin Jowett and her old friends, 'Clarkey' and Julius Mohl, served to keep alive Nightingale's intellectual interests, while Sir John McNeill and Sidney Herbert were trusted and respected counsellors. Dr Sutherland, who irritated her personally, taught her sanitary science; he also served as her secretary when she was too weak to write, and advised her on much of her writing. To Clarkey and Jowett alone she confessed her loneliness, but from others, such as Sir John McNeill, she indirectly sought sympathy. Her letter of condolence to him on the death of his wife soon shifted to her own grief over Sidney Herbert's death many years earlier, before concluding with a full-scale report on how her work was progressing. Jowett and Herbert criticized Nightingale for her harsh judgements of others and her exaggerated opinions; Sutherland chided her for her impatience; Clarkey urged her to spend fewer hours at work;

and Sir John constantly reminded her of how much she had achieved.

Distance was both isolating and safe. Jowett and Clarkey were perfect friends, for they did not live in London and did not expect to see her. Only in the 1870s, when she began to assist a few favourite nurses in their careers, did Nightingale actually begin to suggest that they might visit or come to stay with her. But even then, letters remained her preferred medium. She would sometimes make concessions, but she always expected them to understand the terms of her favour, and the desirability of letters over visits. Only when she mellowed in old age did Nightingale's acerbic wit assume a kinder, more self-deprecating style which emerges in letters to her favourite grand-niece, Rosalind Smith Nash.

Nightingale's extreme dedication to work, her use of collaborators, and the Victorian public's adulation made her an obvious target for later generations. Those most anxious to cast off the dead hand of Victorian hypocrisy and fatuous idealism found her a convenient scapegoat. Her letters provided evidence, an almost overwhelming amount of it, to prove that the 'angel of the Crimea' had clay feet – indeed, that the clay might extend very far; Victorian idolization of her had been at best misguided, at worst destructive. The very tone of Nightingale's letters – her bitter, thrusting comments about men in high command, her confident assertion of the way things ought to be done – have made it easy to find ammunition against her and her pretensions.

The most famous attack on Nightingale remains Lytton Strachey's *Eminent Victorians* (1913). Under his beady eye she became a monster, relentlessly using her friends and family for her own single-minded purpose. After reading his essay, reform – whether of the army, the nursing profession, or hospital architecture – fades into the background, as if these changes occurred naturally without human action, while Nightingale harassed busy men in positions of authority. Strachey's most famous comment is his summation of her character: her mother wept, saying, ' "We are ducks who have hatched a wild swan." But the poor lady was wrong: it was not a swan they had hatched: it was an eagle' (p. 124).

His ironic undermining of the accomplishments of this particular Victorian bird has dominated historical, as opposed to popular, interpretations, of Nightingale. As recently as 1982, F. B. Smith published *Florence Nightingale: Reputation and Power*, yet another damning indictment of her supposed abuse of power. Smith, returning to the mass of letters, interprets them in such a way that he can argue that she was an utter failure in the Crimea, in nursing reform and in the sanitary reform of India. Nevertheless, he concludes,

'Thousands of men in the British army at home and abroad lived healthier, longer lives in better conditions because she acted the bully for them' (p. 108). If Strachey ignored the vital role of individuals, Smith evaluates all women reformers as meddling bullies.

Nightingale was not a neutral figure in her own day; even if the public adulated her, many politicians, bureaucrats and army officers loathed her. It is hardly surprising that she still evokes such strong condemnation. Her faults are too evident. She tended to see all issues in black and white; those who agreed with her were friends and those who disagreed were enemies. Her lack of generosity, even vindictiveness, towards women who disagreed with her was a lifelong habit. She manipulated her friends and family shamelessly; she used her illness to force other people into action. But she was a brilliant reformer who had an indefatigable capacity to study, absorb, and relate material to a larger picture; without her many changes in the army, public health, nursing and sanitation in India would have been far slower, or neglected until scandal forced minimal reforms. As Sir John McNeill wrote to her after the death of Sidney Herbert:

> [Y]ou are destined to do a great work and you cannot die till it is substantially if not apparently done. You are leaving your impress on the age in which you live and the print of your foot will be traced by generations yet unborn. (19 Nov 1861 BL Add 45968: f 169)

Nightingale the person continues to fascinate and anger, but her achievements were considerable; to use a metaphor appropriate to her age, Nightingale was the engine that drove the machinery of sanitation, since she could not be the machinery that performed the work.

Editorial Note

From a very early age Nightingale began making copies of her letters for herself; these form the bulk of her original collection. After her death Rosalind Smith Nash undertook to collect as many of her letters as possible from individual owners. Typed copies were made and were placed on permanent loan to the British Library along with the original Nightingale collection of letters, diaries and manuscripts. Most of the letters written to Henry Bonham Carter, Secretary for the Nightingale Fund, and all the letters written to Mrs Wardroper, Matron of St Thomas' Hospital, as well as letters to favourite nurses, Sir John McNeill and other friends, form the collection of the St Thomas' Hospital Archives, now held at the Greater London Record Office. Photocopies of the letters owned by Sir Ralph Verney of Claydon, heir to the estate of Sir Harry Verney, Nightingale's brother-in-law, are available for use by scholars at the Wellcome Institute for the History of Medicine. Photocopies of smaller collections are also in the Wellcome. These are now often the only available copies; those written to Henry, Cardinal Manning, from the Presbytery of St Mary of the Angels, Bayswater, appear to have been lost.

Nightingale, like most Victorians, used the dash as an all-purpose punctuation mark. Her spelling, especially of personal names, was erratic (e. g. Affghan and Afghan, Paulet and Paulett). For emphasis, she began many paragraphs at the left edge of the page or halfway across the page. In spite of her careful drafting of so many letters, she was repetitious and contradictory, even in the same letter. She also frequently recycled examples, *bons mots* and information. Occasionally she borrowed from friends' letters, passing on the most effective phrases to others. We have not littered our text with *sic*, choosing rather to present Nightingale with all her idiosyncrasies. But the necessities inherent in turning handwritten letters into print have forced some changes. We have normalized her paragraphing. For clarity we have used a full stop instead of a dash wherever the following word begins with a capital; full stops have been added for clarity where no punctuation has been given, but the next word begins with a capital. We have also eliminated the dashes that often follow her commas. Quotation marks have been changed to modern British usage. Abbreviations have been kept, but instead of printing them as superscriptions, as Nightingale wrote them, we have used an apostrophe (e. g. hosp'l, c'd, Dep't). Nightingale used an equal sign where we would use a hyphen (e. g. brother=in=law); we have changed these to modern usage. We have not included material crossed out, except to footnote the occasional significant change. We have included Nightingale's own footnotes in the body of the text, rather than where they appeared in the original letter, squeezed at the bottom of a page. She always marked her footnotes with clear asterisks. We have also done so, but placed them in round brackets. Since Nightingale used both square brackets and round brackets, we have indicated editorial additions by the use of braces { }.

Usually, and invariably during the Crimean War, Nightingale dated her letters very precisely; she also normally indicated to whom the letter was addressed. But when dates are missing this information has been supplied by scholars and sorters of the letters. (For those at the British Library, Rosalind Smith Nash and Sir

Edward Cook; for those at the Wellcome, Sir Ralph Verney and Sue Goldie.) We have in all cases accepted their attribution and/or dating, indicating it by braces. In order to save space we have placed Nightingale's address and date, normalized to day/month/year, on one line. Since Nightingale scholars have all too often quoted Nightingale out of context or out of chronological order – and since she is contradictory herself – we have given the sources and dates of all citations from her letters. The numbered letters are all given in the most complete form available; occasionally only a copy or an edited transcript of the original exists. The source for each letter is given at the end of the letter; dates and sources for the excerpts are given in round brackets following the excerpt.

Everyone who studies Florence Nightingale's letters is indebted, first and foremost, to Sue Goldie's monumental *A Calendar of the Letters of Florence Nightingale* (1983). This invaluable chronological, annotated listing of extant Nightingale letters and their location is the essential starting place for any study of Nightingale. The complete family trees prepared by Goldie are the basis for our abbreviated family trees (we have included only a selection of those cousins important to Nightingale). Goldie is currently preparing a series of edited volumes of Nightingale's letters by topic; these should in time make available in published form all her important correspondence.

We join all who have ever worked on Nightingale in praising Sir Edward Cook's definitive biography, published only three years after her death in 1913. Before her papers had been sorted and catalogued, he sifted through them to produce a judicious and fair-minded evaluation of Nightingale's life and work; the biography is indispensable reading. I. B. O'Malley's biography of Nightingale up to 1856, published in 1931, is valuable because she quotes from letters that were destroyed before the second collection of Nightingale letters was deposited in the British Library (1940). In 1950 Cecil Woodham-Smith published her one-volume biography of Nightingale, using many family papers that had not been available to Cook. Although Woodham-Smith has an irritating habit of quoting a letter without dating it correctly, or of eliding different sections or even different letters as if they formed one continuous thought, her book still remains the most accessible biography. Moreover, she quotes material that appears to have been lost or destroyed since she wrote. W. H. Greenleaf, in his review, has enumerated the errors of fact, transcription and interpretation that mar the biography. All the other biographies of Nightingale derive from these three studies.

Early Years: Family Struggles, 1820–54

Florence Nightingale was born on 12 May 1820, in the Italian city of flowers whose name she bears. Her sister, Parthenope, had been given the Greek name for Naples, where she had been born a year earlier. William Edward Nightingale and his wife Frances – or Fanny as she was called – were on an extended European tour following their marriage in 1818. Florence was born with every advantage of wealth. Her maternal great-grandfather, Samuel Smith, a London merchant, had amassed a fortune. At the age of nine her father, born William Shore, inherited the Lea property in Derbyshire from his uncle, Peter Nightingale; upon coming of age he adopted his uncle's surname. Shrewd investment and the discovery of a lead mine greatly enhanced the property's worth, so that William Edward Nightingale – or W.E.N. – went to Cambridge University with an income between seven and eight thousand pounds a year. W. E. N. purchased Embley Park near Romsey in Hampshire in 1825. The family summered primarily at Lea Hurst on the edge of the Derbyshire hills and spent the rest of the year, except for stays in London, at Embley Park. The moderate scale of Lea Hurst led Florence to claim that even with fifteen bedrooms, the house was small.

Wealth was not the only influence on Florence's life. She also inherited the liberal and humanitarian outlook of the Smiths, as well as Unitarianism on both sides of the family. Together these two traditions produced a progressiveness which was tempered by the rigid respectability that governed upper-class behaviour. Nevertheless, Fanny insisted that the family become Anglican as more appropriate for landed gentry. William Smith, Fanny's father, sat in the House of Commons for forty-six years; an abolitionist, he also battled for the sweated factory workers and the rights of Dissenters and Jews. The young W.E.N. was a supporter of parliamentary reform and declared that Bentham had taught moral truth more effectively than all the Christian divines.

Fanny, a great beauty who was six years older than her husband, grew up in her father's intellectually stimulating circle. All her life she loved entertaining and the arts. Her family did not wholly approve of her marriage to the clever and reflective but unambitious

W. E. N., who enjoyed travel, books and good conversation. He became a charming dilettante whose chief interest was in speculative problems, which he discussed with Florence throughout his life. The outgoing Fanny, on the contrary, loved an active social life, as the nine-year-old Florence wrote to her cousin Henry: 'Mama went to the ball the 11th of January, came home between 5 and 6 o'clock and stayed in bed till after our dinner. She had on a dark green gown, white sleeves and diamonds' (1829 Wellcome).

Neither Parthe nor Florence inherited their mother's beauty. But Florence, a year younger, was both more attractive and intellectually acute; she also appears to have been more anxious to please. Her letters reflect a conscientious, earnest child who filled her time with studies, music, sewing, and a little play. At eight she wrote to her mother, 'I do figures, music, (both Piano-forte, & Miss C{hris}tie's new way too,) Latin, making maps of Palestine, (and such like about the Bible) & then we walk, & play, & do my patchwork, & we have such fun' ({1828} Wellcome). At the age of ten she wrote to her mother, after a long description of a sunset:

> I felt so happy, mama, I thought I loved God then . . . Uncle and Aunt Oc and miss Southwood are all very kind, and so am I, I hope, to my cousins. I do not eat too much, I assure you, and I do not play too much. I lie down sometimes. I have found a very pretty book here, called the Christian's Friend, consisting of short Sermons, and Stories showing the shortness of life, and suddenness of death. (12 July 1830, Wellcome)

Since the Nightingales could not find a governess who would satisfy W.E.N.'s intellectual requirements or Fanny's standard of elegance and breeding, W.E.N. decided to teach the girls Greek, Latin, German, French, Italian, history, grammar, composition and philosophy himself, employing a governess only for music and art. W.E.N. was a demanding teacher; Florence rose to these challenges but Parthe rebelled. Their differences brought Florence and her father into close communion, for they both had a passion for accuracy and abstract speculation, while Parthe, who both wrote and drew well, developed close ties to her mother. Fanny was wise enough to sense the need to send her daughters separately to visit relatives.

Florence's peculiarities revealed themselves early, both to herself and her parents. She self-consciously wrote home at the end of February 1830, 'I think I am got some thing more good-natured and complying' (Wellcome). But impatience and intolerance remained problems. She became passionately involved in the lives of favourite cousins, and continually demanded approval from those she loved. Accuracy, self-discipline, self-righteousness and a sense of justice emerged early. The latter two characteristics are mingled in a letter to her sister Parthe, also known to the family as Pop, on 28 March 1830, from Fair Oak, where she was visiting her mother's sister Aunt Joanna and her family: 'dear Pop, Why don't you write? I should think you had plenty of time, and I write you such long letters, and you, but very seldom, write me 2 or 3 lines. I shall not write to you, if you don't write for me' (Wellcome). Her eye for detail and her ordered mind are reflected in another 1830 letter to her father from Fair Oak, written on Wednesday 24 February, in which she discusses the play activities with her cousins Hilary and Jack Bonham Carter:

> . . . have made a little tool house in our larder, in which we keep, viz. 1. spade, 2 rakes, 2 hoes, 4 baskets . . . Our quarrels are worse than ever. A few days ago, he began an accusation before Uncle Carter but we make out 5 formal accusations viz. 1. Breaking 2 carts. 2. Hurting Hilary's hand. 3. Accusing us of doing it. 4. Beating my legs. and 5. Hurting me. (Wellcome)

Florence's letters to her family during these early years ranged over many topics: the merits of church sermons she had heard, dramatic performances acted at home, the problem of caring for her own clothes and the expense of various articles ('I shall not buy any black ribband, thank you, partly because I think it does not signify' [To Fanny, 24 Feb 1830, Wellcome]). Flowers and animals were frequently mentioned. To her grandmother Florence wrote on 8 January 1832 about a pet squirrel and a pigeon she had rescued. Florence – or Flo, as she was called – grew up apparently surrounded by affection, security and comfort, with all the intellectual challenges and wide-ranging opportunities that life in a wealthy, respectable nineteenth-century family could offer.

Family relations featured prominently in the Nightingale social life. Fanny came from an energetic and pleasure-loving family of eleven children who maintained close relations throughout their long lives. Letters travelled back and forth frequently and visits were regular. Florence was closest to three families on her mother's side: the Nicholsons of Waverley Abbey, the Bonham Carters of Fair Oak, and the Samuel Smiths of Combe Hurst, Surrey. Sam Smith, Fanny's youngest brother, had married Mai Shore, W. E. N.'s sister; Aunt Mai became Florence's particular friend – and defender. Moreover, since W.E.N. had no male heir his property would be inherited by his sister's eldest son, William Shore Smith, born in 1831 when Florence was eleven. Shore, as he was called, was a favourite in the Nightingale household and came to be referred to by Florence as 'my boy Shore'.

Florence's immersion in the life of her extended family is depicted in a letter to her paternal grandmother at Tapton, near Sheffield, written in the late thirties or early forties (see Abbreviated Family Trees):

1. To Grandmother Shore   Thames Bank Friday 28th[1]

My dear Grandmama

I have been intending for many days to write to you, but I have been staying with Mrs. Octavius Smith for the last week, and have had so much to do with the children, in consequence of her delicate state, that I have never been able to find time. Three pleasant weeks I have spent at Combe, while Papa was with you, during which I saw a great deal of the children, as Miss Wicksteed was away during part of the time. Dear Bee is particularly clever and forward in every thing she does and in a few years, I doubt not, she will be able to fix her now wandering attention. She is getting very forward in her German. Shore and Gerard are disporting themselves together at Embley to the improvement of themselves and every one about them. As to the two babies, they are the most good tempered accommodating little things I ever saw and the most beautiful of their family, I think. They do not lose their beauty in the least. Bab[2] is the most affectionate little thing. I have not yet seen Papa whom we expected in London to-day. I hope to spend some more time at dear Combe, where the very atmosphere of love and kindness much improve every one who comes there, after I leave this place. But Aunt *Jane* is again confined to her bed with the excitement produced by William Nicholson's sudden departure to join his regiment in Australia. He was off in three days from the first an unexpected notice which he received from headquarters and called here on his way. This harrowed up old associations in Aunt Jane's mind connected with the poor fellow who was lost and has much weakened her. She requires a great deal of care. The two youngest are nice little girls and are very much with me. I am taking lessons here. I hope to see Papa to morrow. He wrote me many nice letters while I was at Combe and gave very good accounts of you and dear Aunt Evans.[3] The spring is coming on now so fast, that we shall be at Lea Hurst almost before we are aware. The two babs at Combe are much more down stairs than they were, they generally breakfast with the others now. Bertha is very steady at her lessons and does her little practising regularly. They are both very neat work women. The Miss Horners[4] are now staying at Combe whom the children are very fond of. Their favourite game is making *seals* with sealing-wax of which they are never tired or hearing one tell them a story. Dear Grandmama, I must wish you good night, for it is late and I have not much time to write in the day as I have the children here always with me, Aunt Jane requiring the utmost *quiet*. With best love to dear Aunt Evans, believe me, my dear Grandmama, ever your truly obliged and affectionate grandchild.

F. Nightingale

Source: Wellcome

1. In pencil: 1837. March or April 1845 Thames Bank. After Will Nicholson to Sandhurst and Australia *c.* 1844.
2. Bab: dialect for baby.
3. Aunt Evans: Grandmother Shore's sister.
4. Miss Horners: Leonard Horner (1785–1864), eminent geologist and Warden of University College, London, had six daughters; the eldest married Charles Lyell.

On 7 February 1837, a few months before her seventeenth birthday, Florence recorded in her personal notes that she had had a mystical experience. She wrote that God had spoken to her and called her to His service, although what that was to be was unclear. This was the first of four such experiences; clearly Nightingale was not to be satisfied with the conventional life of a Victorian woman.

The Nightingales left for Europe in September 1837 and did not return until April of the following year. They travelled through France, Italy and Switzerland. Everywhere they had friends and letters of introduction; everywhere they attended balls and operas, salons and various social events where high society and the intelligentsia gathered. Mary Clarke was probably the single most important person whom the Nightingales met on the trip. 'Clarkey' was a brilliant conversationalist who, through a forceful and charming personality, had built one of the most noted salons in Paris where distinguished men met every Friday evening. Clarkey quickly developed great respect for Flo's intellect, while the latter, twenty-seven years Clarkey's junior, was captivated by this woman who refused to fit into the traditional feminine mould. Clarkey did not generally cultivate women's friendships; rather, she preferred the intellectual companionship of her learned male friends, such as the medieval scholar Claude Fauriel and the

Orientalist Julius Mohl. Florence enjoyed being Clarkey's exception, and shared her preference for intellectual men.

That Florence's grace, wit and learning impressed European society obviously pleased her parents. But before leaving Paris, Florence wrote in a private note that to be God's servant, she had first to overcome 'the desire to shine in society', a theme she was often to repeat. She wrote her grandmother a letter from Paris that gives the flavour of life abroad with the Nightingales:

2. To Grandmother Shore   Paris 2 Feb 1839

We send this by the Ambassador's bag, or it should have gone before.
Dear Grandmama

It is a long while since we have heard from Aunt Mai or have heard news of you. We are coming home so soon now that she does not perhaps think it worth while to write. We expected to have left Paris before now but are waiting till the weather is a little warmer before we begin the journey. The snow is on the ground but we have not had a severe winter, I hope yours has been no colder. There has been a great deal of interest here lately for Papa, we have been several times to the House of Commons where ladies are admitted here and which is very entertaining. But now the ministry has resigned and the king would not accept their resignations, so he is going to dissolve the House of Commons.

All the drawing-rooms and balls of the Queen have been put an end to by the death of poor Princess Marie, her daughter. All Paris was ready dressed and we among others for the first drawing-rooms when that very day the poor Princess died. It was kept secret for some time from the Queen who was so excessively attached to her that she has been ill ever since. The baby who is not six months old, has just arrived in Paris where it is come to be taken care of by the Queen. The Princess, its mother, died in Italy, but she was brought here to be buried.

We have quite enough going out though without this, and know a great many people. Mama went to a private concert last Wednesday when she heard a girl of 17, Mademoiselle Garcia, (the sister of poor Malibran who died some years ago at the Manchester festival) sing beautifully. We have, living in the same house with us, a Yorkshire lady with her sister whose name perhaps you may know, Mrs Walker Ferrand. She is a widow and very beautiful and very much we like her. There is a most extraordinary actress here at the great French theatre, who promises to be as fine as our Mrs. Siddons, she is only 17, her name is Mademoiselle Rachel. This is the time of the Carnival when there are masked balls at all the theatres, but we have not been to see any. Pray give our best love to dear Aunt Evans, we suppose that she has left Tapton or we should write to her. Papa and Mama send you their love and believe me dear Grandmama, ever your affectionate grand daughter

Florence

Source: Wellcome

Upon the Nightingales' return to England in May 1839, Parthe and Florence were presented at the Queen's drawing room. A large house-warming was held at the renovated Embley Park home for the extended family at Christmas. But December found Flo bored and discontented. Aunt Mai, who shared Flo's intellectual curiosity, humour and philosophical interest, had become a devoted friend. She convinced Fanny that Flo would benefit from a visit to Combe Hurst. The two women studied mathematics, a discipline that Flo felt was good for her because of its concrete nature. Aunt Mai wrote to Fanny, suggesting that a mathematics master might be employed for her daughter, but Fanny disagreed violently and even W.E.N. thought that history and philosophy were more appropriate. But Flo continued its study during the month she spent helping another aunt, Mrs Octavius Smith. After she returned home she studied mathematics, Greek and philosophy on her own in the early morning. The rest of the day was occupied with an endless parade of guests and family affairs. Clarkey, Fauriel and Julius Mohl visited the Nightingales in the summer of 1840. In addition, Lord Palmerston, the future Prime Minister, Lady Emily, and her son-in-law, Lord Ashley, later the reformer Lord Shaftesbury, philanthropist and founder of the Ragged School Union, had become a part of the Nightingale circle. Flo exuded vitality and intelligence; an excellent mimic, she was a charming and entertaining member of the company. But she alternated between exhilarating social success and burdensome doubts about what she ought to feel, what she ought to do, and where her destiny lay. In spite of consorting with some of the leading figures of the time, Nightingale remained oppressed by a growing restlessness that would not be satisfied for another twelve years. To Hilary Bonham Carter, the cousin who had become her confidante, Flo wrote, 'Ladies' work has always to be fitted in, where a man is, his business is the law' (Woodham-Smith, p. 40).

During the early 1840s Flo was the relative summoned to help when there were illnesses, births or impending deaths. But Fanny had to be coaxed to let Florence go, or stay, and was not pleased when her daughter preferred helping the family to attending a social event; after all, Flo was supposed to be on the marriage market. Over the years the Nightingale women became mistresses of exaggeration and manipulation as their most effective tactics to achieve their own desires. While visiting her friend Helen Richardson, whose sister, Hope Reeve, had just died in childbirth, Florence wrote home asking if she could stay longer:

> My dearest. I write to you to bespeak your intercession, which I know you will give, without my asking it, tho' I do not deserve it, because you never think of your own solitude. Helen is sitting opposite to me to make me say that she dares 'not look you in the face it is not to leave her alone now'. I sh'd be missing the only opport'y I ever had of doing real good . ... My dear, I cry unto you, do this thing for me for no one else can do it. You will have me all your life, for I shall never die & never marry. I cannot come either, because my washing at Hampstead does not come up till Friday. ({1843} Wellcome)

Service to God became an obsession. Flo longingly wrote to her cousin Hilary Bonham Carter in an undated note of her wish to transcend the expectations of her family and friends, and to pursue her own aspirations:

> Dearest, I am looking forward to next Saturday, if I can go any how tacked on to some body's apron string – how often I wish for grey hairs – they are the greatest possible convenience – & if they could be had before other infirmities, would be of as much advantage as Brevet Rank.[1] If any body wishes to read about the May of life in the little ink marks of poets, it's all very well, if they wish to read of it in real life, it is a series of scrapes, of dull bothers & sharp remorse, of useless giving of pain, and hopeless perplexity – we reckon our young years by their failures & not by their months & fifty times a day have I remembered, ever since, what an elderly woman once said to me, about the privileges, the joys, the *exemptions* from youth, which her age enjoyed. (3 May 184? BL Add 45794: ff 86–87)

---

1. Brevet Rank: a nominal higher rank conferred on an officer, usually in time of war, but carrying no extra pay.

Her Aunt Anne's sister-in-law, the Evangelical Hannah Nicholson, became one of Florence's strong supports in her spiritual struggles.

3. To Hannah Nicholson   Embley Friday {1844 or 45?}

My dear Aunt Hannah I most gladly profit by your kind permission to keep two of your books, till we have the pleasure of seeing your dear face again. As I have not half done with Mr. Stevenson nor he with me, & Searle's[1] subject is particularly interesting to me in his searches into the Old Testament. I return by William the other two, as I know I can see them in London & Nicholls is a book of reference which is so useful to me in *teaching* to give me hints and suggestions, that I shall get it at the Xtian knowledge. I do not mean to say that it is not equally useful in *learning*.

I think parts of Robinson[2] are very striking particularly man's state of condemnation & his 'inability to save himself' but I confess to thinking, that the fault of us young people is too much groping in our own minds, too much refining on our own particular feelings, & thinking & subtilizing in our own private names – & that the looking into the nature of God, the re-attaching ourselves to the great system of the Xtian dispensation, as parts of it is what we want – which is, what researches into such grand & sublime subjects as Searle's, will one w'd hope, help one to do.

I only say this, dear Aunt Hannah, to shew you that your kindness & your books, are, I hope, not entirely wasted upon me – & that I have not neglected making the most of them that I could. But if you knew how little of the spiritual life there is in me, I often wonder how much the proportion is, whether there are not 99 parts of bread and mutton & only 1/100th of the spiritual part, which will live for ever, in my composition. If you knew too how grateful I am for your interest in me, how your letter will stay by me & warn me, when the dreams of life come one after another clouding & covering the realities of the unseen, you would never think that you could write any word, which would not be received with humility & gratitude by me. One sh'd indeed be thankful, when the invisible Sympathy takes a visible form & speaks to one through the mouth & life of a human creature, when higher things take a tangible shape – & show one the Father. I have been reading lately a Report upon Lunacy, which insists above all upon exercise. In the open air for the patients, upon working in the garden, for instance as having an almost extraordinary effect in soothing the irritation of madness. It says 'gardening' in order to supply them with an interest to take them out & adds that the patients *rarely* resist, it even says, *never*, when it is set about in the right way & in company. That this can only be done in an Asylum, I am afraid, is too evident, but I thought of poor Mrs. Haydon's melancholy depression as just a case in point only that it seems hard to urge the relations to send an Insane person from home. But it says that the company of the Insane, which one w'd think enough to drive a sane person mad, often has just the contrary effect upon the Deranged. The invariable effect of madness in disordering the circulation & depressing the life & warmth of the extremities gives, it adds, the *physical* cause as well, of the wonderful effect of working in the open air upon Insanity. The rich Insane, & especially the female part, are I believe, much worse off than the poor in that way – & have consequently less chance of happiness & of recovery. Pray remember me kindly to Mrs. Copus, & forgive me for having written so much of myself. It seems as if I thought your sympathy inexhaustible – & that it was impossible to intrude on it. Accept all our best loves, & above all, that of my dear Aunt Hannah's grateful & affectionate

Florence Nightingale

Source: BL Add 45794: ff 16–19

1. John Searle of Penrhyn {?}: author of *Human Nature Laid Open* (1836).
2. Hastings Robertson {?}: (1792–1866), an earnest Evangelical churchman. Author of *Church Reform and Christian Principles* (1833). He also edited Archbishop James Ussher's *Body of Divinity* (1841).

Flo's pleasure in her growing reputation in society continued to be checked by the heavy weight of discontent. Several potential suitors circled her, including her cousin Henry Nicholson and Richard Monckton Milnes, who became a noted humanitarian and philanthropist as well as amassing a large collection of pornographic works. Henry proposed during the winter of 1843, and Florence refused him, which strained relations with Waverley for a time. At least Fanny and W. E. N. agreed with her decision. Florence, however, could not accept the coolness of Marianne, who sided with her brother. Florence had adored her for many years; in a series of letters to Hilary she lamented, 'I was not a worthy friend of her. I was not true to her or to myself in our friendship. I was afraid of her: that is the truth . . .' (O'Malley,

p. 104). A little later she was to declare, 'I never loved but one person with passion, & that was her' (O'Malley, p. 124). Throughout her life Nightingale formed emotionally dependent relationships with women who responded sympathetically to her ambitions. But when they failed to support her unconditionally, she never forgave them. In numerous letters she subsequently condemned all women as selfish and unreliable.

In January 1844 Florence became ill while visiting the Nicholsons at Waverley. A letter to W.E.N. suggests that there had been a psychic element in her condition, but it also illustrates Flo's capacity to dramatize her illnesses.

4. To W. E. Nightingale   Wednesday {1844–45?}[1]

Dear Papa

You ask for my 'experience of the Sick Room' so it w'd be very ungracious of me not to give it, (tho' I have not yet set pen to paper) – it is humbling enough.

I felt, as the body fell off, so little of any other life in me, that when any-body came into the room, I was obliged to ask them to read something strong, Channing[2] or the Bible, by way of an excitement to make me care to live on – for the mental life was flickering, flickering, as if it w'd go out.

This makes me feel, that if I had been going to die now, when the call came for me to rise up again, I sh'd kick & struggle a little, like a weak chicken in its shell, & that is all that w'd come of it, because there w'd be nothing strong enough, when the body was gone, to stand up & live on by itself.

Still I do not say – povera natura umana – but only povera natura mia[3] for what *all the* world has sung about the joys of convalescence must be true. Miss Martineau[4] says, the more the body falls in pain & weakness, the stronger the conviction of an independent & unchangeable self – she *should* have said, I suppose – 'There lies the difference between strong minds & weak ones'.

Unsigned

Source: Wellcome

1. In pencil: FN ill at Waverley Jan & Feb 1844 to W. E. N. ? 1845 at Embley.
2. William Ellery Channing: (1780–1842), American Unitarian theologian who stressed unity with God and one's ethical duties to others.
3. povera natura umana/povera natura mia: miserable human nature/my miserable nature.

4. Miss Harriet Martineau: (1802–76), journalist who wrote on political economy, women's work and current affairs. Her sister had taught Hilary at a Unitarian school in Liverpool.

During these years Florence turned repeatedly to Hannah Nicholson in her quest for the meaning of life.

5. To Hannah Nicholson　　　　1 Feb {1846?}

My dearest Aunt Hannah,

I cannot leave this place, without telling you, how *very* sorry I was to learn from your letter, that we have no chance of seeing you before we go. I was in hopes till the last, that you would have come. In answer to your question, as to my feelings about going to London – I really do not care. The day of personal hopes & fears is over for me. Now I dread & desire no more. I should be very glad, if I could have been left here, when they went to London, as there is much to be done, but as that would not be heard of, London is really my place of rest – for people talk of London gaieties – there you can at least have the mornings to yourself – to me the country is the place of 'row' – since we came home in September, how long do you think we have ever been alone? not one fortnight – a country house is the real place for dissipation – sometimes I think that every body is hard upon me, that to be for ever expected to be looking merry & saying something lively, is more than can be asked, mornings, noons & nights, of any one – & then I remember every body's patience with me, & am very much ashamed of myself. I should not have written two pages on this subject, which is just two pages too much, if it had not been for your question, & to explain how London can be really a place of rest.

But there is peace every where. I do not deny it – *peace & food*, there is food sufficient to verify the promise, that 'they shall hunger no more' – when we are fed with the 'meat of doing the will of Him that sent us' – there is peace, when we exchange the search after one sort of sympathy, which begins – *You do not know* how &c for that which begins, *Thou knowest.*

Anxiety however must always remain – though all restless anxiety is from want of trust in God – but when I think that my dear lad might be like St. John, except in Inspiration, it makes

24

my heart burn within me. And do you believe that there is any inherent reason why he should not be? The will of God must be as strong for our sanctification now as it was then. And my boy has such a pure heart and affectionate soul. As for me, I have said to corruption, Thou art my mother & sister. But he might be all that I would have been.

But I must say goodbye, dearest Aunt Hannah, for I have much to do. I am afraid dear Lolli is rather lonely without Mr— – but I do hope the sea may be of use.

My boy left us this morning, Blanch some time since. She reminded me so of my own early days, but she has principle which I never had.

With best love to Lolli, take the same for yourself, my dearest Aunt Hannah, from your ever loving & grateful child

I have delivered Sam's message
Feb 1
I read your 'Mount of Olives' with my boy, who was exceedingly interested by it, which, & the necessity of fitting my readings to him, have prevented me from reading your last little book till now.

I ought to say, forgive me for talking so much of myself. I do ask forgiveness – even from my dear, kind, indulgent friend.

in haste, ever yours.

Source: BL Add 45794: ff 20–23

While the rest of the Nightingale world continued its cyclic journey through the year, moving from Lea Hurst to London to Embley to London to Lea Hurst, Florence continued to sort out the warring elements within her. In an undated letter (1844?), possibly addressed to Parthe, she spoke about the possibility of regeneration giving meaning to life:

> What is life? It cannot be merely a gaining of experience – it is freedom, voluntary force, free-will, & therefore must be a hard fought battle – in order to make a choice, there must be evil & good to choose from. I sometimes think too that we may be expiating in this life the sins of a previous existence, that the disgusts & weariness some people feel may be the natural & inevitable consequence of a reckless ministering, in some previous state, to the morbid cravings of the heart for excitement. Is there any thing so very fantastical in this? (Wellcome)

Some time in the spring of this year Florence became convinced that her destiny lay in hospital work.

In July 1844 Clarkey's special friend, Claude Fauriel, died. In her letter to Clarkey, Florence reveals how her search for meaning and truth penetrated every worldly experience:

> I cannot help writing one word, my dear Miss Clarke, after having just received your note, though I know I cannot say anything which can be of any comfort. For there are few sorrows I do believe like your sorrow, and few people so necessary to another's happiness of every instant, as he was to yours. . . . How sorry I am, dear Miss Clarke, that you will not think of coming to us here. Oh, do not say that you 'will not cloud young people's spirits'. Do you think young people are so afraid of sorrow, or that if they have lively spirits, which I often doubt, they think these are worth anything, except in so far as they can be put at the service of sorrow, not to relieve it, which I believe can very seldom be done, but to sympathize with it? I am sure this is the only thing worth living for, and I do so believe that every tear one sheds waters some good thing into life . . . (Cook, I, 31–32)

Florence was again convalescing in the early months of 1845 when Shore came to visit. Florence 'warned him against lying long in bed, and the temptations of the world, liking to be praised and admired and a general favourite more than anything else . . .' (Woodham-Smith, p. 51), conflicts which described her own state of mind. Indeed, she especially feared that she could not control her habit of daydreaming, and repeatedly vowed she would stop. In her happier moments, however, Flo could still see the humour in day-to-day events:

6. To Hilary Bonham Carter   Undated[1]

My dear,
    This comes hoping that you are well, & will send on *Miss Barnett*, which was left, by Jack, & bring back St. Oldooman & other strays. We saw poor Alf at Alresford, who rushed down, rather woebegone, I thought, that *we* had not rushed to *him*, but of course, you know, it was an affair of the most critical importance to accomplish the journey in the least possible space of time, which brooked *no* delay, as the fates of thousands depended on our

reaching the Romsey Lodge at ten minutes past five o'clock London time (consequently, six minutes past Southampton time). I poured into him as much news as I could in 7-tenths of a minute, a fatal delay at the inn, occasioned by the post-boy's requiring spiritual support, but providentially made up by the increased velocity consequent on such support being administered. I asked him to come to Embley tomorrow, but he, the youthful Daniel, preferred the Saturday after, whereupon we signed a shake-hands to one another, already at the distance of one mile apart, & so parted. At Winchester Mama rushed wildly into a shop, crying 'Buns, buns', & holding out certain coins of great value in one hand, & fell prostrate across the counter into the shop-boy's arms, in her search after food, while I endeavoured, by a preternatural solemnity, to maintain our dignity with two princely men in the shop, & turning my head without an inch of my body, said to the shop-boy, Tardy of purpose, give *me* the buns. Papa all the time imploring her by all the wedding-rings of unpunctual wives, now in a state of fusion on their fingers, left hand, in the *Lowest Circle* & by the 18th of June, to despise the buns & die. But she would not. Lastly we clattered up stairs, (You know mothers always *will* put themselves to rights,) undressing all the way, like Ld. Fitzwilliam, as we went up, & dressing all the way down, that is, our bounch-caps.[2] A demain, [There is a word here which we cannot read.] {?} I will send the Gard. Chron.s pray tell Miss Johnson how sorry I was not to see her. I have had a satisfactory letter from Mrs. Plunkett, which I will send, & one from the Fowlers.   Unsigned

Source: Wellcome

1. In pencil: late 1840s: probably *c.* 1845?
2. bounch-caps: var. bunch; caps gathered in folds.

Seven years had passed between 1837, when Florence first experienced the 'call from God', and 1844 when she concluded that her role lay in nursing. In spite of her considerable experience in nursing the villagers near Lea Hurst and Embley, as well as sick relatives of all ages, Florence felt that she needed some hospital training in order to help people more effectively. She decided to spend three months at the Salisbury Infirmary, located only a few miles from Embley Park, where a family friend, Dr Fowler, was the head physician. When she suggested this plan during a visit from the Fowlers in December 1845, the conflict between Florence's dream and her parents' aspirations for her broke into the open. Florence plunged into the dark night of despair. In November 1845 she had written in her diary:

> Lord thou knowest the creature which thou hast made thou knowest that I cannot live – forgive me, O God & let me die – this day let me die it is not for myself that I say this. thou knowest that I am more afraid to die than to live – for I shall carry myself with me – but I know that by living I shall only heap anxieties on other hearts, which will but increase with time –

Her misery continued, for on 1 December 1845 she wrote:

> No wonder we cannot figure to ourselves identity in the next world without a body. How badly the poor mind comes off in this. Oh if one has but a tooth ache, what remedies are invented, what carriages, horses, ponies, journeys, doctors, chaperones, are urged upon one – but if it is something the matter with the mind, unless it belongs to one of the three heads, loss of friends, loss of fortune, loss of health, is neither believed nor understood, and every different kind of suffering is ranged under the one comprehensive word: Fancy, & disposed of with the one comprehensive remedy, Concealment or Self-Command which is the same thing.

And four days later, on 5 December:

> Dec 5. As for me, all my hopes for this winter are gone & all my plans destroyed. My poor little hope, requiescat in pace no one can know its value to me no one can tell how dear a child however infantine is to its mother, nor how precious an idea, tho' it was an unformed one – but between the destruction of one idea & the taking up of another I can understand now how a soul can die. Ach ich fühl 'es wohl, ein Scheiden Kaum so schwer von wahren Freuden als von einem Ichönen Traum[1]. God has something for me to do for him – or he would have let me die some time ago. I hope to do it by living – then my eyes would indeed have seen his salvation – but now I am dust & nothing – worse than nothing – a curse to myself & others. This morning I felt as if my soul would pass away in tears – in utter loneliness – in a bitter passion of tears & agony of solitude but I live – and God grant that I may live to do this. Oh if our Saviour walked the earth how should I

28

not go to him, & would he send me back to live the life again which crushes me into vanity & deceit, or would he not say Do this. Oh for some great thing to sweep this loathsome life into the past. (BL Add 43402: ff 34–35)

1. Ach ich fühl 'es wohl, ein Scheiden Kaum so schwer von wahren Freuden als von einem Ichönen Traum: A separation from true joys isn't nearly as difficult as a separation from a beautiful dream.

Flo's parents had good reasons for their opposition. The upper and middle classes were nursed by relatives and servants at home; even the poor tried to avoid the hospitals, whose mortality rates were frighteningly high. As long as the connection between cleanliness and infection was poorly understood, a patient was safer at home than in a hospital. Hospitals of that period were often filthy and stank; nurses were said to be immoral and undisciplined; untrained staff were reputed to be drunk and disorderly. The upper classes firmly believed that hospital nursing was the choice of only the desperate and the religious. As Nightingale ruefully wrote to Hilary on 11 December 1845:

> But there have been difficulties about my very first step, which terrified Mama. I do not mean the physically revolting parts of a hospital, but things about the surgeons and nurses which you may guess. Even Mrs. Fowler threw cold water upon it; and nothing will be done this year at all events, and I do not believe – ever; and no advantage that I see comes of my living on, excepting that one becomes less and less of a young lady every year, which is only a negative one. (Cook, I, 44)

The failure of her plan, however foreseeable, was agonizing to Florence. As a dutiful daughter, she was emotionally unable to enter her chosen vocation without her family's blessing. Yet her personal frustration is barely concealed by abstract speculation:

7. To W. E. Nightingale   Embley 27 Jan {1846}

Dear Papa,
   Your account of our old ladies was most flourishing – it is so refreshing to me to be with such a woman as Aunt Evans, who

never formularized her feelings, nor gave expression to her ideas –
in this artistic age, when we find more pleasure in the expression,
than in the feeling itself. Speaking is more like my dog Teazer, who
says, I must evaporate. It works off all our thoughts & feelings.
Out of the effervescence, not the 'abundance', of the heart the
mouth speaketh, now.

In this too highly educated, too little active age, the balance
between Theory & Practice seems destroyed – the just connexion
between Knowledge & Action lost sight of – the inspiration
unacknowledged, which is to be sought in effort, even more than
in thought, the actual addition to our store of *Knowledge*, which is
supplied by every *deed*, & the positive subtraction from Thought,
which a life of thinking suffers – not considered.

In the last century, it does not appear, at least among women, to
have been so. The education of the faculties, & their sphere of
action, were in harmony – & we hear consequently little, in poetry
or fiction, of uneasiness or melancholy.

In this century we have advanced the standard of the one
(Theory) – without that of the other (Action) – for man cannot
move both feet at once, except he jump – & he now seems to stand
askew. May we not hope that, in the next century, without the one
retrograding, the other may be brought up to stand alongside, &
the balance again restored. But for this, trials must be made, efforts
ventured – some bodies must fall in the breach for others to step
upon, failure is one of the most important elements of success – the
failure of one to form a guide-post to others – till, at last, a dog
comes who, having smelt all the other roads, & finding them
scentless & unfeasible, follows the one which his Master has gone
before.

Why cannot a woman follow abstractions like a man? has she
less imagination, less intellect, less self-devotion, less religion than
a man? I think not. And yet she has never produced one single
great work of Art, or Science, or Literature. She has never, with the
exception perhaps of Deborah, the Virgin, & the Mère Angélique,
been deemed a fitting vessel for the Spirit of God – she has never
received the spark of inspiration, & though she may have indirectly
left the impress of her character on the world, yet nothing she has
said or done has had a record in history – & the Song of the Virgin
Mary remains the only expression of female feeling, which has
found its echo in every heart & every church. And why? why is her
frame never deemed a worthy House for the Spirit of Truth? nor
hers a worthy tongue to proclaim the service of the Kingdom of
Good, by which I mean the struggle with Evil? Is it not because *the
habit* of never interesting herself much, in any conversation,

printed or spoken, which is not personal, of making herself & her own feelings the subject of speculation – (& what is the good of studying our own individuality, save as the reflection of the generality) – of making all she says autobiographical, & being always is a moral tête-à-tête, of considering her own experiences as the principal part of her life, renders her powerless to rise to any abstract good, or general view. It cuts her wings, it palsies her muscles, & shortens her breath for higher things – & for a clearer, but sharper, atmosphere, in which she has no lungs to live. She has fed on sugar-plums, her appetite is palled for bread.

But I find these speculations so universally uninteresting – that I will stop, for fear of tiring you.

Mary Oxford's sister is better. Shore leaves us on Tuesday. Kitty comes here tomorrow, to refresh, at Shore's & my invitation.

Sharp's the word here. To Parents – & Guardians – should any desire a locality, where sharp's the principle, & excitement the practice – an eligible opportunity now offers.

ever, dear Papa, your affect'e child

Source: Wellcome

The contradictions in Florence's ideas about women were never resolved. However much she recognized the perniciousness of too much leisure, all her life Nightingale berated women for their selfishness and believed that they were incapable of perseverance. She was convinced that women pursued only personal ends, and were unable to understand public responsibilities. Even though she adulated a few particular women, she appears to have looked to men for her intellectual challenges and thought herself a woman born with a 'male intellect'.

Rising before the rest of her family, Flo studied hospital reports secretly throughout the winter of 1846. From the blue books and reports supplied by Lord Ashley, she collected facts about hospitals and public health. Fanny put her in charge of supervising and preserving in the still-room as well as checking, listing damages, and ordering replacements and repairs in the linen-room and china cupboard – all considerable tasks in a wealthy country home. Unwittingly, Florence was honing organizational skills that would serve her well in later years.

Many themes surface in her writings at this time, including the superficiality of worldly activities and the unreality of one's existence:

All is like a dream, you say, yes, the world, & the pink satin ghosts in it, & ourselves most of all – if we could always be true to ourselves, have a sacred trust in our intentions, we should need no other truth – but we lie to ourselves first, the lying to others follows of itself. That the sufferings of Xt's life were intense, who doubts? but the happiness must have been intenser – only think of the happiness of working and working successfully, too, & with no doubt as to his path, & with no alloy of vanity or love of display or glory – but with the ecstacy of single heartedness – all that I do is always poisoned by the fear that I am not doing it in simplicity & singleness of heart – everything I do always seems to me false without being a lie. ({c. 25 Apr 1846} BL Add 45794: ff 100–101)

However much Florence claimed to trust in God's ways, she always carefully calculated her priorities in regard to friends and work. In a vigorous letter to Hilary she condemned the energy that went into love, marriage and friendship – all obstacles to one's long-term goals:

Are one's earthly friends not too often Atalanta's apple, thrown in each other's way, to hinder that course, at the end of which is laid up the crown of *righteousness* – & so, dearest, it is well that *we* sh'd not eat too much of one another – that word righteousness always strikes me more than any thing in the Bible – Strange that not happiness, not rest, not forgiveness, not glory, not success, sh'd have been thought of that glorious man's mind (when at the eve of the last & greatest of his labours,) but all desires so swallowed up in the one great craving after *righteousness* that, at the end of all his struggles, it was mightier within him than ever, mightier than even the desire of peace. How can people tell one to dwell within a good conscience, when the Chief of all the Apostles so panted after righteousness, that he considered it the last best gift, unattainable on earth, to be bestowed in Heaven. (26 Apr 1846 BL Add 45794: f 103)

Detachment from ego and from social relations became equally important for Florence. Both were distractions, along with the desire for approval, attention and admiration. Her thinking already foreshadowed her decision to become an invalid and work from her bed, but it was a long struggle before she could give up the pleasures of this world for the work of this world.

Since Florence wanted action in the present, future

rewards, such as the Christian faith espoused, held little attraction for her. She gradually loosened her emotional and spiritual ties with Aunt Hannah, whose conventional religion did not seem to require public action. She wrote to Aunt Mai in 1850, '... what man *does* is as much God's will as what he *has*' (BL Add 45793: f 75). Good works described the moral life, and to live thus was to discover truth. Flo could not spurn worldly reality; to Hilary she wrote: 'I am so glad to be in this age – I hope we shall all *greatly* increase in knowledge about the unexamined laws of matter of the connexion between matter & mind – the laws of matter have been patiently sifted already' (26 Apr 1846 BL Add 45794: f 99).

During 1846 Flo met a couple who were to become the most influential and supportive in her life – Selina Bracebridge and Charles Holte Bracebridge of Atherstone Hall near Coventry. She had found a replacement for Marianne Nicholson. Sigma, as Florence came to call Selina, appears to have been unusually warm, understanding and accepting. She became a primary support for Flo, who enthusiastically wrote to Hilary: 'never do I see her, without feeling that she is eyes to the blind & feet to the lame – many a plan, which disappointment has thinned into a phantom in my mind, takes form & shape & fair reality when touched by her' (25 Apr 1846 BL Add 45794: f 103). Florence's enthusiasm for her new friend coincided with short periods of practical work. She wrote in October 1846: 'O happy, happy six weeks at the Hurst, where (from July 15 to Sept. 1) I had found my business in this world. My heart was filled. My soul was at home. I wanted no other heaven. May God be thanked as He never yet has been thanked for that glimpse of what it is to *live* (Cook, I, 64). Her letters to Aunt Hannah indicate that she did much visiting of the sick and teaching in poor schools during this period.

In spring 1847 the Nightingales travelled to Oxford to the meeting of the British Association where the two discoverers of Neptune were being honoured.

8. To Mary Clarke[1]   Lea Hurst, 10 July {1847}

My dearest friend,

I hardly know where to write to you now, but I hope this will reach you somewhere. We have seen your friend M. Mohl at Oxford & in London, & were very sorry not to see him at Embley, as we proposed to him, but hope that he will come here. Papa & I went with him to the Pentonville Prison (on the Solitary system) in London, & he seemed very busy at Oxford – but my opinion of him is, that he is thorough *Weltmensch*, who is labouring under a delusion (you know, they say we have all of us one mental delusion, some two – one monomania, which makes us think ourselves other than we are – in some it takes the form of conducting themselves as tea-pots, in others as Napoleons – one thinks himself a jug – another Jesus Christ) now my opinion of your friend is, that he thinks himself very much interested in the Civil Policy of England – whereas he is a thorough man of the world, who is very much bored by every thing but the things of Society.

We too have been seeing the world, the flesh & the devil during the last month – the first ten days of which we spent in London, hearing Jenny Lind (but it really requires a new language to define her – and meanwhile she must be felt, not talked about,) & doing the Exhibitions – then to Oxford for the British Association – and never any thing so beautiful, as that place was looking, have I seen abroad or at home – with its flowering Acacias in the midst of its streets of Palaces. I sauntered about the church-yards and gardens before breakfast & wished I were a College man. The Astro-nomical Section there was a plum-pudding with-out the suet. Le Verrier & Adams[2] sate on either side the President, like a pair of turtle doves, cooing at their joint star, & holding it between them. And there were {—?} &c &c &c. We worked hard – Chapel at 8 to one of those glorious Services – Sections from 11 to 3 – Colleges afterwards – then lecture. Away at 8. & philosophical tea & muffin at somebody's afterwards. Fowlers, Hamilton Grays, Bucklands, selves &c the muffins – Hallam, Wheatstone, Sewell & the great guns the philosophy. By the bye, I must tell you, that Mr. Hallam has found out that Gladstone is the Beast 666 in the Revelations. It came to him one day by inspiration in the Athenaeum – he tried Pusey & Newman[3] with the Greek numerals & the letters of their names but they wouldn't do – besides any body might have thought of them, the open beasts – but then it came to him that Gladstone was the hidden, the secret beast – at first the epsilon at the end stumped him – but, remembering that no Greek nominative ends with an epsilon, here he is – and no doubt it will cost him heaven or his Election, which is of rather more consequence.

On Sunday we went to church	γ	3
every 2 hours – not being able	τ	30
to 'do it' without – taking a lunch	α	1

at Christ Church, with one of
the Undergraduates on our way. I
asked a little bear of 3 months old,

δ	4
σ	200
τ	300
υ	70
ν	50
η	8
	666

which he had got chained up at his door, in to luncheon. It began
directly sucking our hands, & then proceeded to the butter on the
table – but the butter getting into its head, it became obstreperous,
& (on its master making it put on its cap & gown!) violent. After it
had behaved like a thing possessed, or a Prince in the disguise of a
bear (a thing commonly met with, you know, in the Arabian or –
Oxonian, regions) it was carried out in disgrace. When we came
out, it was still walking & howling on its hind legs, gesticulating &
remonstrating in a state of great aggravation & nervous excitement.
I spoke to it, but Papa pulled me away, lest it sh'd bite. I said, Let
alone, I'm going to mesmerize it. Mr. Monkton Milnes followed
the suggestion, & in 1/2 a min. the infant bear began to yawn, & in
3 min. was stretched fast asleep on the gravel, in a position in
which its master said it never slept naturally. A clear case of
collusion between the infant bear & Mr. Milnes!

Since Oxford we paid a visit at Lord Sherborne's, whose
daughter, Mrs. Plunkett is a great friend of mine, & at Mrs.
Bracebridge's, who is as ever my Ithuriel. She is a thorough woman
of the world without ever having had a worldly thought – give me
the woman, who has built her unworldliness upon the rock of the
world, against which the childish boat of mere unconsciousness
has gone to pieces. I have known many more intellectual, many
more brilliant, but I never knew such an union & harmony of
opposite qualities, she has the heart of a woman, the judgment of a
man – she is practical & poetical – the habits of a man of business,
the imagination of an artist – the hand of earth, the soul of heaven.
She pursues one object with unfaltering steps, yet is ready with her
sympathy to respond to all. She has the steadiness of the
Conqueror & the lowliness of the servant. She has the energy in
action of one, who bears down upon his object as if he had no
other aim on earth, & the serenity in failure of one, who feels that
he has no work at all of his own to do, & says 'I made a mistake.
My Master has other work for me that was not mine' – or rather
she can feel no disappointment – none of that death, which the soul
often dies between the destruction of one idea & the taking up of
another, for she has no idea which she is striving to carry out for its
own sake.

On Thursday we came home, to that dear home, where silence & solitude are such infinite blessings – & as my mother has no housekeeper, I am up to my chin in linen & glass, which have all a life & a soul to me, given them by my dear old Gale. I am very fond of housekeeping though without that. In this too highly educated, too little active age, it, at least, is a practical application of our Theories to something – & yet, in the middle of my lists, my green lists, brown lists, red lists, all my instruments of the Ornamental in Culinary Accomplishment, which I cannot even divine the use of – (I'm sure that list is badly made) – I cannot help asking in my head. Can reasonable people want all this? is all that China, linen, glass necessary to make man a Progressive animal? is it even good Political Economy – (query for 'good' read atheistical Pol Eco?) to invent wants, in order to supply employment? or ought not, in these times, all expence to be reproductive? And the best Versailles service says, And a proper stupid answer you'll get so go & do your accounts – there's one of us cracked.

The Carters are at Embley for the summer, & I trust enjoying it much, all but poor Frances, who does not improve in strength. Aunt Julia is in Bedford Sq. The Nicholsons returned home – except Marianne, who is still in London, as thin, I am sorry to say, as ever. The Sam Smiths are at home – & my boy Shore coming here for the holidays. The Hallams are coming to us – otherwise, I believe, we shall have a pretty quiet summer. We have seen something more of the Archer Clives[4] lately. She, you know, was the V of whom you said, 'Dear me, to think of the creature's having a heart & no legs.' She is now married, has two children, & I never saw happiness so stamped on any human creature's face. I like her exceedingly & admire her husband for disproving the general proposition, that *we* are to be treated as furniture or a piece of clothes for the man's vanity while *they* are to be as ugly as they please, & no one is to wonder at any body's marrying *them*. I was in ten thousand rages at Mr. Hamilton Gray having the impudence to wonder *to* me 'how any man could marry V'. He, who himself is much lamer than she, & has married Pots & Pans, you know – the famous Etrurian lion. Why is woman considered by woman *herself* as more of furniture than man? But how few people judge & discern for themselves. When a person says, I judge, for 'I' read generally Idleness or Prepossession or Conventionalism judges.

Aunt Polly is at Bath. But I must stop, for you will be tired, & so am I of writing such a long farrago. Do tell us where you are, & what you are going to do. I wish we could meet you somewhere – but there is no idea of our going abroad & I hardly wish it. People have left off talking about Ireland, only because they are tired of the subject – there is every prospect of a good & early harvest, but that will hardly relieve her woes. Adieu, dearest friend, with best love from all here, thine ever, whatever else I am 1000 thanks for your letter.

FN.

Source: BL Add 43397: ff 292–95

1. A virtually identical letter was sent to 'My dear' {Marianne Nicholson?}, dated 28 June. See BL Add 45767 ff: 210–15.

2. Le Verrier and Adams: John C. Adams (1819–92), mathematician and astronomer, at twenty-two had discovered Neptune by tracing the irregularities of Uranus. Since he had not published his findings, the French astronomer Urbain J. J. Le Verrier (1811–87) was first credited with the discovery. They met on this occasion to share the honour.

3. Pusey & Newman: E. B. Pusey (1800–82), John Keble and John Henry Newman (1801–90) published *Tracts for the Times* (1833), and were the leaders of the High Church Oxford Movement. After Newman's conversion to Roman Catholicism in 1845, Pusey became the nominal leader, although he had been suspended as a university preacher in 1843 for heresy.

4. Archer Clives: Mrs Caroline Archer Clive (1801–73), author of *Poems by V* (1840) and *Paul Ferroll* (1855), was an invalid who married the Reverend Archer Clive in 1840.

Soon after writing to Clarkey, Flo was delighted to hear that she had married her long-time friend, Julius Mohl.

Dearest friend, To think that you are now a two months' wife, & that I have never written to tell you that your piece of news gave me more joy than I ever felt in all my life, except once, no, not even excepting that once, because *that* was a game of Blind-Man's-Buff, in *your* case you knew even as you were known. I had the news on a Sunday from dear Ju & it was indeed a Sunday joy & I kept it holy . . .

And now for my confessions. I utterly abjure, I entirely renounce & abhor, all that I may have said about M. Robert Mohl, not because he is now your brother-in-law, but because I was so moved & touched by the letters which he wrote after your marriage to Mama; so anxious they were to know more about you, so absorbed in the subject, so eager to prove to us that his brother was *such* a man, he was quite sure to make you happy.

And I have not said half enough either upon that score, not any thing that I feel; how 'to marry' is no impersonal verb, upon which I am to congratulate you, but depends entirely upon the Accusative Case which it governs, upon which I do wish you heartfelt & trusting joy. In single life the stage of the Present & the Outward World is so filled with phantoms, the phantoms, not unreal tho' intangible, of Vague Remorse, Fears, dwelling on the threshold of every thing we undertake alone. Dissatisfaction with what is, & Restless Yearnings for what is not, Cravings after a world of wonders (which *is*, but is like the chariots & horses of fire, which Elisha's frightened servant could not see, till his eyes were opened) – the stage of actual life gets so filled with these that we are almost pushed off the boards & are conscious of only just holding on to the foot lights by our chins. Yet even in that very inconvenient position love still precedes joy, as in St. Paul's list, for love, laying to sleep these phantoms (by assuring us of a Love so great that we may lay aside all care for our own happiness, not because it is of *no* consequence to us, whether we are happy or not, as Carlyle says, but because it is of so much consequence to another) – gives that leisure frame to our mind, which opens it at once to joy.

But how impertinently I ramble on 'You see a penitent before you', don't say, 'I see an impudent scoundrel before me'. But when thou seest, & what more, when thou readest, forgive.

You will not let another year pass without our seeing you. M. Mohl gives us hopes, in his letter to Ju, that you won't, that you will come to England next year for many months, then, dearest friend, we will have a long talk out. If not, we really must come to Paris – & then I shall see you & see the Diaconesses too, whom you so kindly wrote to me about, but of whom I have never heard half enough.

I have just read your P'esse de Cleves – it is a jewel, but were you thinking of that, wretch, when you wrote to me? The Nicholsons are all at Waverley again. Marianne, they say, is getting fatter. Some of the party have been in Scotland. Helen Richardson is not very well. But she has the little Reeve with her, & is very happy at Kirklands. The Bracebridges are at home. She rejoiced as much as we did over your event. Parthe is going at the end of Nov'ber to do officiating Verger to a friend of ours Fanny Hanford, on a like event. Her prospects are likewise so satisfactory, that I can rejoice and sympathize under any form she may choose to marry in. Otherwise I think that the day will come, when it will surprise us as much, to see people dressing up for a marriage, as it would to see them put on a fine coat for the Sacrament. Why should the Sacrament or

Oath of Marriage be less sacred than any other? Do you remember V. (Mrs. Archer Clive) the woman of whom you said 'Only think of her having a heart & no legs' – we have been staying with her, & though my people still keep up a low murmuring grumble of astonishment re: her husband (being singularly subject to the 'caprice des yeux') I maintain that it is not at all astonishing. Though there is another great difference between her & all the rest of the world that while all her fellow creatures are always trying to say something clever, she is always trying to say something stupid. Aunt Patty is at Tenby with, though not in the house of, the Allens. Miss Allen is coming here.

Fortunately for you, my paper is at an end – the house being deficient in that article, & not yet unpacked – fortunately too, (as I am writing before breakfast,) I must go, & lay down rules for the laying down of the carpets, instead of chattering on with you so rudely. Why didn't I write before? Because I thought you would rather be let alone at first & that you were on your travels. And now, dearest friend, with *all* our *best* loves & congratulations to you & your Accusative or Nominative Case, believe me yours overflowingly, ever
  yours,

       Florence Nightingale
  Excuse haste & 'vain repetitions' – I am in the middle of china & linen lists. (13 Oct {1847} BL Add 43397: ff 296–300)

Florence's playfulness was only a façade, for her health worsened under the strain of idleness. She wrote, 'I see the numbers of my kind who have gone mad for want of something to do' (26 Oct 1850 BL Add 45790: f 107). By September, she collapsed after having lost weight and sleep for months. The Bracebridges persuaded Fanny and W.E.N. to let Florence accompany them to Rome for the winter. The party left on 27 October and did not return until the early summer of 1848. The trip was another building block for the future. Florence met the wealthy Anglo-Catholic couple Sidney and Elizabeth Herbert, who were to become key figures in her future work. Congenial friends in their circle were the Reverend Henry Manning and Mary Stanley, both of whom later converted to Roman Catholicism. Equally important, Florence met Madre Santa Colomba of the convent of the Trinità de Monti, who was not only profoundly mystical but also practically efficient. Florence spent much of her time in Rome at the convent, where she recorded the sayings of the Madre who became, in fact, her spiritual guide. During a retreat arranged for her at the end of her stay, Florence had her second mystical experience. She received what she believed to be a direct revelation from God in which she was instructed to surrender her will completely to Him.

But when Florence returned to England nothing had changed, in regard either to her family or to the social evils she saw all about her. She had written to Clarkey as early as 26 July 1848: 'In London there have been the usual amount of Charity Balls, Charity Concerts, Charity Bazaars, whereby people bamboozle their consciences and shut their eyes ... England is surely the country where luxury has reached its height and poverty its depth' (Cook, I, 80).

To make matters worse, after nine years' wait Monckton Milnes made his final offer of marriage; Florence refused him in June 1849. This must have aggravated family tensions, for the match would have been considered brilliant. Florence's decision to remain single arose from her belief that dedication to a higher calling precluded marriage. She attracted and enjoyed the company of men, and in a personal note, she admitted:

> I have an intellectual nature which requires satisfaction and that would find it in him. I have a passionate nature which requires satisfaction and that would find it in him. I have a moral, an active, nature which requires satisfaction and that would not find it in his life. Sometimes I think I will satisfy my passional nature at all events, because that will at least secure me from the evil of dreaming. But would it? I could be satisfied to spend a life with him in combining our different powers in some great object. I could not satisfy this nature by spending a life with him in making society and arranging domestic things. (Woodham-Smith, p. 77)

But the decision was not easy, for 'I know that since I refused him not one day has passed without my thinking of him, that life is desolate without his sympathy.' At the same time, Nightingale wrote: 'I know I could not bear his life ... that to be nailed to a continuation, an exaggeration of my present life without hope of another would be intolerable to me – that voluntarily to put it out of my power ever to be able to seize the chance of forming for myself a true and rich life would seem to me like suicide' (Woodham-Smith, p. 77).

In one of her meditations upon marriage, Nightingale had resolved, 'I must strive after a better life for woman' (Cook, I,

102). She believed that some women were destined for marriage, but that it ought not to be seen as women's only goal. Three years earlier, in 1846, she had written:

> I don't agree at all that a woman has no reason (if she does not care for any one else) for not marrying a good man who asks her, and I don't think Providence does either. I think He has as clearly marked out some to be single women as He has others to be wives, and has organized them accordingly for their vocation. I think some have every reason for not marrying, and that for these it is much better to educate the children who are already in the world and can't be got out of it, than to bring more into it. The Primitive Church clearly thought so too and provided accordingly . . . (Cook, I, 100–01)

Twenty years later she could staunchly declare, 'Unless the union of two together makes their work better for mankind, I cannot call it worth the tie' (to Harriet Martineau, 18 Feb 1864 BL Add 45778: f 242).

The Bracebridges again rescued Florence, taking her along to Egypt and Greece in the winter of 1850. While travelling *en route* to Egypt, Florence met two sisters of St Vincent de Paul who gave her introductions to the sisters at Alexandria. In Athens she met the American missionary couple Mr and Mrs Hill, who showed her their Protestant school and orphanage. She wrote of Mrs Hill, as with her madre in Rome, that she was 'always listening for the voice of God, looking for his will' (5 May {1850} BL Add 45793: f 76). Her powerful sense of destiny led her to seek such opportunities even when there appeared to be no way of achieving her goals. But the Olympian struggle that raged below the surface of the elegant and learned Miss Nightingale only increased in ferocity. How to reconcile her life with the will of God was far from resolved, as her diary entries testify:

> 7 Mar Gale all night & all day. Lying under Gibel Hereedee
> God called me in the morn'g & asked me 'Would I do good for Him, for Him alone without the reputation' –
> 8 Mar Thought much upon this question – my madre said to me Can you hesitate between the God of the whole Earth & your little reputation? as I sat looking out on the sunset upon the river in my cabin after dinner.
> 10 Every day, during the 1/4 of hour I had by myself,

after dinner & after breakfast, in my own cabin, read some of my Madre's words. Can you give up the reputation of suffering much & saying little, they cried at me.

11 Thought how our leaving Thebes which was quite useless owing to this contrary wind (we might have had another fortnight then) but without it I might not have had this call from God.

16–17 Tried to bring my will one with God's about Athens & Malta all the way as we rode in to Cairo. Can I not serve God as well in Malta as in Smyrna – in England as at Athens? perhaps better – perhaps it is between Athens & Kaiserswerth – perhaps this is the opportunity my 30th year was to bring me. Then as I sat in the large dull room waiting for the letters, God told me what a privilege he had reserved for me, what a preparation for Kaiserswerth in choosing me to be with Mr. B. during this time of his ill health & how I had neglected it – & been blind to it. If I were never thinking of the reputation, how I sh'd be better able to see what God intends for me.

Mai 12 To day I am 30 – the age Xt began his Mission. Now no more childish things, no more vain things, no more love, no more marriage. Now, Lord, let me only think of Thy will, what Thou willest me to do. O, Lord, Thy will, Thy will . . .

24–25 Mai God has brought me to Athens to teach me to look for His will. This was His birthday present to me. Surely some great temptation must be preparing that this great privilege has been granted me. This breathing time – if I had been all day long seeing Athens. I sh'd not have remembered my vows for my 30th year. I tho't that not seeing Athens w'd be the preparation for my birth day – it has been so, but in a different way – seeing something better at Athens . . .

9 juillet A miserable week at Berlin. I did not think it worth while to get up in the morning. What c'd I do but offend God? I never prayed. All plans, all wishes seemed extinguished. And now, on the brink of accomplishing my greatest wish, with positively planning it for me, I seemed to be unfit, unmanned for it – it seemed not to be the calling for *me*.

I had 3 paths among which to choose. I might have been a married woman, a literary woman, or a Hospital

Sister. Now it seemed to me, as if quiet, with somebody to look for my coming back, was all I wanted. I did not feel the spirit, the energy for doing anything at Kaiserswerth. To search out the will of God for me seemed so far from me I could not do it. (BL Add 45846: ff 23–24, 26, 41, 44–45, 57–58)

Whether or not Germany was originally part of the tour is unclear. The party travelled home via Berlin, however, where the Bracebridges stayed while Florence visited Kaiserswerth for the first time. A large hospital, penitentiary and orphanage had grown up there through the efforts of Pastor Fliedner and his wife; under conditions of rigorous piety, working-class and peasant women received training in basic nursing and childcare. Florence had first heard about this remarkable institution in 1842 from the Prussian Ambassador to England, but she had had to wait until 1850 to visit it herself. Upon arriving there on 31 July of that year she wrote in her diary:

I c'd hardly believe I was there – with the feeling with which a pilgrim first looks on the Kedron, I saw the Rhine – dearer to me than the Nile. The Fliedners rec'd me kindly. Went over the Institution with Fliedner – returned with him to dinner. Late the afternoon with her & the Russian in the garden. My hope was answered. I was admitted within the Diakonisson Anstalt. Went to the Inn to dismiss Trout[1] & get my things. My first night in my own little room within the Anstalt. I felt queer – but the courage which falls into my shoes in a London draw'g room rises on an occasion like this. I felt so sure it was God's work. (BL Add 45846: f 63)

1. Trout: FN's personal maid for the trip.

When Florence left on 13 August, she recorded: 'Left Kaiserswerth feeling so brave as if nothing c'd ever vex me again & found my dear people at Düsseldorf' (BL Add 45846: f 66). Soon after this visit she published anonymously a pamphlet, 'The Institution of Kaiserswerth on the Rhine', in which she described the work of the deaconesses and urged English women to engage in the same type of work.

The fortnight spent at Kaiserswerth appears to have restored Florence to high spirits, but on returning home she was again brought face to face with family opposition. Fanny was furious about her visit to Kaiserswerth, and W.E.N. had not yet shifted his position of neutrality.

To placate her family, Florence agreed to stay at home for six months to keep Parthe company, for her sister's health had been waning while Florence was travelling. The obedient daughter acquiesced, but she despaired, conscious as never before of cutting herself off from various options she had held open as long as possible. Milnes's marriage to another woman would probably have been of no consequence had her own dreams materialized, but her future continued to look bleak. During the years 1850 and 1851 she wrote some of her darkest private notes.

9. Private note   30 Dec 1850

But let me consider it truly Dec 30 1850.

I have no desire now but to die. There is not a night that I do not lie down in my bed, wishing that I may leave it no more. Unconsciousness is all that I desire. I remain in bed as late as I can, for what have I to wake for? I am perishing for want of food – & what prospect have I of better? While I am in this position, I can expect nothing else. Therefore I spend my days in dreams of other situations which will afford me food. Alas! Now I do little else. For many years, such is the principle of hope. I always trusted that 'this day month' I should be free from it. God, Thou knowest the efforts I have made. Now I do not hope. I *know*. I know that I, my nature & my position remaining the same, same nature can generate but same thoughts. Dec 30 – 1851, I shall be but so much more unable to resist these dreams, being so much the more enfeebled. Starvation does not lead a man to exertion – it only weakens him. Oh weary days. On evenings that seem never to end – for how many long years I have watched that drawing room clock & thought it never would reach the ten & for 20 or so more years to do this. It is not the misery, the unhappiness that I feel so insupportable, but to feel this habit, this disease gaining power upon me – & no hope, no help. This is the sting of death.

Why do I wish to leave this world? God knows I do not expect a heaven beyond – but that He will set me down in St. Giles' at a

Kaiserswerth, there to find my work & my salvation in my work, that I think will be the way, if I could but die.

Source: BL Add 43402: ff 55–56

10. Private note[1]   Undated {1851?}

— what is to become of me?
— I can hardly open my mouth without giving my dear Parthe vexation – everything I say or do is a subject of annoyance to her. And I, oh how am I to get through this day is the thought of every morning – how am I to talk through all this day – and now, I feel as if I should not have strength even to do anything else. My God, I love thee, I do in deed. I do not say it in open rebellion, but in anguish and utter hopelessness – why didst make me what I am? A little later, oh my God, a little later, when I should have been alone in the world or in the next stage – not now, not yet, not here — I have never known a happy time, except at Rome and that fortnight at Kaiserswerth. It is not the unhappiness I mind, it is not indeed – but people can't be unhappy without making those about them so. {Of F.P.N.}[2] oh, if we could but have been alike, either I like her or she like me. Or if my father and mother could but have but

Source: BL Add 43402: ff 64–65

1. The note has been copied (and edited) from an earlier note on 10 South St stationery immediately before or after FN's death.
2. {Of F. P. N.} Frances Parthenope Nightingale.

In April 1851, finally freed from her six-month commitment to Parthe, Florence went to Wilton, the country home of the Herberts, where she stayed throughout Liz Herbert's confinement. While there she met Dr Elizabeth Blackwell, the daughter of a Bristol merchant who had emigrated to the United States; Blackwell had become the first American woman doctor and was now studying in Europe. Florence invited her to Embley Park, but she failed to reassure Fanny, for Blackwell had lost an eye from purulent ophthalmia and her younger sister was planning to don male dress in order to avoid improper advances by medical students. But interest in hospitals had become the topic of the day, and 'shameful' could no longer appropriately describe Flo's aspirations. Florence herself was shifting from unquestioning obedience to the possibility of independent action. In a private note that summer, she observed, 'There are knots which are Gordian and can only be cut' (Woodham-Smith, p. 88).

11. Private note   Undated {c. 1851}

experienced in their own experience. My difficulties. to let me take the food I am perishing for – what makes me so unlike them? These things I cannot help saying to God. I do not say Forgive me, but Shew me the Truth. What is the Truth?

My father is a man who has never known what struggle is. Good impulses from his childhood up – & always remaining perfectly in a natural state, acting always from impulse – & having never by circumstances been forced to look into a thing, to carry it out. Effleurez, n'appuyez pas[1] has been not the rule but the habit of his life. liberal by instinct, not by reflection. But not happy, why not? he has not enough to do – he has not enough to fill his faculties – when I see him eating his breakfast as if the destinies of a nation depended upon his getting done, carrying his plate about the room, delighting in being in a hurry, pretending to himself week after week that he is going to Buxton or else where in order to be in legitimate haste. I say to myself how happy that man would be with a factory under his superintendence – with the interests of 2 or 300 men to look after.

My mother is a genius. She has the Genius of Order, to make a place, to organize a parish, to form Society. She has obtained by her own exertions, the best society in England – she goes into a school & can put this little thing right which is wrong – she has a genius for doing all she wants to do & has never felt the absence of power. She is not happy. She has too much fatigue & too much anxiety – anxiety about Papa, about Parthe's health, my duties, about the Servants, the parish. Oh, dear good woman, when I feel her disappointment in me, it is as if I was becoming insane. When she has organized the nicest Society in England for us, & I cannot take it as she wishes.

Parthe – she is in her Element if she had but health – & if she had but not me she is in her Element. It is her vocation to make holiday to hardworking men out of London, to all manners of people who come to enjoy this beautiful place. And a very good vocation it is –

46

no one less than I wants her to do one single thing different from what she does. She wants no other religion, no other occupation, no other training than what she has – she is in unison with her age, her position her country. She has never had a difficulty, except with me – she is a child playing in God's garden & delighting in the happiness of all His works, knowing nothing of human life but the English drawing room, nothing of struggle in her own unselfish nature – nothing of want of power in her own Element. And I, what a murderer I am to disturb this happiness – it is all that reason, divine reason, can do to prevent me repeating this even now – and I repeat it in my heart, while I no longer repeat it in my conscience.

I what am I that I am not in harmony with all this, that their life is not good enough for me? oh God, what am I? The thoughts & feelings that I have now I can remember since I was 6 years old. It was not I that made them. Oh God, how did they come? are they the natural cross of my father & mother? What are they? A profession, a trade, a necessary occupation, something to fill & employ all my faculties, I have always felt essential to me, I have always longed for, consciously or not. During a middle portion of my life, college education, acquirement I longed for – but that was temporary – the first thought I can remember & the last was nursing work & in the absence of this, education work, but more the education of the bad than of the young.

But for this, I had had no education myself – & when I began to try, I was disgusted with my utter impotence. I made no improvement. I learnt no ways. I obtained no influence. This nobody could understand. You teach better than other people, was the desperate answer always made me – they had never wanted instruction, why should I? The only help I ever got was a week with my Madre at Rome, which I made use of directly & taught my girls Holloway always on that foundation & my fortnight at Kaiserswerth. Still education I know is not my genius – tho' I cd do it if I was taught, because it is my duty here.

But why, oh my God, cannot I be satisfied with the life which satisfies so many people? I am told that the conversation of all these good clever men ought to be enough for me – why am I starving, desperate, diseased upon it? Why has it all run to vanity in me, to – what impression am I making upon them? when it comes to wholesome fruit in others? The concern of my life I have recorded what is the cause of it? Is it enough to say that rice disagrees with one man & agrees with another? that, as (Channing says) the ground of sincerity lies in talking of what you are interested about – so none of the subjects of society interest me enough to draw me out of vanity. Oh what do books know of the real troubles of life? it is all Hebrew & Chinese – death, why it's a happiness – oh how I have longed for a trial to give me food – to be something real. A nourishing life – that is the happiness – whatever it be – a starving life, that is the real trial. My God, what am I to do? teach me, tell me. I cannot go on any longer waiting till my situation sh'd change. dreaming what the change shall be to give me a better food. Thou hast been teaching me all these 31 years what I am to do in this? Where is the lesson? let me read it – oh where, where is it?

All that you want, will come – in one stage or another you (& all the rest of God's creatures) will have all food, all training, all occupation necessary to make you one with God. With this certainty, cannot you wait

You have already learnt something – you say yourself, what do they know who have never suffered?

Source: BL Add 43402: ff 79–83 {incomplete note}

1. Effleurez, n'appuyez pas: Touch lightly, do not dwell on them.

12. Private note   Whit Sunday 8 June 1851

My life is more difficult than almost any other kind. My life is more suffering than almost any other kind, is it not, God?

Let me not try to disguise these two facts from myself, Spirit of Truth – but let me honestly & with simplicity of purpose set to work, not to complain, but to find the means to live.

I must *take* some things, as few as I can to enable me to live. I must *take* them, they will not be given me – take them in a true spirit of doing thy will – not of snatching them for my own will.

I must do without some things – as many as I can – which I could not have without causing more suffering than I am obliged to cause any way.

Let me try to diminish the difficulties of my life knowing that what I do with such struggle as to cause continual dreams of another cannot be well done.

Let me try to diminish the suffering of my life knowing that I *cannot*, what I so truly desire, minister to Parthe's happiness while in such suffering myself. God's law has provided against that – let me venerate & observe that law.

Father, not my will but thine be done. Father of Truth, of Wisdom, of Goodness.

My object being to be one with Thee, to do Thy will, which is, at present, evidently to produce as much happiness, to avoid as much unhappiness as possible in these three, what are the means I can take?

The first is to preserve myself in a healthy state. Myself being in the same state as I was yesterday – & my circumstances the same, which they will be, the same things would occur.

To preserve myself in a healthy or at least a healthier state – my Holy Ghost tells me to do three things.

First, to spend one hour a day at least at the school. Without this, I know it to be impossible for me to preserve my being – & I am more fulfilling their wishes, I shall be more capable of doing what they want the rest of the day, than if I gave way & destroyed myself by doing what they think they wish in company the whole of the day – which I know to be impossible to me. I shall be more cheerful, less worn, more really obedient to their wish.

Secondly, I must keep to my hour & a half's steady thinking before breakfast. Without this, I am utterly lost – with this, I think I could keep myself alive – thro' the day. Whether that thinking shall be writing to Aunt Mai, or writing for myself, experience will decide.

Thirdly, I must place my intercourse with these 3 on a true footing, I mean only as regards myself. What is the true footing, Spirit of Truth? At present I am vibrating between irritation & indignation at the state of suffering I am in – & remorse & agony at the absence of enjoyment I promote in them. I wish for nothing but death, in order to relieve them & relieve myself. This cannot be true. This is childish. What is the true footing? It is impossible for their minds to understand mine. Ought I to be irritated with this? Poor dears – it is impossible – their most earnest desire is for my happiness – let me be sure that I am fulfilling their desire by taking as much of it as I can without altering any circumstances which it is clearly my duty not to alter.

It is impossible for any situation to go on well where one is at the bottom who ought to be either independent or at the top. I am at the bottom & ought not to be there. This aggregate can see farther than theirs is this presumptuous? no more so than to say that I can walk farther. If the Spirit of Truth has led me through suffering which they have not known to see farther, more comprehensively, is it presumption to act accordingly – or would it not be trying to act in a way, which His laws have provided that you shall not act to submit comparative knowledge to comparative ignorance. I might as well say that she ought to leave it to me to lay out the garden. I have been so long treated as a child & have so long allowed myself to be treated as a child that I can hardly assert this even to myself. It is with the greatest effort that I can reach it.

Yet I should love them both much better, if I could. Parthe is a child – let me love her as such in my thoughts as I do Shore.

I must expect no sympathy, nor help from them. I have so long craved for their sympathy that I can hardly reconcile myself to this. I have so long *struggled* to make myself understood, been sore, cast down, insupportably fretted by not being understood (at this moment even I feel it when I retrace these conversations in thought) that I must not even try to be understood. I know they *can not*. I know that to try for it & fail irritates me.

Is it presumption to say that I see farther, can judge better, about some things, than either of them? Then that is to say that the world is to make no progress. Mama says that I am inconsistent – says truly – the nature cannot be cramped & not cramped at the same time. To be inconsistent is to be cramped in some direction.

Parthe says that I blow a trumpet – that it gives her an indigestion – that is also true. Struggle must make a noise – & every thing that I have to do that concerns my real being must be done with struggle.

Now let me see how far the fallacy of intending to will directly affects me. A certain circumstance upon a certain nature must always have a certain, the same & a definite effect. To say that it will have any other the nature & the circumstance remaining the same, is absurd.

I have been brought hither by the laws of God – the circumstances acting upon the nature, it was impossible that I should feel otherwise than I do. I shall be brought through by the laws of God.

It must be only for fun that I try to make them understand me – because I know it is impossible.

Source: BL Add 43402: ff 68–73

13. Private note 15 June {1851}

To be cheerful, tender & gentle with Parthe – that is my object. Now, how is it to be obtained? Not by violent effort, nor by pretence of falsehood – but by a clear understanding of her character & mine & of the laws influencing such characters.

Father save me from this hour. But for this cause came I unto this hour. Spirit of Truth, what is to be done? Father of Wisdom, let me be one with Thee.

Our aggregates sympathize on few points – neither on religion, nor on politics, nor on manners of living (including modes of occupation, ends of life, social systems, characters of persons). We have therefore few points of sympathy – we cannot expect to convert one another. I have no desire to alter her. She, the greatest to alter me. Let me entirely avoid these subjects – it is better to be silent, even when appealed to – or to say, as I do with Shore, what I think best for him.

How do I do with Shore? I do not seek his sympathy. I know that he cannot give it me. I never ask for it. It is just as impossible for Parthe to give me her sympathy as it is for Shore. Let me never seek it.

I am continually trying to sympathize with Shore on his subjects, to make him talk. Let me observe what are Parthe's subjects – the owl – music – literature – art (including my dress & appearance). Let me sympathize with these & try to discover more.

It is difficult to sympathize with her in her health – because she repels it.

Source: BL Add 43402: ff 75–76   {incomplete note}

Florence observed sardonically while accompanying her father to the spa at Umberslade: 'The water-cure: a highly popular amusement within the last few years amongst athletic individuals who have felt the *tedium vitae,* and those indefinite diseases which a large income and unbounded leisure are so well calculated to produce' (Cook, I, 118).

In 1851 her parents agreed to let her return to Kaiserswerth while Fanny accompanied Parthe to Carlsbad for the water cure. Consent, however, did not mean that they were sympathetic to her plans.

14. To Fanny Nightingale   Kaiserswerth-am-Rhein,
16 July 1851

Dearest Mother,

It was the greatest possible relief to me to hear from you. I thought the letter long in coming – & did not write till I heard from you. I am rather glad you did not consult Killian, as he might have set your minds at sea again – & as the long journey seems really rather to agree than not – & I am very glad she has taken to drawing – & that Aschaffenbury & Wurzburg are so pretty. I hope that you will have seen all the Albert Dürers at Nuremberg – & particularly my Crucifixion, which I am so fond of – the forehead has all the intellect of the God, the Jupiter, & the mouth all the tenderness of the woman. Power & Sympathy, the two requisites in a friend are both there. I shall be very anxious to hear how Karlsbad agrees – you have horrid weather.

With regard to me, I am no longer, I am sorry to say, in the room you saw, but I am not at the Pastor's house at all – & therefore hardly ever see them – except when they make their rounds. I eat now with the Sisters in the great dining hall you saw, & sleep in a room in the Orphan Asylum, the same house where my last year's room was. I am afraid any account of what I do would be very uninteresting to you. On Sunday I took the sick boys a long walk along the Rhine – two sisters were with me to help me to keep order – they were all in ecstacies with the beauty of the scenery – it was like Africa turned green – but really I thought it very fine too in its way – the broad mass of water flowing ever on slowly & calmly to their destination – & all that unvarying horizon – so like the slow calm earnest meditative German character.

I have not mentioned to any one where I am – & should also be very sorry that the old ladies should know. I have not even told the Bracebridges. With regard however to your fear of what people will say, the people whose opinion you most care about – it has been their earnest wish for years that I should come here. The Bunsens (I know he wishes one of his own daughters would come) the Bracebridges, the Sam Smiths, Lady Inglis, the Sidney Herberts, the Plunketts – all wish it – & I know that others Lady Byron, Caroline Bathurst, Mr. Nemenheere, Mr. Rich (whose opinions however I have not asked) would think it a very desirable thing for every body. Also the Bonham Carters. There remain the Nicholsons whose opinion I don't suppose you much care for, who would not approve – & many others no doubt. The Stanleys I know would approve. With regard to the time chosen, I grant people will think it odd – & I would willingly have staid with Papa, as you know, & gone another time. But you preferred not. No one can judge of any one's family circumstances but themselves & you know how much better Parthe is without Papa or me – although she will not think so. One must judge for her. One cannot tell people what are the excitements which make it desirable for her to be alone & without irritation. But with regard to telling people the fact (afterwards) of my having been here, I can see no difficulty knowing as I do that all my friends, whose opinion you most value, will rejoice in it as a most desirable thing. The Herberts, as you know, even commissioned me to do some thing for them here. The fact itself will pain none of them. Uncle Nicholson said directly (when that foolish Marianne proclaimed something about Papa & me going with you) – 'I think Nightingale & Florence had much better go to the Hurst if invalids have a good courier & a good maid they are much better alone.' I am so glad the travelling suits her.

The world here fills my life with interest & strengthens me body & mind. I succeeded directly to an office & am now in another so that till yesterday I never had time even to send my things to the wash. We have ten minutes for each of our meals, of which we have four.

The people here are not Saints, as your Courier calls them, though that was a good hit, but good flesh & blood people, raised & purified by a great object constantly pursued. My particular friends are however all on foreign service, which I am very sorry for – all excepting that one precious soul, whom I introduced you to in the Penitentiary. But as we are all too busy to visit each other in our respective houses, I have never been able to go to the Penitentiary since I took you there, dear mother. The Pastor sent for me once to give me some of his unexampled instructions, the man's wisdom & knowledge of human nature is wonderful – he has an instinctive acquaintance with every character in his place. Except that once, I have only seen him in his rounds.

We get up at 5 – breakfast at 1/4 before 6 – the patients dine at 11 – the sisters at 12 – we drink tea, (i.e. a drink made of ground rye) between 2 & 3 – & sup at 7. We have two ryes & two broths – i.e. ryes at 6 & 3 – broths at 12 & 7. breads at the two former, vegetables at 12. Several evenings in the week we collect in the great hall for a Bible lesson or an account of Missions &c. But I must away ever dearest Mother your loving child

thank dear Pop for her letter

Athena[1] must not make blots & she must have sand & not drink the ink.

Unsigned

Source: BL Add 45790: ff 133–36

1. Athena: Florence's pet owl, which she had brought back from Greece.

On 31 August, Florence wrote to her mother:

I sh'd be as happy here as the day is long & wish I could
hope that I had your smile, your blessing, your sympathy
upon it – without which I cannot be quite happy. My
beloved people, I cannot bear to grieve you. Life & every
thing in it that charms you you would sacrifice for me –
but unknown to you is my thirst, unseen by you are
waters which would save me. To save me, I know would
be to bless yourselves, whose love for me passes the love
of woman. Oh how shall I shew you love & gratitude in
return, yet not to perish, that you chiefly will mourn.
Give me time – give me faith. Trust me. help me, I feel
within me that I could gladden your loving hearts which
now I wound. Say to me 'follow the dictates of that Spirit
within Thee.' Oh my beloved people, that spirit shall
never lead me to say things unworthy of me who is yours
in love – Give me your blessing. (BL Add 45790: f 142)

Florence later denied having received training at Kaiserswerth,
although throughout her life she praised the hospital for its moral
atmosphere: 'But never have I met with a higher tone, a purer
devotion than there. There was no neglect. It was the more
remarkable because many of the Deaconesses had been only
peasants – none were gentlewomen (when I was there)' (Note on
flyleaf, 24 Sept 1897 BL copy, *The Institution of Kaiserswerth*).
Her class bias notwithstanding, Florence glimpsed here the possibilities for ideal nursing which she tried to incorporate into her
later work on nursing reform. No equivalent to Kaiserswerth
existed in the general hospitals in England at this time.

The dreary cycle of family conflict resumed when Florence
returned home. W.E.N. requested her company when he went
anywhere; Parthe demanded that she stay home; Fanny pressed
her to consider her sister; the entertaining never abated. And
relatives continued to ask for Flo's help. In a private note titled
'Butchered to make a Roman Holiday', Florence wrote:

Women don't consider themselves as human beings at all.
There is absolutely no God, no country, no duty to them
at all, except family . . . I have known a good deal of
convents. And of course everyone has talked of the petty
grinding tyrannies supposed to be exercised there. But I
know nothing like the petty grinding tyranny of a good
English family. And the only alleviation is that the
tyrannized submits with a heart full of affection.
(Woodham-Smith, p. 93)

The year 1851 ended on a bitter note which is reflected in an imaginary dialogue with her mother:

15. Private note[1]   7 Dec 1851

Why, my dear, you don't think that with my 'talents' and my 'European reputation' & my 'beautiful letters' and all that, I'm going to stay dangling about my mother's drawingroom all my life. —I shall go & look out for work, to be sure.

You must look upon me as your son, your vagabond son, without his money. I shan't cost you near so much as a son would have done. I haven't cost you much yet – except my visits to Egypt and Rome. Remember, I should have cost you a great deal more if I had married or been a son—

Well, you must now consider me married or a son— You were willing to part with me to be married.

Source: BL Add 43402: f 66   {incomplete note}

1. Copied and edited note on 10 South St stationery.

Another unrelated note followed, summarizing her expectations for the next year:

16. Private note[1]   Undated

had not you rather have had all your experience than not? But now this year you will probably spend in the same position you are in now – you will be hardly ever alone – the next 3 weeks you will have company – then a fortnight alone – then a few weeks of London, then of Embley – then perhaps go abroad – then 3 months of company at Lea Hurst – then the same round of Embley company. Now what are you to do? — What you have to look forward to at home is your nightly visit at Holloway to the school, & here – your daily hour at 11. — Remember that you know what is the real object of life better than you did, better than many who have not suffered and, if you like, ruined. Remember that you believe in God that all will become one with him.

to offer a religion to the working Tailors[2]

to translate the Prophets if you could carry out these objects they would keep you healthy. Why can't you get up in the morning? I have nothing I like so much as unconsciousness but I will try —

Source: BL Add 43402: f 67 {incomplete note}

1. Copied and edited note on 10 South St stationery.
2. *Suggestions for Thought* (privately published 1859). See letter 74 to John Stuart Mill.

Florence was not the only thwarted daughter. Vivacious, gifted both as an artist and writer, and the perfect hostess, Parthe had a light touch that Florence lacked. While they might have complemented each other, both instead felt victimized. In a letter of November 1852 to Madame Mohl, Parthe revealed her deep anger towards her sister:

Truth is a good thing, and the history of the last year (the others much like it) is one month with the Fowlers in Ireland, three months with Aunt Mai in London, three more with her at Harrogate and Cromford Bridge, three more with her at the water cure and Grandmama's. Now Aunt Mai is the person she loves the best in the world, and whose metaphysical mind suits her best, so that I hope she has passed a very pleasant year, but meantime those eternal poor have been left to the mercies of Mama and me, both very unwell, and whose talkey-talkey broth and pudding she holds in very great contempt. Now, dear Clarkey, you are a very clever man and wise (which is better) and what you say is very true, I believe she has little or none of what is called charity or philanthropy, she is ambitious – very, and would like well enough to regenerate the world with a grand *coup de main* or some fine institution, which is a very different thing. Here she has a circle of admirers who cry up everything she does or says as gospel, and I think it will do her much good to be with you who, though you love and admire her, do not believe in the wisdom of all she does or says, *because* SHE says it. I wish she could be brought to see that it is the intellectual part that interests her, not the manual. She has no *esprit de conduite* in the practical sense. When she nursed me, everything which intellect and kind intention could do was done, but she was a shocking nurse. Mariette was ten times better. Whereas her influence upon people's minds and her curiosity in getting into the varieties of mind is insatiable. After she has got inside, they generally cease to have any interest for her. (O'Malley, pp. 199–200)

Florence was often called to help relatives, so perhaps she was not as bad a nurse as Parthe claimed. In the shadow of a sister who attracted and demanded attention, Parthe felt misunderstood and neglected. In old age the two sisters were more accepting of each other, but even then Florence remained intolerant and attention-seeking.

Not surprisingly, Nightingale's 1852 birthday letter to her father was an uncomfortable combination of gratitude and suppressed anger:

17. To W. E. Nightingale   12 May 1852

Private

My dear Father
     on my 32nd birthday I think I must write a word of acknowledgement to you.

     I am glad to think that my youth is past & rejoice that it never never can return, that time of follies & of bondage, of unfulfilled hopes & disappointed *in*experience when a man possesses nothing, not even himself.

     I am glad to have lived though it has been a life which, except as the necessary preparation for another, few would accept.

     I hope now that I have come into possession of myself. I hope that I have escaped from that bondage which knows not how to distinguish between 'bad habits' & 'duties' terms often used synonymously by all the world. It is too soon to hollow before you are out of the wood. I like the Magdalen in Coreggio's picture, I see the dark wood behind, the sharp stones in front only with too much clearness – of clearness however there cannot be *too* much. But, as in that picture there is light.

     I hope that I may live, a thing which I have not often been able to say, because I think I have learnt something which it would be a pity to waste – & I am ever yours dear father in struggle as in peace with thanks for all your kind care.

                                                                    FN

When I speak of the disappointed inexperience of youth, of course I accept that not only as inevitable but as the beautiful arrangement of Infinite Wisdom, which cannot create us Gods, but which will not create us Animals & therefore wills mankind to create mankind by their own experience a disposition of Perfect Goodness which no one can quarrel with.

I shall be very ready to read you when I come home, any of my 'Works' in your own room before breakfast, if you have any desire to hear them.

Au revoir, dear Papa

Source: Wellcome

In the summer and autumn Nightingale toyed with the idea of becoming a Roman Catholic convert. The Reverend Henry Manning, himself a recent convert, sympathized with her search for a supportive institution through which to channel her ambitions.

18. To the Rev. Henry Manning
Lea Hurst, Matlock
13 July 1852

Yes, it was very nearly what I expected – nearly, but not quite.

I acknowledge the truth of every word you have said. It is a matter of fact that the Catholic Church has done all the things you say & that no other church has done so. These are facts of history. Would I could believe in more. Empirically but not scientifically I believe in her – she has no more fervent disciple than I. I believe in her with all the power of my eyes, as the early Chaldeans believed in the return of eclipses which they could ascertain by observation, but could not account for.

You will say, as my dear Madre at the Trinità used always to do, And is not that enough? what would you have more? She is too beautiful not to be true. Ye shall know a tree by its fruits.

But there is a difference between conjecturing empirically & knowing certainly. My observation shews me the uniformities which exist in the Catholic Church of faith, of simplicity of aim, of love & self-sacrifice – as the observation of the Chaldeans shewed them the uniformities of the celestial motions. But I hesitate to rely, for want of being able to believe their theories as we waited till Kepler told us the law, which the Eastern had only mistaken.

You would have me snatch at the blessing the Catholic Church

has to give, without having given her my unconditional allegiance –
& make my own conditions (tacitly) instead of receiving hers. So
have I done all my life with the Anglican Church. I have snatched
her Sacraments (a faithless child – but she never asked me why)
tacitly making my own conditions to myself.

I stand now trembling where I stood firm before. Those
I have known left the arms of one church but to go to those of
another – a more faithful mother. I have a precipice behind me. If I
do not reach the Church.

Source: Presbytery of St Mary of the Angels, Bayswater
{Wellcome photocopy}   {incomplete letter}

Conversion faltered when Manning concluded that she had no
understanding of what Roman Catholicism demanded. Adherence
meant submission, a concept that was antithetical to Florence's
approach to life and religion.

In letters to Manning Nightingale seemed to see more clearly the
constraints on women than the renowned figure of later years was
to acknowledge:

> I say, *If* you knew. But you do know now, with all its
> faults, what a home the Catholic Church is. And yet what is
> she to you compared with what she would be to me? No one
> can tell, no man can tell what she is to women – their train-
> ing, their discipline, their hope, their home – to women
> because they are left wholly uneducated by the Church of
> England, almost wholly uncared-for – while men are not.
>
> For what training is there compared to that of the
> Catholic nun? . . . There is nothing like the training (in
> these days) which the Sacred Heart or the Order of St.
> Vincent gives to women. (15 July 1852 Presbytery of St
> Mary of the Angels, Bayswater/Wellcome photocopy)

She despised the Church of England, and longed to go to the work
that she knew was ready for her among the daughters of St
Vincent, but she could not convert:

> The wound is too deep for the Ch. of England to heal. I
> belong as little to the Ch. of England as to that of Rome –
> or rather my heart belongs as much to the Catholic Ch. as
> to that of England – oh, how much more. The only
> difference is that the former insists peremptorily upon
> my believing what I cannot believe, while the latter is too

careless & indifferent to know whether I believe it or not. She proclaims out of the Prayer book what we are to believe, but she does not care whether we do (and we don't) while the Catholic Church examines into the fact. If it were not for that, I might have a home where now I have none. (22 July 1852 Presbytery of St Mary of the Angels, Bayswater/Wellcome photocopy)

Just as Manning was making arrangements for Nightingale to visit a hospital in Paris run by the Sisters of Charity, Parthe had a breakdown. She was put under the observation of Sir James Clark, a leading physician and family friend, who advised Flo to leave Parthe so that her sister could learn to live without her.

19. To the Rev. Henry Manning   30 Old Burlington St
Wednesday {1852}

You were kind enough to wish to hear the result of our sad & degrading history.

After the fullest examination & consultation, the opinion given is that 'imbecility or permanent aberration is the inevitable consequence, unless my sister is removed from home & placed under a firm & wise hand.' My poor mother can be brought neither to see nor understand. They go on ordering their winter clothes & arranging their autumn parties, as if this horrible fate were not hanging over them. They are like children playing on the shore of the eighteenth century. Oh! don't laugh. For it is like seeing people jesting among the mangled bodies of their kin. So we play thro' life among the mangled souls of those we love.

My father cannot even be persuaded to come up to town to see Sir James Clark. I have had to walk by stealth alone at night to get the medical men to come to us. It is well for me that the Sisters of Charity have taught me the way to do odd things.

Under these circumstances, I have but one course to pursue. No one will act but me. My people return on Thursday to their own home in Hampshire – meaning to take me with them to undertake the care of my sister at home. The medical men are decidedly of opinion that my presence at home aggravates the disease. I have therefore said that Sir James Clark having given this awful warning, I cannot think it right to take a part in a way of going on which he has said will have such consequences. If my dear parents cannot think it right to make the change he prescribes, I hope that they will not blame me for withdrawing from taking part in a way of life in which I must either yield to my sister to her destruction (Sir James Clark having expressly stated that the brain is actually in a state of disease & that yielding to her must increase this state of the brain) or by opposition to her wishes & ideas I must be perpetually increasing her nervous excitement & fostering the monomania about me. I have, at the same time, offered to take the whole charge of her, without a nurse, (which the education I have received at different places has made me competent to do) – away from home, at any place the medical men may name – & said that, at any time, wherever I am, they may recall me to do this & I shall consider myself bound to come.

The question remains what am I to do with a stranded ship which appears to be useless now to every body? If I were to go to Paris immediately, I am told that I should hasten the catastrophe by the fits of tears & hysterics I should produce – & which I am well accustomed to, (in re Kaiserswerth). You asked me whether I had anticipated this. Oh! for such *long, long* weary years have I been expecting it that it is almost a relief it has come at last.

I believe I shall go for the present to the duty nearest at hand – to nurse a sick aunt – & wait to see what I can find out to be God's work for me.

I am blamed by every body, most of all by themselves 'for seeking duty away from the sphere in which it has pleased God to place me'. Hardly any body has any idea of the true state of the case, excepting the medical men, for with the cunning of monomania, every thing is smooth outside. It is only known that my sister has bad health & what I can be doing away from home, 'nobody *can* understand' under such circumstances.

I know you will pray for us – for the poor shattered brain – & for the worn & weary spirit, which would so gladly have given its life blood to her.

Forgive me this long story. I think you can hardly complain of my 'reserve' now. I hope that I have told the history of my woes not for the pleasure of talking of myself, but because, in your direction of young ladies, it may really be of some use to know what certain modes of life will lead to. I have not even the comfort of thinking that the organization was defective & that therefore it has come more directly from the hand of God. For I am told that there is nothing here which might not have been prevented, which might not be prevented now. Any story which I tell must sound like a long complaint, which I most earnestly desire to avoid – for God is very good.

You accuse me of reserve. But if you knew how earnestly I have desired a friend & prayed for a counsellor.

I wished to say one thing more about myself – which is that, if you are kind enough to see the Abbé Des Genettes or the Superioress on my account, I should be glad that neither the patients nor the Sisters should know that I was not a Catholic.

I do not ask you to write, for I know well how much you have to do. But if at any time you should kindly have any communication to make,

Source: Presbytery of St Mary of the Angels, Bayswater
{Wellcome photocopy}   {incomplete letter}

In another undated letter to Manning from the same period, Florence wrote:

> Oh if mothers saw what I have seen, had watched as I have the downward course of the finest intellect & the sweetest temper, thro' irritability, nervousness & weakness to final derangement – & all brought on by the conventional life of the present phase of civilization, which fritters away all that is spiritual in women – they would curse conventional excitements, as I do now, instead of rejoicing . . . (Presbytery of St Mary of the Angels, Bayswater/Wellcome photocopy)

Florence went to nurse Great-Aunt Evans, Grandmother Shore's sister, through her final illness. Writing from Aunt Evans's bedside, Flo was strong enough to attempt a kind of reconciliation with Parthe:

20. To Parthenope Nightingale   Tapton, Monday
{Jan 1853}

Oh my dearest Pop,
    I wish I could tell you how I love you & thank you for your kind thoughts as received in your letter today. If you did but know how genial it is to me, when my dear people give me a hope of their blessing & that they would speed me on my way – as the kind thought of Cromford[1] seems to say they are ready to do. I will write to Mama about Paris & Cromford.
    My Pop, whether at one or the other, my heart will be with thee. Now, if these seem mere words, because bodily I shall be leaving

you, have patience with me, my dearest. I hope that you & I shall live to prove a true love to each other.

I cannot, during the year's rounds, go the way which (for my sake, I know) you have wished. There have been times when, for your dear sake, I have tried to stifle the thoughts which I feel ingrained in my nature. But, if that may not be, I hope that something better shall be. If I ask your blessing on a part of my time for my absence, I hope to be all the happier

Source: BL Add 45791: f 274   {incomplete letter}

1. Cromford: Cromford Bridge, near Matlock, home of Grandmother Shore.

In February Florence finally reached Paris. Staying at first with the Mohls, she visited all the major hospitals, collecting data, reports and statistics on hospital organization and nursing arrangements for Europe as well as Paris. Just as she was about to enter the Maison de la Providence to train with the Sisters of Charity, she was called home. Her Grandmother Shore was ill. She and W.E.N. travelled to Tapton, where Florence stayed until her grandmother's death in March.

From Tapton she went to Lea Hurst to make preparations to return again to Paris, while the rest of the family were at Embley preparing to go to London. In April, Liz Herbert recommended Florence to Lady Charlotte Canning, chair of the Ladies' Committee, for the superintendency of the Institution for the Care of Sick Gentlewomen in Distressed Circumstances. Flo was interviewed and Lady Canning was suitably impressed. The Nightingales, upon hearing the news, put forward their usual objections, but W.E.N. then shifted his position. He conceded to Florence an allowance of five hundred pounds a year. Negotiations with the Committee were difficult because of her social position. Unfortunately, one of the committee ladies who knew Flo's cousin Marianne asked her if Florence's family approved. Her distortion of the conflict Florence had caused at home led the Committee to withdraw their offer. When the Nightingales heard that the Nicholsons said Florence was 'going into service' and had begged for the job rather than been offered it, they leapt to her aid. The problem was resolved when Liz Herbert and others convinced Florence to write to the Committee with evidence that she had her father's permission.

21. To Mary Clarke Mohl   Lea Hurst 8 April {1853}

My dearest friend You will have heard from Hillie of my dear Grandmother's death & of her fearful sufferings. I shall never be sufficiently grateful that I came, as she allowed me to do many things in the way of moving & changing her, which perhaps she would have allowed no one else to do, & which made her end less suffering. This was the reason why I did not answer your letter sooner, you will understand. We buried her last Friday & after the funeral Papa & my aunt & I came here for a few days. But I am going back to Tapton (my grandmother's) tomorrow, to settle with the poor old servants & wind up affairs – for a week.

Now for my own affairs. In all that you say, I cordially agree, & if you knew what the 'fashionable apes' have been doing, their 'offs' & their 'ons' poor fools! & asking Marianne Galton's advice, such a sensible idea! You would say so ten times more. I shall be truly grateful if you will write to Pop – my people know as much of the affair now as I do, which is not much. You see the f.a.s (or a.f.s which will stand for 'ancient fathers' & be more respectful, as they are all Puseyites) the f.a s want me to come up to London now & look at them, & if we suit, to come very soon into the Sanatorium, which, I am afraid will preclude my coming back to Paris, especially if you are coming away soon, for going there without you would unveil all my iniquities, as the f.a.s are quite as much afraid of the R.C.s, as my people are. It is no use telling you the history of the negotiations, which are enough to make a comedy in 50 Acts. They may be summed up, as I once heard an Irish shoeless boy translate Virgil, 'Obstupui'. I was althegither (altogether) bothered – 'steteruntque comae' & my hair stood up like the bristles of a pig – 'vox faucibus haesit' & divil a word could I say. Well, divil a bit of a word can I say except that you are very good, dear friend, to take so much interest, & that I shall be truly glad if you will write to Pop, dans le sens du muscle[1].

All your advice, which I sent to Mrs. Bracebridge I give my profoundest adhesion to. I would gladly point the finger of scorn in the liveliest manner at the f.a.s, & ride them roughshod round Grosvenor Sq. I will even do my very best – but I am afraid it is not in me to do it as I should wish. It would be only a poor feint – a mean Caricature. But I will practise – & you shall see me.

My people are now at 30 Old Burlington St. where I shall be in another week – please write to them there, & if you can do a little quacking for me to them, the same will be thankfully received, in order that I may come in when I arrive, not with my tail between my legs, but gracefully curved round me, in the way in which Perugino's Devil wears it, in folds around the waist.

I am afraid I *must* live at the place. If I don't, it will be a half & half measure, which will satisfy no one. However I shall take care to be perfectly free to clear off, without its being considered a failure, at my own time. I can give you no particulars, dearest friend, because I don't know any. I can only say that, unless I am left a free agent & am to organize the thing myself & not they, I will have nothing to do with it. But as the thing is yet to be organized, I cannot lay a plan either before you or my people. And that rather perplexes them, as they want to make conditions that I shan't do this or that. If you would 'well present' my plans, as you say, to them, it would be an inestimable benefit both to them & to me. That estimable matron, Mrs. Douglas Galton, is doing all she can against the poor little infant – I mean my Sanatorium not her baby. Hillie will tell you all I know – that it is a Sanatorium for sick governesses, managed by a Committee of fine ladies. But there are no surgeon-students nor improper patients there at all, which is, of course, a great recommendation in the eyes of the Proper. The Patients, or rather the Impatients, for I know what it is to nurse sick ladies, are all pay patients, poor friendless folk in London. I am to have the choosing of the house, the appointment of the Chaplain, & the management of the funds, as the f.a.s. are *at present* minded. But Isaiah himself could not prophecy how they will be minded at 8 o'clock this evening. I hope Hillie will stay with you till you come to England. I hear from Abraham himself that she is not wanted at home. I would write to her if I had time. (Aunt Ju is at the Holmwood now).

And now what shall I say, dearest friend, for all your kindness to me? Think anything but that I am indifferent when I do not write. Give my love & thanks to M. Mohl. If you could give me a little impression of your & Hillie's plans, I should be very much obliged. I fear that, if I undertake the f.a.s, my people will wish me to spend the intermediate time with them, & so I shan't on account against me for all you have paid for me – & dearest, *if* you want any little presents of cutlery, there are some in my little top-drawer (in Tallboy). I believe you must bring all my goods back with you, as, even if I do go back to Paris, I fear it will not be yet. Perhaps you said a word to Parthe about my not having sate to you. If you come to England after Easter (but I hope you will *not*) I may see you in London, pending my negotiations. It was heaven's mercy that I came, & I shall never regret it, *what e'er betide*. Dear Aunt Mai had never seen a death bed before & this was an awful one to begin her experience. The end however was so calm that, tho' I sate at the head, I did not know the exact moment. More when we meet.

Pay my letters, stays, & all my odds & ends, dearest – let not aught stand against me. God bless you.

I would send you some French money I have still by me, if I knew how.

The letter you forwarded to me was to tell me that Canning was on again.

Put my straw bonnet into my carpet bag. And please say all kinds of things for me to dear kind patient Mr. Mohl. Don't leave behind any of the 'Budgets' he gave me, which are in the Drawing Room. He bought them his own self for me & made me a present out of his pocket. I was so shocked. When I thought he was only going to borrow them.

Adieu, dearest. I am sorry to give you the trouble of bringing home my goods, or any trouble, this particularly.

Papa is at the Hurst with your people. He has been here – she just recognised him – he returns for the funeral on Friday. I am very glad I did not delay an hour. She knew me always, but never took food after I came. I am sleepy & have much to do. Good night – ever, dearest, with love & blessing to dear Clarkey, & something to Fräulein Anna, thy old Flo

I hear M. G's baby is a very little one but not a very bad one.

Source: BL Add 43397: ff 305-09

1. dans le sens du muscle: with muscle.

Florence tried once more to train with the Sisters of Charity. She returned to Paris again at the end of May, and actually entered the Maison de la Providence without her parents' or the Committee's knowledge since this, a Catholic *maison*, was forbidden territory. Her plans for the new Institution, however, moved forward without delay:

22. To Lady Charlotte Canning[1]   120 Rue du Bac, Paris
5 June {1853}

Dear Lady Canning

Many thanks for the plan of the house in Harley St – & for your kind information on the subject, which interests us both so much.

The indispensable condition of a house for the purpose we require is

1st that the nurse should *never* be obliged to quit her 'floor', except for her own dinner & supper, & her patients' dinner & supper – (& even the latter might be avoided by the windlass we have talked about).

Without a system of this kind, the nurse is converted into a pair of legs for running up & down stairs. She ought to have hot & cold water upon her own floor, she ought to sleep upon her own floor – in her own bed-room, she ought to have the requisites for making poultices, barley water, warming all her medicines, dressings &c &c, (&, I should say, for making her patients' breakfasts & teas, & her own,) so that she should never have occasion to leave the floor confided to her. Her bed-room & little kitchen (which may be one & the same) & the other Accompaniment are therefore indispensably on the *same* floor as her patients. At Chandos St. & other places, where the nurses sleep all together on the ground floor, they might just as well sleep out of the house.

2'nd The bells of the patients should all ring in the passage outside the *nurse's* own door, *on that story*, & should have a valve, which flies open when its bell rings, & *remains* open, in order that the nurse may see who has rung. If a nurse must go down into the kitchen for every thing, she has, (if she has 3 patients,) 6 journies for their breakfasts, as many for everything they want &c, besides the waiting in the kitchen, because the cook cannot let her boil their eggs, or make their chocolate, or cut their bread & butter at that moment.

Should it be impossible to spare one small room on *each* floor for the purpose mentioned, there ought to be one large room set apart on the 2'nd floor, where everything for the nurses' use is *ready* & where all the nurses go to fetch what they want & to warm & to mess for their patients.

The carrying hot water all over the house is desirable. The cheapest way of doing it is, I believe, to have a boiler at the top of the house with a small fire to heat it (the boiler replenishing itself) & pipes bringing the hot water to each story, (one cock on each story is sufficient). But there might be a small boiler on *each* story with its little fire of its own (it does not take much fuel) all the boilers replenishing themselves so that there is no danger of burning.

Each nurse ought to have one or two Sub-nurses or Probationers under her, according to the number of patients she has. Where the rooms are properly distributed & all the above precautions observed, I have seen one nurse & two probationers take the care of twelve patients (all in separate rooms), excepting in cases where a patient required a nurse to herself. But, if a nurse has one patient at the top of the house & another at the bottom, besides journeys to the kitchen & to her own bed-room, of course this is impossible.

Dear Lady Canning, I make no apology for writing all these details, as, if you take the Harley St. house, some thing of bell hanging, hot water piping &c &c (to accomplish some of these objects) may be necessary to be done at once. I am sorry I have not time to make it shorter. It is difficult to me to judge of the Harley St. house, without asking a variety of questions which can hardly be answered at a distance. Early in July I shall be back in England, for the sake of serving a short apprentice-ship in the Chandos St. house before it is given up, if they have room for me.

I am afraid my Committee will greatly disapprove of my being at Paris in the enemy's camp, instead of being very much obliged to me for acting as a spy to despoil the enemy of their good things. With the fear that they would not be as grateful to me as they ought, I did not proclaim my intention of going to Paris.

I would further say

1st that the Superintendent ought to sleep in the middle of her patients

2nd the Committee should ask themselves the question whether they wish to train patients or nurses. If it is the patients they wish to train, the Superint't should take her meals with them, if it is the nurses, with the nurses.

3rd if it should be the intention of the Committee to have a house where dyspeptic patients may find a home, where they may amuse themselves & make acquaintances, a drawing room & a dining room are very desirable – but if, on the contrary, it is for grave disease, these rooms may be devoted to the reception of patients, as few, or none, will be able to leave their rooms.

I would make an apology for these remarks which are perhaps not very a propos, & with many thanks, dear Lady Canning, for all the trouble you have taken,

believe me yours very truly

Florence Nightingale
in great haste

Source: BL Add 45796: ff 39–42

1. In pencil: F.N. to Lady Canning on necessary condition in a house for the gentlewomen in answer to Lady C's letter of June 3.

After only a fortnight with the Sisters of Charity, Florence contracted measles and had to leave. While staying with Julius Mohl, she wrote to Clarkey, who was in England.

23. To Mary Clarke Mohl

Rue du Bac 120, Paris
28 June 1853

Back drawing-room! at Madame Mohl's!

My dearest friend,

Do you see where I am? Here's a 'go'! Has Mr. Mohl told you? Here am I in bed in your back drawing-room. Poor M. Mohl appears to bear it with wonderful equanimity & recueillement, like his danseuse[1]. Not so I. It is the most impertinent, the most surprising, the most inopportune thing I have ever done – me established in a Lady's house in her absence to be ill. If Mr. Mohl had any sins, I should think I was the avenging Phooka appointed to castigate him – as he has none, I am obliged to arrest myself at the other supposition that it is for my own. It was not my fault though really. Here is how the things have happened.

But first let me tell you, in answer to yours, that I think Clinton looking a great deal better. Her lip has almost retaken its natural size – & she looks altogether much less scrofulous. Nelken says that she wants her constitution changing by Iodine & Cod Liver Oil, which he is giving her, & that a little more sea or a little more country, tho' very good for her, are not the essential, but that she will get well here. I think her already looking so much better with the good food & the medicine. Nevertheless I write in good time that you may decide whether I am to bring her, as I must be in England the beginning of *next week*, if I can, & shall be too glad to bring her (& pay her journey & expences, of course,) if you will let me bring her.

I go into service at my place in London next week, if I possibly can. Do come & see me there – (1 Upper Harley St) – when you come to town.

To explain

I have had the measles at the Soeurs. And, of all my adventures, of which I have had many & queer, as will be (never) recorded in the x Book of my Wanderings, the dirtiest & the queerest I have ever had has been a measles in the cell of a Soeur de la Charité. They were very kind to me – & dear Mr. Mohl wrote to me almost every day, & sent me tea, (which however they would not let me have) and he lastly, in his paternity, would have me back, (where I came yesterday), & established me in the back-drawing room, to my infinite horror, & now I am getting better very fast, & mean to be out again in a day or two. I hope nobody will catch it here. Mr. Mohl assured me that both the children had had it – & I had got rid of the eruption & all that before I came. Mr. Mohl is *so* kind, & comes to see me & talk, which I suppose is very improper, but I can't help it, & he has been like a father to me & never was *such* a father! I really am so ashamed of all his kindness, & the trouble I give them, that my brazen old face blushes crimson, & I assure you this paper ought to be red. Julie is very kind to me. But I hope not to be long on their hands. As to my calamity itself, it is like the mariage de Mademoiselle, who could have foreseen it? It really was not my fault. There was no measles at any of my posts – & I had had them not 18 months ago, so that, erect in the consciousness of that dignity, I should not have kept out of their way, if I had seen them. The Dr. w'd not believe I could have had them before. Well, I'm so ashamed of myself that I shall lock myself up for the rest of my life & never go nowhere no more. For you see, it's evident Providence, who was always in my way, & who as the Supérieure said, is 'très admirable', (meaning *wonderful*), in having done this, does not mean me to come to Paris nor to the Soeurs, having twice made me ill when I was doing so – & given you all this trouble. For me to come to Paris to have the measles a 2'nd time is like going to the Grand Desert to die of getting one's feet wet, or anything most unexpected.

I hope you are going to the Hurst, where my people are now. I have heard nothing of Hillie.

And now, enough of me. I am so provoked that Mr. Mohl's benign face enrages me, & I am ever, dearest friend, yours repentantly & very gratefully

F.N.

Please write to M. Mohl, & comfort him for his disaster. I am so repentant that I can say nothing – which, the Cath's tell me, is the 'marque' of a true 'humiliation'. Thank you 1000 times for all your kindness. I come to England next week.

Source: BL Add 43397: ff 310-12

1. recueillement, like his danseuse: with composure, like a balancing act.

Upon her return to England, Florence took rooms in Pall Mall and supervised the arrangements for the new institution. On 12 August 1853 she moved into the premises at 1 Upper Harley Street. She gaily wrote to her mother, describing with relish the minutiae of her new job. Old quarrels were submerged in the pleasures of the new tasks:

24. To Fanny Nightingale   1 Upper Harley St 29 Oct 1853

Oh my boots! my boots! dearer to me than the best French-polished, my brother boots! where are ye, my boots! my boots! I ne'er shall see your pretty faces more!

My dear, I *must* have them boots. I can't wear your London-made square-toed corn-begetting rascals. The pair I gave Mariette at Cavendish Sq. was quite new, save a rubbed piece of cloth at the back. I have but one shoe to my feet – & them boots I must have. Why Mariette must have hundreds of my old boots. I had four pair, not at all decrepit when I came home from Paris. Alas! I charged her so particularly not to let that pair I gave her in London out of her hands. But, if she really *cannot* disgorge, Chollocombos must, alas! make me a *new* pair. He has my measure & probably Mariette can find him one old pair of mine as a pattern that he may make no mistake.

Thank you for Duolin's direction. I will have a pair of quilted bottines[1] made there by & bye. Our stone stairs are now very fine & carpeted.

I sent to Sprague's the three Reviews,
> Wicliffe &
> Cloister Life

I wish you would kindly send me the direction of a 'blanchisseuse de fin'.[2] It is quite the cheapest plan to go to the best, because they keep clean so much longer. Mariette's are too 'mow'[3] – so I don't send any to her to be washed, this time – & my own 'blanchisseuse' is horrid – the things are dirty 3 hours after.

I have sent all the boxes back by the rail with 'Empty' on them.

More flowers, more game, more grapes – thankfully received I wd say many thanks for what we've got, but am afraid you wd say la reconnaissance est un vif sentiment des bienfaits futures,[4] &c &c. The old clothes were most magnificent & received 'with a shout' as David w'd say. L'y Caroline Russell is come back to my great joy. With her spicy Irish fun she prevents the other women from tormenting me, & makes a joke of what they say. However they are much improved. And L'y Canning & Mrs. Herbert attended my Committee to-day. They are both come back & they hope war will be staved off.

John, my fidus Achates, was delicate about sending back the

boxes – he thought it such a broad hint, he said. However, the sweet little boxes are gone.

We have no funds to hire an accountant – & if we did, he would off with the money.

Many thanks for my Davenport &c &c &c. Newman has not yet returned Cromf'd Br. mounted & I have heard nothing of the new Mrs. Herbert – tho' her frame is come. Many thanks for the Cromf'd Br. frame. I s'pose the rings must be altered.

The Caxtons are being read aloud in the common room at this moment. But now B. is gone, I have everything to do – for only one of the patients can read aloud & she has only half a lung. The Cs. are much admired.

Many thanks for the envelopes. Little Crossthwaite sticks on stamps for me by the doz.

Your black poplin has clothed the old lady.

I consent to have the £12 book-case *if* it does not come to more, & *if* you will kindly order it, (as Index Expurgatorius can go in) I will get a little cheap 3 shelver to hang against the wall besides.

I have subscribed to Mudie for the patients 15/ for 3 months 3 vols. & take in a newspaper at 4 o'clock (same day) 20/ pr quarter – it sounds very dear. But it seemed to me best.

Unsigned

Source: Wellcome

1. bottines: a high half-boot worn by ladies and children.
2. blanchisseuse de fin: laundress of delicate clothing.
3. mow: a jest.
4. la reconnaissance est un vif sentiment des bienfaits futures: Gratitude is the keen anticipation of future favours.

The same cheerful busyness characterized Florence's letters to Lady Canning, a friend and trusted ally on the Ladies' Committee:

25. To Lady Charlotte Canning

Upper Harley St
13 Sept {1853}

Dear Lady Canning

Mrs. Parez bore the moving like a hero, & was decidedly the better for it! Now however she is failing, & sometimes, I think, cannot live through the night. Miss Robson has not yet returned.

I have parted with the under-housemaid, & I have been obliged to give poor Nurse Bellamy warning, though I had no fault to find with her, farther than that she had nothing of a nurse but the name & the wages. We have now one nurse & one servant less than in Chandos St – we bake, preserve, & do all the needle-work of the new furniture at home – (having made all our blinds, curtains, carpets & linen ourselves) – & we don't find the want of those extra servants.

Your furniture from Mr. Fisher's has not yet all arrived. That which has come we like exceedingly. The curtains for the great ward are all made, & look very gay – but they are not yet *all* up, owing to 3 doz. of Gutta Percha rings being still wanting. I have been to the place in Bond St about them twice. They will not let us have them for less than 2/6 per doz. (but they say the price to other customers is 3/9). I have got those which were sent to your house in Grosvenor Sq – & ordered 5 more doz – which, of course, ought to go to the account of the Institution.

The arm-chairs you ordered from Mr. Fisher's have been the delight of the Patients & are all in use.

I have not seen any of the Committee but Miss Maurice since Ly Caroline Russell's departure. Every body else is out of town. Mrs. Lindsay has not been seen yet.

The workmen are not yet nearly out of the house. The lift & the stoves seem to be stumbling-blocks & stones of offence, as if no one had ever heard of them before.

We have seven patients – two more coming in – two more making application.

With regard to my own share in the business, I have been so busy for the last fortnight that I really had never asked myself the question till your letter came. Now I ask myself, in obedience to your desire, how do I like it? And I can truly say that, as far as the Patients are concerned, my business is full of joy & consolation. They are much easier to manage than I expected, & they are always to be cheered, tho' not always cheerful. Indeed I think we are most fortunate in our Patients – & we are going to lose one on Thursday, who is going home to die, because Dr. Farre can do nothing for her, whose loss I shall regret as if it were my own sister.

I think I have answered all your questions, & I must conclude, in great haste, dear Lady Canning, ever yours most truly & gratefully for all your kindness

F. Nightingale

I believe that some alterations in the way of organization will be required, as you say. But I have not mentioned them yet –

preferring to wait till you & other ladies of the Committee were in town & on the spot again.

Mr. Marjoribanks has been most kind & helpful. Indeed, without him, I don't know how we should have got through. Lady Stuart de Rothesay was so good as to call one day about your furniture & said that she would write to you. We have not been able to take patients into the 'Camp' yet. I fear we shall have to change the 'Fry' nurse. Mr. Fisher is a dilatory gentleman & has not yet! finished putting up our blinds, but at this time of year London workmen 'strike' for their amusement, just as country workmen marry when they are out of work to divert their minds.

Source: Harewood Collection, Lord Canning Papers, 177/Z/5

Nightingale's letter to her father was more revealing than those she wrote to her mother and friend; reforming her small institution involved complicated behind-the-scene machinations that were to become her characteristic mode of operation in the Crimea.

26. To W. E. Nightingale   1 Upper Harley St 3 Dec 1853

Dear Papa

You ask for my observations upon *my* Time of statesmanship. I have been so very busy that I have scarcely made any *Resume* in my own mind, but upon doing so now for your benefit, I perceive

1. when I entered into service here, I determined that, happen what would, I *never* would intrigue among the Com'tee. Now I perceive that I do all my business by intrigue. I propose in private to A, B or C the resolution I think A, B, or C most capable of carrying in Com'tee, & then leave it to them – & I always win.

I am now in the hey-day of my power. At the last Gen'l Com'tee, they proposed & carried (without my knowing anything about it) a Resolution that I should have £50 pr month to spend for the House & wrote to the Treasurer to advance it me – whereupon I wrote to the Treasurer to refuse it me. Ly Cranworth,[1] who was my greatest enemy, is now, I understand, trumpeting my fame thro' London. And all because I have reduced their expenditure from 1/10 per head per day to 1/.

The opinions of others concerning you depend not at all, or very little, upon what *you* are but upon what *they* are. Praise & blame are alike indifferent to me, as constituting an indication of what my-self is, tho' very precious as the indication of the other's feeling.

My popularity is too great to last. At present I find my Com'tee only too easy to manage. But if they could be so taken in by my predecessor?

Last General Committee, I executed a Series of resolutions on five subjects, & presented them as coming from the Medical Men

1. that the successor to our House Surgeon (resigned) should be a dispenser & dispense the medicines *in* the house, saving our bill at the Druggist's of £150 per an.

2. a series of House Rules, of which I sent you the rough copy

3. a series of Resolutions about not *keeping* patients, of which I send the foul copy

4. a complete revolution as to Diet which is shamefully abused at present

5. an advertisement for the Institution, of which I send the foul copy

All these I proposed & carried in Com'tee, without telling them that they came from me & not from the Medical Men – & then & not till then, I shewed them to the Medical Men without telling *them* that they were already passed *in Com'tee.*

It was a bold stroke, but success is said to make an insurrection into a revolution.

The Medical Men have had two meetings upon them, & approved them all, nem. con. – & thought they were their own. And I came off with flying colours, no one suspecting my intrigue, which, of course, would ruin me, were it known. As there is as much jealousy of the Com'tee of one another & of the Medical Men of one another, as ever Napoleon had of Wellington, or what's his name of Marlboro?

I have also carried my point of having good harmless Mr. Garnier, our Parish Clergyman, as Chaplain – & no young Curate as Chaplain to have spiritual flirtations with my young ladies.

And so much for the earth-quakes in this little mole-hill of ours.

Ly Monteagle

Ly C. Murray

& Ly C. Russell are my Standing Com'tee for this month. The S. Herberts are gone to Wilton.

> ever dear Pa
>
> your loving child

Source: BL Add 45790: ff 152–55

1. Lady Laura Cranworth: (1787–1868), wife of Robert Rolfe, Baron Cranworth. During the Crimean War, she and Lady Canning interviewed and hired the nurses and forwarded various necessities to FN.

On 11 January 1854 Florence wrote to Aunt Hannah: 'Our vocation is a difficult one, as you, I am sure, know – & though there are many consolations & very high ones, the disappointments are so numerous that we require all our faith & trust. But that is enough. I have never repented nor looked back, not for one moment. And I begin the New Year with more true feeling of a happy New Year than ever I had in my life' (BL Add 45794: f 72).

The Crimea Years: 1854–56

The Harley Street hospital for gentlewomen soon proved too limited in scope for a person of Florence Nightingale's vision. Within months of her optimistic letter to Aunt Hannah, she was being encouraged by Louisa Twining and William Bowman to apply for the superintendency of the new King's College Hospital. There she would be able to train nurses, a particular interest of hers. But historical events, powerful friends and her considerable reputation combined to thrust upon Nightingale a destiny which she could hardly have envisioned.

The relatively peaceful period in Europe following the defeat of Napoleon at Waterloo in 1815 ended on 28 March 1854 when England and France, in alliance with Turkey, declared war on Russia. They feared that Russia would gain control of the shores of the Bosphorus and perhaps the Dardanelles. The major land route to India lay through this territory; Russia could not be allowed to gain dominance over the eastern Mediterranean. The intransigent Lord Palmerston, Home Secretary in Lord Aberdeen's administration, and Lord Stratford de Redcliffe, British Ambassador to Constantinople, were the major proponents of war in a reluctant government; they were supported by public feeling, whipped up by the London *Times*, which strongly favoured teaching the Russian bear a lesson. In April Prussia and Austria joined forces with Turkey against Russia along the Danube, and the Russians were forced to withdraw from the Balkans. But France and England then decided to break Russia's power in the Black Sea by attacking her naval base at Sebastopol. The decision was made without sufficient consideration of the tactical difficulties an expeditionary force would face. The transportation of soldiers, military supplies and equipment to fight on Russian soil was incompetently planned and disastrously executed.

William Howard Russell, special correspondent of *The Times*, accompanied the troops east. For the first time the telegraph made news from the front almost instantaneous. A patriotic public soon discovered that all was not well. Russell sent impassioned reports describing the heroic efforts of the common soldier and the incredible losses from disease and disorganization. Twenty per cent of the expeditionary force had been hospitalized with cholera and other enteric diseases between June and August 1854, before a single shot had been fired. Nearly a thousand had died (Summers [1988], p. 30).

When the French and British troops finally left camp at Varna and crossed over into Russian territory, Lord Raglan assumed a quick victory at Alma. Horses and wagons – indeed, all the essentials for transporting the tents, food, medical supplies and other equipment – were utterly lacking or ill adapted to the terrain. After the defeat of the Russians at the Alma, the Allied forces were unable to capitalize on their position, and instead marched towards Sebastopol, where they prepared for a long siege. Although the navy brought ample supplies into Balaclava, winter set in with no overall plan to carry these supplies to the waiting troops. Everything had to be hauled up six hundred feet and then carried six miles on dirt roads to the divisional camps, and another two to the front lines. Until the construction of a railway by British navvies brought from England in January 1855, it was impossible to carry sufficient supplies up the hill and on to the troops (Ffrench Blake, pp. 108-10).

Although Russell celebrated the Battle of Alma as a great victory for the British, in early October he sent *The Times* a series of outraged reports of hospital conditions. On 13 October he wrote:

> The manner in which the sick and wounded are treated is worthy only of the savages of Dahomey . . . The worn-out pensioners who were brought as an ambulance corps are totally useless, and not only are surgeons not to be had, but there are no dressers or nurses to carry out the surgeon's directions, and to attend on the sick during the intervals between his visits. Here the French are greatly our superiors. Their arrangements are extremely good, their surgeons more numerous, and they have also the help of the Sisters of Charity who have accompanied the expedition in incredible numbers. These devoted women are excellent nurses. (Quoted in Goldie [1987], p. 18)

Public reaction to the October despatches was prompt and overwhelming. In response to an appeal from *The Times* on 12 October for funds to supply the sick and wounded with necessities, Sir Robert Peel contributed £200 on the 13th, and on the 14th a letter to the editor asked, 'Why have we no Sisters of Charity?' This question had already roused a number of reforming ladies with political contacts. Lady Maria Forester had contacted Florence Nightingale after Russell's 9 October despatch, offering to pay the expense of sending a few nurses out under Nightingale's supervision. In turn, Nightingale wrote to Liz Herbert offering her services to the army as a private citizen:

27. To Elizabeth Herbert   1 Upper Harley St 14 Oct 1854

My dearest

I went to Belgrave Sq. this morn'g, for the chance of catching you, or Mr. Herbert even, had he been in town.

A small private expedition of nurses has been organized for Scutari & I have been asked to command it. I take myself out & one Nurse. Lady Maria Forester[1] has given £200 to take out three others. We feed and lodge ourselves there, & are to be no expence whatever to the country. Lord Clarendon[2] has been asked by Ld Palmerston[3] to write to Ld Stratford[4] for us, & has consented. Dr. Andrew Smith[5] of the Army Medical Board, whom I have seen, authorizes us, & gives us letters to the Chief Medical Officer at Scutari. I do not mean to say that I believe the Times accounts, but I do believe that we may be of use to the wounded wretches.

Now to business -

(1) Unless my Ladies' Committee feel that this is a thing which appeals to the sympathies of all, & urge me, rather than barely consent, I cannot honorably break my engagement here. And I write to you as one of my mistresses.

(2) What does Mr. Herbert say to the scheme itself? Does he think it will be objected to by the authorities? Would he give us any advice or letters of recommendation? And are there any stores for the Hospital he would advise us to take out? Dr. Smith says that nothing is needed.

I enclose a letter from Sigma. Do you think it any use to apply to Miss Burdett Coutts?[6]

We start on Tuesday *if* we go, to catch the Marseilles boat of the 21st for Constantinople, where I leave my nurses, thinking the Medical Staff at Scutari will be more frightened than amused at being bombarded by a parcel of women, & I cross over to Scutari with some one from the Embassy to present my credentials from Dr. Smith, & put ourselves at the disposal of the Drs.

(3) Would you or some one of my Committee write to Lady Stratford[7] to say, 'this is not a lady but a real Hospital Nurse', of me. 'And she has had experience'.

My uncle went down this morning to ask my father & mother's consent.

Would there be any use in my applying to the Duke of Newcastle[8] for his authority?

Believe me, dearest in haste

ever yours

F Nightingale

Perhaps it is better to keep it quite a private thing & not apply to Gov't qua Gov't

Source: BL Add 43396: ff 11–13

1. Lady Maria Forester: (d. 1894), an Evangelical widow of the Honourable Charles Weld Forester who devoted herself to philanthropy.

2. Lord Clarendon: George William Frederick Villiers (1800–70), Secretary of Foreign Affairs in Lord Aberdeen's government.

3. Lord Palmerston: Henry John Temple (1784–1865), Home Secretary in Lord Aberdeen's government; became Prime Minister in January 1855 when Aberdeen's government fell.

4. Lord Stratford: (1786–1880), first Viscount Stratford de Redcliffe (formerly Sir Stratford Canning), the British Ambassador to Turkey.

5. Dr Andrew Smith: (1797–1872), Director-General, Army and Ordnance Medical Departments (1853–58). A frequent opponent of many of FN's reforms, but he had early warned the Horse Guards about the unhealthy conditions in the Crimea. When they failed to take his advice, he was left to deal with the consequences.

6. Angela Burdett-Coutts: (1814–1906), one of the wealthiest women in England; a distinguished philanthropist who promoted education, housing and improved sanitation for the working class, as well as the reform of prostitutes.

7. Lady Stratford: second wife of Lord Stratford; daughter of James Alexander, MP.

8. Duke of Newcastle: Henry Pelham F. P. Clinton (1811–64), Secretary for War in Aberdeen's government. When out of office in 1855 he visited the Crimea to investigate conditions.

In previous wars conditions at the front could be concealed from the public, or at least delayed until long after the events. As Nightingale herself was later to do so brilliantly, Russell successfully used the power of the press to enlist readers in forcing a lethargic or cumbrous government to act, if only to institute investigations. He did not blame specific individuals, but Whitehall was clearly responsible. The government, vulnerable to publicity, sought to palliate the public. Nightingale's long-time friend, Sidney Herbert, responded to the cry for English 'Sisters of Charity'.

On 15 October Herbert wrote to Nightingale, asking her to take out a group of nurses under government sponsorship. As Secretary *at* War, rather than Secretary *for* War, Herbert was technically only in charge of finances and accounting, but his popularity in the Cabinet gave him the freedom to interpret his duties more liberally. Women had never before been allowed to serve officially in the army; now a group of experienced nurses, under the close supervision of a lady, were to supplement the orderlies, comprised of pensioners and recovering soldiers, who traditionally served the sick and wounded during war. Herbert gambled that Nightingale could pacify the public, in spite of anticipated resistance from the military and medical officers. His decision was to have far-reaching consequences for the army, for women nurses – and for Nightingale.

But the utter chaos of the Scutari hospitals could not be resolved by female nursing alone. Inevitably Nightingale drew the attention of the government to problems that went far beyond her specific purview; in the process she exposed the administrative incompetence and disorganization of the British military from the lowly commissariat and purveyors to the highest levels of government. She faced – and created – enemies. Nightingale had a genius for large-scale organizational and administrative reform; she was woefully lacking in tact, patience and compromise. Although she emerged from the war a national heroine, Nightingale was only partially successful in achieving the many reforms that she and Herbert thought essential to improve the army's medical services; she was even less successful in overcoming opposition to women nurses in the military.

Nightingale immediately accepted Herbert's offer to be 'Superintendent of the female nursing establishment in the English General Military Hospitals in Turkey'. The very day she received his letter she wrote home, 'In the hope that I shall see my dearest mother & sister tomorrow, & that they will give me their blessing on our undertaking, I shall leave it to Mrs. Bracebridge to explain what that undertaking is' (Wellcome). The Nightingales were flattered that Flo had been asked; the Ladies' Committee of the Institution for the Care of Sick Gentlewomen was equally impressed and released their Superintendent for war work. Florence plunged into the new challenge, eager to leave the petty squabbles of the small hospital on Harley Street. Lady Canning wrote to Lady Stuart de Rothesay on 17 October, 'No one is so well fitted as she to do such work; she has such nerve and skill, and is so wise and quiet. Even now she is in no bustle and hurry, though so much is on her hands, and such numbers of people volunteer services'(Cook, I, 160). Florence's hour had finally come.

Nightingale and her party of nurses left London on 21 October, a mere six days after she had received the letter from Sidney Herbert. Within this short period, thirty-eight women were selected from a largely unimpressive group of volunteers who came from religious institutions and hospitals. Exceedingly ugly uniforms – unenvied by the nuns – were designed and made up, and numerous other details attended to. Nightingale and Herbert were both anxious to balance Dissenting and Low Church Protestants with Roman Catholic and High Church candidates. Unfortunately, only Roman Catholic and High Church Sisters came forward; ten of the former and fourteen of the latter were selected, along with fourteen regular hospital nurses. The Roman Catholic leadership agreed reluctantly to place their volunteers under Florence's authority.

In spite of obvious problems, Nightingale remained extraordinarily calm throughout the journey across France, a mood remarked upon by the Bracebridges, who accompanied the party to the Crimea and remained there until summer 1855. The French showered the party with attention, providing free accommodation and meals. By the time they boarded the *Vectis* at Marseilles, Nightingale was already a heroine. Readers of *The Times* donated £7000 for her personal use; Nightingale herself donated her annual allowance of £500 to the work. This money became central in ameliorating hospital conditions – but it was also a source of jealousy and anger among the army doctors, officers and others who opposed Nightingale. Those already frustrated with public interference in the military structure could not readily accept her position as an official employee of the government with unlimited private funds.

The party arrived on 3 November in the pouring rain. Upon disembarking, they were escorted to the Barrack Hospital where Nightingale established her headquarters. This vast hospital was beautifully situated on high ground overlooking the sea, with Constantinople across the straits. The quarters they were assigned confirmed the military prejudice which Herbert had feared. Six rooms, of which one was a kitchen and another a closet, space normally occupied by three medical officers and their servants, now had to accommodate the forty-two people in Nightingale's party. The room assigned to the eight Anglican sisters from Mother Lydia Sellon's order in Devonport was found to contain the corpse of a Russian general. No furniture, food, cooking utensils, blankets, or supplies of any kind were provided. Raised wooden platforms around the room served as beds. Fleas and rats were to be a continual problem. While Mr Bracebridge found someone to remove the corpse, Nightingale obtained basins of milkless tea from the hospital. The basins subsequently had to be used for washing, eating and drinking, for the hospital was inadequately equipped. The spirits of all sank, one Sellonite confided to her diary (Woodham-Smith, p. 162).

However dismal their quarters, the hospital was worse. Young officers recognized that problems existed on the battlefield, in the medical services, and in the military operation as a whole, but no one was prepared to voice criticism or to take responsibility, and thereby jeopardize promotion. The arrival of women at a military establishment – jealously guarded male turf – was perceived as a serious threat. The only women with whom the military had had to contend were wives and prostitutes, and the army had been singularly successful in simultaneously oppressing and disclaiming responsibility for both groups. Nightingale's position in society, however, made her much less vulnerable to attack; moreover, she was determined to succeed. After her first offer of help was refused, her strategy was to gain the confidence of the medical officers, her designated superiors. She waited for them to come to her. In the meantime she kept the nurses busy making shirts, pillows, stump-rests and other essentials from the supplies she had brought with her.

The women became restless, but Nightingale did not take people into her confidence. She believed in unquestioning obedience to those in authority. The cramped quarters, the tedious activity, the inadequate washing and eating facilities, the lack of water, and the hospital stench would have tested the most balanced individual as that week dragged by, hour by unceasing hour. But the situation changed abruptly following the Battle of Inkerman, when masses of sick and wounded poured into Scutari on 9 November from the heights above Sebastopol, suffering from malnutrition, dysentery and exposure. Inundated with an influx of sick and wounded soldiers, the doctors turned to Nightingale and her nurses for help.

28. To William Bowman, Surgeon[1]   Barrack Hospital, Scutari 14 Nov 1854

'I came out, Ma'am prepared to submit to Everything. to be put upon in Everyway. But there are *some* things, Ma'am one can't submit to. There is the caps, ma'am that suits one face. and some that suits another. And if I'd known, Ma'am about the Caps, great as was my desire to come out as nurse at Scutari, I wouldn't have come, ma'am'. – Speech of Mrs. Lawfield

Dear Sir Time must be at a discount with the man who can adjust the balance of such an important question as the above – & I, for one have none: as you will easily suppose when I tell you that on Thursday last we had 1715 sick & wounded in this Hospital (among whom 120 Cholera patients and 650 severely wounded in the other Building, called the Gen'l Hospital, of w'ch we also have charge, when a message came to me to prepare for 510 wounded on our side the Hosp'l who were arriving from the dreadful affair of the 5th of Nov'r at Balaclava, where were 1763 wounded & 442 killed, besides 96 Officers wounded & 38 killed. I always expected to end my days as Hospital Matron, but I never expected to be Barrack Mistress. We had but 1/2 an hour's notice, before they began landing the wounded. Between one and nine o'clock, we had the mattrasses stuffed, sewn up, and laid down, alas! only upon matting on the floor, the men washed and put to bed, & all their wounds dressed – I wish I had time or I would write you a letter dear to a surgeon's heart, I am as good as a 'Medical Times'. But oh! you gentlemen of England who sit at home in all the well earned satisfaction of your successful cases, can have little idea, from reading the newspapers, of the horror & misery in a military Hosp'l of operating upon these dying exhausted men. A London Hosp'l is a garden of flowers to it. We have had such a sea in the Bosphorus, and the Turks, the very men for whom we are fighting are carrying our wounded so cruelly, that they arrive in a state of agony – one amputated stump died two hours after we received him, one compound fracture just as we were getting him into bed, in all 24 cases on the day of landing. We have now 4 miles of beds – & not 18 inches apart. We have our quarters in one Tower of the Barrack & all this fresh influx has been laid down between us and the main guard in two corridors with a line of beds down each side just room for one man to pass between, and four wards. Yet in the midst of the appalling horror, there is good. And I can truly say like St. Peter 'it is good for us to be here' – tho' I doubt whether if St. Peter had been here, he would have said so. As I went my night-round among the newly wounded that first night, there was not one murmur, not one groan the strictest discipline, the most absolute silence & quiet prevailed.

Only the step of the Sentry & I heard one man say 'I was dreaming of my friends at home', & another said 'and I was thinking of them'. These poor fellows bear pain & mutilation with unshrinking heroism & die without complaint. Not so the officers, but we have nothing to do with the Officers. The wounded are now lying up to our very door & we are landing 540 more from the 'Andes'. I take rank in the army as Brigadier General, because 40 British females, whom I have with me, are more difficult to manage than 4000 men. Let no lady come out here who is not used to fatigue & privation – for the Devonport Sisters, who ought to know what self-denial is, do nothing but complain. Occasionally the roof is torn off our quarters, or the windows blown in & we are

flooded & under water for the night. We have all the sick Cookery now to do – & have got in 4 men for the purpose, for the prophet Mahomet does not allow us a female. And we are now able to supply these poor fellows with something besides Gov't rations. I wish you w'd recall me to Dr. Bence Jones[2] remembrance, when you see him, and tell him I have had but too much occasion to remember him in the constant use of his dreadful present. In all our corridor I think we have not an average of three units per man, and there are two ships more 'landing' at the Crimea with wounded, this is our phraseology. All who can walk come in to us for Tobacco – but I tell them we have not a bit to put into our own mouths – not a sponge, not a rag of linen, not an anything have I left. Every thing is gone torn to make slings & stump pillows & shirts. These poor fellows had not had a clean shirt nor been washed for two months before they came here & the state in w'ch they arrive from the Transports is literally *crawling*. I hope in a few days we shall establish a little cleanliness. But we have not a basin, nor a towel, nor a bit of soap, nor a broom. I have ordered 300 scrubbing brushes. We are getting on nicely in many ways. They were so glad to see us. The Senior Chaplain is a sensible man, w'ch is a remarkable providence. I have not been out of the Hospital wall yet. But the most beautiful view in the world I believe lies outside. If you ever see Mr. Whitfield the House Apothecary of St. Thomas's will you tell him that the nurse he sent me, Mrs. Roberts, is worth her weight in gold. There was another engagement on the 8th, & more wounded, who are coming down to us. The text w'ch heads my letter was expounded thus Mrs Lawfield was recommended to return home and set her cap, vulgarly speaking, at some one elsewhere than here, but on begging for mercy, was allowed to make another trial. Mrs. Drake is a treasure. The four others are not fit to take care of themselves nor of others in a military Hosp'l. This is my first impression but it may modify, if I can convince them of the necessity of discipline and propriety in a drunken garrison. Believe me dear Sir yours very truly & gratefully
Florence Nightingale
This is only the beginning of things. We are still expecting the assault.

Source: Wellcome {copy}

1. William Bowman: (1816–92), distinguished ophthalmic surgeon at King's College Hospital. From 1848, professor of physiology and general and morbid anatomy. Knighted 1884. He had attended the patients at the Harley St hospital. He was also a leader in the founding of the High Church St John's House, which had supplied several nurses.
2. Henry Bence Jones, MD: (1814–73), physician and chemist at St George's Hospital. Specialist in urine, kidney and diabetic diseases.

Nightingale soon recognized that the destruction of the army was due to illness rather than to battle losses. One of the best surgeons at Balaclava, Dr Blake, treated a total of 3025 cases of sickness as compared with 564 for wounds, and his regiment was one of the most heavily engaged at Inkerman, where the casualties were high (Hibbert, p. 246). Cholera was rampant. Post-war records revealed that men kept at the divisional campsites, in spite of the incredibly bad conditions in makeshift regimental hospitals, more often recovered than did those who were sent to Scutari. The stress of being transported across the Black Sea killed many men. Strapped to mules for the trip to the harbour, the wounded were then transferred to boats and rowed to the ships where they lay on the bare deck or in the suffocating hold for hours before the gruelling eight-day voyage to Scutari; rowed to shore, they were transferred to stretchers for the trip up the hill to the hospitals. Each stage was rougher than the last. The real miracle is that any wounded survived.

British–French relations were poor after the victory at Alma. Their disagreements and delays gave the Russians an opportunity to strengthen their defences and subjected the troops to the worst winter the Crimea had seen for years. Several costly skirmishes occurred. The charge of the Light Brigade is only the most famous of the mistakes made. In battles that the Allies ostensibly won, such as the Battle of Inkerman, the casualties and deaths were so high that they can be considered Pyrrhic victories at best. The weather seems to have colluded with the enemy, for Inkerman was followed by a hurricane which devastated the British camp and sank in the harbour ships whose hulls were filled with winter clothing, medical supplies and ammunition. The British soldiers were in rags, their tents were in tatters, food was scarce and fuel nonexistent. If meals were to be had, they were eaten raw. The men arrived at the hospitals suffering from malnutrition, scurvy and frostbite, as well as the usual dysentery and diarrhoea.

While conditions in the Crimea could be explained in terms of the extraordinary difficulties of maintaining an army on enemy soil, matters were little better in Turkey at the British hospitals. The Commissariat, the Purveyor's Department and the Medical Department, collectively responsible for the health of the British army, were understaffed, and in some cases under the authority of an incompetent veteran. The Commissariat were the contractors for all normal daily supplies, including food, transportation and stores. The Purveyors, through the Commissariat, supplied the hospital with equipment and invalid food. But the respective duties of both were unclear. The Purveyor, at the bottom of the pyramid of authority and dependent upon the Chief Medical Officer for his promotion, had every reason to interpret his duties as narrowly as possible; he had been ordered to govern by thrift, and no emergency would alter his position. To add to the complications, urgent requisitions sent to London travelled through eight departments, and were further delayed if a requested item was not in stock.

The realities of war exposed the weaknesses of the army's system – or non-system. Doctors ordered requisitions from the Purveyor, but they did not follow up to see if these were filled. When an item was 'not in store', the requisition was simply discarded. All requisitions had to be countersigned by two doctors, one of whom had to be a senior official who was inundated with paperwork. The Purveyor and the Commissariat had executive powers, but only 'warranted' goods could be supplied; they could be held personally liable for any 'unwarranted' article. When soldiers reached the hospitals without their packs, the Purveyor refused to consider the requisition for articles such as eating utensils or shirts because they were not warranted.

When Nightingale arrived in Scutari, there were four principal British hospitals. The Barrack Hospital accommodated two to three thousand, while half an hour's walk away was the General Hospital, which held about one thousand. South of the General was the Palace Hospital for officers, over which Nightingale had no responsibility. The hospital at Koulali opened in December 1854; by Nightingale's request, she was relieved of responsibility for this hospital by Lord Panmure when he took over from Sidney Herbert early in 1855. She had no responsibility for the civil hospitals but was often consulted, especially by her friend Dr E. A. Parkes, at Renkioi. Given the chaos at Scutari, she soon found herself taking on many responsibilities that should have been shouldered by the army itself.

Overwhelmed by the hordes of sick and wounded that poured into the hospitals, coupled with the tragic loss of supplies in the hurricane, the hospital administration ground to a standstill. The Commissariat had stopped keeping records after the arrival of the sick and wounded from Alma, which in turn paralysed the Purveying Department. Sidney Herbert sent out a 'Commission of Enquiry into the State of the Hospitals and the Condition of the Sick and Wounded' to establish the facts, but it was given no authority to alter existing arrangements. Members of this Commission were the barrister Peter Benson Maxwell, Dr Cumming and Dr Spence. At this point Nightingale was the only person who had the money and authority to act. Bence Macdonald, in charge of

The Times fund, the Reverend and Honourable Sydney Godolphin Osborne, a friend of Sidney Herbert's who had come out to be a chaplain to the soldiers, and Augustus Stafford, an MP who had come to see for himself what conditions were like, became her assistants.

Over the next twenty months Nightingale bombarded Sidney Herbert with suggestions for modernizing the army.

29. To Sidney Herbert

Barrack Hospital, Scutari
25 Nov 1854

Private

British Sisters Quarters

Dear Mr. Herbert

(1) It appears that in these Hospitals, the Purveyor considers washing both of linen & of the men a minor 'detail' – & during the three weeks we have been here, though our remonstrances have been treated with perfect civility, yet no washing whatever has been performed for the men either of body linen or of bed-linen except by ourselves, & a few wives of the Wounded, & a story of a Contractor, with which we have been amused, turns out to be a myth. The dirty shirts were collected yesterday for the first time, & on Monday *it is said* that they are to be washed, – & we are organizing a little Washing Establishment of our own – for the bandages &c. When we came here, there was neither basin, towel nor soap in the Wards, nor any means of personal cleanliness for the Wounded except the following.

Thirty were bathed every night by Dr. MacGrigor's orders in slipper-baths, but this does not do more than include a washing once in eighty days for 2300 men.

The consequences of all this are Fever, Cholera, Gangrene, Lice, Bugs, Fleas – & may be Erysipelas – from the using of one sponge among many wounds.

And even this slipper-bathing does not apply to the General Hospital.

(2) The fault here is, *not* with the Medical Officers, but in the separation of the department which affords every necessary supply, except medicines, to them – & in the insufficient supply of minor officers in the Purveying Department under Mr. Wreford, the Purv'r Gen'l, as well as in the inevitable delay in obtaining supplies, occasioned by the existence of one single Interpreter only, who is generally seen booted.

(3) Your name is also continually used as a bug-bear, they make a deity of cheapness, & the Secretary at War stands as synonymous

here with Jupiter Tonans[1] whose shafts end only in 'brutum fulmen'.[2] The cheese-paring system which sounds unmusical in British ears is here identified with you by the Officers who carry it out. It is in vain to tell the Purveyors that they will get no 'kudos' by this at home. See Note A

(4) The requirements are, unity of action & personal responsibility.

It is a sad joke here that a large reward has been offered for any one who is personally responsible, barring the Commandant.

(5) Another cause is, the imperfection of distinct order in England as to *packing*. The unfortunate 'Prince' who was lost at Balaklava had on board a quantity of medical comforts for us which were so packed under shot & shell as that it was found impossible to disembark them here & they went on to Balaklava & were lost at the same time as your Commissioner Dr. Spence.[3]

(6) In consequence of the Duke of Newcastle's letter to Mr. Cumming,[4] the latter has not taken the command here, & in consequence of Dr. Spence being lost on board the 'Prince', the Commission of Enquiry has not yet begun its labours. Mr. Maxwell visits us *en amateur*.

(7) Two or three hundred Stump Pillows, ditto Arm Slings, ditto *Paddings* for Splints – besides other Medical Appliances are being weekly manufactured & given out by us – & no provision appeared to have been made for these things before.

All the above is written in obedience to your *private* instructions. Do not let me appear as a Gov't spy here which would destroy all my usefulness & believe me, in greatest haste,

    Yours ever truly

                 F. Nightingale

P.S. Lord Napier[5] & the Visitors generally remark that the Hospital is improved since we came.

Note A –

The habits & the honor of the Purveying Department, as inferior officers, fix their attention upon the correctness of their book-keeping as the primary object of life.

Note B –

Mr. Osborne & Mr. Macdonald have been profuse of offers. We have accepted wine, shirts, flannel, calico, sago, &c – delay being as fatal to us as denial in our requisitions.

Entre nous, will you let me state that Lady Stratford, with the utmost kindness & benevolent intentions, is, in consequence of want of practical habits of business, nothing but good & bustling, & a time waster & impediment. As the Commission is not yet doing anything, the Ambassador should send us a *man* who, with prompt efficiency, can also defend us from the difficulties & delays of mediating between conflicting orders in the various departments – to which I ascribe most of the signal failures, such as those in washing &c, which have occurred.

F.N.

P.S. Mrs. Herbert gave me a fright by telling Mrs. Bracebridge that your private letter to me had been published. That letter was shewn to no one but my own people & it appears to me impossible that it can have found its way into any other hands.

P.P.S. We are greatly in want of Hair Mattrasses or even Flock, as cheaper. There are but 44 Hair Mattresses in store. Our very bad cases suffer terribly from bed-sores on the Paillasse, which is all we have – while the French Hospital is furnished throughout with mattrasses having an elastic couche of Hair between two of Flock & a Paillasse underneath.

Source: BL Add 43393: ff 13–17.

1. Jupiter Tonans: God of Thunder.
2. brutum fulmen: blind strike.
3. Dr Thomas Spence: Deputy Inspector General of Army Hospitals, drowned aboard the *Prince*, Balaclava Bay, 14 November 1854.
4. Dr Alexander Cumming: appointed Inspector-General of Army Hospitals in the East, 27 October 1854.
5. Lord Napier: Robert Cornelis Napier (1819–98), Secretary at the British Embassy in Constantinople. Later, as Governor of Madras (1866–72), he corresponded with FN about sanitation, irrigation and public works.

According to various official reports, Nightingale's party brought about a noticeable change in the two hospitals in which they nursed. Mr Macdonald from *The Times* declared: 'The first improvements took place after Miss Nightingale's arrival – the greater cleanliness and greater order. I recollect one of the first things she asked me to supply was 200 hard scrubbers & sacking for washing the floors, for which no means existed at that time' (Cook, I, 195). According to the Reverend and Honourable Osborne, however, not all the floors could be scrubbed:

> The patients lay either on the floor, or on the wooden divans which surrounded some of the wards. The boards under the thin chaff beds on which they lay, were rotten, and I have seen them alive with vermin and saturated with everything offensive; the orderlies told me, they

could not be kept clean; I was also informed by one of the chief authorities, that if these wards were washed, so rotten were the boards, that they never could be got dry. The bed clothing was in character with the place. (p. 13)

Nightingale and her nurses introduced extra diets of beef broth, custard and other food appropriate for convalescents. They supplied the patients with many essentials such as eating utensils, shirts, sheets, blankets and stuffed bags for mattresses; in addition they purchased operating tables and screens so that operations (mainly amputations and the removal of bullets) would not have to be performed in full view of the rest of the ward. Nightingale used part of *The Times* fund to set up a laundry, employing the soldiers' wives as washers; for the first time clean linen could be supplied. At one point, when diarrhoea was rife and the pipes were clogged, Nightingale had to force the orderlies to empty the open wooden tubs which were substituted for privies.

Nightingale found herself purveying the hospitals and clothing the British army. This involved finding ways to circumvent the system that was paralysing the officials. When negotiations with the Turkish workmen broke down over rebuilding a condemned part of the Barrack Hospital to accommodate another influx of soldiers, Nightingale stepped in and paid the labourers herself. The story leaked out and she was reimbursed, but Colonel Sterling's comments about the affair must have echoed the feelings of many frustrated officers – Miss Nightingale 'coolly draws a cheque. Is this the way to manage the finances of a great nation? *Vox populi?* A divine afflatus. Priestess, Miss N. Magnetic impetus drawing cash out of my pocket!' (Cook, I, 206–07). Yet Nightingale remained a strong believer in regulations; she broke the rules only if she saw no other way.

While her letters to Sidney Herbert discussed all her problems frankly, those to her family only hinted at her difficulties.

30. To the Nightingale family   Scutari 5 Dec 1854

Dearest people
    Could you but see me, you would not wonder that I have no time to write – when my heart yearns to do so. Could any one but know the difficulties & heart-sinkings of *command*, the constant temptation to throw it up, they would not write to me, as good Mr. Garnier does, praying for grace that I may bear the praise

lavished upon me. I who have never had time to look at a Paper since I came.

Praise, good God! He knows what a situation He has put upon me. For His sake I bear it willingly, but not for the sake of Praise. The cup which my Father hath given me shall I not drink it? But how few can sympathize with such a position! Most of all was I surprised at dr. Aunt Mai's sanguine & gleeful view of it. But do not suppose that I shrink. Without us, nothing would have been done here – & I am satisfied. All this is, of course, *private*.

I subjoin a list of small wants

Pray *date* your letters.

Ever yours

F.N.

I should like to hear about Harley St.

Source: Wellcome

31. To Parthenope Nightingale {?}   Undated

Barbarous woman – there is a black *lace* bonnet & a black *silk* gown come, & not my Bear's grease! which was to have come in my box per Imperatrice. Now, if this savor of vanity, *let* me tell you you don't know what this climate is – & as the natives oil themselves, so must I Bear's grease myself. I have been obliged to Cold Cream my hair. So let me have my Bear's grease or I die. I left your Castor Oil Grease behind on the mirror table like an honest woman.

Source: Wellcome

The supervision of the nurses continued to be a vexing problem. The original thirty-eight had proved, not surprisingly, extremely varied in their skills and devotion. Some were clearly unequal to the task and to the living conditions, while others fulfilled the stereotype of the drunken nurse. Still others confirmed the rumour that the women had come out to find a husband; six marched in with their intended husbands to announce that they were quitting to marry. Some complained bitterly about the strict discipline that Nightingale imposed.

At the end of 1854, just as Nightingale was gaining acceptance for her nurses, Liz Herbert wrote to Mr Bracebridge about a second group of nurses who were planning to come out.

32. To Sidney Herbert

Barrack Hospital, Scutari
10 Dec 1854

Private

Dear Mr. Herbert

With regard to receiving & employing a greater number of Sisters & Nurses in these Hospitals, I went immediately, (on reading Mrs. Herbert's letter of the 23rd, addressed to Mr. Bracebridge,) to consult Mr. Menzies, the Principal Medical Officer, under whose orders I am.

He considers that as large a number are now employed in these Hospitals as can be usefully appropriated, & as can be made consistent with morality & discipline. And the discipline of forty women, collected together for the first time, is no trifling matter – under these new & strange circumstances.

He considers that if we were swamped with a number increased to sixty or seventy, good order would become impossible. And in all these views I so fully concur that I should resign my situation as impossible, were such circumstances forced upon me.

For our quarters are already inadequate to preserving in health our number. More quarters cannot be assigned us. The sick are laid up to our door. We had even to give up a portion of those quarters which had been assigned us (at the General Hospital) to the Wounded.

With regard to taking a house at Scutari, the Medical Officers considered it as simply impossible. Regularity could not be preserved, where the Sisters & Nurses were living from under our own eye – the difficulties of transport are what no one in England would believe – & the going to & fro between the two Hospitals is becoming daily less easy. That I should not accept a responsibility, which I could not fulfil, is equally the opinion of the Medical Officers & mine.

If, in the course of the winter, we have out ten or twenty more, & send back some of those we have, the Medical Officers are of opinion that that number will be sufficient, i.e. forty efficient ones being picked out eventually for the two Hospitals averaging 3000 sick.

Lastly, I have found from this last month's experience that, had we come out with twenty instead of forty, we should not only have been less hampered with difficulties, but the work itself would have been actually better & more efficiently done. About ten of us have done *the whole work*. The others have only run between our feet & hindered us – & the difficulty of assigning to them something to do without superintendence has been enormous. It is the difference between the old plough with the greatest amount of power & the greatest loss in its application – & the Gee-ho plough with reins – accomplishing twice the work with half the power & much more efficiently.

We were so alarmed at the general terms in which Mrs. Herbert described the nurses as instantly to be sent off – that we held council & decided on writing the enclosed to the Ambassador as the only means of protecting them & ourselves. In other words we could neither house nor keep them.

English people look upon Scutari as a place with inns & hackney-coaches & houses to let furnished. It required yesterday (to land 25 casks of sugar) four oxen & three men for six hours – plus two passes, two requisitions, Mr. Bracebridge's two interferences, & one apology from a Quarter Master for seizing the Araba, received with a smile & a kind word, because he did his duty. For every Araba is required on Military-store or Commissariat duty. There are no pack-horses & no asses, except those used by the peasantry to attend the market 1 1/4 miles off. An Araba consists of loose poles & planks extended between two axle-trees, placed on four small wheels, & drawn by a yoke of weak oxen.

There is not a Turkish house which is not in a fragmentary state – roof & windows pervious in all directions – there is not a room in our Quarters which does not let in the rain in showers, whenever the weather is bad. We can only buy food through the Commissary & are sometimes without wood or charcoal.

For want of a carpenter & a man to put up a stove, in the absence of all hands (the workmen available being all employed in repairing the sick Wards, the matter of first importance) we have been unable during the last week to effect the move of some of our nurses into the Gen'l Hosp'l, or even to get in a few poor soldier's wives into our little Lying-in Hospital, which the pressure of the misery of these poor women had compelled us to begin.

All this will tend to explain the impossibility of having more women, & especially ladies, out here at present.

Mr. Bracebridge has put down some Memo'a as they occurred to him.

What we may be considered to have effected is

1) the kitchen for extra-diets, now in full action, for this Hospital – with regular extra-diet tables sent in by the Ward-Surgeons –

2) A great deal more cleaning of Wards – mops, scrubbing – brushes, brooms, & combs, given out by ourselves, where not forced from the Purveyor –

3) 2000 shirts, cotton & flannel, given out & washing organized – & already carried on for a week.

4) Lying-in Hospital begun

5) widows & soldiers' wives relieved & attended to.

6) a great amount of daily dressings & attention to compound fractures by the most competent of us –

7) the supervision & stirring-up of the whole machinery generally, with the full concurrence of the chief medical authorities – & the practical proof which our presence has given that Gov't were determined to know all they could & do all they could –

8) the repairing of wards for 800 wounded which would otherwise have been left uninhabitable. And this I regard as the most important.

The Government could not do otherwise than send a number of Female Assistants worthy of it – viz 30 or 40. Of these, at most 16 are efficient. The personal qualities of five or six have effected (under God's blessing) the results already obtained.

I am willing to bear the evil of governing (& preventing from doing mischief) the non-efficient *or scheming* majority, which is my great difficulty & most wearing-out labor – because I acknowledge the moral effect produced, which could not have been produced by smaller numbers. But I am not willing to encounter the crowding greater numbers to exhaust our powers & make us useless & incapable – by wasting our time & nervous energy in governing that which cannot be governed.

Lastly at the moment we came out, the 'Times' commissioner & his fund were prepared immediately to go into opposition – as they have actually done at Balaclava, where the 'Times' supplies have been refused – as well as admission to Mr. Stafford – whereas here, instead of opposition, we have had support. Nothing has been given here except through us & we have had abundant supplies, more than we asked, from Mr. Macdonald & Mr. Osborne – who have held daily consultations with us. Mr. Stafford, who was on the point of going into extreme opposition, has shewn nothing but kindness & zeal.

The great fault here lies in our geography – in our being on this side the water. Four days in the week, we cannot communicate with Constant'e, except by the other harbour, 1 1/4 mile off, of Scutari proper, to which the road is almost impassable.

I add the Pièces Justicatives –

The grand administrative evil emanates from home – in the

existence of a number of departments here, each with its centrifugal & independent action, un-counteracted by any centripetal attraction – viz. a central authority capable of supervising & compelling combined effort for each object at each particular time.

Excuse confusion In great haste
     ever yours

F. Nightingale

P.S. The remedy which was proposed in making Mr. Cumming Inspector General was distinctly neutralized – 1st by his own caution in not assuming a power not legally his & waiting for Ld. Raglan's orders 2nd by the D. of Newcastle's letter assigning him the post of Head Commissioner, which arrived at the same time as Ld. Raglan's reply. The result has been that Mr. Cumming has not acted as Insp'r Gen'l & that the Commissioners were three weeks before they began to sit – having replaced poor Dr. Spence by the selection of an efficient Medical Officer here.

Mr. Cumming's habit of mind & delicacy towards Mr. Menzies led him to be very chary in giving advice till the arrival of your letter, since which he has given it *as* advice.

Source: BL Add 43393: ff 22–32

Florence's response to the intention to send more nurses out arrived too late; in the midst of the increased hospital load and the continuing organizational problems, her old friend Mary Stanley arrived with another group of volunteers. Nightingale sent Mr Bracebridge aboard the ship to tell the Stanley party that the doctors did not want any more nurses and that she could not accommodate them. Her summary rejection of Mary Stanley's group of nurses was to cause enormous grief for her and the cause to which she had dedicated herself (see Summers [1983]). Nightingale lashed out at Sidney Herbert, charging him with breaking their agreement by sending a second group. On 15 December 1854 she wrote:

> When I came out here as your Sup't. it was with the distinct understanding (expressed both in your own handwriting & in the printed announcement which you put in the Morn. Chron. which is here in every one's hands) that nurses were to be sent out at my requisition only, which was to be made only with the approbation of the Medical Officers here. (BL Add 43393: f 34)

The arrival of the Stanley party of nurses brought to a head the question of authority. Nightingale's instructions from the Secretary for War stated:

> Everything relating to the distribution of the nurses, the hours of their attendance, their allotment of particular duties, is placed in your hands subject, of course, to the sanction and approval of the Chief Medical Officer but the selection of the nurses in the first instance is placed solely in your control or under that of persons to be agreed upon between yourself and the Director General of the Army and Ordnance Medical Department. (20 Oct 1854 BL Add 43393: ff 1–2)

Yet Mary Stanley's group appeared to have no intention of submitting to Nightingale. After her rejection given by Mr Bracebridge, they appealed to Dr Cumming. Although he too rebuffed them, they had bypassed Nightingale in her capacity as Superintendent, and undermined her authority.

Before the first party of nurses had left England, the religious orders had agreed, albeit reluctantly, to let their volunteers take orders from Nightingale rather than some head of their own. But with Mary Stanley's party came a group of Irish nuns under Mother Frances Bridgeman, who had refused to agree to this condition. Nightingale assumed the worst of them from the beginning, writing to Herbert on 4 January 1855:

> The R. C. question remains unsettled – *Brickbat*, the Rev'd Mother of Kinsale, refusing to let five of her nurses come here without her to be under our Rev'd Mother thereby shewing that she has some second view besides Nursing – & I refusing to let our little Society become a hotbed of R. C. intriguettes. Of course we shall have a R. C. storm. But *our* Rev'd Mother, heart & hand with us, is doing her best to stop it. (BL Add 43393: f 65)

Although many of the new nurses were to prove every bit as good as the original group, Nightingale was never reconciled to Mother Bridgeman. Both were strong-willed upper-class women; possibly they were too similar to work well together.

The successful introduction of female nurses into the military was of paramount importance to Nightingale, but to realize this goal, she felt that she needed a small controllable group. The slightest degree of incompetence or disobedience jeopardized success. She permitted no discussion or deviance from her approach to the work at hand. In contrast, Mary Stanley and many others felt that the appalling hospital conditions cried out for the immediate introduction of large numbers of nurses. Nightingale's adamant refusal to co-operate with the new nurses played into the hands of the hostile medical and military officials, such as Dr John Hall, Inspector-General of the Hospitals in the Crimea, who capitalized on these divisions in his own war against Nightingale.

A certain inflexibility which bred intolerance and contempt for those who failed to measure up to her own sense of dedication characterized Nightingale. Her first angry letter to Herbert was followed by another ten days later:

33. To Sidney Herbert

Barrack Hospital, Scutari
25 Dec 1854

Dear Mr. Herbert

You have not stood by me, but I have stood by you. In this new situation, I have taken your written instructions as my guide, &, carrying them out with the best discretion which God has given me, I have endeavoured to establish – in circumstances however perplexing & anomalous a consistent action. Had I not done this, we should have been turned out of the Hospitals in a month, & the War Office would have borne the blame of swamping the experiment.

You shall judge for yourself. Such a tempest has been brewed in this little pint-pot as you could have no idea of. But I, like the ass, have put on the lion's skin, & when once I have done that, (poor me, who never affronted any one before), I can bray so loud that I shall be heard, I am afraid, as far as England.

However this is no place for lions & as for asses, we have enough.

The ἦθος[1] of my instructions appears to me to be this –
(1) Establish no separate action from the Medical Men but be their lieutenant & purveyor to carry out their intentions.
(2) Control among your charge all these different sects & views so as to prevent these Hospitals from becoming a 'polemical arena' – I quote your own words.

The first propositions for the utilizing of the Therapians[2] which Miss Stanley makes is that ten of these Protestants should be appropriated as Clerical females by the Chaplains, ten of the nuns by the priests, *not as nurses* but as female ecclesiastics. With this of course I have nothing to do. It being directly at variance with my instructions, I cannot of course appropriate the Gov't money to such a purpose. Mr. Cumming's answer you will probably have by this post.

The second proposition which the Superior of the new nuns (who is obviously come out with a *religious* view – (not to serve the sick, but to found a convent) completely mistaking the purpose of our mission) makes is that the *whole* of the 15 nuns should come in *or none* – they cannot separate & they cannot separate from *her*. Why? Because it 'would be *uncanonical*'. As, by this word, she has brought herself against the barrier of the War Office Instructions, & as, for the good of the service, I consider two Superiors disadvantageous (our former Sup'r being the one whom I prefer,) & as, to house fifteen more nuns is impossible, I have taken the course to be mentioned hereafter.

The third element in the question is (which bears upon the *first* part of my Instructions) that the Medical Men fix positively the No. of females for the two Hospitals at fifty as a *maximum*, in which judgment I entirely concur for reasons which I shall explain hereafter.

Episode 1. The publication of the letter of one of the Sellon Sisters in the Times of the 8th Dec., her Examination & mine by the Commission, which proves her letter to be partly exaggerated, partly untrue, & my determination that she should resign.

Upon these premises, my course is like a proposition in Euclid. And, till I am superseded, I shall carry it out at any expense to me of odium, tho' no human being can stand for two months what I am doing now.

The Candia, the finest vessel in the service, being to sail before night on the 23rd, the day I had all these interviews, in four hours I sent off ten of my old party, 5 nuns, 2 Sellons, including the offender, & 3 nurses. For each one of these I had to stand a *black-guarding* (there is no other word in the English language to express it). Of the one from Father Michael Cuffe for the five nuns, I enclose a Mem'm. He told me that I was like *Herod* sending the Blessed Virgin across the desert. We shall hear more of this.

(And, I assure you that, in the midst of my own overwhelming troubles, my heart bleeds for you that, you, the centre of the parliamentary row, should have to attend to these miseries, tho' you have betrayed me).

My reasons for selecting *these* nuns to go back (out of the whole number) I have written to Dr. Manning.

I then wrote to the Superior of the new lot to offer to fill their places with five of the new party, to work under the old Superior whom we brought out with us & who is invaluable, stating that we could neither house fifteen, nor could I have two Superiors in so small a number. My belief is that we shall hear no more about what is 'uncanonical'. But that they will worm their way in & intrigue with the Priests afterwards. (But I must put in my proviso – viz. that the Bermondsey nuns, who came out with us, are the truest Xtians I ever met with – invaluable in their work – devoted, heart & head, to serve God & mankind – not to intrigue for their Church).

I cannot tell what will be the issue of all these questions. To send back the fifteen new nuns will be awful. To take them in impossible. But, if they will not separate? —

I am now going to incorporate what I can of the Sisters & Nurses – in which I must, in conscience, exercise my right of selection.

I am no nearer distributing any of the party elsewhere. Balaklava has virtually fallen through. Merchant Seamen's Hosp'l has declined altogether. So have the Medical Men for the Convalescent Hospitals.

Here is where we are.

The Sellons are, as may be expected, furious at the dismissal of their confederate, & charge me with tyranny, who acted only under the advice, though perfectly in unison as to judgment, with the Commission. For such letters cannot be passed unnoticed. The Superior has been invited to read over the evidence & declined.

Pray confirm Father Michael Cuffe in his position here! It is the only agreeable incident I have had!

I believe it may be proved as a logical proposition that it is impossible for me to ride through all these difficulties. My caïque is upset – but I am sticking on the bottom still. But there will be a storm will brush me off. None the less shall I do what I believe to be your first will & that of Common Sense.

Unsigned

Source: BL Add 43393: ff 45–50

1. ἦθος : character, essence.
2. Therapians: Therapia was a village on the other side of the Bosphorus where the Stanley party was housed before they were sent to various hospitals. The British Embassy was comfortably situated there.

Nightingale did not carry out her threat to resign, but rather divided her time between infighting and initiating what she hoped would be long-term reforms. On 8 January 1855 she wrote to Herbert:

> As the large proportion of the Army (in which we are told that there are not two thousand sound men) is coming into

Hospital – as there are therefore thousands of lives at stake – as, in a service where the future of the official servants is dependent upon the personal interest of one man, these cannot be expected to peril that future by getting themselves shelved as innovators. I feel that this is no time for compliments or false shame – & that you will never hear the whole truth, troublesome as it is, except from one independent of promotion.

I will just add that this letter I have been asked to write by the best men here. It is no result of an indefinite feeling of feminine compassion. But it is the well-weighed conclusion of men of experience here, who see no provision made for the horrible emergency at this moment standing over us, yet who, if they represented it themselves, would obtain nothing but their own ruin.

I *beseech* you to keep this letter to yourself, while making the enquiries to which it may lead you.

The Commission has done nothing – probably its powers were limited to enquiry. Cumming has done nothing. Lord Wm. Paulet[1] has done nothing.

Lord Stratford, absorbed in politics, does not know the circumstances. Lord Wm. Paulet knows them, but partially. Menzies knows them & will not tell them. Wreford knows them & is stupified. The Medical Officers, if they were to betray them, would have it 'reported personally & professionally to their disadvantage'.

Lord Wm. Paulet, & Dr. Forrest the new Medical Head, I see, are *desperate*.

As your official servant, you will say that I ought to have reported these things before. But I did not wish to be made a spy. I thought it better if the remedy could be brought quietly – & I thought the Commission was to bring it. But matters are worse than they were two months ago & will be worse two months hence than they are now.

The Medical Men are pulled up by the Senior Med'l Authorities for receiving ward-furniture & food from & being purveyed by *me* – & therefore, like naughty children, pretend to ignore that their Requisitions go in to me instead of to the Purveyor & leave me to be rebuked for over-facility. (BL Add 43393:ff 75–76)

---

1. Lord William Paulet: (1804–93), appointed by Lord Raglan as chief commander at Scutari, after he had served in the Crimea. He was succeeded by Sir Henry Storks when he assumed command of the light division in the Crimea.

Nightingale then went on to outline in detail how the system ought to be revised in order to work.

Lord Stratford, the English Ambassador at Constantinople, sent his wife as his emissary to the wounded soldiers, but after her first visit to the noxious hospitals she would only meet them outdoors. The seeming indifference of the aristocratic ambassador and his wife infuriated Nightingale:

> She asked me whether we wanted any thing – & among other things I mentioned that, if we wanted to bring up stone from the beach, we had to make requisition for an 'Araba', which Araba was sure to be confiscated to carry the arms & munitions – or the dead to the grave – that I always answer, 'I am happy to serve Her Majesty' – & allow the goods to be turned out on the road. Well, said she, how many Arabas do you want? Mr. Bracebridge, thinking she meant for the service of the Hospital, said, Oh! about twelve. Well, she said, you shall have them tomorrow morning. She sends her Carvass to the Pasha himself per- haps – Heaven knows. But the next morning arrive five gilt coaches, (Talikas) before the Hospital gate, & seven other vehicles, & halt before the gate. What was to be done? Mr. Bracebridge went out & paid them off with Miss Nightin- gale's money – & this lark of the Ambassadress's cost Miss Nightingale 500 piastres. And so ended the Ambassador's first & last interference in our affairs. But, when this Strat- fordian policy concerns the lives of between four & five thousand of H. M's subjects, it becomes a very serious joke. (14 Jan 1855 BL Add 43393: ff 89–91)

Florence urged Herbert to establish a central authority who would co-ordinate all the purveying departments, but under the existing circumstances such a radical reform was impossible.

34. To Sidney Herbert

Barrack Hospital, Scutari
28 Jan 1855

Dear Mr. Herbert

As the Purveying seems likely to come to an end of itself, perhaps I shall not be guilty of the murder of the Innocents, if I venture to suggest what may take the place of the venerable Wreford.

Cornelius Agrippa had a broomstick, which used to fetch water for his use. When the broomstick was cut in two by the axe of an unwary student, each end of the severed broom, catching up a pitcher, began fetching water with all its might.

Were the Purveyor here cut in three, we might conceive some hope of having not only water but food also & clothing fetched us. Let there be three distinct offices instead of one indistinct one –

(1) to provide us with food
(2) with hospital furniture & clothing
(3) to keep the daily routine going

These are now the three offices of the unfortunate Purveyor – & none of them are performed.

But the Purveyor is *supposed* to be only the channel, thro' which the Commissariat stores *pass*. Theoretically but not practically it is so. (For practically Wreford gets nothing thro' the Commissary, but employs a rascally contractor, Parry – whose acc'ts or no accounts will soon be found out).

Now, why should not the *Commissariat purvey* the Hospital with food? – perform the whole of Purveyor's office, No 1? The practise of drawing *raw* rations, as here seen, seems invented on purpose to waste the time of as many Orderlies as possible, who stand at the Purveyor's office from 4 to 9 A.M. drawing the patient's breakfasts, from 10 to 12 drawing their dinners – & to make the Patients' meals as late as possible – because it is impossible to get the diets, thus drawn, cooked before 3 or 4 o'clock. The scene of confusion, delay & disappointment where all these raw diets are being weighed out, by twos & threes & fours, is impossible to conceive, unless one has seen it, as I have, day after day. And one must have been, as I have, at all hours of the day & night, in this Hospital, to conceive the abuses of this want of system! raw meat, drawn too late to be cooked standing all night in the wards &c &c &c.

Why should not the Commissariat send *at once* the amount of beef & mutton &c &c required, into the kitchens, without passing through this intermediate stage of drawing by Orderlies?

Let a Commissariat Officer reside here – let the Wardmaster make a total from the Diet Rolls of the Medical Men – so many hundred full diets – so many hundred half diets – so many hundred spoon diets – & give it over to the Commissariat Officer the day before. The next day the *whole* quantity, the *total* of all the Ward Masters' *totals*, is given into the kitchens direct. It should be all carved in the kitchens on hot plates & at meal-times the Orderlies come to fetch it for the Patients – carry it thro' the wards, where an Officer tells it off to every bed, according to the Bed-tickets, on

which he reads the Diet, hung up at every bed. The time &
confusion thus saved w'd be incalculable. Punctuality is now
impossible – the food is half raw – & often many hours after time.
Some of the portions are all bone – whereas the meat should be
boned in the kitchen, accord'g to the plan now proposed, & the
portions there carved contain meat only. Pray consider this.

There might be, *besides*, an Extra Diet Kitchen to each Division
– a teapot, issue of tea, sugar &c to every *mess*, for which stores
make the Ward-Master responsible – arrow-root, beef tea &c to be
issued from the Extra Diet Kitchens.

But into these details it is needless to enter to you.

(2) The second office of the Purveyor *now* is to furnish, *upon
requisition*, the Hospital with utensils & clothing.

But let the Hospital be furnished at once, as has been already
described in former letters. If 2000 beds exist, let these 2000 beds
have their appropriate complement of furniture & clothing,
stationary & fixed. Whether these be originally provided by a
Commissary or a store-keeper, let those who are competent
decide. The French appear to give as much too much power to
their Commissariat, who are the real chiefs of their Hospitals,
while the Medical Men are only their slaves, as we give too
little.

But the Hospital being once furnished, & a store-keeper
appointed to each division, to supply wear & tear, let the Ward-
Masters be responsible. Let an inventory hang on the door of each
ward of what *ought* to be found there – let the Ward-master give
up the dirty linen every night & receive the same quantity in clean
linen every morning. Let the Patient shed his Hospital clothing like
a snake when he goes out of Hospital, be inspected by the Quarter
Master, & receive if necessary, from Quarter Master's store, what
is requisite for his becoming a soldier again. While the next patient
succeeds to his bed & its furniture.

(3) The daily routine of the Hospital. This is now performed, or
rather not performed by the Purveyor. I am really cook,
housekeeper, & scavenger, (I go about making the Orderlies empty
huge tubs,) washerwoman, general dealer, store-keeper. The
Purveyor is supposed to do all this, but it is physically impossible.
And the filth, & the disorder, & the neglect let those describe who
saw it when we first came.

This is no time to palliate things. Poor Lord Wm. Paulett hides
his head under his wing. Ly Stratford plays the game of popularity
– & Ld Stratford, angry that the negotiations for peace are carried
on at Vienna & not by him, hardens his heart & shuts up his
despatches.

While, of 54,000 men, 11,000 are fit for duty. And the rest, where are they?

While you are straining every nerve to know the truth, & bring the remedy, at the expense of knowing that which must break the heart, these dreadful people are refusing, some to tell you the truth, some to know it themselves.

I am not 'playing a game to ruin poor Wreford', as I hear said every day – 'Miss Nightingale is bent upon ruining that poor man'. I could easily do that by simply stopping when my present stores are exhausted – & letting it then be seen what the Purveyor will do. But these poor soldiers must be thought of first – & as long as I can do them any good, I shall stay, & shall go on collecting & issuing as long as I can get money & have your licence to do so.

I have had much talk with Mr. Maxwell since the Commission came back. He entirely agrees with all this. He is doing his work well & energetically.

He will tell all this much better than I can tell it myself. And I will leave it to him to right these miserable Hospitals, & to do you justice by telling you the facts *you* are so generously anxious to hear, & *all here* are so ungenerously anxious to conceal. The Commission have written a letter to Lord Wm. Paulet, of suggestions, since they came back. But of this man nothing will come. We are expecting your clerks with anxiety.

I go on to No (3)

Let us have a Hotel-keeper, a House-steward, who shall take the daily routine in charge – the cooking, washing & cleaning us – the superintending the house-keeping, in short – be responsible for the cleanliness of the wards, now done by one Medical Officer Dr. McGrigor, by me or by no one, inspect the kitchens – the wash-houses – be what a housekeeper ought to be – in a private Asylum.

With the French the 'chef d'administration', the Commissary, as *we* should call him, is the master of the Orderlies. And the Medical Men just come in & prescribe, as London physicians do, & go away again. With us the Medical Officers are everything & have to do everything, however heterogeneous. The French system is bad, because, tho' there may be 20 things down on the Carte for the Medical Man to choose his Patient's diet from, *nominally*, the Chef d'Administration may have provided only two – & the Patient has no redress.

Whether, in any new plan, the House Steward have the command of the Orderlies or the Medical Man, which I am incompetent to determine whichever it be, let us have a Governor of the Hospital. As it is a Military Hospital, a Mil'y Head is probably necessary, as Governor.

I could give you pages full of illustrations, if I had time, or you – of Lord Wm Paulett, of the Embassy, the Medical Men. But I have none – except for two, one of Lord Wm Paulett, one of how the Medical Army Education, acting on the Scotch temperament, tells.

(1) I furnished 450 men, going on board the Dunbar, Convalescents for Corfou, with shirts, socks &c &c. Ld W. Paulett having been called upon in vain by me through the Medical Officers to furnish them from his stores. After they were on board, he sent two bales of shirts on board, his theory therefore being that they should go naked from the Hosp'l to the ship. Of my 450 suits, which were of course intended to become permanent Hosp'l clothing, I got back 43 shirts & these only by the energetic interference of Dr. McGrigor, who sent his Sergeant on board for them. This I mention for the sake of the principle, not for the sake of the 43 shirts. It is manifest that all system thus becomes impossible – & all those *duplicates* will be thrown overboard.

(2) I made Cruikshanks put into words his principle about the Nurses. (He is our Senior Medical Officer here). He volunteered to say that my best nurse, Mrs. Roberts, dressed wounds & fractures more skilfully than any of the Dressers or Assistant Surgeons. But that it was not a question of efficiency nor of the comfort of the Patients – but of the 'regulations of the service' 'that *officially* he should think it his duty to interfere, if he saw a nurse dressing sores, because it was contrary to the regulations of the service – tho' *privately* he might wink at it, for the sake of a Patient's life'. What could I say?

But we are only the symptom of what is going on in the Krimea. We are only the *pulse* which marks the state of the army. But this is hardly my business.

If you promote Dr. McGrigor, you will shew that you recognize a *principle* that of preferring man's life to the 'regulations of the service'.

I have been examined by the Commission & sent in my Returns by their desire.

The Sisters & Nurses are all placed

    19 have, at different times, gone home

      8 to Balaklava, who I hope will come back. For it is a mistake,

    16 to Koulalee

    41 here

    —

84 independently of Miss Stanley who always said from the first she did not mean to stay above a limited time – of Mrs. Bracebridge & of me

Could Mrs. Herbert think I was 'jealous of Miss Stanley'? — But that is, oh! such a minor matter *here*.

I never look at the Times, but they tell me there is a religious war about poor me there, & that Mrs. Herbert has generously defended me. I do not know what I have done to be so dragged before the Public. But I am so glad that my God is not the God of the High Church or of the Low – that He is not a Romanist or an Anglican or an Unitarian.

I don't believe He is even a Russian – tho' His events go strangely against us. NB. A Greek once said to me on Salamis, I do believe God Almighty is an Englishman.

Ever yours, dear Mr. Herbert,

F. Nightingale

We have not yet succeeded in getting rid of the depot, an essential measure for the good of this Hospital.

Source: BL Add 43393: ff 113–26

In January Lord Aberdeen's government had fallen on the passage of a motion by the radical MP J. A. Roebuck to form a committee to investigate the condition of the army in the Crimea, including the hospitals. The resulting report essentially censured the government, but Nightingale's mission was condoned, for 'Your Committee in conclusion cannot but remark that the first real improvements in the lamentable condition of the hospitals at Scutari are to be attributed to private suggestions, private exertions, and private benevolence' (Cook, I, 179). While out of office, Herbert continued to exert influence behind the scenes, and asked Nightingale to continue her correspondence with him. His successor was less inclined to sympathize with her plight, and recommended both a cessation of her purveying and a curtailment of her authority over the nurses; the actual situation was one of accusations, inaction and independent decision-making (Goldie [1987], pp. 104–10).

Meanwhile problems with the Stanley party increased. Mary Stanley had planned only to bring her party of nurses out and then return to England, but she stayed when the nurses appeared to be stranded. Mother Bridgeman thought it a part of her nuns' duty to minister to the spiritual as well as physical needs of the many Irish soldiers, an undertaking that had been expressly denied the first group. Furthermore, a Father Ronan had come out separately from

the nuns to avoid appearing as their spiritual adviser, an appointment the government had forbidden in their negotiations with
Manning. In a letter to Sidney Herbert of 15 February, Nightingale
begged for a resolution of the situation regarding the Stanley party
which, now located at Koulali, was creating the expected
problems:

> Now the party cannot be consigned to *no one* – it must be
> either to the Inspector General, or to the Superintendent
> of Nurses, or to Miss Stanley, who is going home.
>   But III – here follows the perverse imbroglio
>   they are 'consigned to Cumming' & not to me – but I
> am to supply them with money & not Cumming. And
> they ride off upon Cumming to avoid submitting to me –
> and they ride off upon me to avoid writing an official
> letter to Cumming, who is expressly designated as the
> person to fix the No. of Nurses by my written instruc-
> tions.
>   Having tried a third party, the Embassy, for money,
> they are forced to come back upon me, & claim the
> orders of the War Office, which don't exist.
>   This is the present web of cross purposes.
>   It is absolutely necessary that you should put the thing
> at once in an official & a definite form, if it is to continue
> to exist. (BL Add 43393: 157–58)

Further on, she added, 'As to the future, I claim to officer & work
these Scutari Hospitals on my plan – tho' only one which
experience teaches can be worked here' (BL Add 43393: f 159).
    By February Nightingale had conceded that Mary Stanley might
be able to manage Koulali and that she might be trusted with any
party she might wish to have, but that none of her ladies was
capable of managing if Mary Stanley left. Stanley herself, feeling
her strength, requested more 'ladies', as opposed to the experienced lower-class nurses. Nightingale loathed amateur nursing,
and tartly wrote to Lady Cranworth on 14 January 1856:

> I shall be very glad of my Rules. It does appear to me that
> the Ladies from Koulali & Smyrna have little other idea
> than that of riding out with the Chaplains & Officers &
> none at all of the work. They seem a little surprised at my
> Regulations, but hitherto we have gone on *very well*.
> And I will do all in my power to reconcile them to rules,
> of the necessity of the strictness of which I am every day
> more convinced. Even our late Command'r, Lord Wm.

Paulet, not celebrated for his prudery, remarked that ladies seemed to come to Koulali to do that which they could not with propriety do in England. (BL Add 43397: ff 76–77)

Raising the standard of nurses became only one of Nightingale's missions. She, along with William Henry Russell, helped to change the perception of the common soldier from that of a drunken brute to a courageous man worthy of respect. In spite of opposition from Lord Panmure, the new Secretary for War, and from military officials, she wanted to give the soldiers an opportunity to send money home. Nightingale organized a service in which she sent all the men's postal orders to Uncle Sam Smith, who forwarded them to their proper destinations in England. Seventy-one thousand pounds were remitted in the first six months. She initiated several other projects that were to improve life for the common soldier. She established the 'Inkerman Café', which gave convalescent soldiers an alternative to the canteen, where alcohol was sold, and provided them with reading material, games, and writing materials so that they could write home. Two school-masters were brought out to lecture and give classes; these were well attended.

Changes in the medical system were more difficult to implement, but she wrote to Herbert enthusiastically:

I. One thing which we much require might be easily done. This is the formation of a Medical School at Scutari. We have lost the finest opportunity for advancing the cause of Medicine & erecting it into a Science which will probably ever be afforded. There is here no operating room, no dissecting room, post mortem examinations are seldom made & then in the dead-house – (the ablest Staff Surgeon here told me that he considered that he had killed hundreds of men owing to the absence of these) no statistics are kept as to between what ages most deaths occur, as to modes of treatment, appearances of the body after death &c &c &c & all the innumerable & most important points which contribute to making Therapeutics a means of saving life & not, as it is here, a formal duty. Our registration generally is so lamentably defective that often the only record kept is – *a man* (sic) *died* – on such a day.

There is a Kiosk on the Esplanade before the Barrack Hospital, rejected by the Quarter Master for his stores, which I have asked for & obtained as a School of Medicine. It is not used now for any purpose. £300 or

£400 (which I would willingly give) would put it in a state of repair.

The young Surgeons here are first-rate Anatomists, as good, I dare say, as any in London, but miserable Pathologists – morbid Anatomy is almost unknown & the science of healing unpractised. At the request & according to the plan of the First Class Staff Surgeons, I gave them some expensive operating & dissecting tables, & I learn from these that they have pulled off the legs & burnt them as fire-wood.

The Kiosk is not overlooked & is in every way calculated for the purpose I have named. The Medical teaching duties could not be carried on efficiently with a less staff than two lecturers on Physiology & Pathology, & one lecturer on Anatomy, who will be employed in preparing the subject for demonstration, & performing operations for the information of the Juniors. If they could thus be interested in their profession (let alone humanity) much vice would be checked, besides saving, in future, many hundreds of lives. (22 Feb 1855 BL Add 43393: ff 173-76)

Florence obliquely admitted to homesickness in letters to her family. She thought she saw her pet owl, Athena, who had died from neglect during her preparations for the East.

35. To the Nightingale family   Scutari 5 Mar 1855

Dearest people

I saw Athena last night. She came to see me. I was walking home late from the Gen'l Hosp'l round the cliff, my favorite way, & looking, I really believe for the first time, at the view – the sea glassy calm & of the purest sapphire blue – the sky one dark deep blue – one solitary bright star rising above Constantinople – our whole fleet standing with sails idly spread to catch the breeze which was none – including a large fleet of Sardinians carrying up Sardinian troops – the domes & minarets of Constantinople sharply standing out against the bright gold of the sunset – the transparent opal of the distant hills, (a color one never sees but in the East) which stretch below Olympus always snowy & on the other side the Sea of Marmora when Athena came along the cliff quite to my feet, rose upon her tiptoes, bowed several times, made her long melancholy cry, & fled away – like the shade of Ajax. I assure you my tears followed her.

On Wednesday 28th Feb, we had the sharp shock of an earth quake. It is indescribable. One does not feel the least frightened, but I felt quite convinced our old towers must come down. Two hundred patients jumped out of bed & ran into the Main Guard – two jumped out of window – some got out of bed who c'd not get in again. When next we looked across to the other side, two minarets of Constantinople had disappeared. Half Bursa is in ruins, & the accts. of killed & wounded there, where statistics are none, vary from 3000 to 800. One man here with comp'd fracture seriously injured himself by scuttling out of bed. We have had several slight shocks since.

Please pay £5 (which torment me) due to Harley St. for board of self & Mrs. Clarke from Michaelmas till the day of our going, *and* my £5.5 Sub'n. for 1855.

ever yours

FN

Source: Wellcome

When the Sultan of Turkey granted permission for a British military cemetery at Scutari, Nightingale was asked to recommend a suitable memorial. She enlisted Parthenope's aid:

36. To Parthenope Nightingale   Scutari 8 Mar 1855

My dearest   I hope you are doing something about the Monument. The people here want to have a Cross – they do not see that immediately will arise the question, Greek or Latin Cross – that we cannot have our own Cross in a country where all Xtians are Greeks – still less can we have the Greek Cross – besides the ill grace of our setting up a Cross at all who are fighting for the Crescent. But these people cannot be made to see this. I should like Trajan's column – or Themistocles' *broken* column, only that nobody would see the sentiment of it.

The whole of this gigantic misfortune has been like a Greek tragedy – it has been like the fates pursuing us. Every thing that has been done has been a failure & nobody knows the reason why – the Gods have punished with blindness some past sin & visited the

innocent with the consequences – for 'our God is a jealous God'
&c how like the Greek & the Jewish Mythology!

But this great tragedy must now, one would think, be near its
close.

Please put yourself *at once* in communication, dear Pop, with the
Chaplain-General Gleig, to get us working drawings for our Public
Monument & Private Chapel in the British burial ground now to be
enclosed on cliff looking over Sea of Marmora – first ascertaining
from Herberts whether Queen wishes to interfere. If she has no
commands, set to work at once. I should like 'Wingless Victory' for
Chapel – one single solitary column for monument to greet first our
ships coming up the Sea of Marmora. It is such a position – high o'er
the cliffs we shall save in vain. I should have liked the Temple of
Sunium – but a miniature never does – & they want a Cross.

I have told Herberts & Chaplain General you will put yourself
in communication with him. *Let us live* at least in our dead. Five
thousand & odd brave hearts sleep there – three thousand, alas!
dead in Jan. & Feb. alone – here.

But what of that? *They* are not there. But, for once, even I wish
to keep their remembrance on earth – for *we* have been the
Thermopylae of this desperate struggle, when Raglan & cold &
famine have been the Persians, our own destroyers. *We* have
endured in brave Grecian silence. *Let* the 'Times' avenge us. I do
not care. We have folded our mantles about our faces & died in
silence without complaining. No one can say *we* have complained.

And as for myself, I have done my duty. I have identified my
fate with that of the heroic dead, & whatever lies these sordid
exploiteurs of human misery spread about us these officials, there
is a right & a God to fight for & our fight has been worth fighting.
I do not despair – nor complain. It has been a great cause.

We cannot yet believe in the death of the Emperor,[1] telegraphed
from Bucharest yesterday – though it is believed at the Embassy –
it is so like the dénouement of a Novel – too good to be true – how
rarely do the fates of Nations hang upon the life of an individual &
how rarely does that individual die in time to be of any use.

ever thine

F.N.

Please date your letters

Source: Wellcome

1. the Emperor: Emperor Nicholas I of Russia (d. 2 March 1855), who had succeeded his
brother in 1825. The British hoped that his successor, Alexander II, would be more willing
to negotiate peace on their terms.

1. Florence Nightingale after her return
   from the Crimea (1856)

2. W. E. Nightingale and Parthenope at
   Embley

3. Sidney Herbert, Lord Herbert of Lea

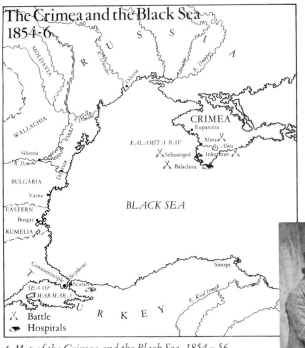

4. Map of the Crimea and the Black Sea, 1854–56

6. Dr John Sutherland and Robert Rawlinson in the Crimea

5. Ward, Barrack Hospital, Scutari

7. Sir John McNeill

8. Typical barracks in India, 1863

9. Mrs Wardroper and St Thomas' nurses

DAILY MEANS OF OCCUPATION AND AMUSEMENT. INDIA *passim*.

I shall myself have no further
communication of any kind
with Mr. Whitfield -
[And I have struck him
out of my Will] It is silly, perhaps, to
mention this. But I only want to express that I can have
myself nothing more to do with him.
I happen to know, par parenthèse,
that he scarcely knows more of our
Probationers by sight -
(that Miss Barclay is one
of these) - I believe she would
refuse to go with him - but have
had no talk with her about it.
I do trust that we shall
begin with Mr. Croft
with the New Year -
But this must form the
subject of another letter.

10. *A page of letter 119 to Henry Bonham Carter*

11. *Florence, Parthenope and Sir Harry Verney at Claydon*

Lady Canning and Lady Cranford, members of the Ladies' Committee at Harley Street, along with Liz Herbert, undertook a variety of tasks, including the recruitment of a continual stream of nurses sent to replace those who were dismissed, fell ill or died.

37. To Elizabeth Herbert

Private[1]

Barrack Hospital, Scutari
16 Apr 1855

Dearest – I am so sorry to be obliged to tell you that Thompson & Anderson, two of the Presbyterian Nurses from Edinburgh, went out drinking with an Orderly on Saturday night. Anderson was brought back dead drunk. But Thompson I believe to be the most hardened offender. This was such a catastrophe that there was nothing to be done but to pack them off to England *directly* – & accordingly they *sail* this morning by the Gottenburg. It is a great disappointment, as they were hard working good-natured women. I sent them to the Gen'l Hosp'l, & alas! I find that under any guardianship less watchful than mine, I can hardly depend on any Nurse. Yet no one else is of any use.

Only one week's wages was due to them, which I have not given them, of course, as by rights they ought not to have a free passage home. There were *no* extenuating circumstances. Should they come to you to have their fares paid down to Edinbro', you will perhaps extend that as a matter of mercy, but pray do no more. They were engaged on March 9. You paid them the first month. I discharge them on April 16.

I think the other five promise well. I like Sinclair particularly. Miss Wear is gone to Balaclava, Miss Stanley rejected her at Koulali. I fear she is too eccentric to be of real use.

Will you tell Mr. Herbert that Milton has with-drawn his paper, requiring me to sell the free Gifts, with an apology, compelled, I believe, by Ld W. Paulet – & that since Mr. Herbert's letter to him, he has been much less red-tapy.

Ever your FN

Source: BL Add 43393: ff 30–31

1. Not in FN's handwriting; the letter was probably copied and circulated among friends.

By early May Nightingale felt that the Scutari hospitals were in sufficient order for her to leave them in Selina Bracebridge's care while she went to Balaclava to inspect the hospitals and female nurses there. During the week-long voyage she wrote home about her continuing concern for the soldiers:

38. To the Nightingale family   Black Sea 5 May 1855

Poor old Flo steaming up the Bosphorus & across the Black Sea with four Nurses, two Cooks & a boy to Crim Tartary (to overhaul the Regimental Hospitals) in the 'Robert Lowe' or Robert Slow (for an uncommon slow coach she is) taking back 420 of her Patients, a draught of convalescents returning to their Regiments to be shot at again. A 'mother in Israel', old Fliedner called me – a mother in the Coldstreams is the more appropriate appellation.

What suggestions do the above ideas make to you in Embley drawing-room? Stranger ones perhaps than to me – who, on the 5th May, year of disgrace 1855, year of my age 35, having been at Scutari this day six months, am, in sympathy with God, fulfilling the purpose I came into the world for.

What the disappointments of the conclusion of these six months are, no one can tell. But I am not dead, but alive. What the horrors of war are, no one can imagine, they are not wounds & blood & fever, spotted & low, & dysentery chronic & acute, cold & heat & famine. They are intoxication, *drunken* brutality, demoralization & disorder on the part of the inferior – jealousies, meanness, indifference, *selfish* brutality on the part of the superior. I believe indeed & am told by admirable officers in the service, that our Depot & Barrack at Scutari – in which to live for six months has been death, is a disgrace to the service & our Commandant the worst officer in the service, (had & solicited for by Ld. Stratford because he would have a man of rank). But our Scutari staff, military & medical, content themselves with saying that the English soldier *must* be drunk & not one thing is done to prevent him. Nothing has been done but by us. We have established a reading room for the Convalescents, which is well attended. And the conduct of the soldiers to us is uniformly good. I believe that we have been *the most efficient* – perhaps the only – means there of restoring discipline – instead of destroying it, as I have been accused of. They are much more respectful to me than they are to their own officers. But it makes me cry to think that all these 6 months, we might have had a trained schoolmaster & that I was

told it was quite impossible. That, in the Indian army, effectual &
successful measures are taken to prevent intoxication &
disorganization, & that here, under Lord W. Paulet's very
windows, the Convalescents are brought in emphatically *dead*
drunk, for they die of it, & he looks on with composure & says to
me, 'You are spoiling those brutes'. The men are so glad to read, so
glad to give me their money to keep or to send home to their
mothers or wives. But I am obliged to do this in secret.

On the 1st May, by the most extreme exertions, our Washing
house opened, which might just as well have been done on the 1st
November six months ago.

I am in hopes of organizing some washing & cooking for the
Regimental Hospitals – & am going up with Soyer, dollies &
steaming apparatus for this purpose for more than for any other.

Mr. Bracebridge goes with us. Mrs. B. keeps the bear-garden at
Scutari. Four vessels of Sardinian troops go up with us – one vessel,
the Argo, with Artillery & horses, ditto – but went aground in the
Bosphorus & could not get her off.

I have more & more reason to believe that this is the kingdom of
hell – but I as much believe that it is to be made the kingdom of
heaven.

Beware of Lady Stratford
    yours ever

                                                            FN

Source: Wellcome

Riding to the front with Alexis Soyer, the French chef who had
accompanied her, Nightingale was cheered by crowds of excited
officers and troops.

39. To Parthenope Nightingale   {Balaclava} 10 May 1855

My dearest/   My days at Balaklava have been so busy as
you may suppose. I have made a tour of inspection of Regimental
Hosp'ls in camp – besides re-organizing the two Hospitals
under our care, which were terribly 'seedy' – Nurses all in
confusion.

The camp is very striking – more so than any one can imagine or
describe. Between 150,000 – 200,000 men in a space of 20 square

miles all obeying one impulse, engaged in one work – it is very affecting. But to me the most affecting sight was to see them mustering & forming at sun-down for the trenches – where they will be for 24 hours without returning. From those trenches 30 will never return. Yet they volunteer – press forward for the trenches. When I consider what the work has been this winter, what the hardships, I am surprised – not that the army has suffered so much but – that there is any army left at all, not that we have had so many through our hands at Scutari, but that we have not had all as Sir John McNeill says. Fancy working 5 nights out of 7 in the trenches. Fancy being 36 hours in them at a stretch – as they were, all December – lying down or half lying down often 48 hours without food but *raw* salt pork sprinkled with sugar – & their rum & biscuit – nothing hot – because the *exhausted* soldier *could not* collect his own fuel, as he was expected, to cook his own ration. And fancy, thro' all this, the army preserving their courage & patience – as they have done – & being now eager, the old ones more than the young ones, to be led even into the trenches. There was something sublime in the spectacle. The brave 39th, whose Regimental Hospitals are the best I have ever seen, turned out & gave Florence Nightingale three times three, as I rode away. There was nothing empty in that cheer nor in the heart which received it. I took it as a true expression of true sympathy – the sweetest I have ever had. I took it as a full reward of all I have gone through. I promised my God that I would not die of disgust or disappointment if he would let me go through this. In all that has been said against & for me, no one soul has appreciated what I was really doing – none but the honest cheer of the brave 39th.

Nothing which the 'Times' has said has been exaggerated of hardship.

Sir John MacNeill is the man I like the best of all who have come out. He has dragged Commissary General out of the mud. He has done wonders. Every body now has their fresh meat 3 times a week, their fresh bread from Constantinople about as often.

It was a wonderful sight looking down upon Sevastopol – the shell whizzing right & left. I send you a Minié bullet I picked up on the ground which was ploughed with shot & shell – & some little flowers. For this is the most flowery place you can imagine – a beautiful little red which I don't know, yellow Jessamine & every kind of low flowering shrub. A Serj't of the 97th picked me a nosegay. I once saved Serj't —'s[1] life by finding him at 12 o'clock at night lying – wounds undressed – in our Hosp'l with a bullet in his eye & a fractured skull. And I pulled a stray Surgeon out of bed to take the bullet out. But you must not tell this story. For I gave evidence against the missing Surgeon – & have never been forgiven.

Sir John McNeill, whom you must not quote, it was who told me that it was . . .

P.S. There is some Cholera in Camp, but not much. I want very much to hear how Blanch is. I was very much disappointed that Aunt Mai did not write. I heard it through a common newspaper, till I had a note from Mama.

Source: Wellcome   {incomplete letter}

1. FN used a long dash for the Serjeant's name.

While in the Crimea Nightingale outlined many ideas for the training and supervision of hospital nurses. Her insistence that the superintendent have sole control over the nurses was to become a cornerstone of her later reforms at home.

40. To Lady Charlotte Canning   Balaclava 10 May 1855

Dear Lady Canning

I would write more at length to thank you for all the trouble you have taken for us – to tell you what an useful person Miss Tattersall, the tradesman's daughter, is turning out, what nice respectable women, two of the Oxford Nurses, Clarke & Howse, these are of the first party – & Logan, the Scotch Presbyterian, I think I like the best of the second party – (their agreements were all right & so were their certificates, excepting that, being expressly designed therein as for *Scutari* Hospital, it gives me no power to transfer them to Balaklava, if found desirable).

Also, I have stated to Mr. Hawes[1] my objections to giving these women 18/ at once, without any power of raising their wages. In this way, women, sent back from hence for drunkenness in a short time, will have almost as much due to them as those tried ones who have borne with me the toil & burden of the day. Or I must raise the wages of the whole of the old set at a great expence to Government. The terms of the old set were 10/ per week with permission to raise up to 25/ : I raised none till they had been with me six months.

I begged Mrs. Bracebridge, who remained at Scutari, to write & thank you for your great kindness in taking so much trouble about the summer clothing – & to say that I have had no trouble about *drinking* with any of your eleven – (the two sets whom you were kind enough to send me) – as yet.

I would like to say much more. But this is principally a letter of business to say – pray prevent any more women being sent out. The 'female troops', as we now are called, are becoming quite the laughing-stock of the Army. (this is strictly 'entre nous') or will be so – if it is continued – to send them out in such numbers. Koulale & Smyrna are so over-stocked that I hear nothing but jokes on the subject – I mean overstocked under present circumstances. Matters are very different now (thank God, as my Mrs. Clarke, now gone home, used always to say & to write, thank *Gog*!) from what they were when I came out. I have plenty at Scutari now to supply Balaklava, even should there be a great & sudden emergency, for I have far too many at Scutari under *present* circumstances. The numbers of sick, including Convalescents, were, when I left Scutari (& they must have decreased since, owing to sending home several more ships)

	Barrack Hosp'l	1100
Scutari	General „	378
	Palace „	240
	Koulale	410

Though there were 1100 in the Barrack Hosp'l, not 100 were in bed – & 10 women could *easily* have done all the work – whereas I had 26.

I am very glad to have a reserve, but I have quite enough to garrison Balaklava. I brought three with me. I had eight here before for the two Hospitals – & such is the difficulty of housing them, such the difficulty of obtaining labour of any kind, & wood (we pay Croats 3/ a day to do, 3 in 3 days, what one English workman does in 1 hour) that, though we only require a hut for the whole party, that hut cannot yet be erected, & I have them still on board a Transport with me. We have here but 400 sick & wounded – of whom but 120 wounded. We are now amply sufficient for this number – as upwards of 100 of the sick are Convalescents – & we are twelve. I have inspected most of the Regimental Hospitals in which the numbers of sick & wounded vary from 4 to 50. Of course it is out of the question to place women there, with an army too which may take the field any day – nor would the authorities, of course, permit it.

Should there be an assault, for which we are all, officers, men, cattle & women, earnestly praying, (for what is the carnage of an assault compared to what we had last winter?) or should the army take the field & march upon Simpheropol or have an engagement which sends us its wounded – we have still at least twenty nurses to spare from Scutari. Two things appear certain that nothing will be done before Napoleon comes if he does come – & when he passes thro' the Bosphorus, it will be time for my Nurses to pass through too from Scutari – the other that it is the intention of Lord Raglan to keep all his wounded up here in the Krimea. (Whether I shall be able to find accommodation such as can keep women respectable is a different question) I wish that there were some combination between Commander-in-Chief, Medical Inspector-General in the Crimea, War Office & its Civil Hospitals. There appears to be none. For, while we hear from Lord Raglan that all the wounded are to be kept here – while the Hospitals, now existing in the Bosphorus, are comparatively empty, we hear from home that three Civil Hospitals, two besides Dr. Parkes' are coming out, of 1000 men each, for the Bosphorus, the Dardanelles or Sinope, we hear from Dr. Parkes, who interests me greatly in his success, that he expects everything but Patients. For there is more than room for sick, already existing.

When I see the camp, I wonder, not that the army suffered so much but that there is any army left at all – not that so many passed through our hands at Scutari – (4000 once in 17 days) but that all did not pass through. Nothing has been exaggerated. But now all is looking up – fresh meat 3 times a week – fresh bread from Constantinople. Sir John MacNeill has done wonders.

Pray believe me, dear Lady Canning,
    yours very truly

F. Nightingale

There is some Cholera in camp – but not much.

Source: LDA: Harewood Collection, Lord Canning Papers 177/Z/2

1. Sir Benjamin Hawes: (1797–1862), appointed Deputy Secretary in the War Office in 1851; he subsequently became its permanent Under-Secretary. FN saw him as a key anti-reformist.

Nightingale's triumphant tour was cut short by her sudden collapse from 'Crimean fever'. Hovering between life and death for several weeks, she was nursed by Mrs Roberts. When she was well enough to travel, Dr Hall and Dr Hadley, the Senior Medical Officer at the Castle Hospital, placed her on the *Jura*, which was returning straight to England, but Mr Bracebridge foiled their plan by transferring her to a ship bound for Scutari. Back at Scutari, Nightingale was received by high officials and carried by relays of soldiers to Mr Sabin's house, where she recuperated slowly. Unfortunately, the Commander of the Forces, Lord Raglan, died during her illness – a loss that she felt keenly, for she never enjoyed friendly relations with his two successors, General James Simpson and General William Codrington.

Upon coming to power, the Palmerston government had appointed several commissions to investigate – and change – defects in the army system. The death rate at the Barrack Hospital had not diminished in spite of the acknowledged improvement that Nightingale and her nurses had achieved. The reason became evident only after the Sanitary Commission – composed of Dr John Sutherland, a sanitarian, Dr Hector Gavin, and Robert Rawlinson, a civil engineer – was sent out with full executive powers. This Commission discovered that the Barrack Hospital was situated on top of clogged cesspools and decayed filth. From mid March until June 1855 they worked to correct the problem; the death rate fell rapidly from that point.

During her long recuperation Nightingale caught up with the many miscellaneous letters written to her as a famous individual who might intervene in the army's bureaucracy. She sarcastically wrote to her family:

> The letters from 'heart-broken friends at home' have begun again – friends who want to know whether a man who died in Feb'y (a time when we were never in from the wards till near twelve o'clock) 'appeared to have any desire to be saved & left a Savings Bank Book for £20'. I am desired to give the minutest particulars of what he thought & did not think at 6 months' distance of time to a 'praying Mother & a father who has feared God many years'. Curiously enough, I remember this man – tho' at that time we were losing fifty to seventy a day. (7 Aug 1855 Wellcome)

In late July the Bracebridges had returned to England. Nightingale's favourite, Aunt Mai, joined her in Scutari until the end of the war; she immediately took up the task of writing letters of condolence which Nightingale signed.

41. To Mrs Maria Hunt[1]

Barrack Hospital, Scutari
6 Sept 1855

Dear Mrs. Hunt,

I grieve to be obliged to inform you that your son died in this Hospital on Sunday last, Sept'er 2nd. His complaint was Chronic Dysentary – he sunk gradually from weakness, without much suffering. Everything was done that was possible to keep up his strength. He was fed every half hour with the most nourishing things he could take, & when there was any thing he had a fancy for, it was taken to him immediately. He sometimes asked for oranges & grapes, which quenched his thirst, & which he had, whenever he wished for them – he spoke much of his Mother, & gave us the direction to you in his last moments. He was very desirous that you should be written to about him. His great anxiety was that his Mother should receive the pay due to him, & should know that he had not received any pay since he had been out, which he wished his friends to be told that they might apply to the War Office for the whole of the pay due to him. He was very grateful for whatever was done for him, & very patient. You may have the satisfaction of knowing that he had the most constant & careful attendance from the Doctors & the Nurses of the Hospital. The chaplain and myself saw him every day. He died very peacefully & sorrowful as this news is for his bereaved Mother. May she find comfort in thinking that his earthly sufferings were over, & in the hope that our Almighty Father will receive him into a better world through the blessed promises of our Lord. With sincere sympathy I am

     Yours truly

Florence Nightingale

Source: GLRO HI/ST/NC1/55/4/1

1. In pencil: FN for M.S. announcing a soldier's death. Written by Miss Nightingale's aunt Mrs Smith, signed by Miss Nightingale.

42. To Lady Charlotte Canning

Barrack Hospital,
Scutari 9 Sept 1855

My dear Lady Canning

I have been waiting only for an hour to thank you very, very much for your most kind letter & to answer the questions contained in it. I have been driven by over-work more than usually of late from the sudden death (by Cholera) of my excellent Matron, who managed the Linen Stores for 1200 Patients & the Hospital Furniture & from the illness of my Assistant at the same time.

I never doubted the sympathy of the Queen for her poor soldiers, & consequently for all those who tried to do them good. Indeed the fellow-feeling at home with these poor fellows has throughout been a great help in their sufferings. And to be assured of the Queen's sympathy was the highest pleasure to them. We feel it the more because on all hands we hear of the pains & the interest she takes in informing herself of all that concerns them.

It seems as if I had been negligent in accounting for the use of the £200 which Col. Phipps desired me to lay out for the Queen in any comfort which it might seem well for her to give. But I have not. The only use I have as yet made of it was to purchase a tent for the Convalescents to air themselves under, which cost £21. Soldiers are strange beings & it seemed desirable that they should have to thank their Queen for something which they did not consider their right. To spend her money in Arrow Roots & socks would not have attracted their attention. At this time too we are amply supplied with every kind of store, very different from what it was when we first came out. Tobacco is, above all, the luxury which the soldier most enjoys – & far be it from me to grudge it him in this miserable war. Still it is not exactly a *Queen's* present. But I look forward to a time next winter, when we shall be less fashionable in all human probability than we are now, when England will be tired of us – & the Queen's kindness will be well applied & fully appreciated by the soldier.
Question I.

It struck me when I read the agreement signed by the Civil Nurses that the last paragraph would not do for a Military Hosp'l. Because the Nurses there must not be placed under the *immediate* direction of the Principal Medical Officer. In Civil Hospitals, the Medical Officer is accustomed to the direction of women – & may be trusted with it – in Military Hosp'ls not. Bind the *Superintendent* by every tie of signed agreement & of honor to strict obedience to her Medical Chief. (I think it has been the defect at Koulale that this has not been done.) But let all his orders to the Nurses go through her. I mean, of course, not with regard to the medical management of the Patients, but with regard to the placing & discipline of the Nurses. I have never had the slightest difficulty about this – tho Medical Men always coming to me & saying, 'I want such & such assistance' – and I always informing them of any exchange or removal of Nurses – & consulting them. But I would never have undertaken the Superintendency with that condition that the Nurses consider themselves 'under the direction of the Principal Medical Officer'. *I* am under his direction. *They* are under mine.

I will give two instances just to explain that my meaning is to attain not insubordination to the Doctors, but a power of explaining to the Doctors.

It has continually happened to me, especially at B'clava, to be asked for a Nurse to attend an Officer where there was *no possibility* for the woman to retire day or night for even a moment – & where it was too far for her to return to her Hospital. And this request has been made by an old married Doctor & a father. In one instance, the Principal Medical Officer of B'clava, when I pointed this out to him, immediately gave up his own room for the Nurse to retire to at certain hours – shewing that it was not indifference but inadvertence. In another instance though, similarly with the first instance, the house was crowded with men, (viz. Officers, servants & doctors &c) & there was not a cranny where a woman could go unseen, yet, though three of the men were Chaplains & the sick man nursed was a Chaplain, it was only by going myself & turning out an Officer's servant – & providing for him elsewhere that I could secure a corner for my poor Nurse – whose Patient required her constantly. These are the things which deaden women's feeling of morality & make them take to drinking & worse – if the Superintendent is not continually on the alert.

The other case which makes me 'stickle' for the Superintendent being first in authority over the Nurses was that of a Nurse whom I removed from her wards on account of an intrigue in which she was slightly to blame & removal was all that was necessary. In the anger of the moment, she said she thought she had been only accountable to the Medical Officer. She immediately repented, saw the justice of the removal & was forgiven. But a Medical Officer would neither have discovered nor removed her for this – & she could have quoted her agreement to prove that she was chiefly responsible to him.

Under these circumstances, therefore, I must suggest that the Form of Agreement should bind Nurses to obedience to their Superintendent, the Superintendent to the Principal Medical Officer by another Form signed by *her*. But, if the Medical Officer conveys his orders, in the first place, to the Nurse, the

Superintendent can only interfere in the second place. And there will be continual quarrelling, which there never has been in the four Hospitals under my charge.

Question II With regard to the wages, a sliding scale is absolutely necessary. At what rate it shall begin I cannot decide. Because I have no doubt that the excitement which has been made about us in England has raised our price – I will only remark that the *lowest* description of Nurses I have had were a Mrs. Gibson who came out at 18/ in the 2nd party, a Mrs. Whitehead who came out at 18/ with the same party & who has not yet returned home, because she has broken her leg, a Mrs. Thompson, & Mrs. Anderson who came out at 18/ each by the 3rd party & returned drunk in 3 weeks, a Mrs. Holmes of the same party, who *was* a woman of bad character, but whom I have kept, because I believe she has really been shocked into reform here – also at 18/– a Mrs. Clarke, from Oxford, of the 4th party, who came out at 16/– & several others, whose names I will not give, because they are not likely to trouble you. These all came out at 18/– whereas some of the most respectable women were of the first party, who all came out at 10/. I do not think their having children to settle has any thing to do with the Government question of providing good & respectable Nurses for their soldiers. But I am not aware, as I have already said, of the present state of feeling in England – & think that your sliding scale may be a necessary one viz 14/ a week for 3 months, to be then raised to 18/ & after a year to 20/.

I have not had a single Nurse yet, either at high or at low wages, whom I could place in a situation of responsibility, excepting Mrs. Roberts & Mrs. Walford, (the latter I found out here & she is the poor woman just dead of Cholera).

I think a mistake has arisen that a Nurse out of a surgical ward means a surgical Nurse. The *nurse* out of a surgical ward is nothing but a maid-of-all-work. She scours, washes the Patients, makes the beds – sometimes the poultices &c. Mrs. Orton, of the 4th party, who came out as a Surgical Nurse from Bartholomew's, is scarcely fit for a maid-of-all-work. She came out at 16/. But she is such a good creature, though silly & vulgar, that I employ her in the Linen Stores under direction.

I send you the first Agreement & first Certificate which I think, after all, were the best.

Question III I see no objection to the 'Drink' rule being left out. Because it is different at different Hospitals. But, without the rule against Presents, no discipline could be maintained. I have had no difficulty in enforcing it. I *know* of many instances where the Nurses have refused money & have never told me so themselves. I *know* of only one instance where money was accepted & that was by an unprincipled woman, Mrs. Lyas, of the 2nd party, whom I was about to dismiss, & who has procured herself a situation as Governess!! in an Armenian family by the agency of the R. C. priest. Experience connected with this woman leads me to the suggestion that it is desirable *never* to send out R. C. *Nurses*, who will always be borne scatheless by their Priests – through any misconduct – & *never* to pay their wages, or any portion of their wages, in any other way excepting thro' the Superintendent. This woman sets all at defiance, has carried off all her new summer clothing, endeavours to seduce away the other Nurses, because I had no check over her – her wages having been paid in London by the W. Office. She sent me word, when she ran away, that she was sure of her wages without me. And she has completely deluded that unlucky Lawfield, of St. John's, whom she converted.

I require, if you please, a large number of new Badges. Ours are worn out & we have no time to work them. Mrs. Bracebridge has the pattern.

I think it undesirable that the Nurses should be allowed to take with them their own outer clothing. It will be a constant struggle to prevent their wearing it.

I would suggest that, if Nurses choose to wear white Petticoats – & white stockings, it should be made a condition that they put them *out* to wash at their own expence. Grey Twill would do very well for petticoats. I have sent for some to Malta.

The rule about wearing the regulation dress applies *particularly* to when they are *out of* Hospital – & therefore the rule as it is written about this is not explicit enough. I have myself heard one soldier address another, 'Don't yo speak to her'n! don't yo know that's one of Miss Nightingale's!' The necessity of distinguishing them *at once* from the camp-followers is particularly obvious when they are *not* engaged in Hospital work.

I think the rule about receiving wages should be – quarterly. I hope that additional rules I sent home by Mrs. Bracebridge will be adopted – especially that about their accepting no other situation out here. People in the East will take a servant, or even a Governess, with no character whatsoever.

The rule about remitting nurses' wages thro' the Paymaster is undesirable for two reasons. 1st the extreme delay. It is stated 'in the same way as soldiers' remittances'. The delay in making these is so well known that the soldiers are in the habit of remitting by me to England in small sums of 20/ or 30/ a *weekly* amount of (now) not less than £150. It is stated that 'the

Genl Agent will, in *due course*, issue the same'. The *'due course'* is one of many months.

2nd the Nurses should be dependent on the Superintendent for their wages – entirely – as she alone can know their deserts.

The Exhortation to the Nurses is excellent. But something might be added. In the rule (4th) about the walking, we are obliged to arrange that they should not go out for exercise excepting with the superintendent, as when two or even three were together, the Soldiers would make appointments to meet them – for we have here the misery of a depot. On the other hand, I have been obliged to waive the rule that two must always be together in the wards. It cannot be always maintained.

The 5th viz. the instructions of the W. Office respecting religious intercourse to Lord W. Paulet has been so completely misunderstood by the R. C.s that it has been, in fact, my principal difficulty – & the less publicity which is given to it the better. The R. C.'s who, before, were quite amenable, have chosen to construe the rule that 'they are not to enter upon the discussion of religious subjects with any Patients other than those of their own faith' to mean – therefore with *all* of their own faith – & the 2nd party of Nuns, who came out, now wander over the whole Hospital out of Nursing hours, not confining themselves to their own wards nor even to Patients, but 'instructing' (it is their own word) groups of Orderlies & Convalescents in the Corridors – doing the work each of ten Chaplains – & bringing ridicule upon the whole thing, while they quote words of the W. Office, which indeed seem to have been left intentionally vague, & to bear this construction.

(1) Aprons may 'well be served out like Towels'. But it is better for the Nurses that each should have her own towels, aprons, &c – as some tear & destroy so much more than others – & the tidy ones ought not to be called upon to succeed to the others' patches or rents.

(2) Etnas &c are very useful.

(3) A good stock of needles, cotton &c &c would be eminently acceptable to me. I am constantly 'emptied out' – as we give a small stock to each Patient returning to the Krimea. He cannot drink cottons. Buttons may be sent us by the million & used – gratefully.

I will send back the Lists of the clothing which the Nurses *have had*. I have not yet got in those from the Krimea, which has caused my delay.

We are truly grateful to you for all you have done for us. I am very anxious that Mrs. Bracebridge should be the person to approve the Nurses sent by Lady Cranworth & that none should come without her approbation – because she knows so exactly what we want.

Death & illness & misconduct have thinned our ranks & I now require

2 Matrons for the Linen Stores
one at each of the two Scutari Hospitals. For we have now undertaken the whole of these immense Stores. There are four Divisional Stores to this hospital only – & each man has now his clean shirt twice a week or oftener and his clean sheets once a week or oftener. These Matrons will have nothing to do with nursing.

1 Housekeeper – who will exercise control over the Nurses *in* the Quarters – not in the wards – she too has nothing to do with nursing.

2 steady elderly healthy Maids of all work: willing to go to B'clava if necessary –

4 Nurses – who must also be willing to go to B'clava, if necessary –

I cannot sufficiently say how much I feel all the trouble you have taken with us – nor how great I feel your loss will be to us. Believe me, dear Lady Canning, most truly & gratefully yours

F Nightingale

P.S.

Many, many thanks for your kind enquiries after my health, which is as much improved, I believe, as I can expect in the time. I have most seriously considered the kind wishes of my friends that I should leave this place for a time. But I believe those about me come to the conclusion that, on the whole, it was best that I should remain here.

Can you pardon this long letter, which I have not time to make shorter, written among interruptions & business of all kinds?

There are of the many good wishes, which will follow you to your command in India,[1] none more *fervent*, at *least*, than ours. I do not know how you will look upon the exile from England. But I cannot help rejoicing at your going to so responsible and important a post.

Many thanks for your encouraging words upon mine.

Source: LDA: Harewood Collection, Lord Canning Papers 177/Z/2

1. Lady Canning's husband had been appointed Governor-General of India at the end of 1855. He assumed the post at the end of February 1856. She died of fever in Calcutta in 1861.

The dismissal of a lady nurse for peculation involved a detailed explanation, in contrast to the simple statement of 'drunkenness' or 'disorderly behaviour' used for the regular nurses.

43. To Lady Charlotte Canning
Barrack Hospital,
Scutari 1 Oct 1855

My dear Lady Canning

I have a very painful duty to perform in giving you some information concerning Miss Salisbury, which is today to be made the subject of a Dispatch from the General Officer commanding here to Lord Panmure.

Miss Salisbury's name is probably known to you through Miss Wyse, (who recommended her to Lady Stratford) & thro' Miss Stanley,[1] as one of the Lady Nurses here.

Miss Salisbury undertook in this Hospital the charge of the 'Free Gifts' store – upon a written understanding that nothing was to be given out of that store, excepting by a written Order from me. I considered it my duty, & it has been my constant practice to keep an account of every Article given – which account could be, at any time, made known to the Public – my responsibility being to the people of England. These accounts have been already printed in the 'Blue Book' up to February 15/55.

Circumstances occurred which made me believe that property from the 'Free Gift' stores was withdrawn by Miss Salisbury, unknown to me. And this suspicion became so much strengthened that I mentioned it to the Commandant who, thinking that I had grounds for it, at once advised me to dismiss her. I did so, paying her her salary, offering to take her passage home to England or to Patras, whence she came & supplying her with money, besides, out of my own pocket.

She refused to go – & offered her services to Mrs. Moore, Superintendent of the Officers' Nurses.

She was about to proceed on the same errand to Lady Stratford at Therapia, when material proof of her dishonesty appeared. Farther evidence against her having come to light, the General Commanding sent men to search my house in Scutari – in which she, Miss Salisbury, slept. Property was found there, which I may safely assert was of above £100 value, concealed in the room of a Maltese couple, who were brought here by the recommendation of Miss Salisbury, & were in my employment.

I must leave it to others to interpret this circumstance for themselves.

Miss Salisbury says that it was her intention to give away this property & acknowledges that she has given away much from the 'Free Gift' stores unknown to me.

The excuse she offers is that the Stores were rotting & eaten by rats. And that Mrs. Bracebridge, when here, had given her & the Nurses leave to take or to give away any thing out of the Free Gift store.

It is my wish to leave the latter assertion to be answered by Mrs. Bracebridge. That rats abound in all these Hospitals is an unlucky fact. But I never heard that Purveyor or Commissariat gave away their stores in consequence.

Be that as it may, Miss Salisbury has broken the agreement which she made, in disposing of the Free Gift stores at her own pleasure – without record or responsibility. And the people of England are not to be left at the mercy of Miss Salisbury.

To this I must add, with the greatest pain, that Articles of my own wearing apparel, which I had missed, have been found in her boxes. It is undeniable that the circumstances are such as would, in any other case, be considered a felony. Five men are now in custody, two of whom she brought to Scutari, in whose possession have been found goods given over to them by her.

It reaches me from various quarters, as being said from one person to another, that a desire is expressed to know the plan that has been & is pursued in the disposal of the Free Gifts & the Queen's Gifts here. I wish that it had been said to myself, as I could then immediately have afforded the information.

For the Free Gifts addressed to me, I have, of course, considered myself responsible.

I have made it a rule in these Hospitals of Scutari to answer all the Requisitions of the Medical Officers, having first ascertained that such Article does not exist in the Purveyor's store. I have then procured it either from Constantinople, Malta or England, if it did not exist in the Free Gift store. I have spent thus upwards of £3000 in Constantinople alone – part of which has been repaid me by Government, part has come out of my own & other private funds. This is wholly independent of the 'Times' Fund. To other Hospitals I have sent *all*, (but nothing else) that was required of me in *any* Requisition, representing things as wanted, either from Medical Officer, Chaplain, or Superintend't of Nurses. Had I sent other things, the public Gifts would have been wasted.

Only in the case of Koulale Hospitals have I deviated from this rule & sent stores unasked.

I have invariably sent, when asked, to all other Hospitals in the East, whether I possessed the Article actually in store or not – & I possess an exact record of what has been sent.

The 'free gifts' & the stores (procured by money at Constantinople), which have been distributed in the Barrack, General & Palace Hospitals of Scutari up to February 15/55 have been published in the Blue Book, as above mentioned.

An exact account is ready for publication up to May 1/55 of the Free Gifts distributed in the same Hospitals.

Also, of the Free Gifts distributed to the Hospitals of Koulale & Balaclava between Nov 4/54 & May 1/55 (It will perhaps surprise some to hear that, in the Barrack & General Hospitals alone, of Scutari, in the first three months of my stay here – were given out by me upwards of

      10,000 Shirts &
      4,000 flannel d'o

independently of all other Articles of Hospital Furniture)

During May, June & July, I was prevented by illness from taking any part in the distribution of the Free Gifts, which was undertaken by Mrs. Bracebridge, who will answer any questions concerning the distribution which took place at that time. From July 28/55 to the present time I have an Account of every Article distributed. And all these Accounts will be published – subjoining that of what is regularly given to each soldier who leaves the Hospital, either invalided home, or convalescent to the Crimea.

Believe me, dear Lady Canning, yours most truly

                Florence Nightingale

P.S. The Queen's Gifts, i.e. those which came to my address, dated Dec '54 & Jan '55, were immediately divided into proportionate quantities among *all* the Hospitals – a double portion only having been given to the Palace Hospital, where were most *Officers*, who would prize most such Articles as the Queen sent. Of the distribution of these, I also kept a record. I have also had a voice in the distribution of her other gifts, particularly of the games, concerning which I can also give an Account – as I made out the List of the proportions to be given to each 'Division'.

I should perhaps add that the correspondence of Miss Salisbury was seized by order of the Commandant here, who thought this step a necessary one – as indeed it proved – & that it laid bare a most conscious system of falsehood, which she had been pursuing in her letters to England. It is so easy for an adventurer of this kind to trade upon people's sympathies in this way.

                           F.N.

Source: LDA: Harewood Collection, Lord Canning Papers 177/Z/2

1. At the top of the first page is a note: 'This is a mistake, as Miss Stanley never saw her or recommended her – CC'.

The autumn of 1855 again brought to the fore Dr Hall and Mother Bridgeman. Mother Bridgeman and five of her nuns had nursed briefly under Nightingale at the General Hospital at Scutari before going to the Koulali General Hospital at the end of January. Disciplined and skilful nurses, they were appreciated by the medical officials. A scandal developed, however, over their issuance of 'extras' – wine, invalid food and clothing – which, given at their own discretion, were seen by the army officers as extravagant. The Principal Medical Officer finally insisted upon the Scutari system, whereby all extras were given out only by the express order of a medical officer. Mother Bridgeman refused, and at Dr Hall's request took her group to the General Hospital at Balaclava in October 1855. In addition, she ordered her four nuns still working at the General Hospital, Scutari, to join her.

Sebastopol had fallen on 8 September, so the end of the war was in sight, but Nightingale decided to go to the Crimea to oversee a satisfactory conclusion. She left on 9 October and remained in the Crimea until the end of November. She returned to Scutari to attend to a cholera outbreak, but again went back to the Crimea at the request of the Land Transport Corps and stayed until the beginning of July, when she returned to Scutari to complete her affairs before sailing for England on 28 July 1856.

Balaclava was the stronghold of her enemies. Dr Hall and the Purveyor, David Fitzgerald, supported by other military officers, made their final moves against her. Dr Hall pounced upon Herbert's mistake in appointing Nightingale 'Superintendent of the Nursing Establishment of the English General Hospitals in Turkey'. Balaclava was in the Crimea, so he and Mother Bridgeman argued that she had no authority there. Now her ally Lord Raglan was dead and his successor had no official letter as to her position. Indeed, the evidence points to a War Office decision in March to limit her authority to Scutari, however vague they were in replying to her letters (Summers [1983], p. 43).

Unfortunately too, Mr Bracebridge had made a speech in England which was published in *The Times* on 16 October. He had bitterly attacked the whole medical establishment in the East and praised his friend. Such an indiscretion was hardly calculated to mitigate the existing prejudices of the medical officers, as the dismayed Nightingale recognized.

A number of stories about Dr Hall suggest that he fitted the role of antagonist. Sidney Herbert had written to Lord Raglan early in the war, 'I cannot help feeling that Dr. Hall resents offers of assistance as being slurs on his preparations' (Cook, I, 288). Hall had undermined Raglan's authority early in the war. In December

1854, Raglan had dismissed Dr Lawson, the Senior Medical Officer in Balaclava, and had rebuked Hall in a General Order for conditions under Lawson. Hall then turned around and appointed Lawson Senior Medical Officer at the Barrack Hospital, Scutari (Hibbert, p. 214). Nightingale's request that Miss Weare be dismissed for inefficiency as Superintendent of the General Hospital prompted Hall to transfer her to the superintendency of the Monastery Hospital for convalescents and ophthalmic cases. In turn, Nightingale was implacable in her assertion of the Superintendent of Nurses' authority; in spite of frequent claims that she and her nurses were obedient to the medical officers' commands, she was arrogant and unforgiving to the end in all her dealings with Dr Hall (Goldie [1987], pp. 229–37).

Angry that her authority had been superseded and anxious that the delicate balance between Roman Catholic and Protestant nurses should not be upset, Nightingale felt isolated. Although prone to exaggeration and self-pity, Nightingale seems at least partially justified in declaring to Aunt Mai: 'Christ was betrayed by one. But my cause has been betrayed by everyone – ruined, betrayed, destroyed by every one alas – one may truly say excepting Mrs. Roberts, *Revd Mother*,[1] *first* & Mrs. Stewart[2] . . .' (19 Oct 1855 BL Add: 45793: f 106).

1. Revd Mother: The Reverend Mother Georgina Moore of Bermondsey, who had come with the first party to the East, and remained a close friend to Nightingale throughout her life.

2. Mrs. Stewart: Jane Shaw Stewart, a trusted (unmarried) lady nurse in charge of the Castle Hospital, Balaclava. Nightingale later had her appointed as the first Superintendent of Military Nurses (see chapter 3).

44. To Elizabeth Herbert

Castle Hospital, Balaclava
17 Nov 1855

My dearest Lizzie

Many thanks for the £1000 information from Wellington, N. Zealand. It is a magnificent tribute from our Colonies – & comes to cheer one's spirits with its kindness, after all the dirt one has to wade thro' here – & the wreck of characters this Crimean war has made.

Now I am going to do a little 'dirty work' myself.

It did very much for our peculiar work the having, as our friends, the great men – Lord Raglan, Gen. Estcourt,[1] & the departure of Sir Richard Airey[2] have been great losses to *our* cause. The man who was born Lord Fitzroy Somerset[3] would naturally not be above interesting himself in Hospital matters & a parcel of women – while the man who was born James Simpson would essentially think it infra dig. Again, a word from the Quarter Master General was quite enough to expedite the Extra Diet kitchen, the draining, flushing, reading-huts for Convalescents &c &c.

Dr. Hall does not think it beneath him to broil me slowly upon the fire of my own Extra Diet kitchen – & to give out that we are private adventurers & to be treated as such.

Remember, please, that this is quite private, that I do not wish to complain of Dr. Hall, who is an able & efficient officer in some ways – & that I think he has been justly provoked by Mr. Bracebridge's 'Lecture' in the 'Times' about English medical treatment – with which I utterly dissent both as to its truth, & as to the propriety of saying it, were it true. The French physicians utterly disown it.

I believe that Dr. Hall is going to India. So that what I say now I say quite generally – & only give a particular instance to shew what I mean.

It is this.

In April, I undertook this Hospital – & from that time to this we have cooked *all* the Extra Diets for 500–600 Patients & the *whole* Diets, for all the wounded Officers by ourselves in a shed – & till I came up this time, (tho' I sent up a French man-cook, to whom I give £100 pr ann –, in July,) I could not get an Extra Diet kitchen built promised me in May, till I came to do it myself viz in October. During the whole of this time, every egg, every bit of butter, jelly, ale & Eau de Cologne which the sick officers have had have been provided out of Mrs. Shaw Stewart's or my private pockets. On Nov 4, I opened my Extra Diet kitchen – but, for 24 hours, I would not bake the Officers' toast in this kitchen, because it disconcerted the Extra Diets for 550 Patients. In those 24 hours, the Officers made a complaint to Head Quarters of our 'ill treatment' in re toast. And Dr. Hall, with the P.M.O. of Balaclava, came down in their wrath & reprimanded the — Cook's Orderly! Whereupon Mrs. Shaw Stewart wrote Dr. Hall a civil formal letter, 'requesting that his orders & reprimands might be given to her', in order that the business might be properly done. Dr. Hall then published to his inferior Officers that the ladies at the Castle Hospital meant to throw off all subordination to the Medical Officers – & that this was the reason he had brought the Nuns to the General Hospital, Balaclava.* (*He has since announced this officially. FN. 21/2/56) He also wrote to Mrs. Stewart that it was his duty to care for the Officers as well as for the men – his paternal care having begun for their toast & them on Nov 7, while he had never enquired how they had been provided for at all since April 25. So that they have perhaps profited more by Mrs. Stewart's & my maternal care than by Dr. Hall's paternal one, which never could be persuaded to issue eggs – or any other comfort, till the Purveyor-in-Chief came up himself.

These things are nothing excepting in as much as they thwart the work.

And, if Mr. Herbert saw no impropriety in it, whose judgment will be far better in this matter than mine, a private letter from some high authority to the Commander-in-Chief or Chief of the Staff to the effect that this work is not a silly display of feminine sensibilities but an authorized set of tools – provided to the hand of the Medical Officers to supply extra diets, cleanliness, clean linen & Hospital comforts to the Patients – might greatly further these objects – by enabling us to obtain the 'de quoi'.

If Mr. Herbert thinks it better not, I am content to work on sottomano,[4] building my Extra Diet kitchens &c myself. *Please* don't say anything about our having provided these things at private expence.

The Irish Catholic rebellion & establishment of the thirteen Irish nuns on an independent footing at Balaclava is what I have been expecting all along, & only wonder it did not take place before. It is the old story. Ever since the days of Queen Elizabeth, the chafing against secular supremacy, especially English, on the part of the R. Catholic Irish. I am very sorry for it. For I think it is fraught with mischief. For these Irish nuns are dead against us – I mean England – the way their priests talk is odious. The proportion of R. Catholics & of Irish has increased inconceivably in the army since the late Recruits. Had we more nuns, it would be very desirable, to diminish disaffection. But *just not* the Irish ones. The wisest thing the W. Office could now do would be to send out a few more of the Bermondsey Nuns* (*This has been done. FN 21/1/56) to join those already at Scutari & counterbalance the influence of the *Irish* nuns, who hate their soberer sisters with the mortal hatred which, I believe, only Nuns & Household Servants *can* feel towards each other.

It reminds me of the Butler who said, 'I am sure, my Lady, you must have observed, your Ladyship, that for six months I have not repeated after your Ladyship the "Forgive us our trespasses &c" in the Lord's Prayer because I could not forgive Mrs. Baker (the Housekeeper) nor will I, my Lady, & by the same token it is now six months since I have spoken to her in the Housekeeper's Room'.

Dearest Lizzie, do not trouble yourself in this matter if you think it is better not. You don't suppose the impertinence of vulgar officials troubles us much – we get the things done all the same, only a little more slowly. When we have the support at Head Quarters, matters advance faster, that is all. During six months, the Castle Hospital, always the *principal* & now the *only* general Hospital in the Crimea, which has always had more than double the number of Patients of any other Crimean Hospital, has had scarcely any thing done for it in the way of all the Engineering necessities of a Hospital. This is the statement of its own P.M.O. But, you know, it would ruin him to say so.

The real grievance against us is that we are independent of promotion & therefore of the displeasure of our Chiefs – that we have no prospects to injure – & that, altho subordinate to these Medical Chiefs in office, we are superior to them in influence & in the chance of being heard at home. It is an anomalous position. But so is war, to us English, anomalous.

God bless you – Thank you
    ever yours

                         F Nightingale

Source: BL Add 43396: ff 40–45

1. Gen. James Bucknell Bucknell Estcourt: (1802–55), along with Airey, was held responsible for the disorder of the Commissariat and Purveying Departments by the McNeill–Tulloch report.
2. Sir Richard Airey: (1803–81), Quartermaster-General to the Crimean Army until November 1855.
3. Lord Fitzroy Somerset: (1788–1855) Lord Raglan, until his death Commanding Officer of the British Troops in the Crimea.
4. sottomano: in secret.

Florence continued to justify herself to her family, seeking an approval that she still felt they denied her. She proudly wrote:

Lord Raglan, in his last visit to me, asked me 'if my father liked my coming out'. I said with pride 'my father is not as other men are – he thinks that daughters should serve their country as well as sons he brought me up to think so – he has no sons – & therefore he has sacrificed me to my country – & told me to come home with my shield or upon it. He does not think, (as I once heard a father & a very good & clever father say,) 'The girls are all I could wish – very happy, very attentive to me, & very amusing'. He thinks that God sent women, as well as men, into the world to be something more than 'happy', 'attentive' & 'amusing'. 'Happy & *dull*', religion is said to make us – 'happy & *amusing*' *social life* is supposed to make us – but my father's religious & social ethics make us strive to be the pioneers of the human race & let 'happiness' & 'amusement' take care of themselves. (14 Nov 1855 Wellcome)

45. To Fanny Nightingale {?}   {29 Nov 1855}[1]

If my name & my having done what I could for God & mankind has given you pleasure that is real pleasure to me. My reputation has not been a boon to me in my work – but if you have been pleased, that is enough. I shall love my name now. I shall feel that it is the greatest return that you can have satisfaction in hearing your child named & in feeling that her work draws sympathies together some return for what you have done for me. Life is sweet after all.

If ever I live to see England again, the Western breezes of my hill-top home will be my first longing – though Olympus, with its snowy cap, looks fair over our blue Eastern sea

Source: BL Add 43402: ff 156–57   {incomplete letter}

1. Note in pencil: Perhaps after meeting in Arthur's rooms Nov. 29. 55.

In early 1856 the differences between Nightingale and her adversaries came to a climax. Miss Salisbury had spread rumours about her in England, and had succeeded in gaining a number of adherents to her cause. Fitzgerald charged to the attack with a 'Confidential Report' to the War Office. He accused Nightingale of insubordination and her nurses of extravagance, inefficiency, immorality and disobedience. He praised Mother Bridgeman and her nuns for their skills, economy and discipline (Woodham-Smith, p. 245). Fitzgerald was easily refuted by Nightingale, who wrote a masterly response to Lieutenant-Colonel John Henry Lefroy of the War Office, rebutting the many inaccuracies and exaggerations. Fortunately Sir John McNeill and Colonel Alexander Tulloch, of the

Commission into the Supply of the British Army, fully exonerated Nightingale in their report to Parliament in January 1856. Nevertheless, the new government in London was thoroughly exasperated with the endless squabbling and less supportive of Nightingale's position than Herbert had been (Goldie [1987] pp. 210–17).

Following Nightingale's illness and her determination to remain in the East at her post until the end of the war, a movement sprang up in England to show some appreciation for the work she had done. The result was the 'Nightingale Fund', a collection which would enable her to set up an 'English Kaiserswerth'. Nightingale was consulted about the use to which she would wish to put the fund but, busy with the war, she refused to commit herself.

46. To C. H. Bracebridge

Barrack Hospital, Scutari
31 Jan 1856

My dear Mr. Bracebridge

In reply to your letter requesting me to give some sign as to what I wish to have done with the money – about to be raised under the name of the 'Nightingale Fund' & as to what purpose it is to be devoted to I can only say –

1. The people of England say to me by this Subscription – 'We trust you – we wish you to do us a service'. No love or confidence can be shown to a human being greater than this – and as such I accept it gratefully and hopefully. I hope I shall never decline any work God – & the people of England offer me. But 2. I have no plan at all, I am not new to these things. I am not without experience – and no fear presents itself more strongly to my mind, no certainty of failure more complete – than accompany the idea of beginning anything of the nature proposed to me – with a great demonstration – a vast preparation – a great man perhaps coming down to the Hospital – to give the first 'Cup of cold water'.

People's expectations are highly wrought – they think some great thing will be accomplished in six months – altho' experience shows that it is essentially the labour of centuries – they will be disappointed to see no apparent great change – and at the end of a twelvemonth will feel as flat about it – as they do on a wedding day, at three o'Clock, after the breakfast is over. But worse than this, the fellow workers who would join me in a work which began with excitement, public demonstration, public popularity, w'd be those whom vanity, frivolity, or the love of excitement would bring – & these would, least of all, bring about the wonderful results w'ch the public w'd be expecting – or rather the results w'd be very 'wonderful' the other way. These are not theories, but experience. And if I have a plan in me, w'ch is not battered out – by the perpetual 'wear & tear' of mind & body – I am now undergoing – it would be simply this – to take the poorest & least organized Hospital in London, & putting myself in there – see what I could do – not touching the 'Fund' perhaps for *years* – not till experience had shown how the Fund might be best available. This is not detracting from the value & importance of the 'Fund' to the work. It will be *invaluable* as occasion arises. I have hardly time to write this letter – much less to give the experience which would prove the deductions to be true. But I could only appeal to two recent instances.

  1. My strength here lay in coming to Hospitals miserably disorganized or rather unorganized, & in organizing them. Had I come to an Institution cut & dry – what would I have done to alter it?

  2. The greater proportion of valuable fellow workers here – came out with the first party notwithstanding the hurry of selection, when the work was obscure – & laborious & laughed at, and the hardships great and *not*, with a few priceless exceptions, with the subsequent parties – when the excitement & popularity were great, & love of glory, of gain, & curiosity, all on the alert. I have no objection to what I say thus in private to you, being repeated to those who have so kindly interested themselves in the 'Nightingale Fund' – & sympathize in her work. The first fruits of a long series (as I expect) of the brick & mortar plans of needy or philanthropic adventurers, who wish to get hold of the 'Nightingale Fund' have already come in upon me. But I hope our inexorable common sense will not be taken in. One more instance & I have done. Compare the gradual but complete success of Fliedner's at Kaiserswerth, with that of the magnificent and pompous 'Bettanien' at Berlin – whose excellent & simple minded foundress was appalled by 'the greatness thrust upon her' and which marred her work. I therefore must decline making any plan whatever, even were I not overwhelmed at present, not with plans, but work.

  At the same time – would I could say (which I cannot) how much I feel the love & confidence of the people of England – in whose service as I have lived – so I shall die.

  I am dear Mr. Bracebridge,
    most truly yours –

Florence Nightingale

Source: BL Add 43397: ff 179–82   {dictated letter}

After reading the Commission into the Supply of the British Army, Florence's family had a better sense of the opposition she had faced. In February 1856 Parthe wrote to Sir John McNeill, thanking him for his support of Florence:

> The effect of it is something quite extraordinary, and good men of every shade of opinion rejoice at the truth being known, and no one except the accused ever doubt for a moment that your calm deliberate well weighed evidence is not truth itself. It is like an earthquake among the well polished fictions and amiable frauds with which Government seems to be generally carried on . . . It is very pleasant to see how when the seed of right is once planted it grows up into a large tree. (GLRO: HI/ST/NC3/SU/61)

But Parthe's optimism was ill founded; Nightingale remained controversial long after the Commission Report. Back at Scutari she was still busy dealing with unfit nurses and, with the help of friends in the War Office and without, defending herself against present and possible future problems.

47. To Lady Cranworth

Barrack Hospital, Scutari
10 Feb 1856

My dear Lady Cranworth

I am deeply grieved to have to send home another of the Nurses, Mrs. Ann Sinclair, for the offence of intoxication.

She was engaged on March 9/55, & was first at *Scutari* for a couple of months, conducting herself perfectly well. I took her up with me to the Castle Hospital, *Balaclava*, in May/55 and she conducted herself also very well there for some time. But when I went up again in October, she appeared quite an altered woman. Repeated offences left no doubt on my mind. And I spoke to her repeatedly on the subject – the offence being not sufficiently decided to compel me to dismiss her, but I forgave her, warning her that such forgiveness could not be repeated, for the sake of the work.

I learn, with deep regret, from Mrs. Shaw Stewart that my warning was not sufficient – & that, on Xmas Eve & Feb 4, Ann Sinclair was again guilty of drunkenness. She is therefore discharged by me & sent home by the 'Golden Fleece' this day.

She has been paid by me up to the day of her departure from

Balaclava (her wages being 18/ per week) & has no farther claim on the War Office whatever. She has returned her *last* Winter Clothing, (which she had not long received,) according to the regulation for Nurses dismissed for any misconduct.* (*If she complains of this, or if she states that she has been deprived of more than this, I will furnish you with the Statement of what has been taken from her.)

As I was confined to my bed when the Ship (the 'Melbourne') which brought her from Balaclava, came down here, I could not see her myself on board. I therefore sent her the Order for her passage home (per 'Golden Fleece') by my Aunt, to whom she did not deny her fault, but said, which gave me great pleasure, that 'she was sorry'.

I am thus particular in stating every detail

1. because, having learnt that it is intended to prosecute me, if possible, of libel in the case of a person dismissed by me, Miss Salisbury, I find that witnesses among the Nurses who return home are sought for this purpose. The evidence of two, Mrs. Sansom & Mrs. Wheatstone, has been separately taken with this view by the gentleman who has undertaken Miss Salisbury's case – Mrs. Wheatstone having been dismissed for drunkenness, acknowledged by herself in writing – I think it not unlikely that Mrs. Sinclair's evidence will now be added to the number.

As a measure of necessary police in this hard & painful, altho' most interesting work, I believe it to be my duty, however, not to shrink from giving true characters of those whom I discharge, not only to the 'grand & distant' War Office, (which little affects the matter,) but to the last employer of the person discharged – the more so as, to many of these Nurses, being heartily tired of the Crimea & the East – & wishing themselves at home again, their return is *in itself* most welcome. I have, therefore, always made & shall still continue to make it my practice, at my own risk, to give the true cause of discharge.

2. May I, therefore, request you kindly to forward this letter to Mrs. Herbert, who will know who recommended Anne Sinclair? It is but just to warn them against what I have so suffered from myself. And this I will never evade. Altho' I find that three of the *four* letters I thus considered it my duty to write concerning Miss Salisbury have been made use of against me – (the fourth being to Lady Canning). The grounds for a charge of libel seem to be laid upon these – one at least of which has been published in a lithographed Statement.* (*which I have not seen, but which I learn is extensively circulated both here & in England.)

As, however, there may be *sixty-four* charges of libel laid against me, I await the result with composure & shall continue to 'do likewise' in a hardened manner.

Believe me, dear Lady Cranworth
ever most truly yours

Florence Nightingale

Lists of Articles of the last Regulation Dress delivered to & now returned by Ann Sinclair, Nurse, dismissed for drunkenness, Feb 6/56

1 badge, burnt

1 brown linsey wolsey dress, deducted from her wages (I repaid her the money – She wore it only a fortnight).

3 Derry Wrappers – she having had one more than the other Nurses, instead of a cotton gown.

2 Prs Sleeves

2 Aprons

2 Collars

2 Best Caps – 1 made up
1 unmade

NB Ann Sinclair's clothing had been recently completed for her by me for the *first year*, she having been with me not quite 11 months.

Source: BL Add 43397: ff 85–90

Nightingale still had not received official confirmation of the scope of her authority, but she was not without allies. Dr Sutherland had remained in the Crimea. Colonel Lefroy, who had come to Scutari in October 1855 as a confidential adviser on scientific matters for Panmure, noted that the medical men were jealous of Nightingale's mission. He observed that 'Dr. Hall would gladly upset it tomorrow' and suggested that a General Order recognizing her position would save her much trouble as it would stop the 'spirit of growing independence among these ladies and nurses who are still under her, a spirit encouraged with no friendly intention in more than one quarter' (Cook, I, 297).

48. To Sidney Herbert

Barrack Hospital, Scutari
20 Feb 1856

Dear Mr. Herbert[1]

I cannot thank you sufficiently for your kind letter.

But I am now about (not to acknowledge your interest for our future work but) to ask it for our present one.

The enclosed I wrote to Mrs. Herbert some months ago. But I did not send it partly because I did not like troubling you, partly because the 'anything-for-a-quiet-life principle' seemed the pervading War-Office rule of action.

I am now, however fighting for the very existence of our work – and whether Peace is to come or not, I desire, for the sake of that work, that it should be placed in 'General Order', so to speak, before the next move whatever it is, takes place.

(1) Col. Lefroy, who has kindly allowed me to refer you to him, will inform you of the attempts which are being made to root us out of the Crimea – of Dr. Hall's official letter to him – of a Purveyor's 'Confidential Report' against me.

Some other facts are known, perhaps, more to *you* than to any one else – viz. that the second Edition of Nuns who came out in December/54, came (as the first did) with the express stipulation that they were to have no peculiar Chaplain to themselves without which condition I would never have received them – that, in direct violation of the treaty, they had, first, the Rev'd Mr. Ronan, & secondly the Rev'd Mr. Wollatt – as their own Director – which latter gentleman managed the affair of their taking possession of the General Hospital at Balaclava for them. Dr. Hall states this affair in the following manner – 'that he had been placed in a painful position about the General Hospital at Balaclava – that, when Miss Nightingale's Nurses were to be removed, a gentleman (the priest above alluded to) called & offered the services of the Nuns, & that he, Dr. Hall, was induced to accept of them & that without any intention of offending any one'.

(2) The Hospitals of the Land Transport Corps, in the Crimea have been & are still the worst in the Camp. The Commanding Officer of the *Left* Wing was desirous that I should send them Nurses – the Medical Officer of the *Right* Wing was equally desirous – I had Nurses *and* Nuns able, ready & willing to go, & was prepared to go up with them myself.

Now arose this question, which is so much better stated by Dr. Sutherland in a letter to me, which he has allowed me to make use of, than I could do that I beg leave to quote it.

'Balaklava Feb 4/56

My dear Miss Nightingale

I have seen Dr. Hall & made the necessary enquiries of him & also of others.

The main question, as it appears to me respecting the Nurses in Hospitals in the Crimea is one of *"responsibility"*. The jurisdiction in the matter, inferred in the letter you received from the War Department, is not, I conceive, sufficient of itself to enable you to claim the support of the Authorities here, for I am told that no official intimation as to your having any charge of the Hospital Nursing in the Crimea has been sent to Dr. Hall, a circumstance which I was not before aware of. And the *responsibility* hence rests officially with him.

I cannot conceal from myself that, such being the case, there is a disinclination to give you any further facilities than those you already have.

Under these circumstances, then, it appears to me that it would be advisable to state the case fully to the War Department, & ask them to place you on a proper footing with the Authorities here. Until this be done, I would advise you not to press for the transference of any Nurses to the Land Transport Hospital at Karani.

In the event of a campaign in Asia & your desiring to go to any Hospital that may be formed at Trebizond or elsewhere, I would still advise you to have yourself placed in an official relation with the Military & Medical Authorities in the Army.

If this be done, every thing will go smoothly, but I fear not otherwise.

In regard to the charges brought against your Nurses at the General Hospital by Mr. Fitzgerald (the Purveyor formerly alluded to) Dr. Hall stated that Mr. Fitzgerald* must be held personally responsible for the statements he had made (*That Dr. Hall would throw overboard Mr. Fitzgerald in this matter I am not at all surprised to learn. I always expected it.)

I am yours ever faithfully
(Signed)
                                                    John Sutherland'

It is obvious that Dr. Hall's statement is only a subterfuge. But it is true viz. 'that *he* had no official intimation from the War Office of the circumstances inferred in the W.O. letter to' me.

It is obvious that my usefulness is destroyed, my work prevented or hindered & precious time wasted by the uncertainty of the relations in which I am left with the Crimean Authorities.

To have the 'jurisdiction', as Dr. Sutherland calls it, of all the Hospitals in & north of the Bosphorus, i.e. the power of placing Nurses in any of the present or future Hospitals with the sanction of the Military & Medical Authorities the power of preventing that these latter should engage any Nurses or Ladies dismissed by or withdrawing from me in other Hospitals is essential to my usefulness – as also to have this signified, (not by myself but) by the War Department to the Military & Medical Authorities. And I would submit that, without this, the responsibilities conferred upon me & the work expected from me by the W. Office are rendered impossible.

If I have served my country well, this is the reward I should wish – the power of continuing that service – of continuing it in Asia, should the war take us there – or of resuming it in any future war – which seems alas! but too likely, if peace comes now.

Might I ask you, dear Mr. Herbert, to crown your enduring kindness to me by, if you see it desirable, conferring with Col. Lefroy in this matter & urging upon the War Department to *telegraph* my powers to the Military & Medical Authorities in the Crimea & to myself? The Hospitals wait.

Believe me ever yours faithfully & gratefully

Florence Nightingale

Source: BL Add 43393: ff 211–14

1. In ink at top: *Miss Nightingale* Feb'y 20 1856 Regarding Mr. Fitzgerald.

49. To Lady Laura Cranworth   Barrack Hospital, Scutari
22 Feb 1856

My dear Lady Cranworth

Thank you very much for the Agreements. You sent me five Copies of my 'Original Agreement'.

With regard to the change proposed, I see many objections – & whatever arrangement may be made for any future war, I shall deprecate any other for the present.

Instead of weakening my position & control over the Nurses (or that of *any* Superintendent) I consider that it requires to be strengthened.

I detailed my reasons at some length to Lady Canning who considered that '*they were unanswerable*'.

It is perhaps hardly worth while to trouble you with them again.

Suffice it to say that 1. the principle, on which the new Agreement stands, that of centralization, is a vicious one & detrimental to all *practical* good working. (It is in fact the system which has ruined us during this War. Now that we have a few men out here who dare to take upon themselves responsibility, look at the improvement). The grand & distant War Office exercises no influence over the imaginations of these women, the most slippery race in existence. They know that the War Office cannot injure their future prospects – that no future employer will go to the 'Secretary at War' for a character of them. To use their own expression, they 'snap their fingers' at the War Office.

2. were I to adopt the new 'Agreement' proposed by Mr. Hawes, I should have two classes of Nurses, the first bound to me, the second to the War Office. It is obvious that this would be productive of every kind of confusion. It is obvious that the latter kind of Nurse would be under no authority but that of the Secretary at War, which is a fiction, & that of the Medical Officer, to whom she would then be directly consigned. And the evils of which latter plan were sufficiently apparent, I suppose, since the War Office sent me out. But, according to this latter agreement, I might as well go home as an amateur adventurer. The experience of 16 months has confirmed & greatly strengthened in me all the above convictions, instead of diminishing them.

And I must beg respectfully, but most firmly to decline any Alteration in the original 'Agreement' with which I came out.

So far from wishing to alter it, I am about to request that *all* the Agreements, kept by mistake at the War Office & which ought to have been forwarded to me, of the Nurses now with me, should be sent me. It has been productive of great inconvenience the not having these. Mrs Shaw Stewart has, especially, deeply regretted it. Some I have & some I have not. And the consequence has been that (but this is strictly *private*) where the Agreement has not been produceable, the Medical Officers have endeavored to allure the woman away, saying that 'all the Hospitals were the same'. This is old, old experience.

As a Comment upon the system of Centralization, I will only add that, had I not given my local Superintendents more authority than the new Agreement would afford me, how could they have enforced any order, system, or discipline whatever?

I have, however, carefully consulted the individualities, (to use a fashionable word), of my several Sub-Superintendents, & am convinced that any other system is a fundamental mistake. Especially, in so trying a situation as this, where the overwhelming proportion of men to women makes, in fact, the real difficulty of our position.

    I remain, dear Lady Cranworth,
        yours most truly

                                Florence Nightingale

Source: BL Add 43397: ff 93–95

Finally, on 25 February 1856, Lord Panmure sent a memo to the Commander of the Forces acknowledging Nightingale's superintendency of all nurses, but contingent upon 'the approval of the Principal Medical Officer in the exercise of the responsibility thus vested in her' (Cook, I, 293).

    In a letter to Uncle Sam, Florence defended herself against the charge that she was impatient of opposition:

50. To Samuel Smith   Scutari 6 Mar 1856

Dear Uncle Sam

    I am very anxious to correct a false impression, which seems to exist in your mind, that I have had a steady & consistent support from the War Office – that, such being the case, I kick against every prick – & am unduly impatient of opposition, inevitable in my or any situation, to my work.

    The facts are exactly the reverse. I have never chosen to trouble the W.O. with my difficulties, because it has given me so feeble & treacherous a support that I have always expected to hear it say, 'Could we not shelve Miss N.? We dare say she does a great deal of good. But she quarrels with the authorities & we can't have that'.

    I have therefore fought my own battle – not only as I can truly say, unsupported by any official out here, with the exception of Gen'l Storks,[1] so that I was amazed the other day at getting the loan of the little Gov't tug for carrying goods – but exposed to every petty persecution, opposition & trickery that you can mention.

    I have never had time to keep any records whatever except in the way of accounts. But I should have liked to have left some record of the way in which officials can torment & hinder a work. And, as they now see, torment, not only unmolested but rewarded, as every man who has been in any way instrumental in our great calamity, has received promotion or honors.

I will give you the slightest, pettiest instance of the hindrance which the pettiest official can make out here, if so minded.

When I came out, an order to furnish me with money was, of course, forwarded from the W.O. to the Purveyors here. I have never availed myself of this to the amount of one farthing. On the contrary, they have been frequently in my debt to the amount of £1500. But the Senior Purveyor at Balaclava refuses to cash my Cheques, for no other reason discoverable than the love of petty arrogance & the hope of injuring my credit, in the minds of ignorant servants.

As I think it is a pity that he should have the pleasure of doing this, I now send up *cash* to the Crimea or take it.

Otherwise I could, of course, if I chose to complain, get an order to compel him not to refuse my Cheque.

This is the little Fitzgerald, who, after a course of successful villany, has like id genus omne,[2] been promoted to be Dep'y Purveyor in Chief, with back pay & all his little soul desires. This is Dr. Hall's doing. But his is only one specimen of the promotions.

I do not like to use hard words. But I have no time to give the facts which would support them. But even to Sir J. MacNeill's Report I could add a few facts which, if they were told (I being now one of the oldest inhabitants in Scutari & the Crimea) would make us feel that the times of the Scribes & Pharisees were nothing to these.

This little Fitzgerald has starved every Hospital when his store was full – & not, as it appears, from ignorance, like some of the honorable men who have been our murderers, but from malice prepense.

I know that you think the Credit of a wild imagination belongs to me. But I cannot but fancy that the W.O. is afraid of the Irish Brigade – and I know that Card. Wiseman,[3] who is supposed, right or wrong, to have some influence over Hawes, has been busy in this matter.

A 'sot' in the hands of 'habiles méchans'[4] can do much, as I know to my cost. And perhaps you do not know that Card. Wiseman has publicly, in his Insults, noticed with praise Mrs. Bridgeman's Insurrection. Now Mrs. Bridgeman & Fitzgerald are one.

Fitzgerald topped up, with his '*Confidential*' Report against me – for which he is rewarded, while a poor little Ass't Surgeon, for a true & public letter in the 'Times', is dismissed the service.

I assure you that our utter disgust at these latter promotions would tempt us, (the few honest men as I hope,) to preach a Crusade against the Horse Gds & War Dep't, feeling as we do now that not one step has been gained by our two years' fiery trial & that more Aireys, Cardigans⁵, Halls & Fitzgeralds will be propagated for the next war.

Believe me faithfully yours

Florence Nightingale

Source: BL Add 45792: ff 17–18

1. General Sir Henry Storks: (1811–74), succeeded Lord William Paulet as commander at Scutari. He worked closely with FN to improve conditions for the soldiers, and later served on the Royal Commission on the Sanitary State of the Army (1857).

2. id genus omne: all such kind.

3. Card. Wiseman: Nicholas P. S. Wiseman (1802–65), Archbishop of Westminster, was active politically in promoting the Roman Catholic Church in English affairs.

4. habiles méchans: skilful operator.

5. Cardigan: Lord Cardigan, James Thomas Brudenel (1797–1868), notorious for his quick temper, led the disastrous 'Charge of the Light Brigade'.

The bitterness that surfaced in this letter overflowed that spring. On 16 March she wrote to Uncle Sam, 'The Gov't asks me to be silent. They refuse me a copy of Fitzgerald's Report . . . But will Fitzgerald be silent?' (BL Add 45792: f 23).

Nightingale felt keenly that the common soldiers, discredited, neglected and maltreated by supercilious officers, were pawns in an inept war. All her life she expressed compassion for the weak, ill-used and powerless – except women of her own class – but the enlisted men remained her favourites:

I have never been able to join in the popular cry about the recklessness, sensuality, helplessness of the soldier. On the contrary I should say (& no woman perhaps has ever seen more of the manufacturing & agricultural classes of England than I have – before I came out here) that I have never seen so teachable & helpful a class as the Army generally.

Give them opportunity promptly & securely to send money home – & they will use it.

Give them a School & a Lecture & they will come to it.

Give them a book & a game & a magic Lanthorn & they will leave off drinking.

Give them suffering & they will bear it.

Give them work & they will do it.

I had rather have to do with the Army generally than with any other class I have ever attempted to serve. (To Lt.-Col. J. H. Lefroy 6 Mar 1856 BL Add 43397: f 217)

Nightingale may have used the cause of the common soldier to cover some of the pain she felt in being the target of concerted attack by Dr Hall and his supporters. She tended to exaggerate her isolation and to accuse her friends of disloyalty. Yet the friends she made in the East – Sutherland, Rawlinson, McNeill, Tulloch and Lefroy – remained close allies throughout their working lives. Towards the end of the war, tired and disillusioned, she felt betrayed and lashed out at the ever-patient Herbert, who had urged restraint in her dealings with Dr Hall, Fitzgerald and the Irish nuns.

51. To Sidney Herbert   Crimea 3 Apr 1856

Dear Mr. Herbert

I received your letter of March 6 yesterday.

It is written from Belgrave Square. I write from a Crimean Hut. The point of sight is different.

I arrived here March 24 with Nurses for two Land Transport Hospitals 'required' by Dr. Hall in writing on March 10, but owing to the severe gales of wind, the Transport could not get up the Bosphorus, & our arrival was therefore delayed – tho' announced by return of mail.

We have now been ten days without rations.

Lord Cardigan was surprised to find his horses die at the end of a fortnight because they were without rations & said that 'they chose' to do it, obstinate brutes!

The Inspector General & Purveyor wish to see whether women can live as long as horses without rations.

I thank God – my charge has felt neither cold nor hunger, & is in efficient working order – having cooked & administered both Hospitals the whole of the Extras for 260 bad cases ever since the first day of their arrival.

I have, however, felt both. I do not wish to make a martyr of myself; within sight of the graves of the Crimean Army of last winter (too soon forgotten in England) it would be difficult to do so. I am glad to have had the experience. For cold & hunger wonderfully sharpen the wits. But I believe that it is difficult to those who never, by any possibility, can have imagined either, (except by the side of a good fire & a good dinner which they will have every day of their lives) to imagine what is the anxiety of being responsible for the lives & healths *and the efficiency* (for the sake of the lives & healths of those we are come to nurse) of those placed under men's charge when the means to feed & warm them have all to be obtained by irregular & private channels. During these ten days, I have fed & warmed these women at my own private expence by my own private exertions. I have never been off my horse till 9 or 10 at night, except when it was too dark to walk him over these crags even with a lantern, when I have gone on foot. During the greater part of the day, I have been without food necessarily, except a little brandy & water (you see I am taking to drinking like my comrades of the Army) the snow is deep on the ground. But the object of my coming has been attained, & my women have neither starved nor suffered.

I might have written to the Commander of the Forces, who came to see me the day after my arrival. But this would only have marred our work by making a quarrel.

I might have accepted presents which were poured in upon us, for all, Military, Medical, Clerical in the Land Transport are our sworn friends. But this would be against a rule which I have been obliged to make so strict that nothing but sheer necessity would induce me to break it.

I might have drawn upon the Extras for the Patients. But then the whole would have gone into the Account of *Nurses'* Expenditure as their extravagance.

I believed it, on the whole, best for our work to do as I have done, notwithstanding the urgent pressure upon me from others to adopt one of these courses. But I do not think that that work can be said, pursued thus, to have been pursued in a 'vehement or irritable spirit'.

I received your letter at 10 o'clock P.M. on my return to our hut upon a pitch-dark snowy night after having been 15 hours on foot or on horseback & almost without food.

I confess it cost me a sleepless night thinking over within myself, Have I injured the work by shewing 'vehemence or irritation', by not bearing persecution, moral & physical rather than not complain, except when the very existence of the work itself was perilled?

I thought & considered – and I determined that I had not. I think I can prove my assertion.

About this matter of the rations, foreseen to a certain extent by me, so that I had brought up with me from Scutari, every article for cooking, furnishing, warming the huts, even stoves, & every article of food that would keep.

Every formality not only of routine but of politeness had been observed by me – within 24 hours of my arrival, the rations had been settled by me in person (after having been 'required' in writing from Scutari) with the P.M.O. of the Land Transport in the office of the Deputy Purveyor in Chief Fitzgerald – had received the approval of Inspector General of Hospitals – & by a curious coincidence of the Commander of the Forces from his calling upon me while in the Purveyor's Office. Every form was observed there & then. Both the Purveyor's Clerks, both the Medical Officers in charge at the two Land Transport Hospitals were visited by me, distant some miles from Balaclava & not together, in company with Dr. Taylor, the P.M.O. Every form was there strictly observed. The rations were to begin from the day before. Every day since, I have ridden some miles, or walked, in the severest weather, with driving storms of sleet & snow, to see the Purveyor in his office on these businesses. I have never brought him a yard out of his office on my business. I have never 'prévaloir'd' myself, even on my quality of woman, to avoid hardships or fatigue, or allow him to say that I had entailed either on him. Never, by word or look, can he have detected that I knew how he had slandered us.

Why do I give you this long detail, you will ask, which can be of no use.

It is not because I ask you to do anything. It is merely because I wish to leave on record some instance of that which nobody in England will believe or can even imagine. But we in the Crimea know it. And we know, & knew at the time, *what* filled the Crimean graves last winter – K.C.B, I believe, now means Knight of the Crimean Burying-Grounds –

As I stood yesterday on the Heights of Balaclava, & saw our ships in the Harbour, so gaily dressed with flags, while we fired the Salute in honor of peace, (it was a beautiful sight), I said to myself, More Aireys, more Filders,[2] more Cardigans, more Halls – we are in for them all now – & no hope of reform.

Believe me when I say that everything in the Army (in point of routine versus system) is just where it was eighteen months ago. The only difference is that we are now rolling in stores. But indeed we were so then only most of them were at Varna.

'Nous n'avons rien oublié ni rien appris.'[3]

2. Those who say that there is a 'Popish plot' are quite mistaken. It is not a Popish plot, but a split of the R. Catholics against themselves.

Of all the Oriental mysteries which I have been made acquainted with since I have been in the East, this has been not the least curious.

The seculars are divided against the regulars. This we have often seen before but never so much as now.

But, as the old Whig families are said always to have a Tory heir apparent, in order to be 'in' both ways, so the R. Catholics have one set of priests & nuns *with* the Gov't & one *against* it.

Mrs. Bridgeman & the Jesuits are against, the secular priests & Bermondsey nuns for.

Mrs. Bridgeman & her 11 Irish Nuns have been instructed to resign & go home & make themselves martyrs, which they will do, I am afraid, on Saturday – tho' I have piped to her & done the Circe in vain.

The Rev'd Mr. Duffy, Jesuit, has been instructed to refuse confession & therefore Holy Communion to, or even to visit those Bermondsey Nuns, whom I brought up with me from Scutari to one of the Land Transport Hospitals, & he calls them, among other epithets in a note to themselves, a 'disgrace to their Church'. For none can be so coarse as a R.C. priest. This note we have forwarded to Dr. Grant, Bp. of Southwark,[4] for approval.

Cardinal Wiseman has recalled the Rev'd Mr. Unsworth, Senior R.C. Chaplain here, who always took part against the Jesuits & Irish Nuns 'under these circumstances'.

On the other hand, the secular priests repudiate the Irish Nuns, & do the civil by the Gov't & me & the Bermondsey Nuns – with principal & interest – & even Father Cuffe, who used to call me 'Herod', now licks my hand, as the Provost Marshal says, 'like a good 'un'.

Irish 'Regulars' are little else than 'Rebels' as has truly been said here.

Such are a few of the premises. You say that the English like to draw their own inferences. Here they have done it already – and here Deputy Purveyor in Chief Fitzgerald is supposed to be the tool of the Jesuits & the Irish Nuns.

The 'Confidential Report' is not a secret to any one here.

3. You say this is but one bud of the bed of roses upon which Secretaries of State are wont to lie. I have just seen enough of Gov't to know what that bed must be. But, till Secretaries of State have known what it is to have the reputations of their wives & daughters slandered, for party purposes, till you have known what it is to be uncertain for many days where you should get food or warmth for those *beautiful children (*My poor Nurses are not 'beautiful' – *Bien s'en faut.*[5] But they are not less my charge.) who are standing round your table, & to feel that grinding anxiety for the

responsibility of the lives & healths of those under your charge, & to doubt whether you are not sacrificing them, in your turn, to considerations for the good of the work, I deny that you can cull one bud from my bed of roses or even imagine its fragrance afar off. Had I told but half the truth in my answer to Mr. Fitzgerald, you would have said, What a fool she was not to make her complaint before!

But no one in England has yet *realized* the graves of Scutari or the Crimea – or their causes.

4. I deprecate most earnestly your judgement that 'the highest proof of success is when a mission is carried thro' without producing attack' as being against all experience & all history from the Sacred history down to the fable of the 'wolf & the lamb', which was the incarnation of a pretty wise experience too. I beseech you to reconsider your opinion. I am not a lamb – far from it. But I have been a lambkin in many instances, & principally in one, & yet have not 'avoided attack'.

I know that yours is the principle of most governments now, & that to steer clear of 'attack' & to promote & praise both sides, if possible is its theory. But I do not see that it succeeds even in averting attack. A '*quarrel*' always, it is true, vulgarizes both sides (witness Sir J. Graham & Napier[6]). But I don't see that the lamb could help the *attack* if Joan of Arc had been said to have had a '*quarrel*' with the D. of Bedford or the lamb with the wolf, it would have been a misapplication of the word.

I will give one 'instance'. In all the Hospitals of our Army which I have seen where women have not been, the Doctors go round so late* (*notwithstanding the Queen's Regulation) that the Diet Rolls cannot be made out in time for the men to have their dinners before 3 or 4, & their Extras before 5 or 6 o'cl. It was (*partly*) on this account that I have insisted so strenuously on our Extra Diet Kitchens. The Drs do not like sending their Diet Rolls in to us late – & the men always get consequently their Extras at 12 & their dinners at 1 from our Kitchens – making the difference for a weakly man between waiting for his Beef Tea from 8 A.M. til 4 or 5 P.M. & waiting till 12 or 1 P.M. I have never, in one single instance, got in my Diet Rolls except as a 'lamb', never reported a Medical officer for being late, but I know the Medical Officers have opposed our Extra Diet Kitchens in many instances like 'wolves', on this account, tho' no single case can be found against us of having given any thing but upon Diet Roll to Patients. Yet this is the ground alledged against us.

5. You may well say that Sir John McNeil's Report is the model of a Report. It is indeed – accurate, lucid, cool & conscientious.

But had Sir J. McNeil made nothing but a Report, he would have done little. But he put his hand to the plough & did much out here. So did Col. Tulloch.

It still remains to be seen whether his *Report* will do *anything*. Hitherto nothing has been done but to promote those reported on – to make Ld Panmure say 'I am very sorry, but I did not know that these men had been promoted', to make Ld Hardinge[7] say, 'I am very sorry. I did hear that the Army had suffered. But I did not know that their sufferings had been at all attributed to these men.'

In 6 months, all these sufferings will be forgotten. And I *indeed* agree with you that, in the presence of that colossal calamity & of the national disgrace of promoting the authors of it, the promotion of that petty offender, Mr. Fitzgerald, tho' in some respects, his offences are not petty, (for none dare offend him, because he can starve any Hospital in the Crimea, & leave, as he recently did, 130 typhus fever cases for 24 hours without wine,) but compared with our other disgraces, *his* promotion sinks into the shade – and I feel more shame than will ever crimson his face at having but mentioned it.

Oh! Lord Stratford – oh! Kars[8] –

And now, what do I want?

Not that you should do any thing, not, ten thousand times *not*, that you should alter your opinion about the Ho. of Commons, still less that you should alter your opinion of me – (though I own I am anxious that you should not pre judge a work because it has been 'attacked' – anxious too to believe that I have not injured the work.)

But all I wish is to leave some record of what will not be believed in the homes of London a twelvemonth hence – of what, tho' a trifling instance, is a true example of what ruined our Army.

Believe me, dear Mr. Herbert, (and if I have used some strong expressions, let me say that there is no more comparison between Sir J. McNeil's case & mine than between the calm review of a historian of the causes of a war, & the officer in the heat of battle providing for his men's safety,) believe me very truly yours,

Florence Nightingale

Source: BL Add 43393: ff 224–33

1. prévaloir: to take the advantage.
2. Filder: Commissary-General at Scutari; he defended himself against the allegations of incompetence put forward by McNeill and Tulloch in *The Commissariat in the Crimea* (1856), in which he claimed that the only major difficulty was a lack of hay for the horses.
3. Nous n'avons rien oublié ni rien appris: We have forgotten nothing and learned nothing.

4. Bishop Southwark: Thomas Grant (1816–70), first Roman Catholic Bishop of Southwark, was known for his learning and zeal on behalf of the poor.

5. Bien s'en faut: It is good that this is so.

6. Sir James Graham: (1792–1861), as First Lord of the Admiralty, was blamed by Admiral Sir Charles Napier (1786–1860) for not supplying him with sufficient gunboats after he had boasted of what the navy could accomplish in the Baltic. Napier, in turn, was accused of poor leadership, due to a capricious humour and intemperance.

7. Lord Henry Hardinge: (1785–1856), was widely blamed for the lack of preparation on the part of the military in the Crimean War.

8. Kars: One of the two main Ottoman army bases, it fell to the Russians on 25 November 1855 when the Allies failed to supply military assistance.

Whatever her actual state of mind, Florence's letters home were often cheerful, even comic.

52. To Parthenope Nightingale   Crimea 22 Apr 1856

Would not you like to see me hunting rats like a terrier-dog? Me!
    Scene in a Crimean Hut
    Time midnight
    Dramatis Personae
    Sick Nun in fever perfectly deaf
    me the only other occupant of the hut except
    rat sitting on rafter over sick nun's head & rats scrambling about.
    Enter me, with a lantern in one hand & a broom-stick in the other (in the Crimea, terrier dogs hunt with lanterns in one paw & broom-sticks)
    Me, commonly called 'Pope' by the Nuns, makes ye furious Balaclava charge, i.e. the light cavalry come on & I am the Russian gun.
    Light cavalry ensconces itself among my beloved boots & squeak – Desperate Papal Aggression.
    Broom-stick descends – enemy dead – 'Pope' executes savage war dance in triumph, to the unspeakable terror of Nun (& of himself.)
    Slain cast out of hut – unburied.
    Fan is a fool to me.

                                                                F.N.

If there is anything I 'abaw', it is a Rooshan & a rat.

Source: Wellcome

Nightingale wrote final reports on each nurse. In all 108 were sent out; 64 were sent home or invalided out; 6 died. About the Bermondsey Sisters of Mercy, she said: 'It is impossible to estimate too highly the unwearied devotion, patience, & cheerfulness, the judgment and activity, & the single-heartedness with which these 'Sisters' (who are from Bermondsey) have labored in the Service of the Sick' ({16 June 1856} BL Add 43402: f 10).

53. To Georgiana Moore, Mother Superior of the Convent of Our Lady of Mercy, Bermondsey

General Hospital, Balaclava 26 Apr 1856

My dearest Rev'd Mother

Your going home is the greatest blow I have had yet.

But God's blessing & my love & gratitude go with you, as you well know.

You know well too that I shall do everything I can for the Sisters, whom you have left me. But it will not be like you. Your wishes will be our law. And I shall try & remain in the Crimea for their sakes as long as we any of us are there.

I do not presume to express praise or gratitude to you, Rev'd Mother, because it would look as if I thought you had done the work not unto God but unto me. You were far above me in fitness for the General Superintendency, both in worldly talent of administration, & far more in the spiritual qualifications which God values in a Superior. My being placed over you in our unenviable reign of the East was my misfortune & not my fault.

I will ask you to forgive me for everything or anything which I may unintentionally have done which can ever have given you pain, remembering only that I have always felt what I have just expressed – & that it has given me more pain to reign over you than to you to serve under me.

I have now only to say that I trust that you will not with-draw any of the Sisters now here, till the work of the Hospital ceases to require their presence, & that I may be authorized to be the judge of this. Unless the health of any of them should make her return desirable, in which case I will faithfully inform you.

I will care for them as if they were my own children. But that you know, and now it is a sacred trust from you.

Sister M. Martha is, thank God, quite convalescent.

Dearest Rev'd Mother, what you have done for the work no one can ever say. But God rewards you for it Himself.

If I thought that your valuable health would be restored by a return home, I should not regret it. But I fear that, unless you give up work for a time, which I do not well see how you can at home, your return to Bermondsey will only be the signal for greater calls upon your strength.

However, it matters little, provided we spend our lives to God, whether like our Blessed Lord's, they are concluded in three & thirty years, or whether they are prolonged to old age.

My love & gratitude will be yours, dearest Rev'd Mother, wherever you go. I do not presume to give you any other tribute but my tears. And, as I shall soon want a 'character' from you, as my respected S. Gonzaga would say, I am not going to offer you a character.

But I should be glad that the Bishop of Southwark should know & Dr. Manning, (altho' my 'recommendation' is not too likely to be of value to you but the contrary,) that you were valued here as you deserved & that the gratitude of the Army is yours.

Pray give my love to S. Gonzaga & thanks for her letter.

Mrs Roberts sends many messages of respect & of sorrow.

Will you thank the Bishop of Southwark with my respectful remembrances for his very kind letter to me?

Will you ask one of the Sisters at home, I dare say S. Gonzaga will do so, to write to me about your health.

And believe me ever, whether I return to see you again in this world or not,

> ever my dearest Rev'd Mother's
> (gratefully, lovingly, overflowingly)

Florence Nightingale

Source: Bermondsey   Wellcome photocopy

Nightingale insisted upon staying until the last soldier had been sent home. She sailed from Scutari at the end of July 1856, travelling as 'Miss Smith' with her Aunt Mai. She refused the public reception that was being planned for her in London and went to Lea Hurst by train, arriving at home unannounced. Her spoils of war included a one-legged sailor boy for whom she found occupation, a Russian orphan boy, a Crimean puppy discovered in a hole in the rocks near Balaclava, given to her by the soldiers, and a kitten which died before it reached England.

The war had ended. Touted as a victory for the English, French and Turks, the outcome was, in fact, a stalemate. The defence of oppressed religious minorities, which had been the excuse for initiating conflict, was not even mentioned in the final treaty. Territorial divisions remained much as they had been. The Danube became an international waterway, and the Black Sea was to be neutral. Sebastopol, over which so many lives had been lost, was returned to the Russians. Little changed in terms of the balance of power.

Florence Nightingale returned to England a heroine and for the rest of her life bore the encumbrances and privileges of fame. Denounced by the Halls, the Fitzgeralds and the Bridgemans, loved by the common soldier, idolized by the people, respected and befriended by the progressive officers, Nightingale was on the threshold of her greatest work. She proceeded to use her fame and experience to effect the reforms that she had initiated in the Crimea. She was to have a profound influence upon government health policies in regard to public sanitation, the army in India, and the Army Medical Corps. She came to dominate nursing reform. But through all these activities Nightingale remained a controversial figure.

For the moment, however, disagreements were forgotten in the triumph of victory. For lack of military heroes, Nightingale became the heroine of the Crimea. Augustus Stafford, MP said: 'Florence in the Hospital makes intelligible to him the Saints of the Middle Ages. If the soldiers were told that the roof had opened, and she had gone up palpably to Heaven, they would not be the least surprised' (Cook, I, 238). Some said that the soldiers would do anything for her – stop drinking, send their money home, or brave a surgical operation. Before the gathering that launched the Nightingale Fund, Sidney Herbert had read excerpts from two soldiers' letters home. One wrote: 'Before she came, there was cussin and swearin, and after it was holy as a church'. The second declared: 'She would speak to one and to another, and nod and smile to a many more; but she couldn't do it all, you know, for we lay there by hundreds, but we could kiss her shadow as it fell, and lay our heads on the pillow again, content' (*Report of Proceedings*, pp. 25–26). Such eulogies, however exaggerated, acknowledge that Florence Nightingale was no ordinary person.

3

Post-Crimea Reforms: 1856–61

(✿)

Florence Nightingale returned from the Crimea a changed woman. She had entered the Harley Street hospital relatively inexperienced, but had soon learned to achieve her goals by behind-the-scenes management of the committees and doctors. She used these strategies again in the East, but Scutari demanded resources she had never before tapped. She rose to the challenge, and was forged in the fires of military and governmental disarray and petty politics. If the circumscribed life of the Victorian woman had prompted Nightingale to seek self-fulfilment through hospital reform, the Crimean experience gave direction to her future work. The years 1856 to 1861 were dominated by efforts to enact long-term reforms of the army, primarily through the Royal Commission on the Sanitary State of the Army.

Out of 97,800 British soldiers in the East, 2700 had been killed, 1800 died from wounds and 17,600 died from disease (Baly, p. 6). Although in desperate need of rest, Nightingale was obsessed by the memory of the Crimean dead. During the summer of 1856 she wrote letters, pursuing Sidney Herbert, on a fishing holiday in Ireland, and Lord Panmure, the Secretary of State for War, shooting grouse in Scotland. Parthe answered the mass of mail that was addressed to her at this time, while Uncle Sam continued to deal with miscellaneous post-Crimea problems. Florence, however, was unable to rest.

On 23 August 1856 Florence received a letter from her old friend Sir James Clark, Queen Victoria's physician, inviting her to Birk Hall, near Ballater, for a month. She seized this opportunity to speak directly with the Queen at Balmoral. On her way there she consulted Sir John McNeill and Colonel Alexander Tulloch about the best strategy to convince the Queen to call for a wide-ranging Royal Commission to examine the sanitary conditions, administration and construction of barracks and military hospitals, as well as the organization, education and administration of the Army Medical Department. She wrote to their ally, Colonel J. H. Lefroy, who worked at the War Office:

54. To Col. J. H. Lefroy[1] Lea Hurst, Matlock 25 Aug 1856

{Answered by 2 Aug}

My dear Sir

The advice I have to ask is fourfold

1. what shall I say to Lord Panmure, to the Queen, & to Sir B. Hawes? The first has proposed to see me at the end of next month in London – the Second at the beginning in Scotland – the third writes asking for my 'suggestions in a shape to

bring our Doctors to consider them & give us sufficent reasons for rejecting them, if they are determined to reject them. It will be hard, no doubt to compel the Doctors to consider & still harder to accept improvements proceeding from a woman'.

In answer to this from Sir B. Hawes, I was going, Hibernicé,[2] to ask you a question. I need not say that – even without knowing the fate of all Memoranda and (alas! that we must say it) of all Commissioners, *if* they are honest and able – I should respectfully decline supplying the proposed 'Memorandum' for the reason which Sir B. Hawes himself anticipates. And you who know something of the workings of our Medical Department in the East will easily anticipate many others – grounded on the one fact that all their passions & all their interests would be enlisted against anything I could propose.

2. But I have another reason – or rather I should like to ask another question. I should wish to be employed in the Military Hospitals of the Peace as I was of the War i.e. in the

Linen

Cooking

Nursing Dep'ts,

to a certain extent which I could define & which would not exclude but facilitate the instruction of the Orderlies in their business, which indeed was one of the main uses of me in the War Hospitals, altho' I am aware that the necessity of training the Male Orderlies, M.S.C.[3] has been made one of the principal reasons, (or shall I say excuses?) for excluding me.

However that may be, even this would not be my principal reason for desiring an official entrance into the Army Hospitals, to the cause of reforming which I feel myself given for life, directly or indirectly. For my principal reason is the *indirect* one of having legitimate means of information by which I could suggest reforms not within my power or province to execute.

Now, should I not cut myself off from all chance of ever obtaining employment in the Military Hospitals by suggesting the necessity of any great reform to my Magnates three *now*? It is certain that I should, were any of the *Medical* Magnates of the Army to have a scent of it?

Would it not be better for me to ask humbly & directly for a Female Nursing Dep't in the Army Hospitals, which I have little doubt the Queen would grant, without making myself more obnoxious than I am – or should I state boldly the whole case at first?

3. I believe you will answer 'you would be much better employed in the London Civil Hospitals to which you now *have* access'. To this I should beg to reply, I am quite convinced that I could do nothing with the Nightingale Fund at present. No reformer ever began with the conditions with which I am called upon to begin. With the buzz-fuzz which is above my name at present, I should succeed in nothing else but in collecting about me much of the vain & needy & frivolous elements of England. Indeed the conditions of success have been removed so entirely out of my reach that I am tempted to say to my Jason, the Hospital Cause, if it asks 'Che mi resta?' 'Io'[4] But 'Io' is alone.

If I could not, therefore, gain access to the Army Hospitals, I should take some small, remote & poor Hospital for some years where I might indirectly but *not* nominally pursue my object of training women.

4. If you should decide for my telling the truth & the whole truth to Lord Panmure & the Queen about their War-Hospitals, viz. that not one step has been made in reform or to prevent the scene of '54 from being acted all over again in any future War – avoiding, of course, all personal assaults upon individual Doctors whose conduct is only the result, to themselves, of the System under which they live. I should, in that case, much like to consult with you, whose opinion is necessarily so far better than mine, as to what reforms are desirable & what are practicable?

Without the entire raising of the Medical Dep't there is little to be done. It is evident that I am unfit to discuss their medical merits. But three things are patent to every body

(1). that, while promotion is a question, not even of seniority but of the caprice of one man, they must be slaves & deficient without any blame to themselves, of that honor & independence which we are accustomed to expect in English men of science. Their standard both of science & honesty is infinitely low. Whether any system of examination and of 'concours' as the condition of promotion would remedy this, I am not qualified to decide.

(2). that they must be better paid & better taught – or no good men will enter or will stay among Army Surgeons.

(3). that a Medical Officer, after having risen to a certain rank, must not cease to do that which he is put there for, in order to do something quite different, i.e. make Requisitions for pots & pans instead of practising Therapeutics. Without falling into the tyrannous system of the French Intendance, but keeping the Medical Officer always, as he is & *ought* to be, supreme in his own Hospitals (& indeed giving him much more executive power as the Sanatary Officer of the Army) it would be easy to take the pots & pans off his hands.

If it is true that the Medical Officer of the Army stands the lowest in Medical Science in all England, there is enough to account for it. I know there are brilliant exceptions. But I know, curiously enough, that the principal exception to this imputation of want of science is the one most anxious to be relieved from the Pots & Pans system. And we have more than one instance of the reverse proposition.

If I could find a mouth-piece, not obnoxious to the same hostility, which the Army Surgeons naturally feel towards me, because, as a General Officer told me, 'they know they have been *found out*', I would gladly give every suggestion which has occurred to me to be worked up & promulgated for the benefit of the Service. I should have much pleasure in conferring (Memoranda in hand) with

Source: BL Add 43397: ff 240–43   {incomplete letter}

1. Col. J. H. Lefroy: (1817–90), was appointed to the War Office as scientific adviser by the Duke of Newcastle, and later sent on a confidential mission by Lord Panmure to report on the hospitals in the Crimea.
2. Hibernicé: Irishism; in the Irish manner.
3. M. S. C.: Medical Service Corps.
4. Che mi resta? Io: What do I have left? Myself.

Queen Victoria and Prince Albert first met Florence on 21 September. Both were impressed with her. The Queen said, 'I wish we had her at the War Office', while Prince Albert wrote in his diary, 'She put before us all the defects of our present military hospital system, and the reforms that we needed. We are much pleased with her; she is extremely modest' (Cook, I, 324). Lord Panmure met her, and asked her to record her experience in the Crimea with suggestions for reform; he also agreed in principle to a Royal Commission.

This victory demanded monumental effort from all the reformers. By early November, Nightingale was living at the

Burlington Hotel in London. Her quarters became known as the 'Little War Office'. Her war experience formed the foundation upon which the reforms would be based. She combined an ability to master detail with a clear vision of the whole picture. An unwavering determination and a phenomenal capacity for work made Nightingale the director of the operation. Sidney Herbert, who belonged to the inner circles of government, became the head of the reform work; he would guide their schemes to realization through his official position. Together they made a formidable team. Nightingale had plenty of time to become acquainted with the dilatory Panmure; six months elapsed between the setting up of the Royal Commission and the issuing of the Royal Warrant granting the Commission. To Sir John McNeill, the impatient reformer wrote, 'Gout is a very *handy* thing – & Lord Panmure always has it in his *hands* whenever he is called upon to do any thing' (15 Dec 1856 GLRO HI/ST/NC3/SU/7). But the reform team used the time to define the scope of the Commission, to meet people who would become collaborators, to select possible candidates to serve on the Commission, and to refine their strategies. Nightingale also gathered information from military stations and hospitals.

In contrast to her experience with women, Nightingale worked well with men even when her patience was stretched. Mixing humour with business, she could prod without antagonizing. But she shrewdly evaluated the problems a woman faced in working with men in a letter of 24 October {1856?} to Sir John McNeill:

I almost regret that I did not make you aware [ie in the Crimea] at the risk of troubling you with trifles, of my experience of the goods & evils of the position of a woman, qua woman, in official life. It is difficult to overrate the disadvantages attached to her means of efficiency, as a public officer among men – public Officers. All their defects, qua men of business, are laden upon her – because 'a woman cannot be a man of business'. Her word is not taken as evidence, because 'I could not contradict a Lady', so that she never hears the counter statement till it comes before her in the ultimate decision. (you both – I know that I have been reported to the Commander of the forces & at home for acts which I have never done, & have never contradicted having done).

If she is perfectly indifferent to all this & allows the authorities at home to throw all the blame upon her, if the measure they have privately enjoined fails, to take all the credit to themselves, if the measure she has privately counselled succeeds, it is difficult to over rate the practical advantages of the position of a woman in an emergency. She is the scapegoat for all experiments . . . (Wellcome)

Nightingale clung tenaciously, even obsessively, to her defined work. The despair into which she fell when situations that could be reformed were delayed for no reason other than a lack of energy found expression primarily in her journals and occasionally to a few intimate friends. Whatever her difficulties with the War Office, Nightingale's wrath more often fell upon women, whom she placed in two absolute categories. A few, such as Mother Bermondsey, she adulated, while the rest were labelled incompetent. She appears to have forgotten the obstacles so eloquently described in 'Cassandra' (1852), or that few women were born with her opportunities, intellectual capacity, physical energy and strength of will. The force behind these attacks was also fuelled by her unresolved relationship with her mother and Parthe, whose presence in the Burlington suite continued to irritate her. In a long letter to one of the few women she trusted, Lady Canning, she combined a familiar tirade with an evaluation of the army nurses and her Royal Commission plans:

55. To Lady Charlotte Canning   30 Old Burlington St
23 Nov 1856

Dear Lady Canning
   I have just received your kind letter 'finished Oct 7. at Barrackpore'. You have been too kind & efficient a Mistress to me & mine for me not to think it an 'official' duty to give you some account of my stewardship, & answer your letter step by step.
   1. *This* seems to me like a dream & not my past 'campaign'. It seems to me like a dream to see the women driving about in little bonnets & big petticoats & hear them saying that 'poor Lord Raglan', (that most chivalrous & noble old man in his disregard of mere public opinion), 'died of the "Times" ' – to see the men playing the game of party politics over the graves of our brave dead, & trying to prevent us from learning the terrible lesson which our colossal calamity should have taught us. Oh my poor men, who died so patiently I feel I have been such a bad mother to

you, coming home & leaving you in your Crimean graves, unless truth to your cause can help to teach the lesson which your deaths were meant to teach us.

2. The public has been, on the whole, very considerate of me. Two or three of my friends have made very great mistakes & been unable to understand what publicity must, by injuring my cause, be painful & worse to me. And puffing always injures any real work, were it only by collecting round it elements of frivolity, vanity & jealousy. On the whole too, the War Dep't has been very kind, & forgiven me my popularity as well as it was able – tho' it was very angry with a speech of Sir John McNeill's at Edinburgh which was made contrary to my earnest and written remonstrance.

3. The Hospitals of the East were, at the end, quite perfect, as also the Sanitary arrangements. I conceive that this year, the Barrack Hospital at Scutari was the finest in the world. Also, the deaths in the second week of January 1855 were 578 per 1000 in the Army – (& this was not our highest mortality, which was in the end of that month). The deaths in the corresponding week of January 1856 were 17 per 1000. The deaths from Epidemics were reduced from 70 per cent of those from all causes to 45 per cent. And the sickness from Epidemics from 60–80 per cent to 16 per cent. This, of course, is attributable to the excellent sanitary arrangements in the Army, introduced by the Sanitary Commission – as well as to those in the Hospitals. The frightful mortality in the Barrack Hospital at Scutari diminished in like manner. During 54–55, that Hospital was literally living over a cess-pool – & the Military Medical Officers ascribed the unmanageable outbreaks of Cholera which took place up to November/55 to a Cemetery 3/4 mile off – !!

To give you some idea of the way in which H.M.'s Ministers are informed of the health of H.M.'s troops the only authorized returns of Cholera (of course Ministers may have had private returns) sent home were (& are) of the Patients who are in Hospital from Cholera on *Saturdays* (Cholera running its course in 3 or 4 hours) & the Patients who are admitted the other six days in the week, dead & buried, of them there is no other record than in the Death Returns & not always then. The excess of burials over recorded deaths was 4000.

4. I am sure that you will be pleased to hear that, of your 'friends', as you kindly call them, Nurses Logan, Sullivan, Cator, Jane Evans, Miss Tattersall, Woodward (from Koulali) Montague, Orton, Maloney etc. turned out 'all right'. Miss Orton so good – & many others honestly anxious to do their duty. I do not mention the virtues of those who were before your reign, as they will be less

interesting to you. But I cannot help just recording the gratitude we owe to Miss Shaw Stewart, the 'Rev'd Mother' of the R.C. 'Sisters of Mercy' at Bermondsey, to Sisters Bertha & Margaret of the Anglican 'Sisters of Mercy' of Devonport & to the immortal Mrs. Roberts.

5. I have not had time to read the Koulali & Smyrna books. But even had I, I would not. For women who have had the happiness of serving God & the honor of serving their country in Her War Hospitals {—}s to make a book about it is to me quite enough, whether that book were prompted by their own vanity or by silly or astute advisers. The Koulali authoress, Miss Fanny Taylor,[1] has now joined the R. Catholic Church, which indeed she had done privately before she went out.

With regard to what you say about the necessity of Chiefs at home having the cause of dismissal always sent them, it is so true, both theoretically & practically, that I only wish it had been more strictly enforced. But, on one occasion, that of Miss Salisbury, a woman proved to be profligate, intemperate & dishonest, the War Dep't did not act upon the character sent home by the Commandant as well as by myself.

6. I am very much obliged to India for their zeal in our cause. I am pleased to hear it, because, ignorant as it is, it is upon a right principle. One is sick of the cant about Women's Rights. If women will but shew what their duties are first, public opinion will acknowledge these fast enough. I dislike almost all that has been *written* on the subject, Mrs. Jameson[2] especially. Let the 'real lady', as you call her, be as much professional, as little dilettante as possible – let her shew that charity must be done, like everything else, in a business-like manner, to be of any use, (a thing I found it more difficult to make my ladies understand than anything) – and all that is good will follow – provided, of course, that the real love of God & mankind is there. And, *with this*, I conceive that we have even an advantage over the R. Catholics. (A vow implies a fear of failure) just as the really sober man is undoubtedly better off than the man who has taken the Temperance pledge. Besides this, R. Catholics, even the best, are essentially incapacitated (from their inherent Manichaean-ism) from doing the best kind of good. They are to console the suffering which evils have produced. They are not to remove the causes of those evils. As a curious instance of this, I will mention that I tried to persuade a great ally of mine, the Superioress of the Sardinian 'Sisters' at Balaclava, Countess Cordero, (one of the most remarkable women it has ever been my good fortune to know,) to join with me in a strong protest against a certain Canteen, up to which we used respectively to see our

respective Patients – in Hospital slippers & clothing – stealing past the (conniving) sentry – out of the Hospital Huts. The protest was to have been addressed to our respective Chiefs of the Staff & would have been easily attended to. But I never could persuade her that it was any use to take any Preventive Measures against drunkenness or any thing else. I have seen this even among the excellent French 'Sisters' at Paris.

You will be glad to hear that Miss Shaw Stewart is hard at work improving herself at Guy's Hospital, where she is training as Nurse. I envy her. For I have much more harassing work to do.

7. I am sorry to hear your account of Indian (middle class) women. But I really think that it might be read aloud here to great advantage, for 'Indian' substituting 'English'.

India is a wonderful field for you. There is very much that we might imitate, with much advantage, out of the Indian Army, & what you say of the Sepoys reminds me of it.

I saw hardly anything of the Turks, as you may suppose. And what little I did see makes me think that poor Turkey's days are numbered. But men, far better informed than I am, say that she is making steady progress onwards. The merest sight of Turkey impresses one, of course, with the immense superiority in civilization which Constantinople has attained over her provinces. The Turkish Contingent was the best thing we did. And I regretted much its being disbanded. They, the soldiers, were getting so attached to us.

How Tropical colouring must call out your artistic feelings. We had small time to look at colouring but even I feel the change to this London sky deaden all my artistic perceptions.

8. You will wonder what is the grievance with us when everything was so perfect about the Army when it left. The fact is we have not made one step towards a system which will prevent the recurrence of such a disaster. If we were to set down at Batoum tomorrow, we should have all /54 over again. I have never heard any sensible man doubt this who was with our Army in the East. We are no nearer having the next Army live on fresh meat at 1 1/2d. per lb. instead of die on salt meat at 8d. per lb – we are no nearer having the next War Hospitals drained & ventilated – the next Land & Sea Transport well organized than if we had not died & lived respectively in the years of Disgrace /54 & of Grace /56. Because the system does not exist to compel it. Nothing has been done but a violent expenditure & the relaxation of all rules & all logical scheme of Government. And the very luxury & expence of /56 was bad for our cause. Because it gave the supporters of the old system (or no system) the right to say, Look what these innovators do.

Lord Panmure is going to give us a Royal Commission of Inquiry into all that concerns the health of the Army at home & abroad. And I have been commanded by the Queen & by him to write a Précis for the Government. I do not feel very sanguine as to the result of either. But I shall '*eat*' straight through. Of all those in Office whom I have had to do with since I came home, you will, perhaps, perhaps not, be surprised to hear that I have found the Queen, Lord Palmerston, & Mr. Herbert the most free from the Office Taint. These are really, (after their different fashions), not officially, interested. I have had much to do with two Taints lately, the Scorbutic[3] & the Office Taint. And the latter is the worse.

The points in my Précis will be to try to show

1. that the Army must be taught to 'do for' themselves – kill their own cattle, bake their own bread, hut, drain, shoe-make, tailor, &c, &c. But in this the Camp at Aldershot is, if possible, behind that in the Crimea. Everything is done for it by civil contract. (Its clothing only is going to be given to it to do). You will hardly believe that, in the Crimea, even when we had fresh meat, we buried one fifth part of it & that the most nutritious. Our Naval Brigade & the French dug up our ox heads & made soup of them – & I dug up the feet, & made jelly of them.

2. that the Commissariat must be put upon the same footing as your East Indian Commissariat which has, I believe, never broken down except during the first Burmese War, which was not its fault, instead of which our Commissariat is made, with other arrangements, to destroy an Army.

3. that the Quarter-Master General's stores must be periodically reported, as to what they contain, to the General Officers of Divisions. You are probably well aware that, while our men were lying in one wet blanket & one muddy great-coat, wet & muddy because they had been 20 hours out of the 24 in the trenches, while they were dying of Scorbutic Dysentery upon salt meat, rum & biscuits, our stores at Balaclava were full of rice, lime-juice, great-coats, coatees, rugs & even blankets.

4. that, in time of war, the Transport must be under military control. For, while stores were daily arriving at Balaclava, & every man in front would gladly have given 1/ to have his blanket carried up to him, & every man in Transport Service could have carried up 10 blankets, we positively never thought either of using or of paying the seamen on board the Transports to carry up stores to the front.

5. that a Sanitary Officer must be attached to every Quarter Master Genl's Office – to advise upon matters relating to encampment, diet, clothing, hutting, sick transport. Even after our

great distress was over, it was found that the 79th, altho' down at Balaclava, was in such a state from Fever that, if matters went on thus, the whole Regiment would pass thro' Hospital 4 1/2 times in 6 months. After the usual recalcitration from Commanding Officers as to 'Military Positions' &c, it was found that by moving the lines 20 yards, which did not alter the military position in the least, the troops were saved from Fever. The boards of the huts were found positively covered with green algine matter. But now a Medical Officer, if he analyses the water & finds it unfit for human health, & remonstrates in writing, may be placed under arrest. Military health, as was written 57 years ago, is sacrificed in an enormous proportion to ignorance.

I have 11 other points which relate

1. to the Government of General Hospitals, which, being in the hands of eight Departments, the Officers of which are appointed by different authorities, ensures delay, irresponsibility & inefficiency. A requisition to mend a broken pane of glass must pass thro' six Departments.

2. the Sanitary Element in Hospitals

3. the Army Medical Department, its rate of pay, education, system of promotion, confusion of its administrative & professional functions, absolute necessity of a *Practical* Army Medical School at home, impossibility of its producing, as at present constituted, good surgical science –

4. the necessity of a Hospital being complete in itself & furnishing a Hospital kit for each man. We positively had no power of inventing any scheme, (when the men were ordered to leave their knap-sacks they never recovered), of clothing these men when they came into hospital with nothing on but an old pair of trowsers & a dirty blanket – nor of feeding them, because it was a Queen's Warrant that they ought to bring their Spoons with them into Hospital

5. Cooking & Dieting of the Army

6. Washing

7. Canteens

8. Soldiers' wives

9. Nursing by male & female

10. Uniformity of Stoppages, the non-uniformity of which engenders a want of confidence in the men, (and justly), as to the accuracy of the balance of pay they receive, there being one Stoppage of 3 1/2 d for the field, another for on board ship, another for wounds in Hospital, another for sickness in Hospital. I have had so much to do with the little money-deposits of the men that I know how badly this works on their moral confidence, without any proportionate saving to Gov't.

11. Engineering of Hospitals
12. Mode of keeping Statistics –
That good little Sardinia has adopted our civil mode of keeping these at the Registrar-General's Office, while we are not allowed to have any sickness in the Army but what they had in Charles II's time. And I could make you laugh at one classification – which seems made to deceive & bamboozle Gov't as to the causes of our disease. Just as the system of the Army Medical Department seems made to prevent it from rising to the level of the Medical Science of the day.

I think, if you could see our *real* Statistics, you would think that I have been moderate in my Statements. In eight regiments in the front, of which the 46th actually lost more than its average strength from disease alone, we lost 73 per cent. in seven months from disease alone. I am not aware that we can show any instance in our history of a similar disaster except in the Burmese War in /26. At Walcheren, which is called the 'ill-fated' expedition, we lost 10 1/4 per Cent in 6 months from disease, in the Peninsula 12 per Cent in a year from disease.

Contrasting this 73 per cent. with the loss in our Naval Brigade, which was scarcely 3 1/4 per cent. from disease, & among our Officers which was 3 3/4 per cent. from disease, shewing that there was no fault in the climate & with the loss, more fearful than ours, from disease among the French this year, when they began to do *on purpose* what we did from stupidity, namely, ill-feed, ill-clothe, ill-shelter the troops; shewing that it was not only over-work in the trenches which killed us, I think we arrive at a pretty just conclusion.

The question is, shall we have any Reform? The queen has been most earnestly interested. So is Prince Albert. But I fear they have taken the wrong sense as to the Crimean Commission. They do not see how, if all the men, therein blamed, were so excellent, what must the system be which killed from disease alone 50 per cent. of all our infantry *in the front* in 7 months – & 39 per cent., taking *all* the Infantry & Cavalry together?

You will wonder at the din & bustle of our English business in your Indian life, &, may I say so?, I think you a little prefer the former in your approbation. I wonder more at the way we have here of making out of the most critical subjects conversation only. I think the proof of this is the degree to which, in England, the newspapers influence people's opinion or rather talk. It is said that the speeches may be counted which, in the House of Commons, have commanded a vote. (That is because an M.P. has an opinion about his vote.) And it is impossible to believe that, if any one has a definite opinion upon any subject, the Article of a newspaper gentleman, who has to get up his opinion before 4 o'clock could alter it. Yet how many people read & talk newspaper – shewing, I am afraid, both how little definite opinion there is, even upon important subjects, & how much these are made mere grinding-organs to grind a talk of.

However, one could not be too thankful for one's own free press when one saw the disastrous consequences to the French this spring of having none.

Lord Panmure has given me six months' work (but no wages or *character*). After that, I go to the nursing business again.

Believe me, dear Lady Canning,
sincerely & gratefully yours

Florence Nightingale

Source: LDA: Harewood Collection, Lord Canning Papers 177/Z/3

1. Miss Fanny Taylor: a nurse with the Stanley party, who wrote *Eastern Hospitals and English Nurses*, by a Lady Volunteer (1856).
2. Mrs Anna Jameson: (1794–1860), well-known writer on art and an early feminist; author of 'Sisters of Charity' (1855) and 'The Communion of Labour' (1856), calling for the employment of women in public service jobs.
3. Scorbutic: affected by scurvy.

Although busy and semi-officially involved in army work, Nightingale ended 1856 depressed and tired. The continued indolence of Lord Panmure, fears about Herbert's powers of leadership, and a belief that her allies lacked her sense of overwhelming urgency led her to write, in an undated personal note:

56. Private note {end 1856}

Oh my poor men who endured so patiently. I feel I have been such a bad mother to you to come home & leave you lying in your Crimean grave. 73 per cent in eight regiments during six months from disease alone – who thinks of that now? But if I could carry any one point which would prevent any part of the recurrence of this our colossal calamity (Walcheren lost only 10 1/4 per cent – same circumstances) then I should have been true to the cause of those brave dead.

You will say, who is this woman who thinks she can do what our great men don't do? But, if I could leave one man behind me, if I fall out on the march who would work the question of Reform, I should be more than satisfied, because he would do it better than I. I have not one now. But I am to have a Commission of ten, out of these, there are, I think, seven, some one of whom may be put up to it.

I have fifteen points, five pertaining to Army reform, ten to Army & Medical Reform mixed.

I shall eat straight through England. I have begun at the highest, my Sovereign & working thro' P. Albert, P. P. N. & H. shall go on thro H. M's Opposition & the Ho. of Commons, till my last appeal which will be like Cobden's with his Corn Law to the Country.

Source: BL Add 43402: f 166

In spite of Nightingale's pessimism, public outcry finally forced the government to acknowledge the work of Sir John McNeill and Colonel Tulloch. Tulloch was given a KCB and McNeill was sworn into the Privy Council. When a British expeditionary force was sent to China, Nightingale was consulted about diet, accommodations, medical equipment and the ventilation of ships. Medical Officers around the country were contacting her to inspect existing hospitals and to criticize plans for new buildings; she was even asked to introduce nurses into the naval hospitals. She assisted Colonel Lefroy in starting reading rooms at military stations; Aldershot established one in June. She worked on statistics with Dr William Farr, a leading medical statistician, comparing mortality in the military with that in civil life; she pioneered the use of graphs for statistical representation.

However satisfying, these were diversionary activities. The impatient Nightingale, ever eager to launch the Royal Commission, rushed to finish the 'confidential report' Lord Panmure had requested. This remarkable work, completed in only six months, became the basis of the Royal Commission's Report. She consulted all the leading authorities of the day, including Sir Robert Rawlinson, the engineer who had served on the Sanitary Commission in the Crimea, Sir Joshua Jebb, the architect of model prisons, Edwin Chadwick, who had worked on Poor Law Reform, and Professor Robert Christison on diet. The facts collected were to prove invaluable to the Commission.

The face she presented to the public was one of determination, but despair filled many pages to friends.

57. To Sir John McNeill

30 Old Burlington St W
1 Mar 1857

My dear Sir John McNeill

I have often thought of Lord Dunfermline's[1] words since we parted, & what I am now going to say will be but too sad commentary upon them.

I think our cause is lost – & that those who deny it feel it even more than those who acknowledge it.

Col. Tulloch will not see that the H. of C. is against or rather indifferent to him. At every successive failure, he promises he will refrain & go abroad. But he never does. and now he will write to Lord Palmerston. Lord Palmerston knows the truth just as well as you or I do. And the real meaning of what he said in the House was 'I would make the Crimean Commissioners both Dukes, if I could. But I cannot do anything to throw odium upon a party which is strong enough to turn me out'. & that he 'disquieteth himself in vain'.

There is less chance of Reform now than before the War – v. H. of C. for the last 3 weeks v. Army Estimates.

Eight months ago, had Lord Palmerston chosen to play a great game & say, 'I will have Army Reform, & if the H. of C. is against me, let me see if the country is for me', – he might have won. Now it is too late. The opportunity is lost & we shall not see another in our life-time.

The Army is strong enough now in the H. of C. to turn out any Ministry as it has always been in the H. of Lords.

For, besides the aristocratic weight & influence it always had, it has now an additional prestige in the late War.

Messrs. Herbert & Gladstone are dead (not in 'tresspasses & sins' but) in indifference & party-spirit. They do not choose to lose a motion in Parl't. which they would do if they moved in this matter. Politically, they may be right. Aesthetically, they are surely wrong. They would stand much better in the country ten years hence, if they did the honourable thing now.

Mr. Herbert is ill & probably going abroad – which will put off the 'Commission' we are going to have, with him as Chairman.

Lord Panmure has no other rule of conduct than that of staving off every question which will give him trouble, till the public interest in it subsides, leaving to the Aristocracy their honors & to the people their money, and 'keeping himself in'.

The Army Estimates cut down every thing that has to do with the scientific element of the Army, with the health, efficiency, morality of the soldier, while it leaves all the Staff appointments.

Lord Panmure has broken all his promises, defeated all reform by his inertia, for his passive resistance, easiest of all to make, is the most difficult to overcome.

Silently, all over the country, no doubt this is sapping the country's trust in the Aristocracy more than any thing else could have done.

Had Lord Palmerston been a younger man, this never could have happened. {He has} not the power to cope with such a multiplicity of subjects alone in the Cabinet, & he sacrifices the gr interests of the nation for those of his Order, for which, at heart, he does not care a Corporal's button.

With our present amount of Sanitary knowledge, it is as criminal to have a mortality of 17, 19, & 20 per 1000 in the Line, Artillery & Guards in England, when that of Civil Life in towns is only 11 per 1000, as it would be to take 1100 men per ann out upon Salisbury plain & shoot them – no body of men being so much under control, none as dependent. And so dependent upon their employers for health, life & morality as the Army.

I want to be out of it as soon as I can. And in three months I shall take service in a Civil Hospital.

All the materials of my Précis are ready, but no criticism upon it which is worth having. Dr. Sutherland has read it. But his opinion was that I must 'confine it to facts & experience for the Army would stand no opinions – & give nothing but propositions for the future, for evidence as to the past would be torn to shreds'. This Paraphrase does not sound strictly logical, but is not the less true for that.

Note: The Précis will do no more good then so many abler & better Reports have done – & I would willingly not send it in at all. But, if I do, I must have a sounder opinion upon it.

Would you write to me, P.O. Great Malvern, & say whether you could now give me that opinion you so kindly promised?

I much wish you could have been in London the last three weeks.

With kindest regards to Lady McNeill and Miss Ferooza

    Believe me always

    faithfully & gratefully yours

Florence Nightingale

Source: GLRO HI/ST/NC3/SU/75

1. Lord Dunfermline: James Abercromby (1776–1858), who served in various parliamentary posts and upon his retirement was active, with Sir John McNeill, in philanthropic work in Edinburgh.

Nightingale focused on the training for doctors and the administration in her reform of the Army Medical Department. She wrote a long letter of encouragement to an old Crimea ally:

58. To Dr Peter Pincoffs[1]

30 Old Burlington St
23 Mar 1857

My dear Sir

I have despatched your Manuscript with many thanks.

I quite agree with you that mere increase of pay, relative rank, &c will not raise our Army Med. Dep. But I fear that it never will be raised to be on a par with that of France & Austria from essential national differences.

In England money is everything. In France, the scientific man, whether he makes money or not, enjoys the position which science gives in France & money only gives in England. Now, you never can pay your Government servants as private practice pays its servants in England. Sir James Clark has a position, not because he is a man of science but because he has made £10 000 per ann. by his Science. Now Army Med. Officers cannot be paid £10 000 a year. And therefore the highest Science will always leave the Army. It matters little how low the French Army Med'l Dep't is paid. It matters little how high the English is paid. The high standards of Science of the former & the low standard of the latter, depend upon other causes – viz. public opinion which is given upon different grounds in the two countries.

Forty years ago, in England, the Army M.O.s were as much before the Civil M.D's as they are now behind them – for very obvious reasons, viz. that our Civil Medical Schools have risen into distinction since that period.

An Army Medical School will never command the same public confidence in England now that our Civil Schools do. And therefore I rather differ with you upon the subject of schools. I would never remove the Army Medical Student from undergoing the usual course in the usual Civil Medical School. But, after he has obtained his Diploma &c, I would then give him a two years' Hospital Course upon Clinical Medicine, Clinical Surgery, Pathology & Sanitary Science in a Military Hospital – where he should receive pay & do the duties of Dresser & Clinical Clerk, under competent Professors who should be Civilians, until Military Medical Officers should be competent. But they should be rather Tutors than Professors. One lecture weekly would be quite enough. Here the Pupils should have every means of learning Operative Surgery & Pathology upon the dead body. The latter especially is ignored by many of our Regimental Surgeons thro' life. Our Regimental system is essentially hostile to science.

Your account of the several Schools abroad is most useful & interesting. I was a little disappointed that you did not enter into a more professional criticism of the practice & Scientific standing of our Army Med'l Dep't. Because this could only be done by a professional man, by one who was not an English man & yet who was intimately acquainted with English practice. In fact, I know no one but yourself who could have done it, & done it in a simple way too, for the public to understand.

e.g. the Sanitary ignorance of our Army Med'l Dep't. What do you think of that?

Our Army Med'l Board of Examiners has so little knowledge itself that our Examinations will be little worth. And a competent Medical witness told me that the discussions at our Army Med'l Soc'y were such pure nonsense that, if he had not seen And. Smith's eye upon him, he could not have kept awake.

Should I ever see a change in our A.M.D. possible, I shall certainly have recourse to you for your official papers on the various Schools.

I hope that your Book will very soon be published. I think that it is so valuable that it must produce a great effect even upon our stolidity. Believe me
    faithfully yrs

                                F. Nightingale

Source: BL Add 45796: ff 154–56

1. Dr Peter Pincoffs: a civilian doctor who worked in the Scutari Hospitals. He wrote *Experiences of a Civilian in Eastern Medical Hospitals* (1857).

While Florence continued to work compulsively, Fanny and Parthe socialized and lounged in the hotel suite. Living intimately together, the three women were soon locked in old battles. Parthe demanded Flo's care and Fanny her social attention. Their quarrels degenerated into squabbles about money. Florence had her allowance from W.E.N. and shared in the cost of the suite, but she wrote to him complaining that Fanny 'tries to smuggle my accounts into hers . . . she sits down and writes items against me, almost at random, often overcharged' (Woodham-Smith, p. 285). Some years later Florence wrote to Clarkey that in the summer of 1857, 'The whole occupation of Parthe and Mama was to lie on two sofas and tell one another not to get tired by putting flowers into water . . . I cannot describe to you the impression it made on me' (Woodham-Smith, p. 288). Family stress became entwined with the lack of government support for the Commission. Florence refused to recognize that she was totally exhausted and lashed out at petty frustrations. She was adept at making herself the martyr of the drama, the sacrificial lamb whom no one understood.

59. Private note {1857}

Two things the Anglo-Saxon cares for
1. to be just
2. that, whatever he suffers (*that* he does not care for) the world should benefit by it. But, if he thinks there is no record of it by which mankind can learn something from his experience, then his sufferings are intolerable to him.

Moses said

Honour thy father & thy mother &c, a sentence which contains 3 lies.

Christ said

My mother & my brethren are those which hear the word of God & do it.

How much farther advanced this was than that.

Words, words, words, says Hamlet. And truly all this generation is Words, words, words.

And while I write I am under the empire myself of words. I don't like to *think* what I say of the 'family' – because I have all my life heard *words* quite different & dear to me from association.

What have mother & sister ever done for me? They like my glory – they like my pretty things. Is there any thing else they like in me? I was the same person who went to Harley St. & who went to the Crimea. There was nothing different except my popularity. Yet the person who went to Harley St was to be cursed & the other was to be blessed. The popularity does not signify much one way or other. It has hurt me less in the Crimea & vantaged me less at home than I expected.

Good public! It knew nothing of what I was really doing in the Crimea.

Good public! It has known nothing of what I wanted to do &

have done since I came home. The 'accident' (?)[1] of my acquaintance with Mr. Herbert has done it all.

Yet this adventitious, this false popularity, based on ignorance, has made all the difference in the feeling of my 'family' towards me.

There has been nothing really learnt by them from experience. But *the world* thinks of me differently – i. e. I have won, but by an accident. That there has been nothing really learnt from experience is proved by their talking of Hilary Carter now in the same strain they used to talk of me.

When we consider what a mother's feeling really is for her child, how flimsy, how unsubstantial it is, when compared with that of some 'Virgin-Mothers' we see the truth. A pretty girl meets a rich man. And they are married. Is there any thought of the children? The children come without their consent even having been asked, because it can't be helped. Sometimes they are not wanted. Sometimes there is need of an heir.

But, in reality, for every one of my 18,000 children, for every one of those poor tiresome Harley St. creatures, I have expended more motherly feeling & action in a week than my mother has expended for me in 37 years.

Oh poor John Bull, don't think as you are (& will be) told every day – that 'nowhere are there such homes & such mothers as in England'. Nowhere are there such mothers indeed. But in what sense.

We have seen what mothers do for their children – and what are children, at least daughters, expected to do in return? To be the property of their parents, till they become the property of their husbands. And I was expected to be not only the property of my parents, but the property of my sister. Because she had the world's opinion with her then. I had not.

Since I was 24 (probably long before, but certainly since then), there never was any vagueness in my plans & ideas as to what God's work was for me. I could have taken different kinds of work – education, Hospitals &c. But each was definitely mapped out in my mind after a plan. I cannot, after having had the largest Hospital experience man or woman has ever had, perceive that the plan I formed, at 24, for learning in Hospitals was imprudent or ill-advised. It was much what Mrs. S. Stewart is carrying out now under my suggestions.

Upon what principle my 'family' opposed this inexorably, overbearingly – I do not know – other than the 'principle' of following the world's *words* & opinion.

In fact, I know they take credit now for having promoted that which they called me unprincipled for proposing. (My mother even taxed me with having 'an attachment I was ashamed of'.)

When I was 30, I had an Adult Evening School for factory-girls, which was, on the whole, the most satisfactory thing I ever did. My sister went into hysterics because I attended this. And my mother requested me to abstain for 6 months from doing *anything* my sister disliked & to give up for that time entirely to her.

To this I acceded. And when I committed this act of insanity, had there been any sane person in the house, he should have sent for Conolly to me.

The rest of the story follows from such a fact as this of itself. When I went to Kaiserswerth the second time for 3 months, being then 31, my sister threw my bracelets, which I offered her to wear, in my face. And the scene which followed was so violent that I fainted.[2]

And, generally, I can remember that I never in all my life, went to the Village School, (that School which they professed to wish me to go to,) except by stealing out of the house unseen, because I was sure to be stopped.

To Harley St, with which they now believe themselves to have 'associations' dear to them, I was all but 'taboo'ed for going. My sister said something to the effect that she could never pass the threshold. And though she did pass the threshold more than once, the first time she ever came was to go almost into hysterics. She hated the place – & treated me like a criminal for taking it. And I felt like one, *then & all my life* till within the last 4 years. That is the extraordinary consideration which should make us pause, viz. the extraordinary hold which 'words' *can have* upon our feelings. And now, what do I tell all this for?

1. & chiefly – To do justice. In all this, I have had a 'spiritual' mother – one, without whom I could have done nothing – who has been always a Holy Ghost to me & lately has lived the life of a 'porter's wife' for me – who left her own people to come out to Scutari to me, to take care of a parcel of unruly servants, while I was 6 months out of the 12 in the Crimea.

2. To shew how fatally untrue the idea of having property in human beings is. Some things are called 'dreadful', & others, twin-facts, which, (if there be any difference, are, if possible, more 'dreadful'), are called 'proofs of affection', of 'family love' &c. Slavery, as to the body, is 'dreadful' – slavery if it includes the mind, is nothing.

And yet we are not man's property but God's property. And even He schemes His whole plan to make us into Gods, not slaves. So far from having this 'treasure in earthen vessels that the excellency of the power may be of God & not of us', it would seem that the whole purpose of His laws & Theodike is to 'work out the "excellency of the power", so that it shall be "of us" & not "of Him"'.

In human life after the Genesis comes the Exodus. There is joy that a man is born into the *world*, not into a 'family'.

3. To shew how words have really come to take the place of things – to be *instead of* feelings. According to this plan, people may come to have & to enjoy emotions, entirely contradictory. They may have both, the satisfaction of feeling that they have made the sacrifice provided they can *say* so, & the satisfaction of having their own way. They may enjoy the emotion that you are dying, that you are living, that you will undertake some great work, that you will never do anything again, they may have the satisfaction that they have prevented you from doing anything & they may have the glory of your having done something.

And how clever is this kind of *talking* folly! How it can continue to throw dust not only into its own eyes but into those of other people! How it will pass a fact which there is no controverting, in order clamorously to assert another which was never denied.

On the other hand, it must be said that there is no need for it to throw dust as to some things. For it is totally blind already. E.g. what blindness can there be similar to that implied in the constant speech of *Society* to *Family*. 'How good you were to give him or her up!' & in the reciprocal self-gratulation of *Family* that it has given him (or her) up.

What! some man (or more generally some woman) has been trying to 'finish the work which God gave him (or her) to do' – & the *Family*, after hindering in every way, after wearing out half his (or her) life by hindrances, after refusing, with-holding or being unable to give any help – dares to say that it has 'given up' him (or her) to *do God's work*, as if he (or she) were its bond-slave & not God's child & fellow worker! Why! even God will no longer call us servants, far less slaves, but joint-heirs, children, co-operators. Thus much have we at least arrived at knowing of the will of God.[3]

'Oh world! oh life! oh time!
On whose last steps I climb
Trembling at that where I have stood before'

if you did but know how you have worn out my life (& not mine only but that of far better men, we who were trying to do your (the world's) work & God's work,) before we had reached the middle of our course with your petty hindrances & chains & the galling & palsying opposition of *disabilities*! So that we have no life now left to do your *work* – if you did but know this, you might change, (too late for me, but not for others).

Even this summer, had I had but ordinary peace & quiet, not to say help, I could have waded through.

'Weep not for me, but weep for yourselves & your children'.

There are some, I know, who can learn no experience from this life – these are they who can take credit to themselves for having prevented a thing & for having accomplished a thing which was done in spite of them. These must wait for another life to learn.

But there are others to whom it is worth while to tell one's own experience, in order that they may save others from the same.

4. I wish to shew how false & cruel it is to make success the test of right.

While I was struggling through the very steps (I am obliged to take again my own experience as illustrative of that of many others) – the very steps necessary to accomplish that for which I am now praised – for want of which same steps others have failed in the self-same thing – all men forsook me – & chiefly my own family. Now, because I have succeeded by an accident which never might have happened, (I speak as men speak – for we know that nothing is an 'accident') all men praise me. What is such praise worth?

But let me say whose support *has* been of 'worth'. 1. my spiritual mother's – 2. that of one who has been a mother to me too in another way – Mrs. Bracebridge – & 3. singularly enough that of Mr. & Mrs. Herbert. They did not wait to send me to the Crimea in order to support me, as far as they could, in doing God's work.

5. I wish to shew how 20 years of doing nothing, of living without occupation & by excitement, may cause to deteriorate the human brain to such an extent that I solemnly declare, (after some experience in Lunatics,) I consider the people in Hanwell who conceive themselves to be tea-pots, or to have 30,000 men fighting in their insides, to be not more the subjects of delusions than the class which thus lives by excitement & not by occupation. These not only persuade themselves but others of their delusion. And I have seen scenes among them quite worthy of Molière, where two people, in tolerable & even perfect health, lying on the sofa all day long & doing absolutely nothing, have persuaded themselves & others that they are the victims of their self-devotion for an other who perhaps is really dying from over-work.

Of these persons, some simulate, (in all good faith) the character for which nature had really intended them, but for which the unfortunate education of absolute idleness had incapacitated them. Some simulate the character – whether of feeling, of imagination, of philanthropy, for which nature had so entirely incapacitated them as to make them unconscious even of their want of the quality they were personating – (also with all naiveté.)

I believe these delusions, bred of idleness, to be absolutely incurable (in this world).

The commonest minor form which this *kind* of *weakness* (in heads of families) takes is to spare the impertinent & knock about the submissive.

Of this we see instances in almost every family. The strongest character is generally the most submissive. Because the affections are also in proportionate strength. And by these it is led. So that the more powerful the character is, the more likely it is to be in subjection to the weaker.

I end as I began. If we are permitted to finish the work which He gave us to do, it matters little how much we suffer in doing it. In fact, the suffering is part of the work & contingent upon the time or period of the world at which we were sent into it to do its work. But surely it is also part of that work to tell the world what we have suffered & how we have been hindered, in order that the world may be able to spare others. To act otherwise is to treat the world as an incorrigible child which *cannot* listen or as a criminal which *will not* listen to right.

Source: BL Add 43402: ff 178–87

1. FN's query.
2. FN deleted 'then first felt the symptom of the disease which is now bringing me to my grave' after I.
3. FN deleted 'We are not the *Family's* children – We are God's children'.

On 27 April 1857 Panmure made an official visit to the Burlington Hotel, bringing a Draft of the Instructions for the Royal Commission for Nightingale to see before he submitted it to the Queen. The official list of Commissioners were all, with the exception of Dr Andrew Smith, progressive pro-reform men. Nightingale had won.

On 5 May the Royal Commission was formed. Behind the scenes the 'Commander-in-Chief', as the men working with her called Nightingale, worked on collating and verifying information. Determined to lose no further time, she drew up conclusions from the statistical material that she and Dr Farr had collected, and familiarized Sidney Herbert, Dr Sutherland, and the other Commissioners with the material. Dr Sutherland admitted to Aunt Mai that she was the mainspring of the work.

Nightingale did not spare herself, and she expected the same dedication from the men on the Commission. Dr Sutherland shared her sanitary enthusiasm and she appreciated his expertise, but he was her antithesis. While she was precise about time and habits, he was careless. While he balanced work with gardening, she never diverted her attention from work. She complained to Sir John McNeill that Dr Sutherland 'does not carry the weight in the Commission which his brains ought to give him. He lets very inferior men put him down owing to his want of pith. It vexes me and upsets the conclusions I want to impress on Mr. Herbert' (Woodham-Smith, p. 292). Nightingale admired Sidney Herbert's quick and accurate perception, and was most attached to him. Yet even he had flaws. He seemed unreliable and lazy; she refused to believe that he was ill, and referred to his complaints as 'fancies'.

Repeatedly she turned to McNeill for advice about how best to treat key witnesses:

60. To Sir John McNeill

30 Old Burlington St
4 & 12 June 1857

My dear Sir John McNeill

This is very nearly the end. This private Mem. pp. 270–288 about the women I feel more doubtful about inserting. You know so much more of human nature than I do that I need not remind you that what we get into scrapes for is (not for saying what nobody believes & every body says but) for saying what everybody believes & nobody says. If my mem'a about women were only for the Queen, it would not signify. But, if it should come out before the H. of C., I should not like it at all. It would do harm. The part about 'Nurses in *Civil* Hospitals' may, at all events, be cut out as irrelevant.

Also, you know better than any one, perhaps you only know how 'scabreux' it is for *me* to get upon the subject of Religion – & how easily I shall be misunderstood.

2. I have looked more at the double columns, & I think they *must* come out.

3. The question whether I should put 'Chapter & verse' to the quotations is, I think, just as board {broad?} as it is long. You know how even educated men will go off upon a word. One does not like the Roebuck Committee, another does not like the Stafford Committee – one distrusts this Commission & another distrusts that – till all thought about the truth is merged in a

discussion of authorities. Socrates says something to the effect that nine tenths of our belief comes from sympathy

<blockquote>
antipathy
authority or
blind assimilation.
</blockquote>

I do not know therefore whether to put references or not. Please tell me. As it is, it may look as if I were quoting from private letters or conversation.

4. I conceive that some remodelling of arrangement must take place – to put all the 'as it is' together & the 'as it should be'.

I understand that Dr. Smith says that he was much afraid of 'the Commission' at first & 'thought it w'd do harm'. But now 'thinks it is taking a good turn'. Is this for us or against us?

My dear Sir John McNeill

I am very sorry to be 'at you' so soon again. But Sir John Hall is to be examined next week. And I have been asked to request you to give some hints, as to his examination, founded upon what you saw of him when in your hands. My own belief is that Hall is a much cleverer fellow than they take him for – almost as clever as Airey – & that he will consult his reputation in like manner – & perhaps give us very useful evidence – no thanks to him.

It is necessary to examine him – and how is it to be done? is the question we would ask you –

I would only recall to your memory the long series of proofs of his incredible apathy – beginning with the fatal letter approving of Scutari, October/54, continuing with all the negative errors of now-obtaining of

<blockquote>
Lime Juice
Fresh Bread
Quinine /c
</blockquote>

& up to his *not* denouncing the effects of salt meat before you. To my mind, with the exception of Gordon, this man is (morally) the worst of the liars.

We do not want to badger the old man in his examination, which would do us no good & him harm. But we want to make the best out of him for our case.

Please help us –

Yours ever sincerely & gratefully

F. Nightingale

29 Old Burlington St
June 12/57 W.
Sutherland & Acland[1] are still in France – I have been down at Netley[2] inspecting. I will report progress.

Source: GLRO HI/ST/NC3/SU/84

1. Dr Henry Acland: (1815–1900), physician at the Radcliffe Infirmary and Regius Professor of Medicine at Oxford (1857).
2. Netley: first general military hospital built. Lord Panmure asked FN to give her opinion of the architectural plans, but when she recommended starting again, he rejected her ideas because of the cost involved.

Nightingale was to give evidence to the Commission in July. After some debate as to what ought to be included, everyone agreed that she would supply written answers to questions. Her evidence, later reproduced with her *Notes on Hospitals* (1859), was a thirty-three-page summary of her report to Panmure. Of Nightingale's report, an army doctor wrote: 'she possesses, not only the gift of acute perception, but that, on all the points submitted to her, she reasons with a strong, acute, most logical, and if we may say so, masculine intellect, that may well shame some of the other witnesses' (Cook, I, 359). The connection was made between the state of army hospitals and the overall health and efficiency of the army. All aspects of organization were treated, ranging from the need for sanitary officers and a statistical department through to the Commissariat, and touching on hospital kitchens, promotions, wives and hospital construction. Army mortality figures in peace and war were compared, with the use of diagrams, illustrations, appendices and supplementary notes. Defects and suggestions for reform concluded her report. Nothing was omitted.

In August Sidney Herbert wrote the Commission Report with Nightingale's help. Essentially an expanded version of her evidence, it showed conclusively that the mortality rate of the military was twice that of the civil population, which included children and old people. The most startling figures given were those for St Pancras, where the civil rate was 2.2 deaths per thousand, while the military was 10.4; and for Kensington, where the civil rate was 3.3 deaths, while at Knightsbridge barracks it was 17.5 (Cook, I, 361). As the Royal Commission's work drew to a close, Herbert generously wrote to Nightingale: 'I never intend to tell you how much I owe you for all your help during the last three months, for I should never be able to make you understand how helpless my ignorance would have been among the Medical Philistines. God bless you!' (Cook, I, 312).

Sidney Herbert warned Panmure that the government should

protect itself by beginning to correct the worst abuses before the Report was presented to the House. He outlined a plan that had been drawn up with the help of Nightingale, giving the reformers responsibility for the implementation of the recommendations. Four sub-commissions, each to be chaired by Sidney Herbert, would be formed. The respective duties of these would be:

1. to put the Barracks in sanitary order.
2. to found a Statistical Department for the Army.
3. to institute an Army Medical School.
4. to reconstruct the Army Medical Department, revise the Hospital Regulations, and draw up a Warrant for the Promotion of Medical Officers. (Cook, I, 363)

Nightingale labelled the fourth sub-commission 'the Wiping Commission', for it was to handle all miscellaneous problems. The sub-commissions were to be given executive powers, as well as financial backing through an interim grant. Panmure subsequently, if reluctantly, agreed to this plan. London emptied as Parliament and Whitehall went on the annual hunting and fishing migration.

Nightingale, disregarding her health, could see only the work ahead. By the end of July she was obsessed with the thought that nothing would be done. Instead of taking a break, as all the other Commissioners were doing, she felt compelled to outline the duties of the four sub-commissions. The proposal to train nurses with Nightingale Fund monies demanded her attention, yet she continued to evade it. Florence found herself overwhelmed, and collapsed on 11 August.

61. Private note   Undated {1856–57?}

My God, my God, why hast thou forsaken us?

What is the characteristic of the present generation? Is it not *words*?

Talleyrand said that words had been given us to conceal our thoughts. Have not words been given us in this generation to conceal our thoughts – *from ourselves*? Is it not come to this that, when a man says a thing, it is because he does not feel it, or does not mean to do it? Is it not come to this that words destroy all feeling, all action – that men may & do talk away all their tenderness, all their idea of right & wrong, all their activity? Our grandfathers & grandmothers did wilful wrong, perhaps more than we do. But they did not make it look so very moral as we do. They did not dress up their wrong with the clothing of right. They did not call their 'bitter sweet'.

Surely this is the age of cant.

Do not men talk *themselves* into a persuasion that they feel what they say. And is not this the most hopeless state of all? the sin against the Holy Ghost?

Take an illustration. We hear it constantly repeated, nowhere are there such homes as in England – nowhere are there such mothers. I say too, nowhere are there such mothers.

In what does this maternity consist?

When the child is about to be born, the grandmother, if there is one, drives about to her morning calls, & enquires for a good Nurse.

The mother does the same afterwards for a good Governess – & then she visits the school-room occasionally & thinks how badly the Governess is doing.

Thirdly, she invites all the young men to the house who, she thinks, will be suitable as husbands for her daughter. And very glad she is when this is done.

Is this a caricature?

The nation has, however, within the last three years, seen & heard the principle of 'words' illustrated/acted out, on the most colossal stage/scale which perhaps it has been ever given to any nation or age to witness.

We are tired of hearing of the Crimean catastrophe. We don't want to know anymore about the 'trenches cold & damp', the 'starved & frozen camp', the deficient rations, the stores, which might have saved the 'great Army of the dead', lying unused & undistributed.

But was this the real bitterness of that death? Is this all the meaning it has to us?

Our men were 'led as sheep to the slaughter & as a lamb before her shearers is dumb, so they opened not their mouths'. The Commander of the Forces was like the drowning Ophelia. Devoted, unselfish & single minded himself to the very highest degree, he let himself & his troops float down to death, unconsciously to himself, with scarcely a struggle against the weeds & the waters which were pulling him down to destruction. As for his principal servants, what shall we say of them? In another age, they would have been tried by court-martial, recalled or disgraced either officially or by opinion. And the least hardened would have become Trappists or retired from life. But what did we see? We came home, with the remains of that lost Army, to see the

Throne taking to its bosom the most distinguished of the malefactors, to hear of a Star-chamber farce which had acquitted them – to find them in all the official posts, honors, & drawing-rooms of the kingdom. Nay more, one of them, a son of a Premier, who had told a lie known to every one who had examined the circumstances to be a lie, for which in the days of duelling, he would have been called out by half a dozen men & shunned at all the clubs, is still regarded by the Sovereign, by the Government, by society with the same eyes as before.

And what do *we* remember of these men in the past tragedy? We remember a General Officer in command, looking out at the dead dogs which were poisoning the atmosphere in which the men lay dying & saying, 'You are spoiling those brutes', meaning not the dogs but the men – we remember him passing over to the Ambassador of England, & 'making', as they expressed it, 'them roar with his stories of the Hospitals'. We remember the highest functionaries of the Head Quarters Staff feeding their horses with the biscuit which the miserable men could not eat, & boasting that it kept these horses fat. We remember indeed hearing of card playing among the authorities, while the men were starving.

But is there any one now living who feels the real bitterness, who learns the real lesson of this?

It is not that 10,000 men, after 6 months, more or less, of mortal agony, which they bore with silent endurance, passed to another and, to them truly, a *better* world. It is that all this only showed, in double relief, a state of feeling & of education which did exist, exists & will continue to exist at home. This no one has 'wept' over, – when we 'mourned'. But you, ye did not weep. This no one has even perceived.

Words were given, in plenty, to the great Crimean catastrophe. But the real tragedy began when this was over. And there exists hardly a being at this moment who has a glimmering of this.

The great town proprietors in England send about broth & blue frocks, but they let the people on their town property live in a condition which leaves no/produces the impossibility of health, of morality, or even of domestic affections.

When these same proprietors or their kin were transferred to a position where the people, viz. the troops, were absolutely dependent upon them, where there was no Poor Law, no market for labor nor for articles of subsistence, no trade, no commerce, & no middle class, these 'people' starved. They actually were then left without the possibility of health or even of life. Yet of personal kindness between the proprietors & the people, even then there was enough. There was plenty (in this case also) of sending about of 'broth & blue frocks'.

But there was not the feeling nor the education necessary to produce a Deliverer.

And this is the remarkable feature of the case. This is the distinction between this & similar historical calamities. Not one man arose, either gentle or simple, out of all those thousands; either Officer or Private, to say This shall not be: to shew How it need not be: to suggest, or, if necessary, to force, at the risk of being shot, an organization to save the Army.

Had the Officer who wrote in January, 1855, a bold & judicious remonstrance in private, to the Commander of the Forces, had he endeavoured to push it further, might he not have succeeded? He could but have been shot, had he failed. Had a Tribune arisen among the Troops who, preserving all their discipline to their Chiefs, had yet led an organization to distribute the stores which would have saved their lives, how much greater such bravery would have been than even that brave endurance!

Such as it was though, it was great. Let them rest in peace.

But far more remarkable is the history of the period which follows.

From Queen, from Minister, from Government, from Opposition, from Houses of Parliament – downwards, no one has felt, no one has seen, not one voice has arisen to tell the state of the race where such a thing could have happened.

Christ has shewn, in strong language, the state of the Scribes & Pharisees? But, taking every word he says about them, what was their state to ours? It surely was not the putting *him* to death which roused his indignation against them. It was the state of feeling or rather of non-feeling which they betrayed.

Moses arose to lead an enslaved race. But we have had no Moses.

Peter the Hermit, Ignatius Loyola, where are they?

This is what constitutes the despair of this period.

We have listened, but there was no Deliverer.

Words have been given to our fate. The people rose & turned out two War Ministers for a worse, far worse, & knitted flannel jackets for us. And the Times wrote a few thundering Articles. And that was all.

The House of Commons has thrown a K. C. B.ship at a man who was, in one sense, a kind of Deliverer, and another honor to a far better man. And that was all.

The War Minister has asked, should he *get rid* of one of the chief miscreants by giving *him too* an honor. And that was all.

Lastly, two or three 'borne the Griefs & carried the sorrows of all & the Lord has laid upon them the iniquity of all'. These too have been in many things useless martyrs. They feel it but they do not regret it. It takes many useless martyrs to make one useful one. But it is better (for the progress of the country) to be an useless martyr than a cowardly deserter. This is the only hope for us – the only consolation that there must be unless the experience of God were in us, useless martyrdoms.

But where shall we seek, when these poor martyrs are gone, one who will find the truth & tell it, in the way that it used to be told, in the way which colors a century, which rouses a generation, which spreads till it becomes an organization of minds?

And, if no one is found, will not the decline of this nation begin?

My God, my God, why hast thou forsaken us?

Everything may be glazed over in these days. A man of a certain class of society may do anything except steal & still be 'received', as it is called.

Source: BL Add 43402: ff 167–72

Nightingale decided to go alone to Malvern for the water cure. Dr Sutherland urged her to refrain from working until she recovered, but she would not stop and demanded that he come to consult with her. Too weak to leave the sofa, pulse racing, sleepless, she obstinately forged on. At this juncture, Nightingale did not expect to live and prepared for her death.

62. Private note   Great Malvern 27 Aug 1857

Father, I do not in the least care whether I die or live. I would wish to know which it is to be, that I may know what Thou wouldst have of me. I do not suppose that there will be any less work for us in any future state of existence; (for us, the salt of the earth – at least, not till after many future states). Thou wilt send us where most work is wanted to be done. Lord, here I am, send me.

Perhaps when I was sent into this world, it was for this, Crimea & all.

Source: BL Add 43402: ff 173–74

Aunt Mai left her family to be with Florence in mid September. Before this breakdown Nightingale had refused to attend public events, but she had visited barracks and hospitals to gather information and attended dinners at the homes of friends. From this time she became an invalid, refusing to go out or to see friends or even collaborators unless they came to her. Aunt Mai, who had before served as the mediator in the family, now convinced Fanny and Parthe that while they were in London, they must stay elsewhere. Florence had an 'attack' if anyone threatened to visit her uninvited. There was, then, no choice. Florence moved into the Burlington Annex, a much quieter part of the hotel, when she returned to London. Aunt Mai, with the assistance of her son-in-law, the poet Arthur Hugh Clough, remained with Flo, spending Christmas at the Burlington while the Nightingales went to Embley.

During November Nightingale wrote letters to be distributed after her death, with detailed instructions as to what was to be given to various friends.

63. To Sidney Herbert 30 Old Burlington St 26 Nov 1857

Dear Mr. Herbert[1]

1. I hope you will not regret the manner of my death.

I know that you will be kind enough to regret the fact of it.

You have sometimes said that you were sorry you had employed me.

I assure you that it has kept me alive.

I am sorry not to stay alive to do the 'Nurses'.

But I can't help it. 'Lord, here I am, send me' has always been religion to me.

I must be willing to go now as I was to go to the East.

You know I always thought it the greatest of your kindnesses sending me there.

Perhaps He wants a 'Sanitary Officer' now for my Crimeans in some other world where they are gone.

2. I have no fears for the Army now. You have always been our 'Cid' – the true chivalrous sort – which is to be the defender of what is weak & ugly & dirty & undefended, rather than of what is beautiful & artistic. You are so now more than ever for us.

'Us' means, in my language, the troops & me.

3. I hope you will have no chivalrous ideas about what is 'due' to my 'memory'. The only thing that can be 'due' to me is what is good for the troops.

I always thought thus while I was alive. And I am not likely to think otherwise now that I am dead.

Whatever your own judgment has accepted from me will come with far greater force from yourself.

Whatever your own judgment has rejected would come with no force at all.

4. What remains to be done has however already been sanctioned by your judgment
       1. as to Army Medical Council
          as to Army M'l School
          General Hospitals scheme
          Gymnastics
       2. as to what Dr. Sutherland must needs do for the Sanitary branch
       3. as to Colonial Barracks – Canadian
                            Mediterranean
                            W & E Indian

5. I am very sorry about the Nursing scheme. It seems like leaving it in the lurch.

Mrs. Shaw Stewart is the only woman I know who will do for Sup't of Army Nurses.

Believe me ever while I can say God bless you
    Yours gratefully

                              F. Nightingale

Source: BL Add 43394: ff 190–94

1. On envelope: 'To be sent when I am dead. F. N. Rt. Hon'able Sidney Herbert M. P.'

Lying on her sofa, Nightingale would see Sidney Herbert and Dr Sutherland daily. Dr Balfour, who was the Secretary of the Royal Commission, Dr Farr, Dr Alexander and others had to be squeezed in between other appointments. Dr Andrew Smith, always a defender of the War Office, fought behind the scenes to eliminate the 'Wiping Commission' while Sir Benjamin Hawes obstructed on the administrative side. Panmure, swayed by opposing forces, revoked the 'Wiping Commission' one day, only to reinstate it the next. Nightingale confessed to Sir John McNeill: 'All that is necessary now is to keep Mr. Herbert up to the point. The strength of his character is its simplicity & candour, with extreme quickness of perception – its fault is its excessive eclecticism. Ten years have I been endeavouring to obtain an expression of opinion from him & have never succeeded yet' (16 Nov 1857 GLRO HI/ST/NC3/SU/94).

Nightingale became convinced that her problems were not simply with a penny-pinching government and recalcitrant bureaucracy. Public opinion needed changing in regard both to the health of the army and to home sanitation. A proper sewage system and good water supply became moral causes; those who refused to reform were sinful reprobates, as this excerpt from a private note written during 1857 suggests:

> Anti-Sanitary Arrangements
> 'Does he think we was all fools afore he came here?' Backed by the collective ignorance, pride, laziness & superstition of A., he shewed to his assistant that terrible front of stupidity against which 'the gods themselves fight in vain'
> 'there's a deal of human natur' in man'.
> 'I'll prove my innocence by not reforming'
> It is hard to make the humiliating confessions which must precede sanitary repentance
> 'I have probably been the cause of half my own illnesses & of three fourths of the illness of my children. It is very much my fault that 2 or 3 of my tenants have died of typhus'.
> & Sanitary reform is thrust out of sight, simply because its necessity is too humiliating to the pride of all, too frightful to the consciences of many.
> 'This new fangled Sanitary reform is all a dodge for a lot of young Government puppies to fill their pockets, & my opinion always was with the Bible that it's a judgment of God & we can't escape His Holy will, & that's the plain truth of it' . . .
> 'to pull down a poor man's pig-sty they might ever so well be Rooshian slaves'.
> 'ever since you've been in this parish, you've been meddling – I'll speak the truth to any man, gentle or simple – & that ain't enough for you, but you must come over that poor half-crazed girl, to set her plaguing honest people with telling 'em they'll all be dead in a month'.
> 'That's a lie!
> Everybody says so.
> Then everybody lies, that's all & you may say I said so & take care you don't say it again yourself – '

To God when He speaks Himself they will listen – not to me. – It is the usual fate of those who try to put a little common sense into their fellow men.

Where she had expected at least a fair hearing, she had been met with peevishness, ridicule, even anger & insult. (BL Add 43402: ff 175–76)

Nightingale declared war within her own house, fighting with her servants about proper sanitary measures. She sarcastically wrote on 16 August 1860: 'If, for one fortnight from this time, I find all the doors shut & all the windows open, (including those of the two water-closets, which also must have the seats shut) I will give the servants a Doctor's fee, viz. one guinea' (BL Add 43402: f 190).

Florence was sometimes too ill to write herself. Dr Sutherland had become an indispensable secretary. She also relied on her family to take down her letters. An undated note in Parthe's handwriting may well have been a reaching out to her beloved Mother Bermondsey.

64. To Mother Bermondsey {?} {Dec 59 or 57}

I never can express what I feel of all that you have been to me & to the work in which we both were engaged. I feel it however presumption in me to say this as you were working for God & not for me. And you required no more reward than I did. But I always felt with you that you understood without my telling you from similar experience at home a great many of my trials which none of my other ladies did & which I never told to you or to any one. And I cannot tell you what a support your silent sympathy & trust became altho I never acknowledged them. I felt that you knew the real difficulty of my position. The praise & blame which have been lavished upon us have been alike so unknowing & so unintelligent. I have been so busy & so ill since I returned.

Source: Wellcome   {copy}

The year 1858 brought progress for the reformers. The Report of the Royal Commission was issued to the public early in the year. Lord Palmerston's government fell in February and Panmure was out. Dr Andrew Smith retired. General Peel took over at the War Office, and at Sidney Herbert's urging appointed Dr

Alexander as Director-General of the Medical Department. Dr Balfour was appointed to establish a statistics department within the War Office. In the spring of 1858, the royal engineer Captain Douglas Galton joined the roster of Florence's men. Occupying an important War Office appointment, he was an invaluable member of the Barrack Sub-Commission. Married to her cousin Marianne Nicholson, he became one of Florence's most reliable co-workers and long-term confidants. Galton became the army's prime expert in barrack construction, water supply, drainage, heating and ventilation. In May Lord Ebrington had been encouraged to move a series of resolutions in the House regarding the health of the army, founded on the Royal Commission Report. Lord Stanley, an admirer of Nightingale, was moved from the office of Colonial Secretary to the India Office. All Nightingale's men were in place. After reading about the debates regarding Ebrington's resolutions, Sir John McNeill wrote to her, 'To you more than to any other man or woman alive, will henceforth be due the welfare and efficiency of the British Army' (Cook, I, 375).

Invalidism kept family and friends at bay, and also forced them to do her bidding. Her limited strength had to be used for her work; the immensity and moral importance of it brooked no opposition. Just as Fanny had made Flo wait upon an ailing Parthe, Florence now persuaded Aunt Mai, Clough, Hilary and others to wait upon her. All who collaborated with Nightingale in army sanitary reform and nursing reform, as well as her extended family, became accomplices in her drama. Their entrances and exits depended upon Florence's cues. Yet they remained loyal, submitting to their brilliant director's wishes.

65. To Fanny Nightingale   Great Malvern 6 Jan 1858

To my dearest Mother

I apply for ease & for help in my present pressing & difficult circumstances. I will explain.

My Father's letter to Aunt Mai asks 'what next?', in reference to plans, & speaks of a 'house in London'. I ought not, therefore, to delay saying that, if you are so kind as to think of a house on my account, it is a kindness I am unable to accept, though I thank you for the thought.

I am obliged now to restrict myself to *one* companion. Or, rather, I should say that companionship can be no more for me, while my work remains unfinished.

In order to keep up to my work, I feel the necessity of having *one* person with me to perform offices, which I am sure my dear Mother & Parthe would feel, each for the other though not for herself, that health would not permit. And, for myself, I should feel such anxiety in seeing either of you attempt the sort of life I am compelled to require in the one person staying with me through this work, (who might not be in full health & strength,) that it would overpower, not help, me. I have no other plan, then, but to ask Aunt Mai to stay with me. I know she will do it willingly.

Such power for headwork as I ever had, I have still, & with that remaining power, I feel called upon to do what I can to rescue the children committed to me from death, from disease, from immorality. This work is in such progress that I may have the hope of seeing it completed, if I can sufficiently save my remaining strength. The details are too small to particularize of what is necessary to do this. Yet they are essential. And I know not how to do without them. This help I can receive, without much anxiety, from dear Aunt Mai. But I could impose it upon no one else.

The help & the ease then, which I ask from *you*, my dear Mother, is not to misinterpret what I am thus compelled either to say or else to give up my work. One person with health for these small but necessary offices is essential to me. More than one I have not the strength to see. During the time I have been in London, I have seen literally no one but those whom the necessities of business have compelled me to see. For these I am obliged to reserve such strength as remains to me.

If I could give companionship or receive it, I would beg you to come & share it with me.

I enclose a little Nasturtium or something else which the good people here give me for nosegays. It makes the prettiest winter vase-ful. I do not remember ever seeing it. You ought to have it.

> Ever my dear mum
> Your loving child
>
> F. N.

I hear that Lady Dunsany is much worse.

Source: Wellcome

In March 1858 Nightingale tried to relinquish her responsibility for the Nightingale Fund. Herbert, however, insisted that she appoint a committee to supervise the investment of the Fund until the nursing scheme could be implemented. He agreed to serve as chair, with Arthur Hugh Clough as the Secretary, and friends such as Sir John McNeill, Sir James Clark, William Bowman and Dr Bence Jones on the committee. Nightingale continued to concentrate on army sanitary reform, carefully protecting herself from Parthe and Fanny:

66. To Parthenope Nightingale   14 May 1858

My dear
    If you have anything to say to (or to hear from) me, will you come between 10 & 11 this morning; or, if that is too early, between 12 & 1; or, if you have any engagement at that time, could Mama come then; or if that is too early for her, could she write?
    But, if there is to be the going backwards & forwards there has been here yesterday & the day before, you will find that I shall not only be unable to help you, but that I shall be unable to live till Whitsuntide.
    ever yours while I can help

FN

Source: Wellcome

Nightingale travelled several times to Malvern for the water cure. From there she wrote to Clough on 30 July 1858:

> Pray do not trouble yourself about my correspondence *not* reaching me. That is the last thing to be feared. The scourge of civilization, the P.O., the worst Detectives, always finds one out. Mrs. Bracebridge used to put her letters into the porter's hands, with the money to pay for them, hoping he would pocket the money & lose the letters. I have no such recourse, tho', if I had, I would refuse to pay a single Postage. (BL Add 45795: f 3)

Most of the summer, however, was spent with Aunt Mai at the Burlington. Florence had many visitors, including the Queen of Holland and the Crown Princess of Prussia, all of whom were seeking her advice on hospitals and nursing. She also grudgingly agreed to be interviewed by Charles Kinglake for his official history of the Crimean War, although she distrusted him.
    In June Parthe married Sir Harry Verney (1801–94), heir to the historic mansion of Claydon House in Buckinghamshire.

Aristocratic, wealthy, handsome, he became a pioneer in rural housing and administration. From 1832 Sir Harry had been the Liberal member for Buckinghamshire. Upon his second marriage, Sir Harry became another of 'Florence's men'. On 17 July 1858 Florence wrote to Lady McNeill evaluating the marriage:

> Thank you very much for your congratulations on my sister's marriage, which took place last month. *She* likes it, which is the main thing – and my father is very fond of Sir Harry Verney, which is the next best thing. He is old and rich, which is a disadvantage. He is active, has a will of his own and 4 children ready-made, which is an advantage. Unmarried life, at least in our class, takes everything & gives nothing back to this poor earth. It runs no risk – it gives no pledge to life. So, on the whole, I think these reflections tend to approbation. My father & mother, who are now in Derbyshire, have both been to see my sister in her new home in Buckinghamshire (Claydon) & were well pleased. But, if you know, as is very likely, the family of the first Lady Verney, you will not 'faire part'[1] to them of my observations. Admiral Hope[2] has been very kind to my sister.
>
> I hope that you and Sir John are pretty strong.
>
> My affairs are going on pretty well. We have gained Alexander, as Director General, & lost Netley, which, in spite of its defects, is to be proceeded with as our Army Hospital. Mr. Herbert went abroad last week, quite done up – or thinking himself so. (GLRO HI/ST/NC3/SU/104)

1. faire part: make known.
2. Admiral Hope: Sir Henry Hope (1787–1863), KCB 1855; admiral, 1858; father of Sir Harry's first wife.

Florence relied upon her family to entertain her friends and allies. Various people arrived at Lea Hurst and Embley for much-needed holidays or as a reward for services they had performed. Specialists could be pressed into service, such as helping with architectural designs or sewerage plans. Fanny had always been generous, and visitors were an outlet for her sociability. These visitors probably also compensated to some extent for Florence's absence.

67. To W. E. Nightingale   30 Burlington St 8 Oct 1858

Dear Papa

I think this School affair such a brilliant opportunity of introducing civilization instead of brutality that I have done a daring thing.

I wrote to Rawlinson yesterday (he who Sanitarized the Crimea & Scutari) the first Water Engineer of the age & saw him this morning. He was going down to the Liverpool Meeting on Monday – & said directly that he would sleep at Lea Hurst on Monday & do your business for you.

He is quite the first authority in Sanitary water-appliances & has an enthusiasm for all these things. Any fee *I* will settle with him afterwards.

Pray forgive him for murdering the Q.'s English. I think it is so creditable to him. He was the son of a private soldier.

Let Beatrice ask him how it is possible to give boys & women an enthusiasm for keeping their own out-offices clean. And he will tell her about Alnwick.

He will go down on Monday by the train which reaches Ambergate at 2.30. And I promised he should be met there. I thought Mama would do it in her daily drive. And it saves strength & health. His is bad. And he must go on to Liverpool on Tuesday. Nevertheless, if you do not like it, could you send a message to the Ambergate Station Master to tell Mr. Rawlinson to go on to Cromford & that he will be fetched there.

Not having time for a reply from you, I have settled these things with him.

He is a man whom I like & respect far more than any one I met in the Crimea except Sir J. McNeill – far, far more than Sutherland.

He has a passion for Art & the country, so will be very easy for Mama to talk to. He would like very much to see the country.

With regard to the appliances, please tell Beatrice that I do not think expence must be considered. From a long experience of large bodies of men, I know that the best things are the cheapest in the end. And I should be very glad to take my share in the expence of proper appliances.

     ever dear Pa

                     Your loving child F.

Source: Wellcome

Worried that her blunt evaluation might be misunderstood, Florence hastily wrote to her father the next day:

A fear came over me that I had expressed myself as if Rawlinson were a kind of foreman & that you would not know where he was to dine or sleep. *[He sleeps with you on Monday night.]*

He is just as much a gentleman as you or I. And I know I shall have all kinds of difficulties in making him take a fee – altho' I expressly told him that I could only consult him professionally & that – no pay, no advice. (9 Oct 1858 Wellcome)

Nightingale kept up a massive correspondence with various reformers. A favourite ally was Sir Edwin Chadwick, one of the few survivors of the Poor Law Commission of 1834; both distrusted the younger generation of sanitarians. As advocates of prevention via ventilation and sanitation, they supported the miasmatic theory that disease arose spontaneously from filth, rather than from disease-specific germs. The growing body of medical men who favoured what we now call the germ theory seemed to undermine their campaigns for greater cleanliness, for this theory suggested that disease could occur in sanitary as well as unsanitary surroundings.

68. To Edwin Chadwick   30 Old Burlington St 6 Nov 1858

Dear Mr. Chadwick

I quite agree with you about the *moral* effect of the superior use of weapons upon our men. And I am glad to think, as I learn from good authority, that our school for teaching rifle-practice &c to the men of all arms is becoming the first in Europe.

With regard to 'Contagion', it is a great advantage to me to hear what people say. For I see no one.

Sanitary experience has so completely disproved the invisible 'seminal' Contagions that I can only see a mania for being wrong in such letters as Greenhow's & Simon's.[1]

With regard to the *material* 'Contagions', I have acknowledged them.

With regard to 'Infection', I believe in it just as much as I do in the emanations from sewage, and put them just on the same footing. But I say, where there is 'Infection', the fault is in those who have charge of the disease not in the disease. Give cubic space, keep your patients clean, ventilate your wards and there is no Infection.

I never knew a case of 'Infection' but there was gross mis-management and care-lessness.

I never heard an anecdote of 'Contagion' but it had *less* evidence than have witch-craft, magic &c to support them.

If I believe the 'auld wives' tales' of {page missing}

be unfit for Surgical cases – by the very Physicians themselves of those Hospitals.

In the well-constructed Hospitals I could mention, I have never heard either Doctors or Patients complain of the bad effects of either light or ventilation being too strong.

Please to look at the answer to Greenhow in to-day's 'Builder'.

I honor the development of the Pavilion system & the ventilation principle in Paris. But there is not a Hospital in Paris where the latrines, the sewerage or the water-supply are not things to be avoided, rather than to be imitated. They are quite behind hand there.

ever faithfully yours

Florence Nightingale

I must just say, with regard to 'cause' & 'effect': I don't want to go into any meta-physical disquisition as to what they are. But just let Messrs Greenhow, Simon & Sir C. Hastings[2] try the ordinary rule, (diminish, increase or remove the 'cause', & the 'effect' will be diminished, increased or removed also) upon 'Contagion' & 'Infection'.

With regard to Patients 'catching cold' in bed, if they did so in fresh air, all the patients in the Crimea must have died. For they lay looking up at the open sky thro' the chinks – & slits. Yet even in the worst time, the Mortality was one half what it was at Scutari & afterwards it became a mere trifle & this with the thermometer near zero.

F.N.

Source: BL Add 45770: ff 77–80   {incomplete}

1. Greenhow and Simon: Edward Hadlam Greenhow (1814–88), lecturer in public health at St Thomas' Hospital. He was much employed by the Board of Public Health and his classification of the causes of mortality were embodied in the Public Health Act of 1858. His eminent and influential colleague at St Thomas', Sir John Simon (1816–1904), was for many years the only London Medical Officer of Health; he was the author of *General Pathology as Conducive to the Establishment of Rational Principles for the Diagnosis and Treatment of Disease* (1850).

2. Sir Charles Hastings: (1794–1866), physician of the Worcester Infirmary and President of the public health section of the Social Science Association at York. He founded the British Medical Association and was editor of the *British Medical Journal* for many years.

In autumn 1858 Nightingale published, at her own expense, two thousand copies of an appendix to the report of the Royal Commission as a pamphlet, and sent these to influential people including the Queen, the Commander-in-Chief, Members of both Houses, commanding officers and doctors. Years later she explained to her friend Benjamin Jowett, Master of Balliol College:

> There is no public opinion – it has to be created – as to not committing blunders for want of knowledge. Good intentions are enough, it seems to be thought. Yet blunders, organized blunders, do more mischief than crimes. Carelessness, indifference, want of thought, when it is organized indifference, as in a family, as in a College or University, as in an Institution, as in a great Gov't office, organized carelessness is far more hurtful than even actual sin, as we may have occasion every day to find out. (8 Aug 1871 BL Add 45783: f 252)

Nightingale was always mistress of the carefully timed confidential leak, skilfully passing on selected information to powerful friends. A reliable ally was the well-known journalist Harriet Martineau, who willingly wrote articles for her. Although they differed about women's rights (Nightingale had tartly informed her, 'I am brutally indifferent to the wrongs or the rights of my sex' [30 Nov 1858 BL Add 45788: f 2]), she admired Martineau's tracts on political economy and trusted her discretion.

69. To Harriet Martineau

30 Old Burlington St
4 Dec 1858

Dear Miss Martineau,

I shall be very grateful to you if you will make use of my Report in the way you mention. All *such* help is most valuable to us. And, for the purpose of putting you in possession of the exact position in which our cause now stands, I shall, if you will kindly allow me, send you in a few days (i. e. as soon as it is out) an answer which I have been forced to make to anonymous attacks & pamphlets, circulated without printer's names, by traitors in our own camp. These are however only mentioned in a note.

The real object of this little thing (which is very short & need not frighten you) is to let our friends know *where we are*.

There is nothing 'confidential' in this – a 'Contribution to the

Sanitary History of the Army'. But, altho' I have inveighed against the anonymous attack, I had rather be kept anonymous myself.

I do not trouble you with any excuses about these things being not literary works & having no charm of style & so on. So long as I can secure some hold upon the minds of those who hold in their hands the remedies we are so urgently seeking, it is only under this aspect that style could be an object of attention to our crying for relief from sufferings so pressing.

The words you use about your own health are also, as far as I have been able to learn, applicable, word for word, to mine; which I only mention to shew that I too have 'no future' & must do what I can without delay.

Believe me Most sincerely yours

Florence Nightingale

P.S. I send you by this day's post, as you mention so kindly your interest in my especial branch, Hospital Nursing, my 'Subsidiary Notes on Female Nursing'. Please put this in the fire either way – i.e. after you have read it, if you feel inclined to read it – or without reading it, if you have no time or inclination that way. I think these manifestos do so much harm in fettering the steps of successors in one's own path. I send it to you only, because there has been so much rant & cant about us, so much misapprehension about what we did do & so much too about what we did not do, & chiefly by the female ink bottles (in which you are very sure I do not include yourself,) that it may interest you to know what a very plain, matter of fact thing Military Hospital Nursing really is.

The most affecting thing I think I ever read (& that must be 20 years ago) was your tale of the death of a drinking woman in one of your Political Economy stories. Since that, I have seen this in real life frequently & in its most terrible aspects. But I have never forgotten the lesson you taught, to work upon it with even friendly interest. F.N.

Source: BL Add 45788: ff 5–8

During these years Florence suffered periodically from a condition diagnosed as dilation of the heart and neurasthenia, then thought to be produced by excessive stress. Her symptoms included attacks of breathlessness and physical weakness, along with an inability to eat and sleep. Although the effects of the Crimean experience were obviously long-lasting, her condition appears to have been closely connected with her determination to control people and events. Uncle Sam finally broached the subject of Aunt Mai's return home; she had been gone for the major part of the time since she had replaced the Bracebridges in the Crimea. He appealed to Fanny, for everyone feared approaching Florence directly. When she heard of his request, Florence ranted about the impossibility of completing her work without Aunt Mai and Clough. All capitulated to her demands, but Clough's health, which had never been good, was now growing worse.

The greatest achievement of 1859 was the establishment of a Royal Commission for India. Ever since the Indian Mutiny of 1857, Nightingale had been collecting and studying mortality rates of the British army in India. Once again the killer was disease, not battle. She prevailed upon the Secretary of the India Office, her friend Lord Stanley, to form a Royal Commission. On 19 May 1859 she triumphantly wrote to Martineau:

> I must tell you a secret because I think it will please you. For eight long months I have been 'importunate-widowing' my 'unjust judge,' viz. Lord Stanley, to give us a Royal Sanitary Commission to do exactly the same thing for the Armies in India which the last did for the Army at home. We have just won it. The Queen has signed the Warrant. So it is safe. Mr. Sidney Herbert is Chairman of course. Drs. Sutherland, Martin, Farr, and Alexander, whose names will be known to you, and Sir R. Vivian and Sir P. Cautley, of the India Council, are on it. (BL Add 45788: f 55)

Lord Derby's government had resigned in March 1859, and Lord Palmerston once again became Prime Minister. Sidney Herbert, already chair of two commissions and four sub-commissions, was now appointed Secretary for War, one of the most demanding Cabinet posts. He was far from well; delays were inevitable.

The year 1860 began on an ominous note when Dr Alexander, Director of the Army Medical Department, died unexpectedly. More personally wrenching for Nightingale was the loss of her 'spiritual mother'; Aunt Mai decided in March to go home. Florence did not forgive her desertion for nearly twenty years. In a petulant letter to her father, written some time in the early 1860s, she complained:

70. To W. E. Nightingale   Undated

Dear Papa – I say nothing about myself. It would have done me so much good to have had one drop of sympathy. I, who for 4 years, have never heard one word of feeling from my own *family* – tho' I am sure they have never seen any one strained to the utmost pitch of endurance of body & mind, as I am. Adieu

FN

No key from home of my Lea desk

Source: Wellcome

There were, however, plenty of reminders that her beloved common soldiers – her children – had not forgotten her:

71. To Elizabeth Herbert   20 Mar 1860

Dearest

Hilary Carter told me of what you said about the men's desire to pray for me – and I believe the Chaplain General has been here about the same thing.

Now I had rather have the men's prayers than a vote of thanks from the House of Commons. And I think there can be no more precious acknowledgement of service done for them. But I should not like a War Office circular to order them to do it. And then you must also have a W.O. Circular to Almighty GOD to tell him to listen. And you must kill a Queen's messenger to take it.

Altogether I think the men had better be left to pray willingly, please. And I know they do it in some regiments.

This is my feeling about the matter – not because I do not value the prayers of the men but because I value them so much.

    ever yours

F Nightingale

Source: BL Add 43396: f 87   {copy}

Florence finally turned her attention to the Nightingale Fund. As an 'invalid', she obviously could not assume the superintendency of the proposed training school. St Thomas' Hospital had come to her attention when she was asked to comment on a proposed new site and building. She had been impressed with Mr Whitfield, the Resident Medical Officer, and with the reforming matron, Mrs Wardroper, who had sent her Mrs Roberts, one of the best of the Crimean nurses. Negotiations were entered into with the hospital to set up the Nightingale Nursing School. In spite of some opposition from resident doctors, who feared the loss of experienced but lower-class nurses, an agreement was successfully drawn up.

The Nightingale School of Nursing was not the first. Fliedner's school in Germany had existed for many years; Elizabeth Fry had established the Institute of Nursing as early as 1840; and St John's House where Florence's friend Mary Jones was the Superintendent, offered training. Nightingale has been called the founder of modern nursing because she created nursing as a trained secular occupation. But, as with sanitary reform, she was one among many seeking change. Indeed, nursing occupied a relatively small part of her time before the 1870s.

The first advertisements seeking candidates for nurses' training appeared in May 1860. The terms of service included uniforms, laundry, room and board, and seemed designed to attract the better sort of domestic servant. Those successful in the year-long course would be placed on the hospital register as 'Certified Nurses'. They then agreed to serve wherever the Fund sent them for five years. The expectations for these new nurses were high, and strict rules covered every aspect of their lives. Greater emphasis was placed on moral behaviour and character than on the acquisition of knowledge. Fifteen applicants for the first group were selected, and on 24 June the school was opened. Although Nightingale maintained that nurses were not housemaids and should not scour, there is little indication in the early days of a concerted effort to attract and retain educated women with leadership potential. Nightingale anxiously consulted her more experienced friend, Mary Jones:

72. To Mary Jones   30 Old Burlington St 15 May 1860

My dear Miss Jones
     As I hope to see you tomorrow at the hour you have been good enough to appoint viz. 3 o'clock, I only mean to trouble you now with three questions, which you may perhaps find it less troublesome to answer at home than here.

1. It is proposed that an age be fixed for our Probationers at entrance.

Yours are, I see, '25 to 40'. Do you approve this? Do you not find it difficult to teach a woman of near 40 any thing like Nursing, if she has not begun before?

2. It has been proposed that a form of testimonials, to be filled up by each Probationer, before she can be received, shall be prepared.

I think testimonials & proofs of character not worth the paper they are written on. What do *you* recommend?

3. It has been proposed not to admit *deserted* wives as Probationers. I think this is hard. Would you, requiring a certificate of marriage, refuse a wife whose husband had left her? Half the respectable Nurses, certainly, I have ever had, have been deserted wives.

4. It was suggested by Mr. Bowman that you thought the payment to your own Probationers for the first three months not enough. Is this so? As I understand you, it is £2.12.6 with all other expenses, (excepting clothing & 5/ per month.)

Enclosed is the sketch of what is offered to our Probationers. But it is still subject to alteration

Believe me

gratefully & affec'tely yours

Florence Nightingale

Source: GLRO HI/ST/NC1/60/2

In 1859 Nightingale had devised model forms for standardizing statistics in hospitals. She and Dr Farr, who was one of the General Secretaries of the International Statistical Congress, worked with several hospitals which agreed to use them on a trial basis. In the summer of 1860 the Congress met in London. Nightingale hosted several breakfasts for members which were presided over by cousin Hilary; a few luminaries were admitted to Nightingale's bedroom to meet her. In regard to hospitality, she was her mother's daughter; every arrangement was made for the comfort of the guests. Notes survive to Hilary, reminding her, 'Take care of your cream – for your breakfast. It is quite turned' and 'Put Dr. Balfour's big book where he can see it when drinking his tea' (Undated BL Add 45794: f 159). Farr and Nightingale drew up the programme for the Second Section of the Congress on Sanitary Statistics. Her scheme for Uniform Hospital Statistics was the principal subject of discussion. The Section discussed and approved her model forms, and the Congress resolved that her proposals be communicated to all the governments represented. But her forms proved too complicated, and were soon abandoned by hospital officials (Cook, I, 431–33).

73. To W. E. Nightingale

30 Old Burlington St
12 July 1860

Dear Pa

The 'International Statistical Congress' (of which I am a Member & for which I write papers) meets in London to day & for the next ten days – delegates from every civilized country come. Quetelet[1] is the Belgian one.

They meet at my rooms a good deal for business (I of course not seeing them) under Dr. Farr's Presidency – and I am obliged to give them to eat.

Lord Mayors, H.M's Ministers, P. Albert & all the Institutions of the country also give them to eat (but *not*, I suspect, for business.)

Now I want you to send me all your flowers, all your fruit, all your vegetables, in fact *all* you have got, for this great occasion – which is to 'cement the peace of Europe'!!!!

Also, Oat-cake or anything, you think, of our savage productions will do to shew our 'distinguished' foreigners.

If you did not dislike travelling, I should almost have thought it worth your while to run up & chatter French & Italian to them here, & take a brace of them back with you.

　　　ever dear Pa

your loving child F.

Source: Wellcome

1. Adolphe Quetelet: (1796–1874), Belgian astronomer, meteorologist and statistician who pioneered the application of statistics to social problems; he was a major influence on FN and Farr.

Religion was clearly a source of strength for Nightingale. She felt that the laws of God were discoverable by experience, research and analysis. But she distinguished between the character of God, which, she claimed, was knowable, and the essence of God, which would always remain a mystery. In a long letter describing her belief system, she wrote to her father:

> Granted we see signs of *universal* law all over this world, i.e. law or plan or constant sequences in the moral & intellectual as well as physical phenomena of the world – granted this, we must, in this universal law, find the traces of *a* Being who made it, and what is more of the *character* of the Being who made it. If we stop at the superficial signs, the Being is something so bad as no human character can be found to equal in badness. And certainly all the beings He has made are better than himself. But go deeper & see wider, & it appears as if this plan of *universal* law were the only one by which a good Being could teach his creatures to teach themselves & one another what the road is to universal perfection. And this we shall all acknowledge is the only way for any educa- tor, whether human or divine, to act – viz. to teach men to teach themselves and each other. (6 July 1859 BL Add 45790: ff 186–87)

Her friend Benjamin Jowett occasionally pressed her to be more specific, chastising her: 'During the ten years & more that I have known you, you have repeated to me the expression "character of God" about 1,100 times, but I cannot say that I have any clear {idea} of what you mean, if you mean anything more than divine perfection...' (31 Oct {1872} Quinn and Prest, p. 234).

Somehow during the busy years of the late 1850s Nightingale found time to complete and publish privately *Suggestions for Thought* (1859), written to provide a rationale for religious belief for intelligent artisans. She sent the 829 large octavo pages to McNeill, Milnes, Jowett, and the philosopher John Stuart Mill, for their advice about wider publication.

74. To John Stuart Mill   30 Old Burlington St 12 Sept 1860

Dear Sir

Taking advantage of your extreme kindness (an article which nobody ever fails to take advantage of) I have sent you, by Book Post, Vol 1 of the religious work in question. There are, I am sorry to say, two other 'devils', (I mean Vols:,) 'worse than the first'.

But, as I fear you will never read five pages of the first, I have, with admirable caution, sent you only one.

From a word you have used (in your very kind note to me,) I do not think it is quite the sort you expect. But that will not make it the less tedious.

Without farther discussion, I accept, from so great a master of language as yourself, the interpretation you have put upon some words in my 'Notes on Nursing', & will alter these words in the next Edit'n. But, as a matter of fact, I protest against your assertion that there is no such class as the one I designate as talking a 'jargon'. You have not seen, as I have seen, a 'scratting' female, (I use the significant old Derbyshire word) among a world of 'scratting' females (& very odd ones too).

To every word of an Article, called by your name, on this subject, I heartily subscribe & defer. *This* is not the 'jargon' I mean. I refer to an American world, consisting of female M.D.s, &c, & led by a Dr. Eliz'th. Blackwell, and, though the latter is a dear & intimate & valued friend of mine, I re-assert that her world talks a 'jargon', & a very mischievous one – that their female M.D.s have taken up the worst part of a male M.D.ship, of 30 years ago – & that, while Medical education is what it is – a subject upon which I may talk with some 'connaissance de cause',[1] – instead of wishing to see more Doctors made by women joining what there are, I wish to see as few Doctors, either male or female, as possible. For, mark you, the women have made no improvement – they have only tried to be 'Men', & they have only succeeded in being third-rate men. They will not fail in getting their own livelihood, but they fail in doing good & improving Therapeutics. I am only here stating a matter of fact. I am not reasoning as you suppose.

Let all women try. These women have, in my opinion, failed. But this is no *a priori* conclusion against the principle.

allow me to be faithfully & gratefully Yours

Fl. Nightingale

Source: BUL N62: Box 2, Folder 4

1. connaissance de cause: knowledge.

Anxious to conciliate the great man, in a later letter Nightingale conceded: 'I *quite* agree that "the more the entrance to the Med'l Profession is widened, the more chance of its being reformed"' (28

Sept 1860 BUL N62: Box 2, Folder 4), but she could not bring herself to approve of women doctors.

Nightingale was clearly flattered when Mill agreed to read the entire *Suggestions for Thought*. She admitted to him: 'I am sure you will not suspect me of false modesty, when I say that the "want of arrangement" & of "condensation" I feel to be such, that nothing but my circumstances can excuse my submitting it to you in such a state' (28 Sept 1860 BUL N62: Box 2, Folder 4). Although Mill recommended publication with minor changes, Milnes, McNeill and Jowett all felt that considerable revision was necessary. Nightingale knew that she wrote repetitiously, for writing remained a springboard to action. Impatient with revision, she went no further than private publication.

Nightingale's opinion on hospital architecture continued to be sought by people around the world. In *Notes on Hospitals* (1863) she attacked the unsanitary conditions of existing hospitals, and recommended her favourite 'pavilion' plan. Separate pavilions or wings for each ward would prevent infection by confining a specific disease to a wing and providing cross-ventilation and ample sunshine through a double row of windows. The Sister or head nurse could see clearly every patient in her wing. The hospitals had to avoid becoming repositories of both physical disease and moral degeneration.

75. To Robert Rawlinson   Hampstead NW 27 Sept 1860

Dear Mr. Rawlinson

I have only just read over Dr. Combe's[1] paper in the 'Builder' describing a plan for a Regimental Hospital. There are some points in it, which I do not like to pass over, without writing to you. Perhaps you would think well to write to Mr. Godwin[2] about them. I cannot enter into any controversy. But principles are at stake. And as there is an *appearance* of knowledge in the paper, I ought at least, to state my opinion on the plan, in order that, at all events, you may not think that I acquiesce in it.

The *appearance* of truth consists in using Pavilions with windows on opposite sides – and in stating broadly the obvious fact that care & discipline cannot be maintained in 'small' wards.

The *error* is in the proposed arrangement. For no one conversant with Hospital construction would ever build a Hospital in three radii with closed angles.

There are new Regimental Hospitals, about to be built, in which the sick are to be *in line*, as they ought to be. In fact, Dr. Combe's plan is only a bad version of these new Hospitals, *plus* the radius at right angles.

2. Again, his ward dimensions are not by any means good. And he does not make the best of the '1200 cubic feet per bed', allowed by the new 'Medical Regulations'.

3. It is impossible to understand on what principles he has placed his W.C. in the middle of the length of one side, & his Scullery opposite.

The result would be that the Scullery would become a mere gossiping place for Patients & Orderlies. And, whenever the Wind blew against the side, where the W.C. is, the foul air, incident to Military Hospital W.C.'s, would be carried directly into the wards.

4. I am not able to go into the errors of detail in the Offices. There are 30 separate apartments (or places) for 92 beds – or nearly one for every 3 Patients. Of all things, avoid unnecessary holes & corners in Military Hospitals – additional places to clean (also to skulk in.)

5. The large hall is an unnecessary expence.

6. The Hospital Serjeant is placed exactly where he ought *not* to be, viz. at the greatest distance from the wards. The Hospital Serj't ought to overlook his wards *by day & by night*. Military Hospitals are to cure the sick, not to be married in.

7. There are two wards of 4 beds each, which have only one window each, & are not ventilated enough for a dog to sleep in. Dr. Combe, it is true, condemns the wards, but at the same time counts the beds into his 'ninety-two beds'. The first thing I should do in an old Hospital would be to close them altogether. I have seen such (in a Brit. Mil. Hosp.) for Ophthalmic Cases, (as he recommends,) which were nests of disease & of *Ophthalmic* disease too.

8. The administrative Offices are so placed that, besides there being an entire absence of anything like Architecture in them, they would increase the difficulty of administration.

9. I am no Engineer, but I would ask you whether his drainage is not as original as it is unnecessarily costly.

10. I am told that his Estimate of £100 per bed is nearly double that for which better (one-story) Hospitals have been already estimated for.

11. Lastly, Dr. Combe appears never to have apprehended the idea of a 'General Hospital'; he considers it necessary to 'agglomerate' sick together, in order to realize a 'General' Hosp'l.

The Pavilion structure was introduced expressly, in order to make possible a General Hospital, without any one of the risks of 'agglomeration'. There are General Hospitals at this moment with fewer sick under one roof than Dr. Combe puts in his 'Segregation', which he justly insists upon, will be effectually carried out in the new *Woolwich* Hospital – if by 'segregation' he means the placing but a small number of sick in each building, & the isolating each building so as to form houses *much more* separate than the houses in a street are.

I am quite sure that Mr. Godwin is not taken in by these Neo-Hospital Constructionists. But I am sorry that he lends the great authority of the 'Builders' to them.

Upon another subject, I see

1. that Dr. Combe, who is an extremely able Medical Officer, supposes that the new Woolwich Hospital is to be an 'agglomeration' of 'Regimental Hospitals'. Such is not the case. It is to be a *General* Hospital under the new Regulations. [An agglomeration of Regimental Hospitals is simply an absurdity.]

2. that, judging by the style, the same hand has several times supplied the 'Builder' with a criticism on the Woolwich Hospital site.

Once, he proposed a site which would have required the Repository, where men are drilled to their duties, at Woolwich, to be abolished.

He proposed another, past which the Mortar practice takes place.

He proposed a third, which Sir Thomas Wilson would not sell; and now he objects to the site chosen, 'because it is on clay', *which it is not.* It is, I am told, on the Woolwich pebble bed, clay mixed with shingle, to obviate even the risk of damp from which the whole building will be raised on a basement, mostly above the level of the ground.

It would have better served the public interest, had Dr. Combe said where a better site was to be had.

I merely mention this, because I have taken at least as much interest in it as Dr. Combe has. And I watched anxiously for every hint the 'Builder' might contain, & *found none*, only helpless objections.

This letter is, of course, only for yourself (&, should you choose to shew it to Mr. Godwin, for him).

Discussion always does good. I have no pretension to 'lay down the law'. Nor has Mr. Robertson, to whom I see Dr. Combe attributes my papers in the 'Builder'.

The 'Builder' *had already*, & *has since*, enunciated sound principles of Hospital construction. But, alas! it does not follow that principles, however sound, necessarily involve their being comprehended or applied in practice. I wish the present case were the only one I knew (of such failure), since the 'Builder' first advocated Hospital reform.

I think I shall follow your advice of getting out, as soon as possible, a Manual of Hospital Construction – when, as I shall be obliged to make use largely of my Articles in the 'Builder', I suppose Dr. Combe will accuse me of plagiarizing Mr. Robertson, a man I greatly respect & admire.

Thank you very much for your two parcels of Books & Reports. Your Article on 'water' I had not seen. Most of the others (by you) I have. Yet not the Woolwich one. Marked by you, they are the more useful to me. But I would return them to you, if you want them – for presents.

Thank you very much for the beautiful little compasses.

Ever, dear Mr. Rawlinson Yours very truly

Florence Nightingale

R. Rawlinson, Esq.
Dr. Combe invites criticism in express words. And I believe is very fairly open to it. He is one of the best Officers the Dep't has. There are some curious little errors about *orderly attendance* on sick. But I don't think these are things for the Builder's pages.

Source: BUL N62: Box 1, Folder 1, #17

1. Dr Matthew Combe: (1824–89), served as a Surgeon Major in the Royal Artillery in the Crimea; appointed to the Army Medical Department in 1866.
2. Mr George Godwin: (1815–88), editor of *The Builder* from 1844. He was particularly concerned with the housing and sanitary conditions of the poor. Author of *London Shadows* (1854).

By the end of 1860, Sidney Herbert's health had broken down. Florence was obviously frightened at the prospect of losing her most powerful ally, and resorted to denying the medical reports. Common sense, fresh air and rest would solve all Herbert's health problems.

76. To Elizabeth Herbert   Hampstead 5 Dec 1860

Dearest
I cannot help writing to you of what I think of night & day, tho' perhaps I ought not to write.

I. I do trust you will make Mr. Herbert have farther advice. All that he told me on Sunday makes me only wish this the more.

The reason Bence Jones gives for *not* consulting Williams[1] appears to me the strongest reason for doing so.

Williams is an old 'muff', I know; but he is one of the cleverest Pathologists we have – and he has known Mr. Herbert a long time, which is the main reason.

It is difficult to me to say why, in so important a matter, Bence Jones's opinion ought not to be considered *a verdict*; altho' the fact of there being albumen I do not in the least doubt; & the necessity of Mr. Herbert giving up the Ho: of C. is, alas! I believe, paramount.

But I will try to give you the reasons

1. Bence Jones is a chemical doctor; the best we have. But a chemical Doctor's opinion is not always the best. I can only shew this by taking the converse. I have known B. Jones make up a diet for a Patient by the purest rules of Chemical Science – only the Patient's stomach did not think so. And this *only* was every thing.

Take the converse. B. Jones tries his Patient (Mr. Herbert) and condemns him on chemical evidence furnished by himself (the albumen). I want to know how many men there are, suffering from London 'Cachexia', (which is only a fine word for ill-health – i.e. imperfect nutrition) who would *not* shew albumen, if they were tried. Why is nature parting with all this albumen? Generally because she is *helping herself.*

Give her fair play to help herself, but don't despair of her.

2. You do not know how strong a temptation it is to a conscientious Chemical doctor, like Bence Jones, to give such an opinion as he has done. Because it would be relieving himself of such a terrible responsibility, if he could persuade Mr. Herbert into giving up all work.

You do not know how often this is done with Patients who are merchants or professional men. And what happens? Nine times out of ten the man dies within a year after 'retiring', as it is called. This is quite a proverb I believe that leaving political life or any life-interest *altogether* is more likely to kill than to cure – always.

3. You will not find that these opinions as to *mere Chemical* doctors, or *mere Pathological* doctors, are unique. The best, those who have most common-sense of these men, will say so *of themselves.*

II. I wish Mr. Herbert would see Williams the latter being acquainted with Bence Jones's opinion & in concurrence with him. These need not meet till after they have seen Mr. Herbert separately.

If they differ, then I do wish Mr. Herbert would see some doctor of strong common-sense himself & let *him* settle the difference.

Brodie[2] is the best, but Brodie is blind, and though I had rather have blind Brodie than another man with his eye-sight (for a *consultation*) perhaps Brodie does not think so himself.

Christison[3] is the next best; i.e. the best Chemical doctor with the strongest common sense. But perhaps Christison is not so much acknowledged as to make it worth while to have him from Edinbro'.

Watson[4] is the next best. And Watson is at hand, has got his eyes & has an acknowledged reputation.

What you want is somebody to take Nature's part.

I do not say all this by way of comforting you but because it is the truth. I tried to tell Mr. Herbert this on Sunday. But I did not feel I made myself clear.

I would not the least undervalue the danger of Mr. Herbert going on as he is now.

It is imperative that he should leave the Ho. of C.

I believe it is imperative that when in London, he should sleep just out of town every night – even if he dined in London. Many professional men, who have, of course, not the command of horses & carriages he has, do this, who are compelled to keep up a house in town too. I deprecate Belgrave Sq. for him. But only *sleeping* out of it would be a great thing.

[I doubt the rightness of his riding. It irritates just those parts which are now irritable. But this is solely an old Nurse's opinion. And I should be the first to give it up, if Doctor's, in *his* case, say 'yes']

The other things I have said are matters of almost *universal experience*.

      ever dearest yours

                                  F.N.

Source: BL Add 43396: ff 89–96

1. Charles James Blasius Williams, MD: (1805–89), Professor of Medicine and physician to University College, London. Physician Extraordinary to Queen Victoria.

2. Sir Benjamin Brodie: (1783–1862), Surgeon and Professor at St George's Hospital. President of the Royal Society of Surgeons (1858–61).

3. Sir Robert Christison, MD: (1797–1882), Professor of Medicine, University of Edinburgh and specialist in chemistry and toxology; Queen's physician in Scotland.

4. Sir Thomas Watson, MD: (1792–1882), a leading London physician; active member of the Royal College of Physicians.

At Nightingale's urging, Herbert gave up the House of Commons and became a member of the House of Lords so that as Secretary for War, he might continue their reforms. He had already surrendered to Lord Stanley the chairmanship of the Royal Commission on India. In January 1861 Sidney Herbert issued a new Purveyor's Warrant and Regulations in which the duties and regulations were well defined, as well as their relation to the Army Medical Department. All the necessities and comforts for men in the hospital were provided on a fixed scale. Committees were set up to study how coffee rooms, lecture rooms, reading rooms, soldiers' workshops and recreational facilities could be provided. Improvements Nightingale had initiated unofficially in the East were now part of army regulations.

The reformers had concrete evidence by this time that their recommendations paid off. Statistically, between 1859 and 1861 the mortality rate at home stations had been halved. The China expedition, another test case, showed a marked drop in the army's death rate from disease. Other reforms that had been begun or accomplished by this time included the formation of an Army Sanitary Committee, a cookery school at Aldershot, the maintenance of General Military Hospitals, an Army Medical School at Fort Pitt, Chatham (moved to Netley in 1863), the publication annually of Army Medical Statistics, the improvement of the status of Army Medical Officers, and a regularly organized Medical Staff Corps. New barrack and hospital construction was being undertaken.

But the bureaucratic structure of the War Office remained beyond change; Nightingale wrote sorrowfully to Harriet Martineau, 'To me the blow is even more severe than it is to him. {Herbert} Because I know he is a man not of organizing capacity (my heart is sick when I think nothing is yet done to re-organize the War Office . . .' (4 Jan 1861 BL Add 45788: f 104). As Sir Edward Cook said,

> To reorganize the War Office on paper is an occupation which, during fifty following years, was to beguile the leisure of amateurs, and to fill with disappointed hopes the laborious days of many a Minister. To carry out any such scheme into practice is a task which only a Minister, in full fighting force, could hope to accomplish. It was beyond the power of a dying man. (Cook, I, 403)

In spite of the break with Aunt Mai, Uncle Sam still continued to work for Florence on the Nightingale Fund. In February 1861, when a maverick reformer she admired died unexpectedly, Florence turned to him as a sympathetic family member.

77. To Samuel Smith

30 O. B. St 25 Feb 1861

Dear Uncle Sam

Adshead of Manchester is dead – my best pupil.

I wrote to condole with a friend of his – intending my letter to be sent to his widow whom I do not know – saying how great the loss was – & how I hoped that Manchester would pay his memory the tribute which, of all others, he would have liked – the carrying out his plans (all finished) for a Country Hospital.

The friend writes me back the answer (enclosed) asking me to let my letter be published.

And this is what I want to consult you about.

I am afraid you do not know who Adshead is. So I must explain.

How often I have called him my 'dear old Addle-head'. And now he is dead.

I had a letter from him about his plans – perhaps the last he ever wrote – saying he was 'better'. And then the next thing was – a pair of black gloves and a fine white Mausoleum painted on a black card – from the Undertaker – dear old custom of my North country – which I have so carefully fulfilled for my own old people & cannot laugh at – minus the Mausoleum.

Adshead was a man who could hardly write or speak the Queen's English (I believe he raised himself) & was now a kind of manufacturer's agent in Manchester. He was a man of very ordinary abilities; common-place appearance – vulgar but *never* unbusiness-like which is, I think, the worst kind of vulgarity.

Having made 'a competency', he did not give up business, but devoted himself to good works for Manchester. And there is scarcely a good thing in Manchester of which he has not been the main-stay or the source.

> the Schools
> > Infirmary
> > Paving &
> > > Draining
> > > Water-supply
> > > &c &c &c
> > > &c &c &c

At 60, he takes up an entirely new subject, Hospital Construction, fired by my book, & determines to master it. This is what I think is peculiar to the Anglo-Saxon.

He writes to me whether I will teach him – (this is about 18 months ago) and composes some plans for a Convalescent Hospital far out of Manchester to become the main Hospital, if the wind is favourable.

He comes up to London to see me about these.

The working plans passed eight times thro' my hands and gave me more trouble than anything I ever did. *Because* Adshead *would not* employ a proper Builder but *would* do them himself – which is part of the *same character*, I believe.

The plans are now quite ready – but nothing more.

He meant to *beg in person* all over Lancashire – & had already some promises of large sums.

Now all this is cut short.

He had been ailing for about a year – but never intermitted anything.

I don't know whether you remember that I had a three months' correspondence with him (and oh! the immense trouble he took) about the transplantation of the Spitalfields & Coventry weavers to Manchester & its districts, Preston, Burnley &c. And how ill Miss Sellon behaved. It never came to any thing about *her* people. I hate Miss Sellon now for it, because I think it hastened his death, tho' *he* would not have minded it, if it had come to good.

He was 61 when he died.

This is the character which I believe is quite peculiar to our race – a man – a common tradesman – who, instead of 'retiring from the world' to 'make his salvation' – or giving himself up to science or to his family in his old age – or founding an Order – or building a house – will patiently (at 60) learn new dodges & new fangled ideas in order to benefit his native city.

Oh how superior I do feel this sort of character to the Sutherlands who pursue the same things for the love of science & capriciously – to the Sellons who cut themselves off from the world & from all progress in ideas to found 'Orders' – to the statesmen, like Lord Spencer, & to the R. Catholics like Pascal, who retire from their life's business for their own 'individual salvation'.

And how I do feel that it is the strength of our country, & worth all the R. Catholic 'Orders' put together. I hate an 'Order' & am so glad I was never 'let in' to form one.

Do you know that St. George's Hosp'l have embezzled A. Morley's legacy for a Convalescent Branch? and that Adshead was actually employed when he died, upon my information, in trying whether it were legally possible to institute Chancery proceedings against them. For it was *not only* Manchester that he cared about.

However, that is all over now. And his plan for Manchester is the only one which will fulfill my ideal of a Country Hospital.

Now, what is to be done? For that is the question.

I don't want to be dragged into holding subscription Lists –

neither into an opposition to all the Manchester Doctors. There is a hot controversy in the Manchester papers now. *Every* day one side or the other sends me an Article.

Please return the enclosed
    Ever yours gratefully

F. N.

Source: BL Add 45792: ff 135–43

In February Nightingale was working on a more uniform system of statistics. She seized the opportunity of a census year to include questions relating housing to the number of sick in different parts of the country. Locked in a struggle with Sir George Lewis, the Home Secretary, she was unable to gain supporters who would speak effectively in either House. No one could understand the value of the information she wanted, and the battle was lost. She transferred her labours to the Secretary of the Colonies and began collecting facts there, particularly on India.

78. To William Farr   30 Old Burlington St 9 Apr 1861

My dear Dr. Farr

As you justly said that the perfect working of the Census must depend upon the detail, I think I am doing you a service in mentioning how the detail was worked here.

(I should say that this vast Hotel, 'Burlington Hotel', consisting of three large houses, besides *this*, (which is the 'private' house) is composed mainly of *family* suites of rooms.)

On Sunday morning (the 7th) a verbal message was sent up to me, *not* by the occupier of the Hotel but by his fac-totum, (a kind of house-steward,) desiring me to write my age (& my maid's) on a bit of paper – *nothing more*. This was the message, verbatim et literatim.

I swallowed the answer which rose to my lips – not thinking it worth while to have a war of words with this person – and, after ascertaining from his assertion that no Schedules had been left for the Families in this Hotel, I took one of the Specimen Forms you were so kind as to give me, & wrote the information fully & accurately therein concerning myself & maid (the man servant does not sleep in the Hotel) & sent it down to him.

I leave you to think, if the message sent up to the other families occupying apartments in these 4 houses, were similar to that sent to me, of how dependable & valuable a nature is the information filled in by this person on his Sheet.

He appeared to consider the Census Act as an invention designed to afford him the amusement of asking people their ages – and of drawing upon his imagination for the rest of the information required.

As you know how much interested I am in the proper working of the Census & that I had rather the information required of us (as regards our healths & houses) were more than less complete, I venture to suggest that all heads of families, whether that family consist of one, two or more persons, wherever living, whether in hotels, lodgings &c should be required to fill up their own paper.

Believe me, (from my personal experience of what happened here) people who have not reflected much on the value of a Census have a very different conscience, as to affording *accurate* information, when called upon to do so by an ignorant Hotel servant, & when called upon directly by the law, which all English people obey. And this observation I think applies rather more to the 'upper' than to the 'lower classes', as they are called.

Believe me sincerely yours

Florence Nightingale

You are quite at liberty to make any use of this.
N.B. The terms 'heads of families' should include single persons, living in Hotels & lodging-houses, all of whom should have the opportunity of filling up separate papers.

You will say that you would then have to send papers to every lodger in a two-penny lodging-house.

But might you not place on the Superintend'g Registrar the duty of ascertaining or deciding what class of Hotels and Lodging-houses should have separate papers for their inmates – the Enumeration being then directed to leave the required number?

Source: BL Add 43399: ff 10–12   {copy}

After years of struggling against poor hospital architecture Nightingale's ire was easily roused.

79. To Captain Douglas Galton

30 O. B. St.
20 June 1861

My dear Capt. Galton

This defies criticism. There is no improvement possible. If the object is to build a suitable Hospital where people are to have a chance of recovery – & not to cover a particular bit of ground with buildings – what can one say to this but condemn it utterly?

Even with this particular bit of ground – even with the condition of combining a Lock[1] with a General Hospital – this is the very worst construction possible.

And a different & better plan might be made even on the same piece of ground.

Where you can't improve, you don't know how to criticize.

E.g. that there should be no closed angle in any Hospital building is a first principle. Therefore this Architect bisects the angle with an extraordinary spike. And then he crams up the *two* angles thus formed with out-Office-buildings – why? that there may be no closed angle.

2. Then, having made a gully for the wind to blow into, he places Lavatories & W.C's just where when the wind blows in that direction, it will blow all into the wards.

3. For a Hospital of 60 beds, of whom half Lock patients, what a ridiculous Surgical establishment – nearly one third of the building.

4. Are the people in Devonport born triangular? or on an average how many are born so? or what is the meaning of these triangular wards?

5. Is the Architect's ideal the profile of a revolver-pistol? If you look at the block plan in this point of view, it is very good.

But as he asks me my opinion, it is that I would much rather be shot outside than in.

As Hospital principles are beginning to be well known, it would be quite enough to engrave this plan on the card of solicitation, to stop all subscriptions.

No Patient will ever get well here. And as I don't approve of the principle of Lock Hosp'ls, I had much better let it go on.

Seriously the plan is unimprovable. And if he wants me to criticize it, he must make one upon the (now) well-recognized principles of construction.

You show him your Regimental one. And he produces this!!!!!

Yours ever truly

F.N.

Source: BL Add 45759: ff 228–29

1. Lock hospital: for patients with venereal diseases.

Sidney Herbert struggled with his obligations until the very end. Florence saw him for the last time on 9 July, when he paid her a visit before going abroad to a spa. He died on 2 August of kidney failure. Florence was determined to continue 'his' work at whatever personal cost in spite of her profound grief. Beneath the self-pity which gave so much credit to herself and so little to others, one can sense her inconsolable pain.

80. To W. E. Nightingale   Hampstead NW 21 Aug 1861

Dear Papa

Indeed your sympathy is very dear to me. So few people know in the least what I have lost in my dear master. Indeed I know no one but myself who had it to lose. For no two people pursue together the same object as I did with him. And when they lose their companion by death, they have in fact lost no companionship. Now he takes my life with him. My work, the object of my life, the means to do it, all in one, depart with him.

'Grief fills the room up of my absent' master. I cannot say it 'walks up & down' with me. For I don't walk up & down. But it 'eats' & sleeps & wakes with me.

Yet I can truly say that I see it is better that God should not work a miracle to save Sidney Herbert, altho' his death involves the misfortune, moral & physical, of five hundred thousand men – & altho' it would have been but to set aside a few trifling physical laws to save him. And altho' he killed me, on whose life that of the Army hung. And nothing but his own life made this worth while.

If you would like to read the enclosed to Sir {missing page} what it should be to a man of that stamp –

Lord pity us – for we know not what we are about.

'The righteous perisheth & no man layeth it to heart' – the Scripture goes on 'none considering that he is taken away from the evil to come'. *I* say 'none considering that he is taken away from the good he might have done'.

Now, not one man remains (that I can call a man) of all those whom I began work with, five years ago.

And I alone, of all men 'most deject & wretched', survive them all. I am sure I meant to have died.

Pray be careful how you write this heavy news. For Bertha has not been very well & they keep it from her.

The news was only received at Combe this morning.

ever dear Pa your loving child

F.

Parthe has found time & strength to write me 8 closely written pages of worry, worry, worry because I said that *her* house was 'devoted' to 'talk'. I cannot think who could have told her that I said so. I hope, dear Papa, that it is quite understood between us that my letters to you are *for you alone*. I always thought that you desired this as much as I do. It is indeed quite necessary. This is the reason why I was so unwilling to come into any house of Parthe's, to accept any obligation from her. This is the *third* time this fatal year that she has chosen my time of deepest misery & distress to give me a scold 8 pages long.

Source: BL Add 45790: ff 217–21

As if to justify her refusal to recognize the seriousness of Herbert's illness, Nightingale wrote long letters to all her friends seeking sympathy. She confessed to Martineau: 'And I too was hard upon him. I told him that Cavour's death . . . was a blow to European liberty, but that a greater blow was that a Sidney Herbert should be beaten on his own ground by a bureaucracy. I told him that no man in my day had thrown away so noble a game with all the winning cards in his hands' (24 Sept 1861 BL Add 45788: ff 134–35). Nightingale, who so often reused phrases from her own letters, was quoting Sir John McNeill's letter of 18 June 1861, when he had written to her about Herbert: 'No one in my day has I think thrown away or at least failed to play out with success so noble a game of which all the winning cards were in his hand' (BL Add 45768: ff 138–39).

When unfavourable obituaries appeared, blaming Herbert for the Crimean War deficiencies, Gladstone asked Nightingale to write a memorial. She identified Herbert as an army reformer and astutely mentioned the work that had not been completed. No opportunity was missed to nudge the government.

81. To William Farr   Hampstead NW 10 Sept 1861

My dear Mr. Farr

We are grateful to you indeed for the memorial of my dear master which you have raised to him in the hearts of the nation. Indeed, it is in the hearts of the nation that he will live – not in the hearts of the Ministers. There, he is dead already, if indeed they have any. And before he was cold in his grave – Gladstone attends his funeral & then writes to me that he cannot pledge himself to give any assistance in carrying out his friend's reforms. The reign of intelligence at the War Office is over. The reign of muffs has begun. The only rule of conduct in the bureaucracy there & in the Horse Guards is to reverse *his* decision, *his* judgment & (if they can do nothing more) his words.

Lord de Grey maintains the fight well. He said to the Commander in Chief, when he was asking Sir G. Lewis (*the* muff) to reverse one of my dear master's acts, Sir, it is impossible: Ld Herbert decided it & the House of Commons voted it.

But what is Ld de Grey against so many?

We have nothing more to expect from that quarter of Ministers.

But you, & such as you, will make my dear master's acts live in the memory of the nation. And it shall be the nation who will carry out his work. The first gleam of hope I have had was in hearing your paper.

You say truly that it was his work, not his reputation, which he cared for. (He had *no* ambition) – & that the best tribute, the only one he would like, would be to carry out his work. His last articulate words, often repeated, were, 'Poor Florence – our unfinished work' – words too sacred to be repeated, but that they shew the man. That was his last dying thought. Other men's is a selfish anxiety after their own salvation.

Oh if he could have said, 'It is finished', how willingly we could have given him back to God. But he could not. Even I did not know till the last how the failure of his energy to carry out the finishing stroke, which was wanting, the re-organization of the War Office, had broken his heart – & how it hastened his death. I blamed him – but not so much as he blamed himself. And I think it is a tribute to his great simplicity to say how little he thought of what he had done – how much of what he had left undone. It was this failure in re-organizing the War Office which has left his work now to be upset *there* by any clerk.

But it is for his friends now to see what they can do *out of* the War Office. You loved him. No one loved & served him as I did. But you & many more will stand by his work, which *is* his memory.

To me & (I may say) to himself, his death, as you may well suppose, was nothing. It was the resignation, of Office, without having re-organized the Office, which was the bitterness of death, both to him & to me. Five years, all but one week, had he & I worked together at the health of that noble Army.

I felt very down-hearted about the Indian Commission since his resignation. But, since your paper, I feel that his friends will rally round his memory to carry out that most important part of the work as he would have wished.

The Barrack Commission starts tomorrow for the Mediterranean Inspection – one of his last official acts. Till the day fortnight of his death, do you know, he struggled on, doing to the last what he could in the Office.

That I should have survived him seems to me most curious. He who could do so much without me. I who can do nothing without him.

My last tie is severed with that noble Army, which I have served so faithfully seven years next October – in weariness oft, in watchings oft, in prisons, I can truly say with St Paul.

For last month makes four years that I have been imprisoned by sickness.

The Army's work has cost three useful lives. But when I hear what you say, I hope that it is not over. On the contrary, that it is rooted by you & yours in a nation's mind.

ever yours sincerely

Florence Nightingale

I venture to send for your host one of my little books. He is known so well by reputation that I think he will not despise it for his poor.

Source: BL Add 43399: ff 41–43

Whatever may have been her feelings about severing her ties with 'that noble Army', other causes demanded Nightingale's attention. In September 1861 a portion of the Nightingale Fund was used to start a midwives' school at King's College Hospital under the superintendence of Mary Jones. Once again she turned to Harriet Martineau to publicize the new project.

82. To Harriet Martineau   Hampstead NW 24 Sept 1861

My dear Mrs. Martineau

I think you will be glad to hear that we are about to open (in

October) a Training School for Midwife-Nurses at King's College Hospital, London.

They are to be persons selected by country parishes, (whether personated by clergy, ladies or Committees or Boards,) between 26 and 35 years of age, of good health & good character, to follow a course of *not less* than 6 months practical training, & to conform to all the rules of St. John's House, (which nurses at King's Coll: Hosp:), while there.

No farther obligation is imposed upon them by us. They are supposed to return to their parishes & continue their avocation there.

I am sorry that we shall be obliged to require a weekly sum from their board – but which will be merely the cost price – not less than 8/ or more than 9/ a week.

Our funds do not permit us, at least at first, to do this cost free. For (the Hospital being very poor) we have had to furnish the Maternity ward & are to maintain the Lying-in beds. In fact, we establish this branch of the Hospital, which did not exist before.

The women will be taught their business by the Physician Accoucheurs themselves – who have most generously entered, heart & soul, into the plan – at the bedside of the Lying in Patients in this ward, the entrance to which is forbidden to the men-students – and they will also deliver poor women at their own homes, Out-Patients of the Hospital. The Head Nurse of the ward, who is paid by us, will be an experienced midwife, so that the pupil-Nurses will never be left to their own devices.

They will be entirely under the Lady Sup't of the Hospital – certainly the best moral trainer of women I know. They will be lodged *in* the Hospital, close to her.

If I had a sister of 18, I should gladly send her to this School – so sure am I of its moral goodness -- which I mention because I know poor mothers are quite as particular as rich ones, not merely as to the morality but as to the propriety of their daughters.

In nearly every country but our own, there is a Government School for Midwives. I trust that our School may lead the way towards supplying a want, long felt in England. Here we experiment & if we succeed, we are sure of getting candidates. I am not sure this is not the best way.

I hope we shall begin very quietly. And if we turn out a few good country Midwife-Nurses we shall be sure of having more candidates than we can accommodate. The first expences have been heavy. I hope another year we shall be able to give board free to a certain number from poor parishes.

Yours ever,

F. Nightingale

Source: BL Add 45788: ff 131–32

1861 saw the loss of another of her men; on 12 November Arthur Hugh Clough died.

83. To Sir John McNeill   32 South St 18 Nov 1861

My dear Sir John McNeill,

I should be sorry that you should see first in the newspapers our great loss, you who have been so kind to us.

Arthur Clough is dead at Florence on Nov. 12. His wife had rejoined him some months before & his sister three days before.

They seemed not to realize the danger till a very few days ago. And there is something unexplained about the rapid end.

He had been so much better at first for going abroad.

He was a man of a rare mind and temper. The more so because he would gladly do 'plain work'. To me, seeing the inanities & the blundering harasses which were the uses to which we put him, he seemed like a race horse harnessed to a coal truck. This *not* because he did 'plain work' and did it so well. For the best of us can be put to no better use than that.

He helped me immensely, tho' not officially – by his sound judgment, & constant sympathy. 'Oh, Jonathan my brother Jonathan, my love to thee was very great – passing the love of women'.

Now, not one man remains (that I can call a man) of all those whom these five years I have worked with. But as you say, 'we are all dying'.

ever, dear Sir John,

Yours sincerely & gratefully

Florence Nightingale.

Bertha Coltman, Blanche Clough's younger sister, who is slowly recovering her confinement, has not yet been told this heavy news. By excess of precaution, I tell you this, altho' it is hardly likely that you should be writing to her family.

If you will change your mind about the meeting on the 28th
(Lord Herbert's) & come here – you know how glad I should be.

F.N.

Source: GLRO HI/ST/NC/SU/143

Again Sir John McNeill seemed to have the most comforting
words to say to Florence when he replied to her letter:

> his death leaves you dreadfully alone in the midst of your
> work but that work is your life and you can do it alone.
> There is no feeling more sustaining than that of being
> alone – at least I have ever found it so . . . So I doubt not
> it will be to you, for you have a strength and a power for
> good to which I never could pretend. It is a small matter
> to die a few days sooner than usual. It is a great matter to
> work while it is day and so to husband ones powers as to
> make the most of the days that are given us. This you will
> do. Herbert and Clough and many more may fall around
> you but you are destined to do a great work and you
> cannot die till it is substantially if not apparently done.
> You are leaving your impress on the age in which you live
> and the print of your foot will be traced by generations
> yet unborn. Go on – to you the accidents of mortality
> ought to be as the falling of the leaves in autumn. (19 Nov
> 1861 BL Add 45968: f 169)

Nightingale, however, was not so easily consoled. The deaths of
'her best men' exacted an emotional toll that was aggravated by
exhaustion. Clarkey had just written a book on Madame Récamier,
praising her and her women friends. For Florence, the book
seemed to mock her close working relations with men. She
unleashed a flood of contempt and anger upon her old friend:

84. To Mary Clarke Mohl   32 South St 13 Dec 1861

My dear Mme. Mohl,
    I have read your book thro' last night and am immensely
charmed by it. But some things I disagree with and many I do not
understand. This does not apply to the characters. I understand the
character of Mme. Récamier, Mme. de Staël, Mme de Maintenon

&c, &c as I never did before. But to your conclusions. E.g. you say, 'women are more sympathetic than men'. Now if I were to write a book out of my experience, I should begin, *women have no sympathy*.

Yours is the tradition. Mine is the conviction of experience. I have never found one woman who has altered her life one iota for me or my opinions. Now look at my experience of men. A statesman, past middle age, absorbed in politics for a quarter of a century, out of 'sympathy' with me, remodels his whole life and policy – learns a science, the driest, the most technical, the most difficult, that of administration as far as it concerns the lives of men, not, as I learned it, in the field, from the stirring experience, but by writing dry Regulations in a London room by my sofa with me.

This is what I call real sympathy.

Another (Alexander, whom I made Director-Gen'l), does very nearly the same thing. He is dead too.

Clough, a poet born if ever there was one – takes to Nursing-administration in the same way, for me.

I only mention three, whose whole lives were remodelled by sympathy for me. But I could mention very many others, Farr, McNeill, Tulloch, Storks, Martin, who in a lesser degree have altered their work by my opinions. And most wonderful of all, a man born without a soul, like Undine – Sutherland. All these elderly men.

Now just look at the degree in which women have sympathy – as far as my experience is concerned. And my experience of women is almost as large as Europe. And it is so intimate too. I have lived and slept in the same bed with English Countesses and Prussian Bauerinnen with a closeness of intimacy no one ever had before. No Roman Catholic Supérieure has ever had the charge of women of the different creeds that I have had. No woman has excited 'passions' among women more than I have.

Yet I leave no school behind me. My doctrines have taken no hold among women. Not one of my Crimean following learnt anything from me – or gave herself for one moment after she came home to carry out the lesson of that war or of those hospitals.

No woman that I know has ever appris à apprendre.[1] And I attribute this to want of sympathy.

You say somewhere that women have no *attention*. Yes. And I attribute this to want of sympathy.

Nothing makes me so impatient as people complaining of their want of memory. How can you remember what you have never heard?

They don't know the names of the Cabinet Ministers. They don't know the Offices at the Horse Guards. They don't know who of the men of the day is dead, and who is alive. They don't know which of the Churches has Bishops and which not.

Now I'm sure I did not know these things. When I went to the Crimea, I did not know a Colonel from a Corporal.

But there are such things as Army Lists and Almanacs. Yet I never could find a woman who, out of sympathy, would consult one – for my work.

Nay, since Sidney Herbert's death, I have not seen a newspaper. Because I could not bear to see his name. Yet somehow or other I know things. And they do not.

The only woman I ever influenced by sympathy was one of those Lady Superinten'ts, I have named. Yet she is like me overwhelmed with her own business.

A woman once told me that my character would be more sympathized with by men than by women.

In one sense, I don't choose to have that said. Sidney Herbert and I were together exactly like two men – exactly like him and Gladstone.

And as for Clough, Oh Jonathan, my brother Jonathan my love to thee was very great, *passing the love of women*.

In another sense, I do believe it is true. I do believe I am 'like a man', as ____² says. But how? *In having sympathy*. I am sure I have nothing else. I am sure I have no genius. I am sure that my contemporaries, Parthe, Hilary, Marianne, Lady Dunsany were all cleverer than I was – and several of them more unselfish. But not one had a bit of sympathy.

Now Sidney Herbert's wife just did the Secretary's work for her husband (which I have had to do without) out of pure sympathy. – – – She did not understand his policy. – – – Yet she could write his letters for him 'like a man'.

I should think Mme. Récamier *was* another specimen of pure sympathy.

What follows perhaps I may draw too much from observations in my own family, viz:

Women crave *for being loved*, *not* for loving.

They scream at you for sympathy all day long, they are incapable of giving *any* in return, for they cannot even remember your affairs long enough to do so,

they care much less for knowing a truth than for disguising that truth from others, if it is a painful one. Hence they never do 'learn to learn' what is truth.

When you tell them anything, they reply, 'Oh I thought

otherwise – so and so I thought' and they will go on to tell you why they thought so, and are incapable of listening to your fact in return, altho' they themselves may have applied to you for the information.

They cannot state a fact accurately to another – nor can that other attend to it accurately enough for it to become information.

Now is not all this the result of want of sympathy?

(2) You say of Mme Récamier that her existence was 'empty but brilliant'. And you attribute it to want of family. Oh dear friend, don't give in to that sort of tradition. People often say to me, you don't know what a wife and mother feels. No, I say, I don't. And I am very glad I don't. And *they* don't know what *I feel*.

I am sick with indignation at what wives and mothers will do, the most egregious selfishness. And people call it all maternal or conjugal affection and think it pretty to say so.

No, no, let each person tell the truth from his own experience.

Ezekiel went running about naked, 'for a sign'. I can't run about naked, because it is not the custom of the country. But I would mount three widows' caps on my head, 'for a sign'. And I would cry, this is for Sidney Herbert, I am his real widow – this for Arthur Clough, I am his true widow (And I don't find it a bit of comfort that I had two legs to cut off whereas other people have but one). And this, the biggest widow's cap of all, is for the loss of all sympathy on the part of my dearest and nearest. (For that my Aunt was. We were like two lovers.)

(Do you know Clough was so like M. Mohl, only on a smaller intellectual and moral scale – or rather I would say on a smaller scale altogether.)

I heard a Greek say to Mr. Wyse at Salamis in 1850, God Almighty is surely an Englishman. Now I don't think he is. He has taken the only man among Ministers. What would it have signified if all the others had been taken?

He has taken the only man in one family. Oh how well we could have spared the whole family! He has taken (and all in five short months) the only man at the Palace. What would it have signified if the whole lot had gone, excepting only Albert?

I could tell you a great deal about that. He neither liked nor was liked. But what he has done for our country no one knows.[3]

The Queen has really behaved like a hero. Has buckled to business at once. After all, it is a great thing to be a Queen. She is the only woman in these realms, except perhaps myself, who has a *must* in her life – who must set aside private griefs and attend to the res publica.

On Sunday ministers were appalled. They thought it was going to be a case of Joanna of Spain. Now everybody is reassured.

Albert was really a Minister – this very few knew. Sir Robert Peel taught him.

We are shipping off the Expedition to Canada[4] as fast as we can, I have been working just as I did in the times of Sidney Herbert. Alas! he left no organization, my dear master. But the Horse Guards were so terrified at the idea of the national indignation, if they lost another Army, that they have consented to everything. But I have wandered from your book.

(3) I cannot understand how Mme. Récamier could give 'advice and sympathy' to such opposite people e. g. Mme. Salvage and Chateaubriand.

Neither can I understand, how she could give 'support' without recommending a distinct line of policy – by merely keeping up the tone to a high one.

It is as if I had said to S. Herbert, Be a statesman, be a statesman – instead of indicating to him a definite course of statesmanship to follow.

Also I am sure I never could have given 'advice and sympathy' to Gladstone and S. Herbert – men pursuing opposite lines of policy.

Also I am sure I never could have been the friend and adviser of Sidney Herbert, of Alexander, and of others – by simply keeping up the tone of general conversation on promiscuous matters.

We debated and settled measures together. That is the way we did it.

Adieu dear friend. How glad am I to see this miserable year come to a close. This is the shortest day. Would it were the last.

Ever yours,

F. N.

Dec 21/61

I read Jules Simon's Ouvrière.[5] The Political Economy is, I have no doubt, quite true and has been said elsewhere. But these books always astonish me by their ignorance of what workmen and workwomen actually say and feel and think. It is not a bit like that.

I am worse. I have had two consultations (Medical) – Brown Sequard[6] in one. And they say that all this worry brought on Congestion of the spine, which leads straight to Paralysis. And they say I must not write letters – wherefore I do it all the more.

Source: Woodward Memorial Library   {typed copy/Wellcome}

1. appris à apprendre: learned to learn.

2. Identified as Parthe by Cook, II, 15.

3. Crossed out on transcript: 'The P. of Wales is very like George III. Only he has absolutely no power of acquisition and is fond of pleasure. Poor comfort for us to look forward to.'

4. Footnote on transcript: Sent because of the American Civil War.

5. Jules Simon: (1814–96), French philosopher and statesman. An opponent to the Emperor Louis Napoleon, he lost his position at the Sorbonne when he refused to take an oath of loyalty (1852). Later Minister of Public Instruction (1870–71), senator for life (1875), premier of France (1876–77).

6. Brown Sequard: Charles Edouard Brown-Séquard (1817–94) had discovered the sensory decussation in the spinal cord (1849) and was the leading specialist in spinal diseases.

'In Office': Government Reforms, 1862–70

After the deaths of her key supporters, Florence Nightingale felt that her work was finished. She wrote to Sir Harry Verney two years later, still bitterly lamenting her loss: 'God has taken away my "five just men" {Prince} Albert, Gen'l Bruce, Sidney Herbert, Alexander & my dear Clough – all within a few months & left none but men who don't know their right hands from their left – & *likewise much cattle*' (30 Jan 1863 BL Add 45791: f 22). Nightingale exaggerated the virtues of her favourites and was at best only tolerant of those who, she felt, possessed limited talents; with others, she was frankly mean-spirited. Lord de Grey, Under-Secretary for War, was an ardent reformer, as was Captain Douglas Galton, who had recently been appointed Inspector-General of Fortifications. Sir George Lewis, however, drew Nightingale's wrath. A classical scholar of unquestionable integrity, Lewis had little understanding of the army when he was appointed Secretary for War. Nightingale labelled him a 'muff' and unfairly accused him of being cowardly, lazy and weak.

In spite of her conviction that her reforms would perish, Nightingale could still write to her mother about countless obligations:

85. To Fanny Nightingale

9 Chesterfield St W
7 Mar 1862

Dear mother

So far from your letters being a 'bore', you are the only person who tells me any news. I have never been able to get over the morbid feeling at seeing my lost two's names in the paper, so that I see no paper.

I did not know of the deaths you mention, (excepting of course Galton's baby,) & am very glad to hear of them, yes really glad. As for poor Galton's baby, it is a deep loss to him. And I cannot be glad. All his future he had built on it. And he would have made it such a good father. I don't know when I have been so sorry for the dropping of such a little life on earth. But Laura's husband & baby's father & others do not know how much they are spared by having no bitterness mingled with their grief. Such unspeakable bitterness has been connected with each one of my losses – far, far greater than the grief.

Then I have lost all. All the others have children or some high & inspiring interest to live for. While I have lost husband & children & all. And am left to the weary hopeless struggle with Hawes at the War Office & Lord Stanley in the Indian Sanitary Commiss'n. While it is an aggravation to everything to think that I predicted to my poor lost chief exactly what has happened, if he left the War Office *without* an organization & *with* a Hawes.

Sometimes I wonder that I should be so impatient for death. Had I only to stand & wait, I think it would be nothing – tho' the pain is so great that I wonder how anybody can dread an operation. If Paget[1] could amputate my left *fore quarter*, I am sure I would have sent for him in half an hour.

But it is this desperate Guerilla warfare, ending in so little, which makes me so impatient of life. I who could once do so much. And that wretched Sir G. Lewis, writing Latin *jeux d'esprit*.

Yes, the Canadian expedition was very well done. But Lord de Grey & I did that together. And we did it by means of the very machinery, constructed by me & Sidney Herbert, which Hawes is now wanting to destroy.

When I hear the street band playing 'Auld Lang Syne', & think that these five last years of my life are indeed now *auld lang syne* – it takes a deal of faith to make God's will mine. For indeed I don't see how in any world there could be such a combination for good as that which existed between me & my lost ones – here. And as it in no way depressed my joy in it to suffer so much as I did even during that time, so it in no way comforts me to think that *I* shall soon be past my sufferings. For the Army will not be better because I am dead.

2. Beatrice is going to see Miss Clough[2] before she leaves her school at the Lakes which I am very glad of.

From the very first moment I ever saw either Miss Clough or her lost brother (the 'man of God') – I felt, 'these people are quite of a different clay from ours. They move in quite a different order of ideas & feelings from what we do'.

I think what I have felt most (during my last 3 months of extreme weakness) is the not having one single person to give me one inspiring word or even one correct fact.

I am glad to end a day which never can come back; gladder to end a night – gladdest to end a month.

I have felt this much more in setting up (for the first time in my life), a fashionable old maid's house in a fashionable quarter (tho' grateful to Papa's liberality for enabling me to do so) because it is as it were deciding upon a new & independent course in my broken old age – which I never have been called upon to do even in my vigorous youth. Always before my path was so clear to me, what I ought to do, tho' often not how to do it.

But now it was quite doubtful to me whether (when all was broken up,) I had better not have left the Army altogether.

The question was decided in my mind by my being so much worse that I *could* do nothing else – & by Lord Stanley throwing all this Indian Commiss'n business upon us. I have now written the biggest part of their Report. But I have not begun my own Evidence; nor the Digest of the Reports from our Indian Stations, 150 in number.

But oh! if I were now able to do what I could do 5 years ago, or even what mothers can do for their children, how little my griefs would be to me, except to inspire me to do more.

In the Medea, Jason says, 'What remains?' And Medea answers, 'I'. I remember when I came home from the Crimea, 5 1/2 years ago, writing this from Lea Hurst to those who would have deterred me from stopping in the Army. All are now gone. And there remains only half 'I'.

I did all (& more than) I intended when I had 'I'; & got up that Commission, having only 'I' to begin with.

But now – – – ? 'what remains'?

3. The Queen, poor thing, is more 'bowed to the earth' (her own expression) than ever.

She is never able to see but one person at a time – never to sit down to dinner with more than one person – which used to be Princess Hohenlohe or Pss Alice. Even her uncle, K. of the Belgians, never dined with her when he was here. She told Lord Palmerston that she should not live long. But I hear there is no reason for fearing this. L'd P. says she is half the size she was.

She fronts the work gallantly. But there are such serious doubts whether she can even get through the daily routine of work, without Albert, that the Cabinet considered every constitutional possibility of creating an Office, to be filled by Lord Clarendon. It was found to be unconstitutional & that she must do the work herself with her Private Secretaries. Albert arranged that Pss Alice should stay 2 years in England after her marriage.

People say that time heals the deepest griefs. It is not true. Time makes us feel what *are* the deepest griefs every day only the more by showing of the blank (which nothing now can fill) every day more & more of the evils which there are none now to remedy, every day one more.

4. Thank you very much for the weekly box. And tell Burton that I ate a piece of her rabbit pie, which was the first real meat I have eaten for 3 months. The smallest contribution is thankfully received – even a sausage, when you kill a pig.

I could not help sending the game, chicken, vegetables & flowers to King's Coll-Hospital.

I never see the spring without thinking of Clough. He used to tell me how the leaves were coming out – always remembering that, without his eyes, I should never see the spring again. Thank God! my lost two are in brighter springs than ours.

Poor Mrs. Herbert told me that her chief comfort was in a little Chinese dog of his, which he was not either very fond of, (he always said he liked Christians better than beasts) but which used to come & kiss her eyelids & lick the tears from her cheeks. I remember thinking this childish. But now I don't. My cat does just the same to me. Dumb beasts observe you so much more than talking beings; & know so much better, what you are thinking of.

You may send this letter to Lea Hurst, if you like it. Papa wanted to know about the Queen. But don't send it anywhere else. If you could send me up some snowdrops, primroses, anemones & other wild spring flowers with roots, I have a fine balcony here looking on Chesterfield Gardens where I mean to take out a license for rural sports & kill Cats.

ever dear Mum Your loving child

F.

Parthe told me you wanted to know whether the Dresden Raphael had come in its new frame. Yes, it did, seven or eight months ago (for I remember I had it before August 2, when my dear Master died). The frame is beautiful. It is just what that kind of print wants to lighten it – an open work frame. I always think good prints are spoilt by framing them in solid work – & made to look heavy.

I have turned out all Mrs. Plumer Ward's performances in her bedroom which is mine. (I had as soon be in the room with bugs & fleas) & hung up your Dresden Raphael & Murillo Virgin, Mrs. Bracebridge's Annunciation (from the Papal Chapel) an unframed Guercino Ecce Homo, & Sistine Isaiah – and two Chromo-lithographs from Roberts & a Norwegian.

And Sutherland said I was 'a vain thing, to have decorated' my room. There are some people who always say the wrong thing.

Source: BL Add 45790: ff 253–64.

1. Sir James Paget, MD: (1814–99), Surgeon at St Bartholomew's Hospital, Surgeon Extraordinary to Queen Victoria, Vice-Chancellor of London University, 1883–95.
2. Anne Jemima Clough: (1820–92), sister of Arthur, a leader in women's higher education who became the first head of Newnham College, Cambridge (1872).

After her illness at Malvern, Nightingale had established a routine which she insisted kept her alive. Duty to God's will was primary, but duty to one's country – defined as the public good – was hardly distinguishable from it. God and work were inextricably connected. She had proudly written to Sir Harry Verney about her public service, 'Other nations may do it for glory – we for duty' (8 Oct 1861 Wellcome). Since duty to God and country had priority, Nightingale was able to justify her neglect of her family; she repeatedly reminded them of her multifarious responsibilities, while clamorously demanding their approval. She never accepted her family's lack of understanding or their unwillingness to support her work before she became famous. Nor was she loath to tell Fanny, Parthe and even W. E. N. of their past and present failures.

86. To Fanny Nightingale {?}   Undated[1]

These are the poor little Patients in King's College Hospital.
I should like you to know how much pleasure your spring things give – to those who *never* see the spring, or never will again.

F.N.

Please send this on to Papa. With the exception of yourself & him, I do think our family loses so much pleasure, by never thinking of giving pleasure – poor Hilary excepted, who wastes her life in doing nothing else. Without one penny of expence, with only half an hour's trouble, oh the pleasure that would be given by the able-bodied, of our family with nothing worthy to occupy their time, who would just pick a nosegay of 'Daf-a-down-dillies' on

Sunday; & send it to one who has been nearly confined to 4 walls for 4 1/2 years, like myself – (and *I* have taken for *them* all that time) or to the poor little inmates of a London Hospital.

Please thank Mrs. Watson & Mrs. Burton for the trouble they have taken. And tell them that every minute of the existence of the gifts they make gives pleasure to every minute of the existence of some poor human being.

F.N.

Source: BL Add 45790: ff 267–68.

1. FN enclosed a note from Mary Jones dated 13 March, thanking her specifically for the 'Daf-a-down-dillies'.

When Fanny ventured to suggest that she might spend more time with her friends and family, Florence replied:

But I confess I have felt that my people might give me more credit, at least for deliberation, especially when the event has so dreadfully justified me. Never was life & health employed or given up so deliberately as I have mine . . .

I only ask that my people will think themselves & say to others, At least she did deliberately what she thought right. 'She is of age: ask her'. No woman ever before directed the labours of a Government office. She must be the judge as to the when & the how, if a woman chooses to undertake to direct men over whom she can have no legitimate or recognized control, she shall do it. No one else can judge how she shall do it.

My looking back, the things I regret are not these. I regret that I have let visitors talk to me to the last moment before a meal, thereby incapacitating me for food & sleep altogether, that I have let them say, with a little scornful smile, 'I suppose you can't eat before me'. Alas if they were to see me after eating, they would never wish to see it again. I regret that I have received two visits on the same day – or after 5 o'clock – things which always bring on my spasm &c. These & such like are the things I regret & not that I have done my work, as long as God would let me. (6 Sept 1862 Wellcome)

Sir Benjamin Hawes, who had long been an obstruction to the

reorganization of the War Office, died on 15 May 1862. Two positions were created for the one he had occupied, and Captain Galton, over much opposition, was created Assistant Under-Secretary in charge of health and sanitary administration of the army. When Sir George Lewis suddenly died in April of the following year, Nightingale pressed her old friend, Lord Palmerston, the Prime Minister, to appoint Lord de Grey Secretary of State for War. She succeeded, and once more her men were in position. Reform hopes again rose.

The Sanitary Commission on India, which was promulgated in May 1859, began sitting in autumn 1861. Nightingale worked closely with Lord Stanley, who had succeeded Herbert as chair. Progress was slow. The great distances and the difficulty of obtaining facts and figures were complicated by the rivalry between various factions, such as the Queen's troops and the East India Company's troops, the India Office and the War Office, and the civil and military government officials. Pro-reformers, however, such as Sir Charles Trevelyan, Governor of Madras, could be found in India.

Sanitary reform in India was a monumental task since it meant bringing sanitary knowledge to the native population. Furthermore, it was dependent upon the co-operation of the War Office, the India Office and the government of India. Nightingale wanted a Sanitary Commission appointed for each of the three Presidencies and a Sanitary Department at the India Office to implement changes. Alternatively she recommended a Sanitary Committee at the War Office with two representatives from India. She also recommended a Sanitary Code for all of India. Her more sweeping proposals at first met opposition but were eventually accepted, although the Commission remained under the military.

Nightingale drafted and sent a *Circular of Enquiry* to every military station in India through which masses of evidence were collected over the next ten years, giving an unprecedented picture of the country. She wrote an abstract of the Commission's two-thousand-page report; her 'Observations by Miss Nightingale', popularly known as the 'Red Book', became a primary reference for politicians and Indian administrators. The most astonishing and deplorable fact was that 'Besides deaths from natural causes [9 per 1000], 60 per 1000 of our troops perish annually in India . . . a company out of every regiment has been sacrificed every twenty months' (Cook, II, 32). This was over three times higher than the death rate for troops at home before the reforms of 1857–61 had been instituted. Nightingale rightly declared that at such a mortality rate England would not be able to produce enough soldiers to hold India.

Nightingale, prompt as always in her press campaign, sent advance copies of the Commission Report to influential journalists. Both the War Office and the India Office were furious at what they saw as her interference. Some of the facts revealed were so incriminating that an attempt was made to suppress the report. A 'Précis of the Evidence' omitting the most damning information was offered for sale to the public and distributed to Parliament. The type of the orginal report, of which only a thousand copies had been printed, was broken, and the original, 'reserved' by the government, was available to Members of Parliament only upon application. Nightingale wrote to Sir James Clark, 'the two folio book is not to be sold, not to be had, not to be published, not to be presented to Parliament . . . ' (Woodham-Smith, p. 415).

87. To Sir Harry Verney   Hampstead NW 19 Sept 1863

My dear Sir Harry
    In answer to your kind letter:
1. For carrying out the recommendations of the India Army Sanitary Commission, all depends upon the promptitude of Government in forming the four *working* Commissions of Health – one for each Presidency in India; and one at home, to be attached to the India and War Offices.

You yourself know how Sidney Herbert halved the Death-rate of the Army at home by his 'Barrack and Hospital Improvement Commission' (among other measures) which still exists.

To this the India Office has already appointed Sir Proby Cautley,[1] & is about to appoint two other members. This is to be the advising body of the India Office in all matters relating to the Sanitary improvement of stations &c.

But this Commission is of course for nothing more than to give its advice when asked for. It can execute nothing. All practical work must be done in India. And not a day should be lost in appointing the three Presidency Commissions, or rather, 'departments of Public Health', as recommended by the R. Commission, to take official charge of the great work to be carried out in India.

2. You know what an impression the Report has made in England; even deeper than that of Sidney Herbert's first Army Sanitary Report. People ask if the state of things revealed 'is to last another

day'. M.P.s are burning to take it up. It is *out of*, rather than *in* the I. O., that the outcry is loudest. It is amazing how easily officials are satisfied of the truth of anything it is held desirable to assert. And therefore it is a simple conformity with the tradition of a Government office to denounce as extravagant and exaggerated the lamentable exposures made by this enquiry. Would that our facts could vanish before their denunciations!

But Lord Elgin,[2] (altho', I take it, it is not a subject which interests his mind,) is too enlightened a man to put it by in this way.

The Government *of* India *in* India must take steps itself, and not wait for pressure from England. It must take the initiative well and willingly. It will never sit down quietly under such a weight of responsibility, nor rest till these deplorable evils are removed.

3. The object is: to have a Department of Health under a responsible head, for each Presidency, to be constituted out of the required elements, Civil
> Military
> Engineering
> Sanitary
> Medical –

to place this Department in the relation of receiving aid and advice from the I. and W. O. Commission at home – and in the position of advising the Public Works Department and local authorities in each Presidency, on all matters connected with
> Barracks
> Hospitals
> Stations
> Bazaars
> Native Towns &c

at home we would gladly help with a plan for working out the details.

But first let India find the best men and constitute the Commissions.

There are some good men to begin with, such as: Dr. T. E. Dempster, Inspector Gen'l MacPherson. Of Madras – Dr. Norman Chevers and Dr. Joseph Ewart. Of Bengal – Dr. MacClelland &c – who would be efficient on these Commissions as Sanitary or medical members.* (*Of course Officers of Health there must be to act under the Commissions. Good names could be given for these too)

4. Unless the Death rate & Invaliding rate of the Indian Army can be reduced, to hold India by British troops will become impossible.

Already this next year, 1854,[3] we want 25,000 recruits. And I have just seen a letter from the Horse Guards who wish to extend re-enlistment by an increase of pay, because they do not know where to turn to keep up the Army.

But a better method than this, would be to improve the Sanitary condition of India. And this is the key to holding India by British troops. And on the India Government now depends the possibility of doing so.

5. There is the native population too. It is surely something to stir us all, to know that Indian pestilences are of Indian manufacture – that the causes which give rise to them are removeable – now that Indians are as much our own fellow-subjects as Londoners.

What is wanted is to drain India, to water-supply India, to cleanse India by something more than surface-cleansing.

What is wanted is that it should not be said now of us as Burke said ?[4] ago – that if we were to leave India to-morrow, we should leave behind us no more traces of our civilization than if India had been in the possession of the hyaena or the tiger.

6. The question is, in short, nothing less than to create a Public Health Department for India. What a glorious work for an India Government!

The difficulties are great. But see what Sidney Herbert's confidence in a good cause enabled him to do. He halved the death-rate of the Army at home. Lord Elgin can do much more than this – the India death-rate can be reduced to much less than half.

For *everything* is there to be done, as every thing had to be done in the Crimea. And this makes it the more, *not* the less hopeful.

The discovery, so to speak, of the R. Commission is that the cause of ill health in India lies, *not* in the climate, but in the absence of all works of sanitary civilization. This produced the very same diseases in Europe, when there was no water-supply, no drainage, no sewerage here – & the results are intensified in India by climate.

Let this not go on. Ever yours

Florence Nightingale

Source: Wellcome

1. Sir Proby Cautley: (1802–71), sat as an Indian representative on the Royal Commission on India and on the Army Sanitary Committee. He was best known for the successful completion of the Ganges canal in the 1840s.

2. Lord Elgin: James Bruce, 8th Earl of Elgin (1811–63). He served as Governor of Jamaica, Governor-General of Canada and envoy to China, before becoming Viceroy of India in 1863. He died in office before any reforms could be effected.

3. FN's error.

4. FN's question mark.

While the India Commission remained her primary enthusiasm, Nightingale found time to respond to an amazing array of
issues.

88. To Captain Douglas Galton
Hampstead NW
21 Sept 1863

My dear Capt. Galton

People are complaining that:

when a Regiment sails, many of their wives & children are left
behind, & the soldiers are unable to make any provision for their
support until they have reached their destination, say China or
Calcutta (after a four months' voyage, round the Cape,) & have
been able to send money through their Captains to their families at
home. Meanwhile the families have gone through five or six
months of distress.

For sailors leaving a port in England or Ireland, the Admiralty
provides power to leave a standing order that a certain amount of
pay is to be sent regularly to their families.

The W.O. objects that a similar arrangement would 'involve a
change in their book-keeping'.

It would involve no 'change'. It would involve a small addition. I
am willing to go the length of six-pence to furnish an account-
book to the W.O., which would enable them to keep these
additional accounts.

The W.O. also objects that it would deprive the Captains of the
chance of fining the soldiers for any military offences.

But they can learn the Admiralty system, & whilst there are
other ways of 'doing' the soldiers, their pay is the only means of
providing bread for their families starving (or doing worse) at
home.

Surely, the soldiers might be allowed to leave for the probable
duration of their voyage, & for a month or two beyond it, a sum to
be paid weekly to their representatives at home.

Sir E. Lugard¹ has been tried & failed.

Pray set this right. But the W.O. would not be the W.O., if such
things as these were not. And when they have ceased to be; the
W.O. will have ceased to be.

ever yours

F.N.

Source: BL Add 45761: ff 122–23

1. Sir Edward Lugard: (1810–98), military under-secretary who served throughout India, 1846–88. FN found him wanting in sanitary zeal.

The Liverpool philanthropist William Rathbone had originally contacted Nightingale in 1861 about providing nurses for the poor. After the successful opening of a Training School and Home for Nurses at the Liverpool Royal Infirmary, he approached her about introducing trained nurses into the Liverpool Workhouse Infirmary.

89. To William Rathbone   115 Park St W 5 Feb 1864

My dear Sir

I will not delay another day expressing how much I admire & how deeply I sympathize with your Workhouse plan.

First, let me say that Workhouse sick & Workhouse Infirmaries require quite as much care as (I had almost said more than) Hospital sick. There is an ever greater work to be accomplished in Workhouse Infirmaries than in Hospitals.

[In days long ago where I visited in one of the largest London Workhouse Infirmaries I became fully convinced of this.

How gladly would I have become the Matron of a Workhouse.

But, of a Visitor's visits, the only result is to break the visitor's heart. She sees how much could be done & cannot do it.]

Liverpool is of all places the one to try this great reform in. Its example is sure to be followed. It has an admirable body of Guardians; it is a thoroughly practical people; it has, or soon will have again, money.

Lord Russell[1] once said (what is quite true) that the Poor Law was never meant to be/supersede private charity.

But, whatever may be the difficulties about pauperism, in two things most people agree – viz. that workhouse sick ought to have the best practicable nursing, as well as Hospital sick – & that a good wise Matron may save many of these from life-long pauperism by first nursing them well, & then rousing them to exertion, & helping them to employment.

In such a scheme as you wisely propose: – there would be four elements:

1. the Guardians, one of whose functions is to check pauperism.

They could not be expected to incur greater cost than at present, *unless* it is proved that it cures or saves life.

2. the Visiting or Managing Committee of the Guardians, whose authority must not (& need not) in any way be interfered with.

3. the Governor, the Medical Officer & Chaplain.

4. (and under the Governor) the proposed Sup't of Nurses & her Nursing Staff.

There is no reason why all these parts of the machine should not work together.

You propose the funds to pay the extra Nursing for a time.

The difficulty is to find the lady to govern it.

When appointed, she must be authorized – indeed, appointed – by the Guardians. She must be their Officer; & must be invested by the Governor with authority to superintend her Nurses in conformity with Regulations to be agreed upon.

So far I see no more difficulty than there was in settling our relations as Nurses to the Government officials in the Crimean War.

The cases are somewhat similar.

As to funds, it is just possible that eventually the Guardians might take all the cost on themselves, as soon as they see the greater advantage of economy of good Nursing.

If Liverpool succeeds, the system is quite sure to extend itself.

The Fever Hospital is one of the Workhouse Infirmaries. That is the place to shew what skilful Nursing can do. The Patients are not all paupers. How many families might be rescued from pauperism by saving the lives of their heads, & by helping the hard-working to more speedy convalescence.

Hopefully yours

FN

Source: BUL N62: Box 2, Folder 2

1. Lord Russell: John, first Earl Russell (1792–1878). From a wealthy Whig family, he filled several different Cabinet posts, and was twice Prime Minister.

Trained nurses deserved financial security after their working lives were over. Her old friend Mary Jones was trying to start a pension scheme for nurses, a plan that fitted well with Nightingale's advocacy of helping people to help themselves. In the meantime the women nurses, introduced into the military hospital at Woolwich in 1861, were facing difficulties. Their matron, Jane Shaw Stewart, described in the Crimea as 'mad' because of her quick temper, was proving unable to cope with military protocol.

90. To Mary Jones   27 Norfolk St Wednesday morning
Private

Dearest friend:

I am so overwhelmed with work & illness – & so ashamed of myself for being so overwhelmed – but I will try to help (as you have so often helped me in similar things) tho' I am afraid what I have to say will not help much.

I think that in our race, (I set aside R. Catholic races & institutions for the moment) all working people ought to be helped in both ways, viz. Savings' Banks & Deferred annuities, to obtain an independence. I think neither way complete without the other. [And I believe that in time & with a wise Government, poor-laws might be dispensed with under such a régime. But this does not concern you & me now]

All that Mr. Gladstone is now doing in this line I think is dictated by the wisest policy.

In such an Institution as yours, the details may be settled in many different ways. But I should always, in all Institutions, aim at these two things; viz. 1. that the Nurse should have a store in Savings' Bank, to enable her to help a relative temporarily, to help herself in an emergency, & also to pay the premium to the Deferred Annuity, when she is incapacitated by sickness from earning wages (this would not apply to you). 2. that she should have a Deferred Annuity in expectation. Suppose every worthy Nurse could have an Annuity of (say) £50 at the age of 55, this would be affluence.

[St. Thomas' grants such.]

There are various ways of doing this: You might make the Nurse pay to both, Savings' Bank & Deferred Annuity – gratuities for good conduct from the authorities going to both. Or you might devote subscriptions to the Deferred Annuity, & let her own savings go to the Savings' Bank, with or without any gratuities for good service from yourselves, the authorities. Whichever way you adopt, I think, to give an English woman that proper feeling of independence & self-help, which you so wisely encourage, she should have *both* (Savings' Bank deposits, & Deferred Annuity) to look forward to.

[It would take much more time than either you or I have, if I were to tell the mischiefs I have seen in R. Catholic orders, arising from a want of acknowledging the principle of individual independence in their dependents.

The miserable old ages of their Nurses in the Salpêtrière, where they are entirely provided for.

The absolute helplessness of big girls of 20 & upwards, brought up in their Orphan Asylums, (in which I have lived & served). It is not, as is generally supposed, that the Orders themselves are destitute of the principles of Political Economy – *quite the reverse*. All over France, Orders actually make money by the work of their dependents – & quite right too. But these dependents are *perfectly incapable*, when they leave the Institutions, whether Educational, Penitential, or what not, of governing themselves, so as to earn a single sixpence even at the very work they have been used to do for the nuns, or so as to keep themselves from falling into the arms of the first man who tempts them. Pardon the crudity of my expressions.]

I therefore entirely conclude for the English principle, which you have carried out so well, of helping people to help themselves. I would do this both ways, both by Savings' Banks & Deferred Annuities.

I think all experience teaches *your* principle, viz. of definite engagements, 3–5–7 years, to be renewed, if desirable, *not* of indefinite engagements, to be broken off, if undesirable.

I send you what I am afraid will be of little use:

1. the principles which guided us as to the Army Nurses, both in regard to wages & pensions (please burn the detached sheets – & send me back the 'Regulations')

2. a sketch by Mrs. S. Stewart which please burn, when read. It is an old thing; & she would be 'mad' with me for sending it you.

3. a book of Dr. Farr's which you will have neither time nor inclination to go into – & which please return to me.

Tho' of course, I would not tie down Institutions & private families & societies to the strict principles of the value of money & life of Life Insurances & Government Annuities, yet I incline to think that, the nearer we keep to money-&-life-values in our private transactions, the safer we shall be in doing good. & not in doing harm.

If, as you cannot possibly be expected to study Dr. Farr's thick book, you would like to write to him (our Army Nurses pension-rates, &c, were all calculated by him) – or would wish me to write to him, to ask some such question as follows:

whether, seeing that Government has provided both for savings & deferred annuities, it would not be best to adopt both plans, say, a deferred annuity accruing at 55 (or 60?) – and the remainder to be placed in a Savings' Bank. Or the Nurse might place all her savings in the Savings' Bank, and the subscriptions might go to a Deferred Annuity. [The chief difficulty in any scheme is in the want of security that the Nurse will continue in her work till she is 55.]

[Between the leaves of my copy of Dr. Farr's big book are some photographs of the Cyclone at Calcutta, sent me from Calcutta, which it may amuse & distress you to look at].

I had already written to Embley to send me Christmas greeneries for you on the 23rd. But I will write again to ask particularly for hollies in berry, *if they are at all*, & perhaps the box had better go straight to you (?)[1] I am so sorry you are so sad for your Christmas.

God bless you ever yours

F.N.

Confidential

Dearest friend

I will tell you (what I have told no one) what has overwhelmed me so much this last fortnight. In addition to our usual work, particularly heavy just now, I have had to do the most painful thing that I ever had to do in my most painful life.

Col. Wilbraham[2] has accused Mrs. S. Stewart of manslaughter – *because* she interfered to prevent every Patient from choosing his own Orderly to sit up with him, from ordering said Orderly to be attached to him alone, & forbidding the Ward Night-Orderly to enter his Ward!!! Half an hour after this insane proceeding had been put a stop to, a Patient dies, and Mrs. S. Stewart is accused of his death. [In addition, she is accused of Anglicanism, 'Foaming-at-the-Mouth', Manslaughter, 'Snapping her Fingers', Insanity, *Drink*, Being Silent in an Omnibus, General Incivility, Not accepting an Invitation to tea, &c &c &c]

I have gone thro' all these papers, which were sent me officially, like a Chief Justice, & not like a Counsel.

To-day a War Office Commission of 3 members goes down to Netley to examine all the parties.

The worst of it is, not that Mrs. S. Stewart should be accused, (for the accusations are too absurd,) but how can her post be of any use to the service after such a scene as this?

F. N.

P.S. In addition, in an *official* letter *to the Secretary of State*, asking for the 'dismissal of Mrs. S. Stewart', dated Sept 27, (but sent to me only a fortnight ago), Col. Wilbraham quotes a *part* of a *confidential* conversation he had with me, (in which I acknowledged Mrs. S. S.'s defects of temper,) taken out of its connection, which was, to soothe him – as a ground for calling for her dismissal. There is no safety with such a man. And I only mention this, in case you should have further communication with him – he may quote you *officially*.

F. N.

Source: GLRO HI/ST/NC1/64/24

1. FN's question mark.
2. Col. Richard Wilbraham: (1811–1900). He served in the Crimea and was then appointed Governor of the general hospital at Woolwich (1861–63); Commandant of Netley (1863–70). He was later knighted for his services.

In January 1864 Dr Sutherland, Dr Farr, and Sir Robert Rawlinson helped Nightingale write 'Suggestions in regard to Sanitary Works required for the Improvement of Indian Stations', which outlined the work that had to be carried out in regard to drainage, sanitation, water supply, and barrack and hospital construction. This was sent to the War Office; from there it was to have been forwarded to the India Office. But months passed. When Sir John Lawrence, then Viceroy of India, wrote to Nightingale asking what had happened to the instructions she had promised, it was discovered that the India Office, offended by the War Office in December, had filed the report and forgotten it. Nightingale printed and forwarded her own instructions to Sir John before Lord Stanley, the Colonial Secretary, and Sir Charles Wood, Secretary of State for India, resolved the differences between the two offices. She had drawn up the instructions for the Presidency Commissions, widening their scope to include the towns near the military stations. Amidst her struggles with contending bureaucracies, Nightingale drew comfort from correspondence with a few pioneering doctors in India who strongly supported sanitary reform.

91. To J. Pattison Walker, MD[1]   32 South St 3 June 1864

My dear Sir,
    I thank you much for your kind letter of April 23 & its most interesting account of the proceedings of the Commission. It is doing its work vigorously – & will be a blessing to India.
    The establishment of a Chair of Hygiene is of the greatest importance for the future progress of the cause and the same

should be done for Bombay & Madras. While teaching Europeans the laws of health, do not forget the natives. Could not the question of public health be brought before any Institutes or Native Societies for discussion? A well-written little book or paper addressed to natives in their own language, explaining the very simplest laws of health – how it is that their present habits lead to fever & cholera – (if the causes of these two diseases are made head against all the rest will follow –) could not this be compiled & circulated among the natives? I have already felt that, if you could take the heads of castes into your counsels, disarm their prejudices – how much might be done? I do not pretend to say how. But you have now, at the head of the Government, the man of all others, who *can* do this & who *will*. Never had a Governor General before such knowledge & such power: I mean particularly with regard to the native races.

It is urgent that some enlightenment should be brought to those districts round Calcutta where the remittent plague prevails – in order to lead them to improve their own sanitary state & to allow it to be improved.

Could not hints, shewing a kindly interest in them by the Government, be put forth by the Government?

With regard to the very important question of disposing of the dead, would not the best plan be to confer with the different castes and ascertain what really constitutes religious burial. [This is what even the old Indians at the India Office here seem not exactly to know]. Then the whole question would resolve itself into the best practicable & most wholesome method of doing work.

If cremation were adopted, suppose your Commission were to send a Minute home, desiring that the War & India Office Commission here (Barrack & Hospital Improvement Commission) should send them out the best plans of apparatus from this country, where the process has been applied to almost every purpose, except burning dead bodies. [And even that has been considered.]

I was delighted to see Mr. Strachey's[2] Minute (April 5) which was sent by the India Office to the 'Barrack & Hospital Commission' in a letter of May 20, desiring them to send out plans &c of sanitary construction to you – because we are so slow (they talk of Hindoos being slow – but War Offices & India Offices in England are slower). These plans are however nearly ready. And they will be sent out almost immediately with general suggestions.

I wish you God speed with all my heart. You will have much opposition to encounter. But great works do not prosper without opposition.

[Do you remember what, (by a curious coincidence) Pope Paul III said to a predecessor of yours in the Missionary work in India: St Francis Xavier, viz. that God would always find means to carry out a work which was really God's – that indeed he, Xavier, would find much to suffer – but that the 'affairs of God' succeed only by the way of crosses & difficulties.

I did not think Pope Paul could have said so good a thing. And I suppose Xavier was half a madman. But, for all that, I think it is true, is it not? for *every* work engaged in for the good of men.]

Believe me Your faithful servant

FN

I need hardly say that any papers or letters from you will always be most welcome to me.

F.N.

I have just had a communication from Delhi (& my brother-in-law, Sir Harry Verney, has seen an officer in London, just arrived from Delhi from his son's Regiment there, who speaks to the same effect) viz. that a disease called 'Boils' is very prevalent among the troops there, & causes much inefficiency. One officer had no less than 80 Boils on his body. The people there attribute the disease to bad water & a bad site – and say that there is good water, tho' at a considerable distance, & a good site for a small Barrack in Delhi. This is just one of the cases with which your Commission could effectually deal. The cause of 'Boils' is very little understood. If you could contrive a careful enquiry to be made to find out the cause at Delhi, & remedy the evils, much good might arise to the Service.

(Of course we do not take implicitly every word we hear from Military Officers, unacquainted with sanitary things.)

F.N.

Source: BL Add 45781: ff 219–22   {typed copy}

1. J. Pattison Walker: (1823–1906), Surgeon and Surgeon-Major in the Indian Army in Bengal (1855–70), worked for an improved prison system and served as Secretary of the Bengal Sanitary Commission. Later Deputy Inspector-General.

2. Mr John Strachey: (1823–1907); Sir John Lawrence, Viceroy of India, appointed him president of a permanent sanitary committee for India in 1864. He had previously investigated the causes of the 1861 cholera epidemic, and would later initiate land taxation reforms.

92. To Dr Charles Hathaway[1]   32 South St 18 June 1864

Private

My dear Sir

I am extremely obliged to you for your letter of May 3 – & for its enclosure (Minute on Calcutta Jail) – & especially for your good news of Sir John Lawrence's health.

Your account of the Military Department reply to the Indian Army Sanitary Report is much what we thought it would turn out to be. The whole question at issue is simply this: 'what *is* a fair formula of mortality?' The Registrar General's Department & the Royal Commission say that, the longer the term of years you take (within limits), the safer you are – simply because the law by which men die everywhere is not ruled by days, months or years, but by 'epochs'. If any one says that the epoch should coincide with one, two, three, five years, he simply shews that he has not sufficiently studied the subject to give an opinion.

The Registrar General's Office & the Royal Commission in making up the Table 10. page lxxxviii for their Report, Vol I, used all the Annual Tables at their disposal. (It is rather hard to be blamed for not using what they could not get. Altho' they applied to India for tables subsequent to 1856 & suspended their proceedings for a whole year to wait for these, none were sent subsequent to 1856.)

It is no reply to the Commission's Tables to adduce years subsequent to 1856. They should shew that the Returns used for Table 10 are either incorrect or improperly used.

I could not help laughing at *your* critics who 'exclude' specific diseases, such as 'Cholera' accidents 'proving fatal' &c.

(It is very convenient indeed to leave out all deaths that *ought not* to have happened, as *not having* happened. And it is certainly a new way of *preventing preventible* Mortality to omit it altogether from any statement of Mortality.)

Then they would 'exclude' 'deaths above 60'. Their principle, if logically carried out, is simply to throw out all ages & all diseases; & then there would be no mortality whatever.

It is clear that all ages & all diseases must be included in every set of Mortality tables, & then, by comparing the whole population at each age with the Deaths at each age, an estimate of the Mortality will be gained.

I wait with impatience for the copy of your Report, (the new Prison Committee) which you kindly promise me.

Mr. Strachey's Minute on the Calcutta Jails exposes a state of horrors altogether inconceivable – & which, if known, would make a great outcry. You should have a fully detailed Report drawn up, with plans shewing what the Jail is – the length, width & height of its rooms – the number of inmates in each – the cubic space & superficial area per prisoner – the state of the fittings, bedding! drainage, latrines &c – with proposals for abolishing utterly the present state of things, & introducing a better one to meet our days's requirements. If you like to send us any plans, we shall be only too glad to get for you every information & practical assistance possible in improving them.

Since I began to write, I have to thank you for the Third Section of Mr. Strachey's Cholera Report. I have only had time to glance at it. There is much experience in England about cholera which might be useful to India (Dr. Budd's[2] paper is of no practical value, & does not represent the present amount of experience. It is purely theoretical, & by a man who has seen little of the disease.) I think we could have improved the practical Instructions in some important particulars.

With all good wishes, believe me yours very truly

Florence Nightingale

Source: BL Add 45782: ff 153–55   {typed copy}

1. Dr Charles Hathaway: (1817–1903), Sir John Lawrence's private secretary in India. Author of *Punjab Jail Manual*.
2. Dr George Budd: (1808–82), Professor of Medicine at King's College, London, from 1840; author of *Diseases of the Liver* (1845) and *Diseases of the Stomach* (1855).

India had been in financial and administrative chaos following the 1857 Mutiny, but by mid 1864 Nightingale was expressing satisfaction at the progress being made in sanitary affairs. Lord Stanley had written to her in July: 'Every day convinces me more of two things; first, the vast influence on the public mind of the Sanitary Commissions of the last few years . . . and next, that all this has been due to you and to you almost alone' (Woodham-Smith, p. 428). The Commander-in-Chief, Sir Hugh Rose, had indeed improved conditions in the army, but the civil side remained unchanged.

93. To Sir John Lawrence   32 South St 26 Sept 1864

Private

My dear Sir John Lawrence,

I always feel it a kind of presumption in me to write to you – and a kind of wonder at your permitting it. I always feel that you are the greatest figure in history, and yours the greatest work in history, in modern times. But that is my very reason. We have but one Sir John Lawrence.

Your Bengal Sanitary Commission is doing its work, like men, like martyrs, in fact. And what a work it is! All we have in Europe is mere child's play to it. Health is the produce of civilization – i.e. of real civilization. In Europe we have a kind of civilization to proceed upon. In India your work represents not only diminished Mortality, as with us, but increase of energy, increase of power, of the populations. I always feel as if God had said: mankind is to create mankind. In this sense, you are the greatest creator of mankind in modern history.

Your Bengal Commission must be the model of the other Presidency Sanitary Commissions. I see that, on the Bombay one, is no Civil member. And so far as I know of its proceedings, it seems to direct its attention not so much to sanitary works as to matters of ordinary police. Now the main business of your Sanitary Commissions should be: construction, not police. Improvement in India mainly depends on works (police regulations are, of course, necessary).

2. Would there be any impropriety in your Sanitary Commissions sending copies of their printed Minutes to the Barrack and Hospital Improvement Commission here, through the India Office – merely for information? As far as your Bengal Commission goes: these men don't want urging: they have not now to be taught. Anything which might even appear to interfere with the responsibilities of your Commissions, unless at their own request, is not only undesirable, but, as far as the Bengal Comm. is concerned, useless. But, if you saw no objection to sending the Minutes for information to the War Office Commission here, I am sure they would very much like it . . . [1] or, if that would be too formal and official, (as regards the India Office here) if they, the Minutes, might be sent to me, with permission to shew them to one or two, such as Lord Stanley, (our late Chairman of the Royal Commission), Dr. Sutherland, Capt. Galton, of the War Office, etc., it would answer the same purpose.

The India Officer here does not shew now the least jealousy of the Barrack and Hospital (War Office) Commission. On the contrary. One can scarcely help smiling at the small things it is glad to throw off its responsibility for upon said Commission.

3. There are three glaring (though lesser) evils in Calcutta about which I know you have been employed – lesser tho' they are – and your attention and Dr. Hathaway's have been aroused by them.

These are:

(1) the Police Hospitals (or state of Hospital accommodation) for sick poor at Calcutta. The police establishments seem about as bad as possible. Indeed the poor wretches are brought in mostly to die.

The Parisian system of relief is very good: every Police Station at Paris has means of temporary help in cases of emergency until the sufferers can be removed to hospital. Some such arrangement, with a thorough reform of the Hospitals, and such additional accommodation as may be wanted, might meet Calcutta's case.

(2) the condition of Jails and Lunatic Asylums in India. Certainly it is not for me to draw your attention or Dr. Hathaway's to this. Probably he knows more about them than any man living. The reports and recommendations of one or two of the Jail Inspectors shew that they want experience: as I am sure Dr. Hathaway will agree with me.

Perhaps we might help you by sending out such Reports on the subject as may be useful.

(3) the seamen at the Great Ports.

You have already done so much. But Rome can't be built in a day.

Bad water, bad food bought in Bazaars, and bad drinks, cause a vast amount of disease and death.

Self-supporting Institutions, such as our Sailors' Homes, (of which indeed I believe you have already founded more than one) would give the men wholesome food and drink – and lodgings and day rooms at little cost.

So many men perish for want of this kind of accommodation at Calcutta, where the evil seems greatest.

It seems to me so base to be writing while you are doing. Oh that I could come out to Calcutta and organize at least the Hospital accommodation for the poor wretches in the streets. There is nothing I should like so much. But it is nonsense to wish for what is an impossibility.

I am sure that you will be glad to hear that one of my life-long wishes, viz., the nursing of Workhouse Infirmaries by proper Nurses, is about to be fulfilled. By the munificence of a Liverpool man, (who actually gives £1200 a year for the object, but desires not to be named) we undertake next month the Liverpool Workhouse Infirmary (of 1000 beds) – the first Workhouse that ever has been nursed – with 15 Head Nurses, trained by ourselves, and a lady (Volunteer) Matron, who underwent a most serious course of training at our Nurses School at St. Thomas' Hospital, 15 Assistants, and 52 ex-pauper women whom we are to train as Nurses.

I am sure it is not for us to talk of civilization. For I have seen, in our English Workhouse Infirmaries, neglect, cruelty, and malversation such as can scarcely be surpassed in some semi-barbarous countries. And it was there that I felt I must found a school for Nurses for Workhouses, etc. The opportunity has come too late for me to do the Workhouse Nursing myself. But, so it is well done, we care not how.

I think with the greatest satisfaction upon your re-union with Lady Lawrence and (some of) your children.

God bless you.

I am yours devotedly

Florence Nightingale

P.S. The Calcutta Municipality does not seem yet to have wakened up to a sense of its existence. It does not know that it exists: Much less, what it exists for.

Still, you are conquering India anew by civilization, taking possession of the Empire for the first time by knowledge instead of the sword.

F.N.

Source: BL Add 45777: ff 49–53   {copy}

1. FN's ellipsis.

Sir John Lawrence sent enquiries about the feasibility of placing nurses in military hospitals in India. For a while it seemed as if this old dream would materialize. In a letter dated 10 February 1865 Nightingale wrote to her cousin Henry Bonham Carter, Secretary of the Nightingale Nursing Fund, about the difficulties involved:

> Of course it is vain for us to think of sending out Nurses by the hundred. What I wish we *could* think of, is to send out trained Training Matrons, wherever we are asked.
>
> But it seems to me that, the more the cant about Women's Missions, the fewer the really efficient women

become. It makes me mad to hear the din about unemployed women. If women are unemployed, it is because they won't work.

But I am sure, from my own experience of Governesses in Harley St, these women had rather shamble on in their ill-paid, ill-performed work, than go through the training we offer, (or half the training I went thro' myself) to become highly-paid Matrons.

[The only Matron they ever had in India was paid £360 a year, (& everything 'found', as the servants say.)

The highest salaries women receive at all, (Queens and actresses excepted) might be secured by women trained by us.] Sir John Lawrence says, 'whatever expence is requisite, must be met'. (BL Add 47714: ff 89–91)

Ten days later, she again appealed to Harriet Martineau:

94. To Harriet Martineau   27 Norfolk St 20 Feb 1865

Dear friend

I do think that an Article from you, as you so kindly propose, *would* help us very much. But the facts look so very small. And the possibilities, which are every day held out to us, are so enormously large – & these we have no right to lay before the public.

It is not money we want; it is workers. The public would give us money; they won't give us workers. Every body is tarred with the same stick. There is the 'Times', congratulating itself on the thousands it has got subscribed this winter. But where are the workers?

No: we don't aspire, altho' they are needed by the hundred & the thousand, to sending out Nurses by the hundred or the thousand. What we want to do is to send a small staff of Trained Nurses & a *Trained Training* Matron, wherever we are asked, proper opportunities being guaranteed to us. But the material, especially for the latter, (the Matrons,) does not come to us.

We have 23 Nurses in training now at St. Thomas' – our largest number. 18 is the largest number we can entirely support at St. T.'s – but this is no difficulty at all: even at this moment some of our 23 are supported by others. We should never lack the money. Wherever people really want Nurses, they will give the money to maintain them. [Of course, the Training costs are paid by us for these.] But we want the workers. The only other limit is put: not by want of money, but by the undesirableness of having too large a proportion of Nurses to Patients. Under St. Thomas' temporary diminution of beds, I think 23 Probationers should not be exceeded. But, by the goodness of King's Coll: Hospital-Superintend't, we not only train Midwifery but general Probationers there now. We have 10 for Manchester training there now – of these, as of the Midwifery Probationers, the cost of *board* is willingly paid by those who send them.

[For the sake of having more beds, it is proposed, & seriously thought of, that we take on another Hospital. But this again is private.]

A higher calibre of woman is required for a Training Matron than for a Midwifery Nurse. I will not say higher, but a finer & a larger sort of calibre. She, the Training Matron, must have some power of organization & of authority. And hitherto women of this stamp have never thought of learning the technical Hospital detail, which it is quite necessary to know.

Now see our opportunities. Messrs. Villiers & Farnall[1] would gladly (I have seen them again) form Schools of Nursing in all the London Workhouse Infirmaries with our Trained Nurses as heads – & Pupil Nurses from the larger Union Schools – i. e. the bigger girls. [I think this plan most promising.]

India would take from us any number of Trained Matrons & Nurses, & pay highly. As it is ridiculous of us to think of sending them out by ship-loads, the more reason why we should send out a high stamp of Matrons & Head Nurses, as nuclei, to form *in* India a sort of 'Covenanted Service' of Nurses *for* India.

I think I will send you (privately) a copy of a private paper I am preparing for Sir J. Lawrence.

[I have got 7 millions – did I tell you? – for Barracks in India. Sir J. Lawrence says it must be 10 millions. And Mr. Massey[2] says it shall be 10 millions. My dear millions – How well it looks – six noughts after a 7 – £7,000,000. Like the man henpecked by his heiress wife, who used to retire to comfort himself with her Banking book, I am married to the India Off., confound it. But I retire to comfort myself with the look of my dear millions]

I am afraid you will think I have given you no materials at all for the Article you are so very good as to propose. But you see my difficulty.

I shall be so glad if you see Lady Elgin.[3]

One question of yours I have not answered. We have no superfluity of applications at all from any description or class of persons wishing to be trained. We can scarcely make up our number of the right sort. But not many of *any* sort apply to be trained. We never once have rejected one of the right sort for want of room. But really not many come of any sort, to be rejected. Yet they are not only maintained, trained, & paid wages, free of cost – but they have a certainty and a choice of well-paid places, when certificated – for we have always 10 times as many situations offered, as trained persons to fill them. Indeed I am sorry to say that Nurses of ours have been made 'Superintendents', who were totally unfit for it, & whom we earnestly remonstrated with, as well as with their employers, to prevent their being made 'Superintendents' – but in vain, such is the lack of proper persons. And this again, you will see, is private.

ever yours gratefully,

F Nightingale

Source: BL Add 45788: ff 284–90

1. Villiers and Farnall: Charles Villiers (1802–93), appointed President of the Poor Law Board (1859–66) by Lord Palmerston and H. B. Farnall, Poor Law Inspector for the Metropolitan district of London, were reformers who consulted with FN about improving workhouse conditions.
2. W. N. Massey: (1809–81), Sir Charles Trevelyan's successor as Financial Minister in India (1863–68).
3. Lady Elgin: Lady Louisa Marie Lambton, daughter of the Earl of Durham, wife of Lord Elgin, Viceroy of India.

Florence's self-doubts surfaced again during 1864 and 1865. In January 1864 she had melodramatically written to Selina Bracebridge:

> You know that I always believed it to be God's will for me that I should live & die in Hospitals. When this call He has made upon me for other work stops, & I am no longer able to work, I should wish to be taken to St. Thomas' Hospital, & to be placed in a bed *in a 'general' ward* (which is what I should have desired, had I come to my end as a Hospital Matron). And I beg you to be so very good as to see that this my wish is accomplished . . .
> (BL Add 43397: f 195)

She seemed unable to stop herself from advertising her desire for anonymity: 'I have taken effectual means that all my papers shall be destroyed after my death' (25 June 1864 BL Add 45798: f 243). The past obsessed her. Later that year she wrote in a personal note: 'It is 10 years to day since Inkerman. It is 10 years yesterday since we landed at Scutari. It seems to me like 3 lives – tho' I have spent 7 of those 10 years in bed . . .' (5 Nov 1864 Wellcome).

To Clarkey Florence admitted the loneliness of her position. Yet she refused to see Clarkey when she visited in the summer of 1865, and sent notes to her downstairs where her old friend was sitting, hoping to be admitted:

> Clarkey Mohl darling – How I should like to see you now. But it is quite, quite, quite impossible. I am sure no one ever gave up so much to live, who longed so much to die, as I do and give up daily. It is the only credit I claim. I will live if I can. I shall be so glad if I can't. I am overwhelmed with business. And I have an Indian functionary now in London, whose work is cut out for him every day at my house. I scarcely even have half an hour's ease. Would you tell M. Mohl this, if you are writing, about the Queen of Holland's proposed visit to me? I really feel it is a great honour that she wishes to see me. She is a Queen of Queens. But it is quite, quite, quite impossible . . . (Cook, II, 89)

When Clarkey protested that solitary confinement was more detrimental than beneficial to her health, Florence responded:

> Darling . . . if you think that my living the Robinson Crusoe life I do is the effect of Stoicism, there never was a greater mistake. It is entirely the effect of calculation. I cannot live to work unless I give up all that makes life pleasant. People say, 'Oh see the doctors have said these 8 years she could not live 6 months – therefore it is all a mistake'. They *never* say: she has lived 8 years when the doctors said she could not live 6 months by adopting this kind of life, of sacrificing everything else in order to work . . . But I have ceased to try to make anybody understand this. I do hope I am getting wiser in this respect – not *explaining* . . . I NEVER said it was 'best for me'. All I said was, it was best for the work – or rather it is the only way in which the work could be done. (Woodham-Smith, p. 430)

The Queen of Holland was not admitted either.

Jowett treated her with a frankness that few others dared express. Nightingale responded warmly to his honesty: 'It does make a great difference to my life to know that you are in the world . . . you do do me good. I wish I did you credit. I hope no one, except a Judas, will ever be so near despair as I have been' (24 May 1865 BL Add 45783: f 30). He repeatedly reminded her of her very real achievements, and wrote on 8 September 1865: 'Considering what ministers are, instead of wondering at their not doing all

you want, I wonder at their listening to a word you say. A poor
sick lady, sitting in a room by herself – they have only not to go
near her & never to read her letters & there is an end of her. And
yet you seem to draw them' (BL Add 45783: f 54).

95. To Benjamin Jowett   34 South St 12 July 1865

Dear Mr Jowett[1]

My deepest reverence, my warmest sympathy are yours.

If you were happy, I could part good friends with life, after all –
tho' that this world is hell; that is, the lowest place in God's
universe, I do assure you – [on the best authority.]

I thank you very much for the books – & especially for the
Sermons. I will keep Spinoza for a(n unreasonable) time – as you
are so good as to wish it. But what is the use of making it mine? My
heirs are the War Office clerks. Not even my 'pupils' would take
anything from me, if they knew I read Spinoza. One of them wrote
to me 12 pages, beginning: 'How is it that while no one denies
your philanthropy, every one doubts your Christianity?' – to
which I answered, with the utmost sincerity, that she was quite
right in thinking me a very poor follower of Christ. And we have
been the best of friends – & she made me dispose of her life – and
she is now Matron of one of the largest & poorest & hardest
Nursing Establishments in the Kingdom.[2]
[Do your pupils write to you in that way? Or is this exclusively
feminine? Perhaps we have found out the 'difference' between men
& women.]

You are quite right in what you say of me. I mar the work of
God by my impatience & discontent. I will try to take your advice.
I have tried. But I am afraid it is too late. I lost my serenity some
years ago – then I lost clearness of perception, so that sometimes I
did not know whether I was doing right or wrong for two minutes
together – the horrible loneliness – but I don't mean to waste your
time. Only I would say that my life having been a fever, not even a
fitful one, is not my own fault. Neck or nothing, has been all my
public life. It has never been in my power to arrange my work. No
more than I could help having to receive & provide for 4000
Patients in 17 days (in the Crimean War) and how easy that was
compared with what has happened since!) Could I help – in the
two R. Commissions I have served, in the 9 years I have served the
W.O. exclusive of the Crimean War, my whole life being a hurry:
if the thing were not done to the day, it would not be done at all.
Nursing was a good apprenticeship.

Patients won't wait to die, or better, to be made to live, and operations won't wait till I am less in a hurry. And my whole W.O. work has been of the same kind.

{from a second draft, not in FN's handwriting}
As in receiving & providing for 4000 patients in 17 days (and that was easy!) so in both the R. Commissions, in all my 9 years in the W.O. the work, and not of my own arranging – must always be done to the day or not at all. Then what with the intolerable sleeplessness. But I don't mean to excuse myself. I wish I could do better. But instead of that I think I do worse every day.

I do think God 'descending into hell' – whatever that word may mean in the Creed – is perfectly true in two senses: that God making his worlds *is* God descending into hell – & that to do his work does entail upon some people descendng into hell. They deteriorate under it. Still it is their fault – – – – –

Mine has been such horrible loneliness. But many women, maids of all work and poor Governesses, have been more lonely than I – and have done much better than I. I think if I had had one friend – such a friend as you have been to me for the last 6 months {Returns to FN's handwriting} I should not have been so wrong. But I am afraid it is too late now. Let us hope however that I should have been much worse without you.

The sermon which struck me so much was that one upon: God is loving – God is just – God is true – & upon what a man might expect from God's friendship, if he did God's work, & lived in harmony with His laws.

I think, if I had felt God loved me, I could have borne anything. But I never could feel it.

I am even more broken in mind than in body, tho' I don't think my mind ever was a strong one.

Yet I believe I am willing now to do God's work anyhow & leave all the rest to Him.[3]

Source: BL Add 45783: ff 35–44   {incomplete and edited letter}

1. Note on letter: Very private and autobiographical.
2. Note: The pupil who wrote about FN's doubtful Christianity was Agnes Jones.
3. Note: A second or third draft of the same letter (a later part) is similar, with some omissions and slight changes. The shorter draft has 'what with the horrible loneliness & the intolerable sleeplessness'. and 'I hope you will forgive me, tho' I do not forgive myself, for being so hopeless' before 'let us hope &c'.

Some days later Nightingale wrote more cheerfully to Jowett,

I think the Elections are pleasing – specially Mr. J. S.

Mill's – & Mr Goschen's[1] being at the head of the poll – & Sir. J. Acton's[2] – & Mr Hughes',[3] tho' I think he is a goose.

I don't think anything of you at Oxford – because you vote 'genteel', like those wretched Lords. Unless you have to fight your way up to the Polling-booth & go in for the drinking & pelting & hooting like a Briton, I think nothing of you.

Same for women: If your pupil, Mr. Williams gives us the suffrage, tell him we must have the drinking & the hooting. Or we shall think nothing of it.

How I wish *I* had the combative faculty. It *is* such a power to carry one through life. Some one said of Roebuck: he was qualified by his fight with the wild beasts of Sheffield to become member for Ephesus.

How I wish I could qualify to be member for Ephesus. {end July 1865} (BL Add 45783: f 41)

1. Rt. Hon. George J. Goschen: (1831–1907), a Liberal Unionist; President of the Poor Law Board, 1868–71.
2. Sir John Acton: (1834–1902), Liberal MP who favoured the secret ballot in elections. Professor of Modern History at Cambridge.
3. Thomas Hughes: (1823–96), Christian Socialist, author of *Tom Brown's Schooldays*. Liberal MP for Lambeth, 1865–68; for Frome, 1868–74.

On 6 September 1865 Florence's cousin Hilary died. To Clarkey she wrote, 'There is *not a single person*, except yourself, who dares not think that Hilary's family were quite right in the most monstrous of slow murders – and all for what?' (V. Bonham Carter, p. 106). She could only shudder when she compared her own narrow escape from the family with Hilary's slow destruction by hers. The artistically gifted Hilary had always been at the beck and call of not only her family but also anyone else who claimed to need help. Both Clarkey and Flo felt that Hilary had sacrificed her talent to the service of others. Liz Herbert became a Roman Catholic and relations between the two women tapered off. Palmerston, who had for many years been supportive of Florence's work, died 18 October 1865. Her 'men' could no longer be summoned at the snap of her fingers; she opened a letter to Captain Galton with, 'Is that unfortunate Christian, Capt. Galton, come back?' (30 Oct 1865 BL Add 47714: f 87). And she never forgot that she had drafted a letter outlining a practical scheme for the sanitary administration of India for Lord de Grey which had reached him just twenty-four hours after the government had had to resign. She blamed the late delivery of her memo on Dr Sutherland, who was in Algeria on an inspection tour for the army sanitary reform team. Every change of government meant different ministers, many of whom were not equally dedicated to – or knowledgeable about – the reform programme. Even her India friend, Dr Pattison Walker, was failing in health and talking about returning home.

96. To J. Pattison Walker, MD   34 South St 18 Oct 1865

Private

My dear Sir,

I am sorry to hear you are so far from well. But I hope that you have taken holiday in time.

John Bull is a conceited ass, & thinks the climate ought to take care of him, instead of him taking care of the climate. The French fare much better.

Anglo India has made its capital of a place where the Moguls used to send their state-prisoners to die. And people fall ill in Calcutta, and then say: it's the climate.

The R. Commission never told you all to live in Calcutta. But you abuse them for not having laid sufficient stress on 'climatic influences'.

We are spending just five millions sterling to empty that small gutter, the Thames, of sewage. And this in a temperate climate.

What are *you* doing?

It is not that Calcutta might not be made much more healthy than it is, if you were willing to spend several millions. The main question is: to keep the sub-soil moisture at a certain distance below the ground varying with latitude & local circumstances. This costs money. If it *costs too much* (as perhaps in a place like Calcutta) then the place ought to be abandoned, or never have been chosen. This is the only real determination of localities, as far as healthy surface of ground is concerned.

But people in India, tho' they are always raving against the 'climate', actually tolerate a state of things in their palaces which we have ceased to tolerate in the poorest village in this healthy climate. And yet we have always Typhus & sometimes Cholera – and at this moment the Poor Law Board is meditating a sweeping

Bill (for London) for next Session, because the Vestries are not doing their duty. And the Poor Law Board is quite right. (I tell you this – but it is a secret.)

There are 120 ways of boiling eggs (this *anent* 'climatic influences'). Climate is good everywhere. But man and his habits & his manner of selecting places to live in & to build on are as bad as possible – (as I say, John Bull's a conceited ass, & his conceit is that climates are made to obey him). And hence he confounds climate with his own want of care. He ought to boil his eggs better.

Batavia was the most deadly place in the world. And now, people go there for their health. Can anything be stronger than this?

In the Table of Mortality for 1859–64, shewn in its distribution by months, which you have been good enough to send me, are appended notes as to the climatic elements, which are assumed as causing the increasing death rates during certain months. I think this is a pity. They belong to a method of determining causation which in this country we venture to think we have improved upon. High temperature & moisture are nothing per se. As influencing other causes, they are a great deal – they have immense power. To place them as *causes* is much the same thing logically as it would be to make the perfection or imperfection of roast beef depend on the quantity of coals raised at Newcastle – as if you said, the more fuel the sun puts into his grate, the more unhealthy India becomes.

I have to thank you for your most kind note of Aug. 16, & for its enclosure from Dr. Bryden.[1]

There is a growing conviction in Europe that, when Cholera seizes a population living in bad sanitary conditions, its influence may extend hundreds of miles atmospherically from the centre where it began. And there is a diplomatic proposition to suppress or regulate the Mecca pilgrimage, in order to prevent its becoming the epidemic centre of the West, which it has always been hitherto.

The moral is this: that unless you improve the sanitary condition of the Civil populations, you cannot insure immunity for the soldiers from epidemics.

I have to thank you, which I do most cordially, for the valuable Draft No. 262 about railway travelling by troops – also for the Extract of a letter No. 247 about the Jails in the Lower Provinces. How curious & instructive that is – & how terrible! It shews that some one must again set hard to work to reform the management & laws of those Jails, like Howard, & never leave off till he has done. The contrast between the men's & women's health, & between the cubic space for each, startles even me.

But my mind is full of Lord Palmerston's illness. He may be

passing away even at this moment. He will be a great loss to us. He made a joke about every thing. But, tho' he made a joke – when asked to do the right thing, he always did it. No one else will be able to carry the things thro' the Cabinet he did. I shall lose in him a powerful protector. Especially in Poor Law & wide sanitary views, he was so much more in earnest than he appeared. He did not do himself justice.

His *presumed* successor is so queer tempered that he cannot manage the Cabinet.[2]

I most sincerely hope that this note will find you quite restored in health.

I will write again by next mail.

Pray believe me ever yours most truly

Florence Nightingale.

Source: BL Add 45781: ff 296–99   {typed copy}

1. Dr James L. Bryden: (1833–80), was the author of *Vital Statistics of the Bengal Presidency* and numerous pamphlets and reports. He achieved the rank of Surgeon-Major (1873).
2. Palmerston's successor: Lord John Russell.

In November 1865 W.E.N. finally found a permanent home for Florence, close to the Verneys' London house. She was bedridden, weak and virtually helpless from 1862 to 1866; Dr Sutherland was indispensable to her. Yet she continued to berate him both to his face and to others. At one point she had written to her mother: 'Please ask Hilly to make me the roughest pen & ink sketch of Jess, the mare, with my face, dragging a cart, & Rab, the dog, with Sutherland's face, pulling behind the other way & "nearly strangling himself to spite" me. It is to shew Sutherland (when I am too ill to speak) what he does' ({June 1864?} Wellcome). To Dr Sutherland himself, she opened a letter with: 'I am sorry you are ill. But I suppose, as I have not heard again, that you intend me to believe that you are either well or dead. I am so busy that I have not time to die. Here are three things . . .' (12 Sept 1870 BL Add 45755: f 46).

Jowett at last persuaded Florence to go to Embley, where she stayed with her mother during autumn 1865. This was her first visit home in nine years. Now that her mother was seventy-seven,

Florence could see her differently. 'I don't think my dear mother was ever more touching or interesting to me than she is now in her state of dilapidation', she wrote to Clarkey in August. 'She is so much gentler, calmer, more thoughtful' (Cook, II, 119).

97. To Fanny Nightingale   35 South St 31 May 1866

Dearest Mum

I forgot to say that I sent your 'Alex. Scott' & 'Moncton Milnes' by Monday's box.

I read A. Scott with the greatest pleasure & interest and I presumed to mark it – hoping that it would have not the less interest for you, my dearest mum, if your poor old child had marked it. I know Papa justly dislikes books being scribbled on. But I thought these were for your own especial reading.

What a life-time it seems to me since I knew Alex. Scott – hard upon 30 years.

I was glad to see: 'The aisles of blessed Peter are open all the year' – my old friend, again.

We have the most inveterate East wind & gloom here I ever knew.

Rev'd Mother is better. But I fear that her life, like mine, is a burden to her – that is, each step of the day's work is a burden.

I hope I am a help to Sir John Lawrence. For indeed the cool way people speak of his immense difficulties & the intense way in which *he* feels them *himself*, makes me mad with the desire of helping him.

Should you ever have to spend August & September at Embley, dearest mum – [may the time be long first – I hope you will, for *many* years & *many more*, go on spending the autumn at Lea Hurst. God forbid that it should be otherwise]. But if you should ever spend August & September at Embley, I might perhaps come & spend them with my dearest mother if I live.

I think I shall live, somewhat on the principle that the Jew thought Roman Catholicism must be true, on the ground that it had survived the horrors of Rome. So *I* think. I *must* live some time longer, because I have survived the sufferings of last winter.

I don't suppose the journey to Embley would kill me – if I had some man to arrange it entirely for me.

I shall never go to Hampstead again, now the Sutherlands are gone.

I could not leave London before Parliament is up. For all Government purposes, Norwood is quite as far as Embley.

Sutherland may be sent to the Mediterranean for Inspections in August & September. In that case, it would be just as easy for me to do the Government Indian work for those two months at Embley, if I only could once get there. But all this is a castle in the air. God only knows. And I know that I hope it will be many, many years before you spend your autumns at Embley.

Ever, my dearest Mum's loving child

F.

If I came to Embley, it would have this advantage, that I should get rid of the dirty old prig, Delany, for the time, & bring only Temperance.

F.N.

Source: Wellcome

Her alliance with the sanitarian and former Poor Law administrator Edwin Chadwick continued, as they consulted each other frequently on issues of public health.

98. To Edwin Chadwick   35 South St 9 July 1866

Private

Dear Mr. Chadwick

I have read your admirable letter with the greatest interest & with the greatest pleasure. And let me say, first of all, how, among the inestimable & most various services you have done our country, I think none greater than what you are trying to do her now – & how I rejoice to see your clear judgment & vigour at work again on this subject. I agree entirely with the administrative principles for the care of the sick poor which you have set.

It is a subject which is familiar to me. And, during the last 18 months, I have been in practical contact with the present system of affording Infirmary relief to sick poor, both in London & elsewhere.

Of course my primary object was: the introduction of *trained*** Nurses into Workhouse Infirmaries – as many as possible. (*I object to the word '*paid*' Nurses. It is not the paying but the *training* of a man which makes him a Medical Officer. It is only the *training* of a woman which will make her a Nurse.) But this happens just to be a test point of the present system of administration. The result of all my experience is that, if the existing Workhouse management is allowed to continue, anything like efficient nursing of the sick is utterly impossible. Indeed it is not nursing at all.

It is true that Guardians might (and I dare say will) employ paid, instead of pauper, Nurses. They might even appoint so-called 'Lady Superintendents'. But so long as a sick man, woman or child is considered *administratively* to be a pauper to be repressed & not a fellow-creature to be nursed into health – so long will these most shameful disclosures have to be made – disclosures which have made our (so-called) local government a bye-word; while the rate payers will be deluded by what is really a false pretence.

The care & government of sick poor – and, indeed, of all persons labouring under physical or mental disability to win their bread, is a thing totally different from the government of paupers.

[Why do we have Hospitals in order to cure? – and Workhouse Infirmaries in order *not* to cure? Taken solely from the point of view of preventing pauperism, what a stupidity & an anomaly this is. 'Penny wise & pound foolish' as even a maid-of-all-work could understand]

This is the very first lesson which our legislators have to learn.

[But our legislature always mixes up administration with party.]

In order that you may not think me sentimentalizing or political-izing, I will try to answer your questions, one by one:
A. to insist on the great principle of separating the sick, insane, infirm & aged, incurable,* imbecile, & above all the children from the usual pauper population of the Metropolis (*how many of those called incurable are *not* incurable a life's hospital experience has taught me. Old age, is, of course, incurable)
B. to advocate a single central administration
C. to place all these classes, (especially those suffering from any disease, bodily or mental,) under this distinct & responsible administration, amenable directly to Parliament – these are the A.B.C. of the reform required

Uniformity of system in this matter is absolutely necessary, in order that the suffering poor should be properly cared for, & in order that vacant beds & places may be filled up, wherever space exists.

All the Officers of these Infirmaries & Asylums should be appointed by & should be responsible to the central authority, which is responsible to Parliament.

Sickness, madness, imbecility & permanent infirmity are general inflictions affecting the entire community – [mainly, too, brought about by the wretched sanitary state of our streets] & are not, like pauperism, to be kept down.

The sick or infirm or mad pauper ceases to be a pauper, when so afflicted.

The past system of mixing up all kinds of poor in workhouses will never be submitted to in future.

The very first thing wanted is classification – classification & separation of the lazy, able-bodied, immoral paupers, living on other people's labour – from the sick, & infirm.

You must thus have two kinds of administration – one for sick, for infirm, aged & invalids, for insane & imbeciles, & above all for children – and another for paupers. Once acknowledge the principle of this separation – and you must have suitable establishments for the care & treatment of Sick & Infirm. For these purposes, consolidation is absolutely necessary unless the rate payers intend to incur an unknown cost.

Any attempt to treat the classes I have named, as they ought to be treated, would, in the existing Work-houses, involve an amount of expence which even London could not bear.

Hence comes the necessity – necessity as I think it, of consolidating the entire medical relief of the Metropolis under one central management, which would know where vacant beds are to be found, & so be able to distribute the sick as to use all the Establishments in the most economical way.

The administration of these Hospitals should be specially organized (as we have done in the Army.) The best Medical & Surgical advice should be found for them – and, as said above, there should be *direct responsibilities* in all Officers from below upwards, ending in Parliament.

The advantage to Medicine & Surgery of such arrangements would be very great indeed.

We know that, in this way, *6000 cases of disease & injury would be constantly undergoing examination & comparison in a few large Hospitals – (which can be built as healthy as the smallest Hospitals & far more economically) instead of the experience being frittered away in a few dark dirty rooms here & there, as at present. (*The last return in my possession gives 6,039 cases more or less acute – and 6,403 old & infirm requiring more or less *constant medical treatment. Total* Medical & Surgical cases 12,442.)

And as part of the general administration, a thoroughly efficient system of nursing Sick, Infirm, Incurables, Idiots, Insane, could be introduced.

This is *impossible* in existing Workhouses. To carry it out, you

must have a sufficient number of Patients, a certain number of
Nurses & Probationers (many of whom, by the way, might come
from the girls* brought up in the Schools) – and, over these, Head
Nurses ('Sisters') and a Superintendent. (*This is impossible now,
because you cannot put girls of 14–16 to be trained as Nurses in
existing Infirmaries)

Sick, infirm, idiots, & mad persons require special constructive
arrangements, special medical care & nursing, & special dieting.
[Of all these, they have little or none that is worthy the name in the
present London Workhouses.] They are not 'paupers'. They are
'poor & in affliction'. Society certainly owes them, if it owes
anything, every necessary care for recovery. In practice, there
should be consolidated & uniform administrative arrangements.
Sickness is not *parochial*; it is general & human.

For sick you want Hospitals as good as the best Civil Hospitals.
You want the best Nurses you can find. You want efficient &
sufficient Medical attendance. You want an energetic & wise
administration.

[All the great Parisian Hospitals, the Schools for half the Medical
men of Europe are managed by *their* central authority].

Dear Mr. Chadwick, this letter is already a great deal longer than
I wish. Yet, tho' there is much repetition in it, I cannot re-write it.
And I have omitted much that I wanted to say.

I have written it at intervals, and, because I am so driven by
business, almost as soon as it was light in the morning. This must
account for its incoherency.

It is for yourself alone, or, if you wish it, for Mr. Mill.

But, if you desired it, I should be very glad to express my
conclusions more in detail, in answer to written questions (as I
have done to two R. Commissions) – should the Committee of the
House of Commons think it worth while.

Much that I have not time to put here I could then say. And I
should then have time to make it shorter. I have scarcely ever been
so busy as I am now.

    Pray believe me dear Mr. Chadwick
    ever your faithful & grateful serv't

                      Florence Nightingale
P.S. If anything were wanting to prove the absence of the very
foundations of knowledge as to what ought be the principles of
administration for the sick poor, you can find it in the evidence of
the very officials of the Workhouses, (including more than one
Medical Officer – & in one instance, a Chaplain.)

To my mind, infinitely more horrible than the horrible cases
which have come to light – (including that of the laying-out of a

living baby) – are these statements of the officials of what *they* considered their duties & their offices.

I can truly say that I have lived among horrors. Yet nothing that I have ever seen in the old Military Hospitals or in the worst-nursed Civil Hospitals in the world, ever came near, (to my mind,) to the horror of hearing Matrons & Masters & Guardians & Medical Officers declare these things to be the normal, proper rule of their lives & offices.

Are they really there, then, to kill & not to cure?

It is the first time, I should think, in the world, that this has been *said* tho' it may too often have been *done*.

F.N.

Except to re-echo your opinion, I would not enter here, upon a matter of detail, (tho' an important detail) viz. the reckless extravagance & waste of the present Workhouse Infirmary system, which can only be rivalled by its miserable 'parsimoniousness'.

But I should have much to say on this point, if examined.

I don't believe it to be at all certain that an improved & efficient system of Hospitals for the sick would cost more than the present disgraceful no-system of betraying the sick.

F.N.

Source: BL Add 45771: ff 102–10

During 1867 Florence again spent several months with her family, where almost inevitably her depression deepened. Jowett encouraged her to pursue interests other than War Office work, writing gently,

> But indeed it grieves me really to see you who have done so much dispirited & desponding. It is hard to say to a person who is ill & alone 'Get another attitude of mind. give up none of your plans & proposals but wait & trust to time & have faith in God, and don't seek to move the world by main force, but give the world a push when it is going your way'. (Feb 1867 BL Add 45783: f 111)

Over several years Nightingale wrote many drafts on the subject 'What is the Character of God? . . . but to create a world according to a certain, definite plan by which each & every one of us is on the way to progress towards perfection, i. e. happiness' (17 Aug 1871 BL Add 45783: f 258). This abstract problem was particularized in terms of family conflicts, if we read between the lines of a draft of a letter to Jowett:

99. To Benjamin Jowett {1867?}

Men & *especially* women 'should never suffer themselves to be diverted from forming a real estimate of a man's character by what is termed "respect for his office"'.

[This which is said of the Clergy & their Bishop *I* say of everybody, especially every body stationed in families. (I really was not aware that any body still did this above Bishops.]

It certainly requires great strength of mind for a woman to 'form a real estimate of' her husband's 'character' & to behave the better, instead of the worse for it. Most women prefer to remain in an amiable fog, thro' which they can see what they like about their husband's character.

But I believe half the misery in families would be done away with, if women could really rise to 'forming a true estimate' of their husband's or their father's & mother's characters, as the case may be. Because there is none of the reverence left of the Patriarchal times – & which certainly existed in the last century in England.

On the contrary, there is scarcely a person in the world so much criticized as a husband by his wife, a father by his son, a mother by her daughter. And yet there is a constant effort to act a lie, if not to say one, about them.

It is all a 'muz' and a maze – the eternal vagueness of the present day.

It is just like Review-writing & reading. People make no effort to 'form a real estimate of' the book. But they criticize it all the more severely & admire it all the more indiscreetly because they know nothing of it but the review. Now, it is not *criticism* that is here recommended of the husband's & parents' character. It *is* a *true estimate*. Nothing else will ever make the life of families endurable. Nothing else will ever prevent that willing martyrdom which does no good to the person who accepts it but only harm.

The martyr sacrifices *her*self (*him*self in a few instances) entirely in vain. Or rather not in vain; for she (or he) makes the selfish more selfish, the lazy more lazy, the narrow narrower.

Now all this would be saved if the martyrs could but see that it was right, it was a duty, to form a 'real estimate' of the characters of those they live with. The martyrs are often paralyzed by those they sacrifice to. Almost always they deteriorate & are deteriorated. Often their martyrdom is only acting a lie. They have a kind of dim conviction some where that the others would be much better without them. (I should be sorry to say in how many instances this has been openly expressed to me.) Now this always deteriorates. Because nothing ennobles martyrdom but a strong conviction that it is for some noble purpose.

The other is only like the poor little weak fag who allows the big boys to run pins into him because he can't help himself.

No less would the Devourers be saved than the Devoured, if they did but form a 'real estimate' of character. For it was often not thro' selfishness, it is from a lack of knowledge of the true value of a human being that they accept the sacrifice, which 'profiteth nothing'.

To how many of these martyrs will the persecutor say, in the next world 'And you knew it – and you let me do this'. It is really a wrong done to the persecutor.

I see no improvement or reform likely to arise in this matter at all. Calas'[1] death opened the eyes of thousands. His death was worth dying. But death, in this matter shuts people's eyes. If they had some small inkling of the truth before, after death it is all to be hushed up, every body is to be perfect, not the slightest remorse is to be felt. And so men's eyes are to be blinded for ever & ever.

Source: BL Add 45783: ff 181–82   {draft}

1. Jean Calas: (1698–1762), a Protestant merchant of Toulouse who was tortured and legally killed on suspicion of murdering his son to prevent him from converting to Roman Catholicism. Voltaire took up his case, and after three years the family was vindicated.

For Nightingale nursing was an art and a calling. She was outraged when Elizabeth Garrett [Anderson], the first English woman doctor, spoke in favour of women doctors at the annual meeting of the National Association for the Promotion of Social Science, and later published an article in *Macmillan's* (April 1867) arguing for the training of ladies as doctors, and defining nursing as an occupation suitable for domestic servants. An avalanche of letters to friends followed the meeting, including her old ally, Dr William Farr, to whom she indignantly wrote, 'Will she forgive me if I say that I know none but the *most* fanatical of R. Catholic Archbishops who would write as she does on this? Certainly no R. Catholic order' (20 Oct 1866 BL Add 43400: f 128).

My principle has always been: that we should give the best training we could to any woman of any class, of any sect, 'paid' or unpaid, who had the requisite qualifications, moral, intellectual & physical, for the vocation of a Nurse. Unquestionably, the educated will be more likely to rise to the post of Superintendents, but *not* because they are 'ladies', but because they are educated . . . I have unquestionably said (and I still hold) that 'Lady Nurses' or 'Lady Superintendents', *un*trained, do more harm than good, & that it is a destructive fallacy to put a 'lady' over Nurses, who does not know their work as well as they do themselves, merely because she is a 'lady'. (13 Oct 1866 BL Add 43400: f 114)

The necessity of training, no matter what the social class of the woman, was a principle Nightingale repeatedly emphasized, for 'Three fourths of the whole mischief in women's lives in England is that they suppose themselves exceptions from the laws of training to which men bow' (20 Oct 1866 BL Add 43400: f 130).

When the Ladies' Medical College, founded in 1865, began to agitate for the proper licensing of trained midwives, Nightingale sensed a rival to her plans. Always an opponent of any form of licensing, she fastened upon Garrett's desire for proper credentials as evidence of her untrustworthiness.

100. To Sir Harry Verney   16 Apr 1867

Private

My dear Sir Harry
      You see I differ upon every word of Miss Garrett's note.
      But it is not a subject on which I am (or fancy myself) an authority.
      And therefore I write this for you only.
      I could not if I would, and I would not if I could, enter upon any controversy with her.
      But then neither must they ask me for advice or co-operation (as they have often done)
      1. *She* starts on the ground that the *summum bonum* for women is to be able to obtain *the same* Licence or Diploma as men for medical practice.
      Now I start from exactly the opposite ground.
      Medical education is about as bad as it possibly can be.
      It makes men *prigs*.
      It prevents any wise, any philosophical, any practical view of health & disease. Only a few genius-es rise above it.
      It makes a man a prig,
      it will make a woman a prig-*ger*.
      But – all that women have hitherto said, is:

I will take the same *kind* of education a man gets, but less in *degree*.

Where he studies years, I will study months.

Against that I set my face.

But – what I want to see is – not, as Miss G. seems to wish – women obtaining exactly *the same* education as men, & exactly the same Diploma – & practising indiscriminately between the sexes as men do.

Very far otherwise.

Not that I conceive it is much more indelicate for a woman to doctor men than for a woman to nurse men.

But the last is necessary.

The first is totally unnecessary.

Indeed female (American) practitioners have told me with their own lips that they should 'consider it an insult if called in to attend a man-Patient'.

That is as it should be.

What I want to see is women attending as Physicians their own sex – especially in lyings-in & in diseases peculiar to women – or children.

The good of a Licence or Diploma is this: that you *can't get it*, except after *years* of a certain course.

& that this ensures you against the superficiality, (said to be) common to all women.

But, if this good result could be brought about by women's own good sense, where would be the necessity of the 'Licence'?

Do you suppose Miss Garrett gets one more Patient by being a 'Licentiate'?

Do you suppose that a thoroughly educated experienced female Doctor would lose one Patient by *not* being a 'Licentiate'?

I don't,

I think English women have too much sense.

It is quite true that a *special* education (i.e. for female cases only) is always disadvantageous.

It is quite true that every Oculist, Dentist, Accoucheur, practises much better for having had a *general* Medical education.

But Miss Garrett does *not* say this.

She does not say: how can we give women the best general Medical education?

She says – how can we satisfy the 'Examining Boards'?

Now – every old fogey, like me, knows that, if a man is a genius, he can't pass – (these 'Examining Boards')

that what makes a man pass is memory, chique – words –

that 'Examining Boards' are just so many charlatans.

[Poor Alexander, the Director-Gen'l, told me of a man who passed the 'Examining Board' triumphantly – & who did not know, one from the other, the heart from the liver, when these valuable Articles were placed before him in the flesh. Every Examiner is full of similar stories.

It was for this that, in 1861, we took so much pains to organize, & Sidney Herbert to start, a Practical Army Medical School (now at Netley) where men who *have* passed *all the regular* Medical course are instructed by the bed-side. For, even the *four years* necessary in Civil Hospitals are no sufficient text. Only the dressers & Clinical Clerks get much thereby – while the hundreds who follow in the train of such a man as Fergusson[1] (the 'great Carpenter', as Sidney Herbert used to call him) get next to nothing for their 'four years'.]

2. Who is to organize it then, if Miss Garrett does not?

It appears as if she wished to be another Ferguson – i. e. totally useless except to Patients.

3. Whether we can do this or not will depend upon our calls & our supply. At present we are engaged years deep to Leeds, Sydney, India &c &c &c &c

I see no prospect of our doing for years to come – what Miss G. wishes.

I have myself had the regret of refusing *two General* Hospitals within the last month – besides many smaller applications.

We should certainly not think it right to sacrifice some great centre like Sydney, &c &c &c &c, which wishes to form a Training-School, for a scheme so unlicked as the present one under discussion.

For we had rather, of course, have a Training-School in a large General Hospital – whenever we have Nurses to spare.

And as to *Midwifery* Nurses: at our humble little Institution at King's College, the education is far better than any thing that could be given us.

[E.g. at Q. Charlotte's & other Lying-in Hospitals, a certificate as *Accoucheuse* is actually given after a month's *or less than a month's* attendance. The lady who is going out to practise at Delhi actually got hers in this way]

4 – Certainly it does

It 'increases the expences' *just by the expences of those Nurses* in training.

If a Nurse is learning, she can't be *in the place* of another Nurse.

Mr. Rathbone proposes to give us £400 a year to train just 10 Probationers at Liverpool Workhouse.

We spend £1000 a year at St. Thomas', £500 a year at King's College.

Ask the Maternité at Paris what *it* spends.

Not one Midwife is saved by having Pupil Midwives.

The utmost that is saved is the expence of '*Extra*' Nurses in any of these Institutions – fevers & operations requiring 'Extra' Nurses, you put on your Probationers (*not*, however, *raw* Probationers) for whom it is excellent practice – or when a regular Nurse is sick or on leave.

ever yours

F.N.

Confidential

In 1860 it took me *months* of very hard work, *assisted as I was* by all the first Civil & Army Medical authorities, to make the Programme & scheme of the Army Medical School. [Of course I took nothing from my own authority. All I did was to collect & sift the best opinions.]

Now I am quite sure that it would take *any* one months of very hard work to make the Programme of a Female Medical School.

I neither can nor mean to do it.

Miss Garrett, I am sure, neither sees the necessity of this close application, nor means to give it.

[The paper on Nurses which she read at the Social Science was crammed full of errors in fact, which half a day's enquiry would have enabled her to avoid – & which cost me a whole week's work to answer *after* the fact.] to different enquiries, including Dr. Farr.]

The great error of these Medical ladies appear to me to be: that they not only put the cart before the horse, but that they expect the cart to drag the horse.

How is a woman to get a man's Diploma? – *that is all they ask*.

It is just the same as if I, instead of qualifying myself to assist Sidney Herbert in the War Office, had bent all my energies to:

how is a woman to become a Secretary of State?

How do people in Paris do these things? for 50 years there has been a succession of Lady Professors at the Maternité, who rank (I was going to say, just as high) but who in fact rank) much higher than Simpson or Locock[2] here.

Their works are quoted as authorities all over Europe.

They command any practice they please when they leave the Maternité. Their names have even been forged – & establishments set up in their names by quacks.

There is no struggle with the men-Doctors.

How have they done all this?

Not certainly by trying for men's Diplomas –

not by a paper war.

not by struggling to get into men's colleges.

Simply by working a female School on female Patients to perfection

& letting all controversy alone.

But then, the School is absolutely complete. An 'élève sage-femme'[3] cannot be certificated *under 2 years*, instead of *in one month*, as in England.

The female Professoriat, the 'sage-femme' en 'chef' & 'sages-femmes aides' reside in the Hospital.

The élèves sages-femmes de 2ème année are made to help in training the 'élèves sages-femmes de 1ère année'.

No Medical School of men ever known is anything to be compared to its perfection in point of instruction, *both*

practical & scientific.

And all this they have done – – – how?

Not by *aping* a man's Medical School.

Just the reverse.

By simply doing the very best to form good Midwives – & not thinking about men at all.

[To ensure the standard of free public opinion. There *is* a man-Professor besides – generally the best Accoucheur in France – but who does not reside, of course.]

[I believe the female head of this School has usually attended the Queens & Royal Duchesses of France in this century. And it was said that the Empress Eugénie desired it very much, & would have gone on quite well, if the Emperor had not insisted on her having a man-Doctor]

If I were forming a Female Medical School in England, I should just cut the Gordian knot at once, & avoid all collision with men, by beginning as closely as possible on the Parisian model, & then afterwards, if you extend it to all diseases of women & children, so much the better – or even to a more general education still.

But it is absurd to tell me that 'Madame la Sage-femme en chef' at Paris requires a Diploma to obtain her a practice among Queens and Empresses – or that it is not trying to make your cart draw your horse. It is not your 'Bishop's Commission' that makes the 'apple-woman' a Deaconess – nor your 'Licence' which makes the lady a Doctor.

As long as Medical ladies go on in England in this way, I have no hope. One sensible woman, like Miss Garrett, may now & then win her way to practice. But even she is as senseless as the others about Female Medical Schools.

Let women begin by that branch of the Profession (Midwifery) which is undoubtedly theirs.

let them do it as well as possible – let them conquer their place in it – instead of, as now, as it seems to me, lady Doctors affecting to despise it.

All the rest will follow.

But *none* of the rest will follow, if their only aim is to be to extort from men a man's place.

N. B. Let me explain what I said about a Nurse Training-School being merely an extra expence.

The pupil Midwives of the 2nd year (at Paris) instruct the pupil Midwives of the 1st year.

I have never made any calculation of the kind.

Still I think I must be much beyond the mark in saying that, if the Maternité were *not* a Training-School, one sage-femme en chef & half the number of pupils de 2de année as sages-femmes would be more than sufficient as a Working-Staff – so that you at once sweep off as 'increases to working expences' all the pupils de 1ère année, half those de 2de année, & all the Head Staff but one.

As to St. Thomas':

tho' I have often found fault with them for turning a penny out of us, it has *not* been for employing our Probationers as 'extra' Nurses – for severe cases – (which is excellent practice)

– not for employing them to take the place (temporarily) of sick or absent Nurses –

– not even for working a whole ward with our Probationers, as has *not never* been done –

but for helping themselves, as they have frequently done, to our *un* certificated Nurses (Probationers who had been with us only a few months) to fill *permanently* vacant situations as Nurses & Sisters – at St. Thomas'.

In such a case, either St. Thomas' or the woman ought certainly to re-fund to the N. Fund.

But we have been obliged to submit. Because it has been the choice of having our own women or a stranger as Head Nurse over our Probationers.

I need scarcely say that, as a rule, you must pay Probationers wages.

F. N.

Source: Wellcome

1. Sir William Fergusson: (1808–77), Professor of Surgery, King's College, London, 1840–70; became the premier surgeon of the day, pioneering surgery for cleft palate and harelip. He was created baronet in 1866.

2. Simpson and Locock: Sir James Young Simpson (1811–70), Professor of Midwifery at University of Edinburgh. Discovered the anaesthetic properties of chloroform, which he introduced to midwifery in 1847. Sir Charles Locock (1799–1875), First Physician Accoucheur to the Queen. Physician to the Westminster Lying-in Hospital.

3. élève sage-femme: student midwife.

Nightingale felt beset by enemies and losses during these years. The Royal Commission's 'suggestions' were treated as such in India, whereas she would have been happier had these been seen as 'orders'. When she recommended designing the new barracks with windows for ventilation, the officials in India opted for doors, a choice that was based on experience of the Indian climate. Nightingale disagreed, not only with this but also with the way in which the Viceroy reached the decision; he had consulted the authorities in the various regions which was, according to her, 'administration by universal suffrage' (10/11 July 1867? BL Add 45781: f 199). To Captain Galton, she wrote:

101. To Captain Douglas Galton

35 South St
30 July 1865[1]

Private

My dear Capt. Galton

I send you the enclosed note, merely for you to see the exact position in which the matter is.

If I don't hear soon from Sir S. Northcote,[2] I shall begin again, through you & thro' Sir B. Frere.[3]

But I should like to be guided by you *as to the time*.

[I am afraid of pressing the matter while they have this fag end of the Reform Bill still in hand.] for fear of being forbidden to press afterwards.

Will you talk to Sir S. Northcote?

Have you talked to Sir S. Northcote?

He *had not* seen Lord de Grey's Minute.

That is the India Office all over.

I am told they are in a great fright about the Orissa affair[4] – & 'really' think that 'something' must be done (about Indian administration) which gives us a favourable opportunity.

I have read the Orissa papers. *Simplicity* & *direction* {direct?} *action*; these are the two things wanted. Hindoos are not English. And, even if they were, simplicity & direct action are two good things.

Sir C. Beadon's[5] defense is pitiable.

But the fault is in the system of administration.

The G. G.[6] sits at Simla like a great hen – and lets all his chickens scratch all over India. And if there is a grain of corn too deep, for them to scratch up, he gives a dig with his claw to help them; that is all. Ld Dalhousie & Ld Canning had made a step towards better administration. Ld Elgin let it all slip back.

Sir J. Lawrence has struggled (in vain) against the dead weights around him.

Please send me back the enclosed.

ever yours truly

F. Nightingale

Source: BL Add 45764: ff 98–99

1. FN has given the wrong date: 1867.

2. Sir Stafford Northcote: (1818–87), succeeded Lord Cranborne as Indian Secretary in 1867. An ally of FN's, he commissioned her to draft various sanitary papers.

3. Sir Bartle Frere: (1815–84), was a highly respected civil servant. He served in Bombay, 1834–56. He returned when the Mutiny broke out and was appointed member of the Governor-General's council in 1859; Governor of Bombay 1862.

4. Orissa affair: A major famine, which local officials failed to anticipate. When the monsoon broke, transportation into the province was impossible and the death rate soared. Later, when excess grain was delivered, it rotted in warehouses.

5. Sir Cecil Beadon: (1816–81), Lieutenant-Governor of Bengal (1862–66). He underestimated the seriousness of the Orissa famine, and failed to make emergency plans; a later investigation held him responsible for the massive loss of life.

6. G. G.: Governor-General of India, Sir John Lawrence.

Her letter to Sir Stafford Northcote was more tactful:

102. To Sir Stafford Northcote   31 July 1867

Dear Sir Stafford Northcote

I am very much alive to the great kindness of your note of July 30.

And it would be most ungrateful of me to press for a decision now at such a moment of pressure of business.

But I do not.

What I venture to say now is suggested by a passage in your very kind note. And is only written in the hope that it will be taken into consideration when the time comes for you taking the whole subject into consideration (of the India Public Health Service.)

In carrying out any measures for protecting Public Health in India, you most truly say that due regard should be had to local information & local peculiarities – & even to local 'habits & prejudices'.

It is just because we had this principle so intensely in view that we have been so confounded by the turn that things have lately taken.

The principle, it is needless to say, applies rather to detail than to great leading Sanitary works.

The immediate question which occasioned my writing to trouble you was precisely one of this nature.

It regarded the application of a great general principle to suit local circumstances – and the gist of the whole out-cry I am making (against the method pursued by the Government in India) is this: that, instead of proceeding to apply the principle to suit local circumstances, they threw the question broadcast over all India to all classes of persons. And after having received opinions from all manner of persons (including Medical Officers who understand the point) the Government in India passed a Minute in the teeth of advice they had asked for – & determined to apply an iron rule to the almost infinite variety of circumstances to which ventilation has to be applied.

But, more than this –

we venture to object to the method of application of principles which the Government of India has adopted in this case, because it is known to be intrinsically mischievous, & because we have a decision of a R. Commission, presided over by Ld Herbert & Ld Stanley, which points out what the administrative principle ought to be. Three Presidency Health Commissions were recommended & appointed. And, connected with these, there were to have been Officers of Health & Executive authorities.

Health questions in India comprise two classes:
1. those of Military stations & the populations about them
2. those of groups of population where there are no Military stations

Both have to be provided for.

Both require authorities to administer under the advice of the Commissions on all special questions –

& also was & regulations to be administered

Both require inspection.

Both require funds.

And, what is of great importance, the India Office here should keep its hand so over the work in India that it should know, almost by every mail, what is being done to improve Stations & people.

And it ought to be able to check the work & to report annually to Parliament.

[Even in France, this is done as regards Algeria. And the Reports are published annually to show the progress in well-being & health of the whole community, civil & military. Almost every case of disease is reported, at least of special diseases. These are noble Reports & might well excite our ambition to 'go & do likewise' for India].

I send the Algerian Report by the W. O. Commission.

The practice now in India has been little more than playing with one of the greatest questions of our foreign Empire. Because people must live, in order to work. And a Secretary of State for India who really set about this great question might have as many lives as the first Napoleon destroyed lives.

[It is a melancholy fact that we English die out everywhere because we will not learn what the natural laws are which we must obey in order to live e. g. in Bermuda, in Demerara, Mauritius – and in India itself.

It is a miserable thing which constantly comes before me in my small way, when called upon to send out Trained Nurses to our foreign possessions.

We can't depend upon the off-spring of Europeans living – the girls to be trained (say) as Nurses – nor the boys even to be drummers.

We must be always importing from England – & importing only to die].

Recurring epidemics are the result solely of want of civilization – of neglect in applying preventive agencies, ready to our hand.

It is not as if the questions were new.

Everything is known.

There is one thing only wanting, viz: – 'intelligent doing'.

There is no question of the land so great as this Indian health question.

I know from educated natives themselves that we have made the natives think more about it than we have been able to induce Government to *act*.

And now is the time to begin.

Great hopes have been entertained since you have assumed the S. of S. ship.

[But, above all, I would not be understood to be worrying just now for action this minute.]

If I might venture to suggest, it would be that the subject should be considered here before Sir J. Lawrence is written to.

Sir J. Lawrence's great kindness to me has enabled & encouraged me to write to him privately on all these Sanitary matters and I have written to him on this very point (this famous 'doors & windows' paper).

But what we really want is – not so much to deal with the

present case as to enter on a new phase altogether – & to organize a Health Service once for all.

What we really want is re-consideration & re-organization – re-consideration on the part of the S. of S., of course in conjunction with the G. G. & the Presidency Governors afterwards.

It is not a difficult matter to do. only it requires to be done.

And it ought to be considered just as much in the Estimates – and, (if I might take the great liberty of saying so) be considered also just as much a part of the current work of the S. of S. for India in Council as any other part of the Public Service.

At this moment there is a member of Council just come home from India & of ye largest Indian experience – who thoroughly understands the whole subject.

I am afraid that it will require a very large measure of your indulgence to enable you to pardon, if you do pardon, this long letter.

I scarcely venture to say that, having had this work well 'grimed in' to me from the beginning, I should esteem it the greatest favour to be allowed to communicate with you on the subject, at any time or in any way least inconvenient to yourself.

F. N.

{In reply to his letter of 30 July 1867 – the draft prepared by FN and Dr Sutherland. Written out by FN}

Source: BL Add 45779: ff 105–08   {Draft letter}

When John Stuart Mill approached Nightingale to serve on the board of the new Women's Suffrage Society, she revealed her complex attitude towards women's rights issues and her own special case:

103. To John Stuart Mill   35 South St 11 Aug 1867
Private

Dear Sir

I can't tell you how much pleased I was, nor how grateful I feel, that you should take the trouble to write to me.

And, if I ill-naturedly answer your note by asking a question, it is because I have scarcely any one who can give me a 'considered opinion', (since those who were always with me are dead).

That women should have the suffrage, I think no one can be more deeply convinced than I. It is so important for a woman, especially a married woman, especially a clever married woman, to be a 'person'. But it will probably be years before you obtain the suffrage for women. And, in the mean time, are there not evils which press much more hardly on women than not having a vote? And may not this, when obtained, put women in opposition to those who withhold from them these rights, so as to retard still farther the legislation necessary to put them in possession of their rights? I do not know. I ask the question very humbly and I am afraid you will laugh at me.

Could not the existing disabilities as to property and influence of women be swept away by the legislature as it stands at present? – and equal rights and equal responsibilities be given as they ought to be, to both men and women? I do not like to take up your time with giving instances, *redressible* by legislation, in which women, especially married poor women with children, are most hardly pressed upon now. I have been a matron on a large scale the greater part of my life, and no matron with the smallest care for her nurses can be unaware of what I mean e.g. till a married woman can possess property there can be no love and no justice.

Is it not possible that, if woman-suffrage is agitated as a means of removing these evils, the effect may be to prolong their existence? Is it not the case that at present there is no opposition between the two elements of the nation – but that, if both had equal political powers, there is a probability that the social reforms needed might become matter of political partizanship – and so the weaker go to the wall? I do not know. I only ask and very humbly. And I can scarcely expect that you will have time to answer.

I have been too busy for the last fourteen years (which have never left me 10 minutes' leisure – not even to be ill) to wish for a vote – to want personally political influence. Indeed I have had, during the 11 years I have been in Gov't offices, more administrative influence than if I had been a Borough returning two M.P.s – (notwithstanding the terrible loss I have had of him who placed me there).

And if I thus draw your attention to myself, it is, only because I have no time to serve, on the society you mention, otherwise, there is scarcely anything which, if you were to tell me that it is right to do politically, I would not do.

But I could not give my name without my work. This is only personal [I am an incurable invalid.] I entirely agree that women's 'political power' should be 'direct and open'. But I have thought that *I* could work better for others, even for other women, off the stage than on it.

During the last 6 years that I have worked hard at the India Public Health Service, I have often wished for an opportunity to ask Mr. Mill for his influence in it. Is it wrong to take the opportunity of asking you now to ask him for his invaluable help.

and so to beg him to, believe me (tho' in haste)

ever his faithful servant,

Florence Nightingale.

Source: BL Add 45787: ff 38–42   {copy}

Mill persuaded Nightingale to join the Society, and later to have her name placed on the General Committee, but she was never an active member.

Work on sanitary reform continued slowly, hampered by the continued rivalry between the government of India and the India Office at home. Moreover, events in India often overtook what little progress had been made. When cholera struck in 1867, Nightingale could only remind Northcote of what might have been, had proper measures been taken.

104. To Sir Stafford Northcote   London {28} Sept 1867
Draft for *Consideration*

Dear Sir Stafford Northcote

I have no apology for again writing to trouble you (And therefore I may as well not attempt any) but the urgency of the business. You have no doubt received the same deplorable accounts of the Cholera in the N.W. Provinces, as I have from Sir John Lawrence.

Up to the date of the last accounts several companies of the best soldiers in the British Army had perished at & near Peshawur – the regiments losing as many men from Cholera as usually fall in a great battle.

We have besides had a great many papers (after Indian fashion) on the subject, which show that the Sanitary arrangements are just as unsatisfactory now as they were years ago – & that there is no reasonable hope of any thing really efficient being done, unless there be established a properly constituted Public Health

Department at the India Office and in India – as a recognized branch of permanent administration.

On this general subject, printed papers sent to me from India in answer to my own letters – all shew that, whatever has been done in the way of improving the Public Health, has been done by fits & starts – & without any system.

It is true that Barracks are being built & that some Stations are being improved. But these things do not constitute Public Health administration, any more than building houses in London.

E.G. why are Meean Meer & Peshawur so deadly to Regiments quartered there? It is not the first time that these catastrophes have happened. Men have been perishing by Cholera year after year. And we who have been asking & receiving deluges of information, both public & private, on this matter, cannot nevertheless at this moment give an opinion as to the causes of unhealthiness at either Station. No document in our possession gives the slightest hint as to what steps have been taken to remedy the unhealthiness.

Surely the most costly of all administrative proceedings is – to send these strong Highland Regiments into districts of country where the causes of unhealthiness ought to be perfectly known – when no efficient steps are taken to remove them.

Years ago we were told that at both Stations the troops died, because they had no wholesome water to drink. The late experience would show that the same deficiency exists still.

It is obvious that such calamities ought not to recur – neither in the Army nor among the Civil population. Our present position is simply this: that, four years ago, the Report of the R. Commission was sent to India – that everything promised fair in the first instance – that the beginning of a Public Health administration was first made & then unmade, before the administration itself was organized.

Something has been done on no definite system, and without any defined responsibility – so that in all probability (to quote my Nursery) 'all the Queen's horses & all the Queen's men' could not find out who or what was to blame for either Meean Meer or Peshawur.

In Madras Presidency alone was any definite method proposed for organizing a Public Health Department – viz. by Officers of Health & Inspectors, acting under the Presidency Commission. But it was first discouraged, then rejected. And the Head of the Commission, Mr. Ellis, who proposed the plan, was so disheartened that he intended to resign, because he could do no good. He is now Sec'y to the Gov't of Madras.

This great question being now in this position – Sir John Lawrence who has done the very best he could under the circumstances will be home in a year or little more. And there will be no security that the work which he has been doing his utmost to forward, will make progress for a single day after he has returned – that is, not unless there is some Executive machinery in India to do the work – & some Controlling machinery here to know that it is being done.

We have now ample experience to guide us as to what should be done.

The first step towards improvement is: – (what you kindly informed me you proposed) – the Public Health Committee at the India Office.

It is perfectly true that you cannot improve the Public Health in India except by local action in India – in the places where causes of disease exist. But your committee would forward the systematizing of local effort. And, from the perfect command of the whole Indian subject of its Head, he would be able to advise on all administrative points connected with the reform of Stations, Bazaars & towns – while he would also aid in the consideration of methods of procedure, Sanitary laws, & all the machinery, so requisite, which may be proposed in India for the future improvement of the country. All persons in India having any Public Health functions to perform would know that their proceedings were watched by a special Department of the India Government. [Nothing stimulates them so much] And such things as have happened at Peshawur could scarcely pass without rigid scrutiny & discovery of the causes of their ultimate removal.

As Mr. Ellis is now Sec'y to Gov't at Madras – would it be possible & advisable to allow him to make a trial of his Health organization, (by districts, Officers of Health & Inspectors, followed by the execution of works & measures) – with such modifications as farther consideration may have enabled him to make in the plan.

This would bring us farther administrative experience.

But – – – what we really want is a thoroughly comprehensive organized system of proceeding.

[The things to be done are all laid down in the Report of the R. Commission, over which both Lord Herbert & Lord Stanley presided.]

And the time has certainly now come when Indian administrators should take this great subject in hand, & define the *methods in which* these things *are to be done*.

F. Nightingale

Source: BL Add 45779: ff 114–19   {Draft}

Even Nightingale's modest nursing scheme for India was rejected when an army officer ignored her small-scale plan and projected excessive expense.

105. To Sir John Lawrence 35 South St 18 Sept 1867

Dear Sir John Lawrence

I hope that you will forgive me for addressing you directly on the subject of Female Nursing in India.

I take the liberty of doing so because, having received at various times from the Presidents of the Bengal Sanitary Commission printed papers relating to the employment of female Nurses in Hospitals in India, I see that the last contains the decision of the Government of India, Mil-Dep:, No. 232, June 10, 1867.

It appears to me to call for a direct reply addressed to yourself personally, which I will make as short as I can. But I fear I shall be obliged to trouble you in this with stating the facts of the case, in order to show that there is really no connection between the humble proposal I made at the request of the India Gov't, and the scheme which was condemned without even having been referred to me. But, had it been referred to me, I being *entirely* 'de l'avis de Monsieur pour la raison contraire'[1] – should without doubt or hesitation have condemned it quite as emphatically as H.E. the G.G. of India in Council – not only on the score of its cost – but because I never could have lent my aid or sanction in any way, humble as they are, to giving effect to any such system which the experience of my whole life tells me contains proposals which would swamp every principle of good nursing.

I will recur to this.

From the voluminous Indian documents which have been sent me, I gather that Female Nursing in General Hospitals in India, so far as it has yet been tried under very unfavourable circumstances, has been found to be of inestimable advantage to the Patients. On this point the evidence of Dr. Beatson, P.M.O. of the British troops in India and of Dr. Bruce, Principal Inspector Gen'l of the Indian Med: Depar't, is conclusive. Both consider a trained Department of Nurses essential and feel confident that the very greatest benefits to the sick will result from its adoption, if properly carried out. No one, in short, from the Gov'r Gen'l & Com'r in Chief to the heads of the Med: Depart't and the Sanitary Commission, seems to have expressed or entertained any doubt on this subject, until Colonel Broome's estimate of the cost of the 'complete scheme' which the Gov't had called for and the Sanitary Commission had submitted startled the Gov't of India by its extravagance.

But the scheme on which Col: Broome founded his estimate is totally inconsistent with the course of proceeding which, at the request of the Gov't of India, I had suggested and for which that Gov't had stated its readiness to provide the requisite funds. The scheme on which Col: Broome's estimate is based proposes the immediate introduction of a complete Nursing establishment in *seven* General Hospitals in Bengal, *five* of which are convalescent Hospitals. In my letter of February 24, 1865, (the only communication of mine that is referred to) I recommend that the experiment should be tried in only one Hospital and that it should be regarded merely as an experimental or tentative measure. The proposal to employ trained Nurses in convalescent Military Hospitals is altogether foreign to my suggestions and indeed to my most settled convictions.

It thus appears that the estimated expenditure, which so much alarmed the Indian Gov't as to cause it to renounce in toto its intention of extending to any portion of the Army in India the acknowledged advantages of Female Nursing, was founded upon a scheme devised in India and has no relation to or connection with the course of proceeding which I, when consulted, recommended as the best.

The most singular part of the story is that the Gov't of India, having done me the honour to ask my advice with a view to be guided {by} it [it is false humility & an incivility to the Gov't for me to disparage this step of theirs] – having no experience of their own to guide them, should have set aside my recommendation to begin with only one Hospital as a tentative measure in order to obtain the experience & knowledge required for future guidance in a new & peculiar country –

that it should have altogether disregarded my distinct intimation that it was not only inexpedient but absolutely impracticable to carry out at once an extended scheme –

and that, it should have called upon some of its own Military Officers, who could not have the requisite practical knowledge or experience – [not being Matrons, any more than Matrons would have the power of advising *them* on Engineering or Artillery points] to submit for consideration a 'complete scheme for the employment of Female Nurses in Military Hospitals', which was understood to mean, & no doubt did mean, all the Military Hospitals in the Bengal Presidency.

Thus called upon to submit 'a complete scheme' for the Bengal

Presidency, the Sanitary Commiss'n submitted such a scheme prepared by Capt'n Williams of the R. Engineers and approved by Major Malleson; and the Gov't, considering that scheme too expensive, thereupon resolved – not to fall back upon the comparatively inexpensive tentative course which I had recommended but –

that no attempt should be made to afford to the sick of the Army in India what the evidence before them from the highest medical authorities represented as an inestimable advantage.

It is not for me or for any one to doubt the duty of the Gov't of India to avoid and to prevent undue expenditure – and there is a limit to the burthen that can be justly imposed on the people of India even for the purpose of promoting the welfare and efficiency of the British Army in that country; but summarily to reject as inadmissable & useless any attempt to introduce, even as a tentative measure, in India, the trained Female Nursing which has been adopted in almost every civilized community – [and an application has now been made to me by a portion of the native community even in India to introduce it there] – and to reject & disparage it merely because a specially extravagant & impracticable scheme, submitted by persons necessarily imperfectly informed on the subject, was considered too expensive, is a course of which the advantage might perhaps be doubted, while there was the alternative of adopting the more safe, judicious and inexpensive course which I had from the first ventured to recommend.

The only account we have of the grounds on which the Gov't may be supposed to have acted is that contained in Dr. Farquhar's Memorandum. That paper, while it condemns the extravagant scheme, (as I should do), hardly attempts to deal, either one way or the other, with the course which I, when I was asked, took the liberty to recommend. The chief objection urged against it is that it might interfere with the Ladies' Committee at Calcutta.

I do not read the Resolution of the Gov'r Gen'l in Council – Par: 2 – as holding out any prospect of the employment of any other description of Nurses than those who have hitherto been employed; it only contemplates putting 'existing establishments' on a better footing.

So far as I am aware, the course I ventured to suggest, in obedience to the Gov't's desire, as the best, has never been considered at all by the Gov't on its own merits.

Unsigned

Source: BL Add 45777: ff 149–55

1. de l'avis de Monsieur pour la raison contraire: of Monsieur's opinion for the opposite reason.

Fortunately Lord Napier, Governor of the Madras Presidency, began a scheme of employing women nurses on a limited basis in this same year. This small-scale beginning received Nightingale's wholehearted support.

On 19 February 1868 tragedy struck on the civil scene: Agnes Jones, matron of the Liverpool Workhouse Infirmary, died of fever; another experiment in reform appeared doomed to failure through the death of an irreplaceable leader. But by her early death Jones provided Nightingale with a nursing martyr who might have glittered less brightly had she lived longer: 'In less than 3 years – the time assigned for our Savior's life – she had done a Savior's work. She had reduced the most disorderly Hospital population in the world to a state of Christian discipline, which even the police wondered at' (To Fanny Nightingale 8 March 1868 Wellcome). Nightingale published an anonymous eulogy, 'Una and the Lion' in *Good Words* in June 1868, which served both as a memorial and as publicity for ladies to take up nursing. Her letter reminding her father of his and Fanny's fiftieth wedding anniversary ended on an angry note at the slow progress made in nursing reform.

106. To W. E. Nightingale   13 June 1868

Dear Papa

I write to you to remind you that this is your Golden Wedding-Year.

On June 15 or 18, 1868, (which is it) you will have been married 50 years.

There is a letter of Bunsen's to his wife, on the anniversary of his Wedding Day, which I think is worth all the rest of the book put together:

'Our pilgrimage is now in the *downward vale* of life: let us try to secure *frequent moments of solemn consecration*, of taste for the higher consciousness, which presupposes leisure & repose' – – –
'With you I desire ever more & more to share the highest reach of spirituality – – – to find the response to my better self' – – 'I pray to be enabled to see more clearly & that the way may be shown me – – – think over our life' – –

I wish I could copy for you the whole letter, which ought, I think, to form part of an Anniversary Wedding Service.

The tragedy of *my* life is so deep that I must put off writing to you about this.

I hope to see you on the '26th, 27th, 28th', as you propose – you & 'the boy'.

Oh dear Papa – 'ye gentlemen' & ladies 'of England who sit at home at ease' – does it appear to you that *that* was the moment (when my 'Una' was hardly cold in her grave) to say that she was gone to 'harder work'? What I had to say to the women of England was: Why did she die? *Because you would not help her.*

If I mistake not, the passage you object to was this: 'let her not merely "rest in peace", but let hers be the life to stir us up to fight the good fight against &c &c &c'. That sentence I would repeat, if I could, like a street preacher, to all those lazy, selfish women in carriages whom I see blocking up the Park at this moment before my eyes, *who killed her* – not tell them that *she* is gone to 'harder work'.

And as for myself, I am so weary & heavy-laden that, if the next existence for me were that of an owl, so that I could live for 100 years at rest, without any men throwing their business upon me which they ought to do themselves, I should be glad.

At this moment I am days & weeks in arrear.

So must close – but shall be ever, dear Pa,
    your loving child

                                                  F.

I will write, if I can, so that you shall have it on your Golden Wedding.

Source: Wellcome

Throughout her life Nightingale repeatedly looked for approval from her mother. Only a month before she had written to W. E. N. she had complained to her:

107. To Fanny Nightingale   35 South St 13 May 1868

Dearest Mum

It has been a dreadful disappointment – not to hear from you to-day or yesterday – & not even to have the weekly flowers – or things, from you.

It is the first birth-day I have ever had without hearing from my dearest mum.

And indeed I may say that, except one Tuesday, I have heard from you every Tuesday. I have been so terrified. I don't think I ever was so frightened in all my life.

But I have just received Watson's telegraph – for which God be thanked – I can write no more.

    ever dearest Mum
      Your loving child

                                    F.[1]

Source: Wellcome

1. At end of letter in Fanny's handwriting: One of those miserable lapses of Memory to which I am so subject & perhaps the worst May/68.

Nightingale was like a puppeteer moving various lines simultaneously; perhaps she felt that if she stopped manipulating the lines, the play would come to a standstill. But since the script could not be written beforehand, events that threatened or destroyed carefully laid plans kept occurring. The main action in the 1860s was repeatedly disrupted by failures on the part of her protégées. Most troublesome was Jane Shaw Stewart. Shaw Stewart had insisted upon Nightingale's Crimean model of authority when she became Superintendent of Nurses for the army. The nurses were to be directly responsible to her, and she to the Secretary of State for War. This hierarchy bypassed both Colonel Wilbraham, the Governor at Netley, and the medical officers. Inevitably conflicts arose, focusing on Shaw Stewart's erratic temperament and the high turnover of nurses. Nightingale remained loyal to her old friend, whom she had urged to take the job against Shaw Stewart's better judgement (Summers [1988], pp. 73-90).

108. To Captain Douglas Galton

                                35 South St
                                1 May 1868

Col. Wilbraham

My dear Capt. Galton
    Tho' I can't say that you and I have wasted much of the Queen's time & paper on one another in the course of the last two years –

yet I don't see what I *can* do with the (enclosed) extraordinary letter from Col. Wilbraham but send it to you.

I might make a yard of comments upon it. But I will only make a few inches.

[A lawyer seeing this letter, coupled with the fact that Mrs. S. Stewart has never once to any of her friends breathed a word against Col. W., while he has filled the air with his complaints & to people who had as little to do with it as the Queen of the Sandwich Islands – would at once say that it was he & not she who ought to resign.]

[Of course I know of the 'row' there has been at the W.O. And I have heard most of the particulars].

Refer to enclosed letter:

1. Col. Wilbraham's last letter to me about Mrs. S. Stewart was not only entirely 'couleur de rose'. It was in the highest degree of complacency.

2. Col. W.'s mind has been constantly rankling on certain refusals of Mrs. S.S. to come to tea.

3. There have not been so many changes among the Nurses as there are in every Civil Hospital.

4. The 'none staying above a few months' is a flower of rhetoric – disproved by the Reports.

4. I have heard a great deal of these 'implorings' of 'dying men' – 'implorings' to keep brandy-bottles under their pillows, & to have favourite friends (orderlies) to sleep with them. [I am rather too old a bird to be taken in with this chaff]

5. This again is a flower of rhetoric. I have this moment seen letters from Dr. Maclean & others saying that the 'Nursing is perfect'. Do they mean that the cooking is 'perfect' *in spite of* the cook?
P.S. I have had for 3 weeks the Report & papers of Mrs. S. Stewart – but have not had time even to glance at them.

Possibly now it may be vain to do so till this 'row' is settled.

I must apologize for this delay. But as the papers came to me unaccompanied by any letter from yourself or Sir E. L., & as I was over-done with cares & business, (since the death of our Sup't at the Liverpool Workhouse, I have had 7 or 8 hours a *day* writing additional) I thought there was no hurry. And I put it off.

My advice to the W. O. is:

Sentence

Order Mrs. S. S. to bed for a week

Order Col. Wilbraham, Dr. Maclean, Dr. Anderson, Mr. Longmore, & all those who made the 'row' in the ward, to bed for a week –

Then order them to kiss & shake hands all round.
Could you return me Col. W. in the course of the day?
   yours truly

                            F. Nightingale

Source: BL Add 45764: ff 119–21

Nightingale must have realized she could not fight the united military medical staff. Shaw Stewart resigned. Her replacement, Mrs Jane Deeble, was the widow of an Army Medical Officer; she did not press for independent control of the nurses and willingly conceded to the doctors' rule.

An indiscreet letter was much easier to squelch. Lucy Osburn, matron of the Sydney, Australia, Infirmary, had written a letter home that nearly brought about her resignation. As Nightingale explained to Sir Henry Parkes, who had arranged for the reforming nurses to undertake the work at Sydney:

> She {Miss Osburn} wrote a relative of hers here a gossipping letter about her voyage & the Duke of Edinburgh[1] &c &c. And this goose of a man printed & circulated it 'for private distribution only'. I dare say there is not a wise man in history who has not written a sillier letter. But I question very much whether there is a goose in history who has ever printed a sillier letter. We, the wise men, are saved not by our wisdom but by the non-existence of such geese to print us. My brother-in-law, Sir Harry Verney, M.P., who is a persuasive sort of person & also firm in his purpose, went to the gentleman-goose, & shewed him how, if the printed letter reached the newspapers, & the notice of the Queen or the Colonial Office, or was copied into the Sydney papers, how much mischief it might do. To do the poor goose justice, nothing could exceed his fright & annoyance – at what he had done. And he instantly consented to withdraw the copies.
>
> This is the whole story.
>
> [A great foreign administrator once said to me: 'I had far rather have to do with a knave than a fool. The knave one can tell what he will do. The fool – one can never tell what a fool will do.' This has been exactly the case with us. This one excellent fool has thrown a shell among all of us, who consider ourselves sensible, active,

well-judging people, which had nearly blown us up.] He told Miss Osburn himself. She declared she would not remain at Sydney, if the letter became public. I also corresponded with her about it.

The whole danger has now blown over. (9 Oct 1868 Mitchell, C362)

1. Duke of Edinburgh: Prince Alfred, the Queen's second son, was shot by an Irishman only ten days after Osburn and her nurses had arrived in Australia, and so was their first titled patient.

Osburn went on to become one of the most successful of the reforming matrons, but Nightingale never trusted her again. In contrast to her unfailing support of Shaw Stewart, she repeatedly referred to Osburn's letter as typical of women's follies.

For years before proceeding to India, viceroys and numerous other high officials made a pilgrimage to South Street to be advised and admonished by Nightingale on sanitary matters. When Sir John Lawrence's viceroyalty was nearing its end, his successor, Lord Mayo, visited her. When Jowett heard of this interview, he addressed Nightingale: 'Florence the First, Empress of Scavangers, Queen of Nurses, Reverend Mother Superior of the British Army, Governess of the Governor of India'. But Florence herself said: 'Rather, Maid of all (dirty) work; or, The Nuisances Removal Act: that's me' (Cook, II, 169).

Jowett remained her greatest comfort. He urged Florence to write popular articles to influence a wider audience, telling her that she had more ideas than anyone he knew: 'I often steal from you' (28 Feb 1871 BL Add 45783: f 236). He humoured, cajoled, criticized and supported her; she opened herself to him as she did with few other friends.

109. To Benjamin Jowett   Undated {1869?}

Somebody says (D'Israeli) that tact can only exist in the absence of deep feeling – & that a family agree together much better, if they will only wish to please each other & be pleased, than if there is deep affection among them.

That I am sure is true. And I am sure that people, even not common-place people, especially men, very much prefer, especially among their females, that there should be *only* that desire of pleasing & being pleased – & no deeper feeling or purpose in life.

Sometimes a book & not even a clever book, is like a revelation (to one) of the whole of one's past life.

I have lived 49 years in this world. And I never understood before things which this Life of Miss Edgeworth makes me see quite plain.

[He says exactly the proper thing – exactly what ought to be said (at the death of each wife). And you see that he felt: nothing at all]

Upon my honour I think this is the best way of doing things – try to please all & care for nobody.

Type & explanation of the want of higher interest.

[She says that in/at her father's case/death, her own private loss put every idea of public benefit lost out of her head.

I have endured the bitterest loss that ever woman had, except the Queen's. And I can truly say that now as then – for I feel its intensity more & more every week I live – my own loss is nothing, is gladly borne, compared with my ever-increasing feeling of the irreparable loss to the country – *how* irreparable I know now far more deeply even than I did at the time.

She sums up her brother's perfect wife:

'good sense, good manners, *good conversation*, good principles'.

That is like a new light to me.

What a fool I have been.

Now I see that that is really all that fathers want in their daughters, all that the world wants in his wife – good sense (meaning of course sense to think like him) good manners, *good conversation* (how enormous is the importance attached to that now-a-days – one would think the world was moved by talk!) good principles (for they don't want their women to run away & get into the Divorce Court.)

And with the four g s, even the better sort of people are satisfied – they *don't want* any deep feeling, any higher purpose in life, any deeper hold on things.

It is rather in their way.

It breaks up the family – & does not contribute to 'good conversation' – to pleasant Society.

Christ's whole life a war upon the family

I see now how it could not be otherwise.

People must almost always please their own families – not by the best which is in them but by that which is not best.

The higher sort always have to give way to the lower – not the lower to the higher.

In the Edgeworth family, there does not seem to have been anything higher in them than what came out to please & amuse one another.

This was their really amiable peculiarity.

But, in their lives as in their books, there was wholly wanting – the Ideal.

And it is, I should think, almost wholly wanting in the World now – but more especially in the Family, in Marriage & in the Novel – and in Government Administrations.

But there is more of the Ideal in *Indian* Governors than at home.

I am the ever grateful fellow servant of one who has taught me again to believe in the Ideal.

Source: BL Add 45783: ff 153–54   {Incomplete draft}

Captain Douglas Galton, the last of Nightingale's confidential allies at the War Office, retired in 1869. As direct communication with the Secretaries for War ceased, her involvement with the War Office decreased. But India remained an absorbing interest. Nightingale's work for *The Annual*, a yearly report on the sanitary work done in India from 1869 to 1874, enabled her to keep abreast of all details and made her knowledgeable to a degree that intimidated viceroys, governors, commanders-in-chief and sanitary commissioners with whom she was in correspondence. Under her eagle eye, all military stations received copies. Sir John Lawrence paid Florence a visit in April after his return. Her admiration for him was undiminished: 'He is Ramses II. of Egypt. All the Ministers are rats and weasels by his side' (Cook, II, 160). In December 1869 Nightingale met Lord Napier of Magdala, who had been appointed Commander-in-Chief in India. A dedicated sanitarian, Lord Napier agreed with everything she said. Around this time Nightingale wrote a tract for the village elders on sanitary reform, addressed to the 'Peoples of India'. Submitted to the Bengal Social Science Association in 1870, it was translated into several Indian languages and she was elected an honorary member of the society.

Colonization had become another interest for Florence, largely in connection with the problem of urban paupers. As with her approach to other reform schemes, she projected a characteristic expectation of major progress but also of tragic failure.

110. To Sir John McNeill   35 South St 8 Feb 1870

My dear Sir John McNeill

Your great kindness encourages me to ask you to help me as no one else can:

I will refer to some points in your conversation:

1. If there are, (as you say & as I entirely agree,) great objections to Government interfering directly in Emigration, would there be the same objection to: the following? – – – –

Poor Law Guardians in England have moved surplus labour out of their parishes into the manufacturing districts with great benefit to all. Instead of paying land conveyance, might they not pay ship passages? Could not a scheme, in which Guardians & private persons in the parish might co-operate, be framed whereby, through the medium of the Colonial Office & the Colonial Governments – emigrants, children & others, might be conveyed & be trained in the Colonies for Colonial life – & so take their place as agriculturists, stock-keepers &c – and the girls, as they grow up, as women where they are so much wanted.

I confess, tho' I have always tried to help, as far as I could, those fine fellows among the unemployed workmen who will pinch & pawn to help themselves out, & afterwards their families, to the Colonies – that I think these are the men whom we should the least wish to part with. If Emigration is only practicable in this way, it may almost be said that it is only practicable as far as it is unnecessary. It is the orphan & deserted children who *can't* help themselves – the young girls, not yet vicious, who are as it were predestined to sin & pauperism in the Old Country, who might be good & industrious & happy in the new; it is these who want our help – but then they must have industrial training in the Colonies to make them do well there.

Would it be impossible, as Glasgow sends its children to Arran, for any scheme to be devised by which London might send its children to Canada? (Melbourne once offered to our Government to form Industrial Schools for our pauper children, 'not yet confirmed in pauper habits'.)

2. *India*

Might I ask you to glance over this good natured but startling letter from Lord Mayo (which I received just after I had the pleasure of seeing you)? – startling, because it shows that not one of the men, from Lord Mayo downwards, understands the question.

[I shall not answer Lord Mayo till I have seen Dr. Cuningham,[1] as he desires.]

I know Dr. Cuningham by correspondence. He is a good, excellent man, who has gone head foremost into all the 'theories' against which we have warned them – but who is clever & candid – & now acknowledges that he 'knows nothing' – a great step in knowledge.

The causes of the failure in healthiness of the 'new Barracks' we could tell them, every one.

Yes, surely: I remember your Mem'o on preparing the ground! We made great use of it. Also: you will perhaps remember that we sent them out 'Suggestions', asked for & approved by the India Gov't here – asked for & approved by the Gov't of India there – on water-supply, drainage, sewerage, Stational improvements, every kind of matter affecting the Public Health. And the Gov't sent a copy to every official whom it concerned. And this is the result.

We have greatly succeeded in native & Civilian health. The Military alone is: *stupid*.

Should anything suggest itself to you as to what questions I should ask Dr. Cuningham – as to how I should fix him to stating (to us) the objections to the 'new Barracks' &c – would you kindly tell me?

It was hardly necessary for me on Sunday to put in words to you how much I am discouraged.

As for the War Office, one may say that they have 'crucified' Sidney Herbert afresh, & 'put him to an open shame'.

The sticking up a man's statue in the Court Yard, & destroying his work within is an organized hypocrisy which Jesuits might envy.

India is after all our best hope. But, when the work there does not progress, it retrogresses.

For me to see you is at once the highest hope & the deepest pain. It reminds me of days when a great career was just begun, when great works & great purposes seemed so prosperous, when the goal seemed in view. Now, all our hopes seem blasted & all our plans destroyed. But it reminds me too of your patient courage & devoted endurance in a long life of successful sacrifice to the good of our country. And, tho' it will not be given *me* to see of the fruit of my toil, of the travail of my soul, yet, who am I that I should complain?

Pray believe me my dear Sir John,
ever yours affect'ly & gratefully,

Florence Nightingale

MOST PRIVATE

I hesitated, when you told me what Mr. Rathbone had said of the failure of the Liverpool Workhouse Nursing, whether I should tell you the facts. It seems to me that a short summary is due from me to you, as you are so good as to be on our Council.

They have not now one woman left there of *our* training.

All our Trained Nurses whom dear Agnes Jones took with her they have now got rid of – not because they deserve dismissal but because they 'deserve promotion'. To us it appears madness. Some we have taken back – at their urgent request – I mean, at Mr Rathbone's – one is gone as 'confidential' Nurse to Agnes Jones' mother – three have just been taken as 'Sisters' at Middlesex Hosp'l. Not one has left in disgrace.

(Another, I regret to say, (whom I do not know,) who was sent there after Agnes Jones' death, as Assistant Matron, they allowed my Committee to recommend to a Liverpool Hospital, saying that they had no fault to find with her – as Matron. And she has disgraced herself – & been dismissed – for intoxication.

With her, of course, our connection is quite at an end. She is struck off our books. After her being struck off, I received a letter from Liverpool Workhouse, stating that we had 'recommended' her after we had been 'faithfully warned' of her character.

I simply answered that the statement was so entirely new to me (I having been in constant confidential communication with them the whole time – & never heard a word of it) that I should submit the statement to my Committee.

A reply immediately came, withdrawing the statement & asking me to accept their apology.

Lastly the Sup't (Matron) there, *is* I regret to say, of our recommending – not of our training. I am sorry to say that I believe all (and more) of what is said against her. After Agnes Jones' death, Mr Rathbone put us to the torture to find a successor. He admitted no reason – he accepted no delay. We found this woman. He would scarcely allow us to give her 3 months trial & training, tho' we told him a year was not enough. (We had already made many searches & many trials.)

[Two very unwise but most excellent old ladies, Agnes Jones' aunts, were meanwhile (most praiseworthily) keeping the Workhouse Infirmary.]

I look upon Agnes Jones' work as completely wrecked. In a few days she will have been dead 2 years. And as these days come round, I cannot even think of her without tears which I have not time to shed.

But I have striven, tho' in vain, to uphold her work. For more than a year I am certain that I gave Mr. Rathbone, the two aunts & the successor more time in answering their questions than was taken by my correspondence with the whole of the Hospitals in the Crimea – sometimes as much as 8 hours a day. It was all in vain: there was not one of them who had the smallest idea of Hospital organization. I do not blame Mr. Rathbone. I do not see how, in any particular thing, he could have done otherwise *except* in his headlong haste. Some time ago, he was seriously angry with *us*! that we would not incorporate Liverpool Workhouse (under this untried woman) as a Training School of our own recommending their Probationers with our own to Institutions. And, shortly afterwards, he said it was unfit to exist at all. (in which I believe him to be right.)

Please consider this as *private*. It seems to me an explanation due to you but to no one else. It has been one of the great misfortunes of my life.

F.N.

Source: GLRO HI/ST/NC3/SU/161

1. Dr James McNab Cunningham {*sic*}: (1829–1905), author of *Sanitary Primer for Indian Schools* (1879) and *Cholera: What Can the State Do To Prevent It?* (1884).

Florence had long corresponded with M. Mohl independent of her friendship with Clarkey. To him she could mock her machinations with the leaders of India.

111. To M. Julius Mohl 35 South St 1 Apr 1870

Dear M. Mohl

You don't know what a happiness & comfort your letter was to me, because you don't know what a fright I was in, having heard accidentally of your illness. But I dare say you are tired of hearing of that.

I don't think I have written since I have become the dog and intimate of Sir Robert Napier (Lord Napier of Magdala) who is just gone out to my great joy as Commander in Chief to India. Ah there *is* a man, a statesman with more practical ability in his little finger than all our Ministers have in all their heads. What overgrown schoolboys do Messrs. Gladstone, Cardwell,[1] Goschen, Lowe[2] & Argyll (Duke)[3] appear compared with such men as Sir John Lawrence, Ld Robert Napier & even Sir Bartle Frere. What they think they say, what they say they do. And all three, the thinking, the saying, the doing is the ever increasing result of 30–40 years' well-used experience – & not the momentary battledore & shuttlecock work of party. [As for Mr. Gladstone's 2 Irish Bills (the Coercion & the Land) they are each just an apple of legal discord thrown down to that unfortunate Erin. No one will reap any benefit from them but the Attorneys. And perhaps, I don't know, Mr. Gladstone wished to conciliate the Attorneys.] (Mr. Maine[4] says that the Sikhs are as litigious a people as the Irish – & that the whole Punjab would have been converted into nothing but one vast litigation by *their* Land Act, if the Attorney's fee had not been fixed at half a rupee. Is that true?)

But to return.

Sir R. Napier & I were like a brace of lovers on our Indian objects or rather passions & even our rages (which concern – this between ourselves – the things, or many of them, that Lord Mayo has been doing lately – about Finance & stopping Public Works &c &c &c.

Lord Mayo is most anxious & disinterested or, it may be, ambitious. He is always consulting us. He sent a man home (the Sanitary Commissioner with the Gov't of India) on purpose to consult us just now. He writes & writes – and we write & write – and our letters are masterly. And nothing is done. That is, the work always sticks somewhere, generally at some Clerk quite low down. But now Sir R. Napier is gone out, we shall see something done.

It is quite extraordinary, his practical knowledge of & love for the native races. And he knows them in Scinde, Punjab, Bengal, Bombay, Guzerat, N. W. Provinces &c &c. Anglo-Indians all talk of (& to) the native races as we do to children, servants & poor people, with a sort of affected tone of condescension. Not so Sir R. Napier or Sir B. Frere.

When Sir R. Napier & I fell into our mutual rages (at Indian doings) I felt: 'there's sympathy' – 'there's more sympathy' – (don't you remember Sir John Falstaff's letter to Mrs. Ford – they both like 'sack' – 'there's sympathy').

He actually spent his last morning in England with me, starting from this house. And I sent away the C. in C. to India without anything to eat! He said he had too much to talk about to waste his time in eating. I wish I could tell you a little of what he said. some day – perhaps.

There is a man in London now, a Hindoo Keshub Chunder Sen,⁵ the leader of the Bramho-Somaj, a great writer & preacher about whom I dare say you know a great deal more than I do. Sir B. Frere says he is a real true man in earnest. But he is made a lion of.

I forget to say that your Queen of Holland came to see me. I liked her even better than usual. But – she asked me for my book again. [Sir Harry Verney took K. C. Sen, the Hindoo, to see her.]

Now I hope you are near the end of Shah Nameh.⁶ *Please tell me.*

ever yours

F. Nightingale

Too much to do, they say, bars progress as much as too little to do. That is my case. I don't feel my work advance. Yet I feel more & more how much it takes out of me.

Excuse a worthless scrap of confusion from a woman overwhelmed with business & illness – who must send this or nothing in her necessity.

Source: GLRO HI/ST/NC1/70/4

1. Cardwell: Edward, Viscount Cardwell (1813–86), served as Secretary of State for the Colonies; in 1868, as Secretary for War, he undertook the reorgnization of the army.
2. Robert Lowe: (1811–92), long-time Liberal MP who opposed the extension of education and suffrage.
3. Duke of Argyll: George Douglas Campbell, Seventh Duke (1823–1900), who served in both Aberdeen's and Palmerston's Cabinets. He was Secretary of State for India under Gladstone's government (1868–74).
4. Mr Maine: Sir Henry James Sumner Maine: (1822–88), was legal member of the Council of the Viceroy of India (1862–69) and a leading writer on legal matters.
5. Keshub Chunder Sen: (1838–84), was later dismissed from the reforming theistic Hindu sect, Brahmo Samaj; his own society pressed for more reforms in Hindu marriage laws, temperance and female education.
6. Shah Nameh: Mohl's life-work, a translation of the great Persian epic by Firdausi, which he never finished.

The Franco–Prussian War of 1870–71 brought out Nightingale's old military zeal, for she was consulted by the Prussians, the French, and numerous relief organizations. She sent a Nightingale nurse, Florence S. Lees, to help the Crown Princess of Prussia in her hospital war efforts, as well as other groups of nurses to help the wounded on both sides. She also worked closely with the National Society for Aid to the Sick and Wounded. For her efforts, Nightingale was awarded the bronze cross by the French Société de Secours aux Blessés in July 1871 and the Prussian Cross of Merit by HM the Emperor and King in September.

112. To Mrs Cox[1]   7 Aug 1870

it is 14 years to-day since I came back from the Crimea

My dear Mrs Cox

Many thanks for your two most interesting letters. You will have seen by this time that, if I was represented as acting only for the *Prussian* 'wounded', that was a false accusation. I joined the Ladies' Association you saw in the 'Times', with the express understanding that the funds raised were to be 'common', i. e. impartially distributed where most wanted among both belligerents (which they have been) for the relief of the Sick & Wounded. And I so joined because that Association was first in the field.

But now, as you will see, I have formally joined the Central Committee (of which the Prince of Wales is President). And all our interest will be given to sick & wounded soldiers as such, irrespective of nationality. France & Prussia will receive our funds alike. On Thursday night the Committee sent off one of their Secretaries to place them in communication with the Convention at Geneva, to return to Paris & put them in communication with the Central French Committee there which sits *en permanence* – would that all this had been done 3 weeks ago! This, as you know, is an authorized agency, in communication with every charitable agency at the Seat of War – supplies information as to what is most wanted – receives & distributes the grants, both in money & kind. It would be little use to the Wounded if we were to send Hospital supplies to the Seat of War, if they were to be seized by the enemy. They must be neutralized, as the Ambulances are neutralized. And we must all be placed under the 'Red Cross'.

As soon as the London Central Committee's arrangements are completed – they ought to have been so long ago – I will place your application before them.

Excuse a hurried note. Since my letter (most unwillingly) appeared I have been deluged, as you may suppose, with applications of all kinds, including Ladies volunteering to go out to nurse at the Seat of War Hospitals.

O that I could go out myself to the Seat of War to work, instead of all this writing, writing, writing!

But that is an unresigned wish!

I am so overwhelmed with business that I must be brief. In 17 years I have had 2 weeks' holiday – excepting what God gave me in Typhus Fever in 1855. I was just going to take a third week – when this awful cloud of war which darkens the world came over us. And all that *can* be, how little, *must* be done for the sufferers by one already overladen with business & incurable illness. How willingly would I die to save any portion of this awful misery.

My kindest regards to Col. Cox – ever yours most truly

Florence Nightingale

Source: GLRO HI/ST/NC1/70/6

1. Mrs Cox: wife of Colonel Cox, an organizer of war relief in northern France.

Nightingale's statement, 'O that I could go out myself to the Seat of War to work, instead of all this writing, writing, writing!' characterizes these busy years of the famous 'invalid'. In an undated fragment of a letter written around 1868, possibly to Jowett, she wrote:

God is always at work in the midst of this 'silence'.

I entirely repudiate the distinction usually drawn between the man of thought & the man of action, between the seeker of the ideal (philosopher) & the political man . . .

I too should be a much happier & better woman, if I were to be *thinking* only of the *Ideal*, if I were to be writing about an ideal moral Army – instead of struggling daily, hourly, with the selfishness, indifference, wilful resistance, which are all that surround me now – while you (my Interlocutor) are in the calm regions of the Ideal. It is the difference between swimming against a strong current, with the waves closing over your head, (which is my state) & standing on the bank, looking at the blue sky.

But where would the army be, if I did not think of incarnating the Ideal in political life – which *ought* to be the 'mission' of *every political* man.

No: let the Ideal go, if you are not trying to incorporate it in daily life: if you seek it only for your own calmness sake. (Wellcome)

5

'Out of Office': Nursing and Hospital Reform, 1870–80

The curtain was beginning to lower. During the seventies Nightingale repeatedly defined herself as old. The deaths of so many friends and relatives only accentuated her isolation. Charles Holte Bracebridge died in August 1872, followed by W.E.N. in January 1874. Selina Bracebridge died only a few weeks after Florence's father. The 'Bison' or Panmure, by now Lord Dalhousie, died in July 1874, and Dr Parkes, Professor of Hygiene at the Army Medical School, in March 1876. Florence wrote to M. Mohl that Panmure's death marked 'the last breaking up of old associations, of strife and struggle for noble aims and objects; the last ghost disappearing of my Sidney Herbert life . . . He used to call me "a turbulent fellow"' (Woodham-Smith, p. 531). Then in January 1879 M. Mohl, her cherished friend and correspondent, died.

The old antagonisms in the family circle had given way to tolerance in the face of feeble, aged parents. Nightingale observed her ailing parents through her nursing eyes.

114. To W. E. Nightingale Undated {1870}

Private

While my dear mother loses her memory (consciously, alas! to herself) she gains in every thing else – in truth of view, in real memory of the phases of the past, in appreciation of her great blessings, in happiness, real content & cheerfulness – and in lovingness.

I am quite sure that, during the nearly half-century in which I have known her, I have never seen her any thing like so good, so happy, so wise or so really true as she is now.

I hope to remember throughout eternity things she has said to me this year & last, such as:

('Your father has never had a cross') '*I have been his Cross.*' 'He has been a better husband to me than I deserved.'

'My lot has been the happiest of lots. I did not deserve it.'

And, with regard to me, her views are so clear, so generous that I do not like to repeat them, because *I* too feel they are not 'deserved'.

But I do not dwell upon these things so much – (to mark the great change that has taken place) – as upon her constant expressions of appreciation, grateful appreciation, of you.

She has learnt from life.

Many, perhaps most, have no more idea of the phases of their past life, than if that life were the life of another, a stranger.

A memory, not of trivial facts but of appreciation of what life has been, is the only true memory.

This is: *truth of mind.*

How often I remember that 'People are such martinets about the truth of their words – but truth *of mind* they never think of.'

My mother's memory & appreciation of *life* – especially of *her life with you* – is in fact better & truer now than it has been during the whole of her half-century with you.

Most Private

One little thing I ought to say which you may – which you *will* think a matter quite trifling – & yet which I see by experience may make the whole difference in her remaining life.

This sort of conversation only arises when she is lying quite quietly in bed & I am sitting close to her quite quietly. *Never* when she is walking about the room, or when she makes me walk about the room looking at things. Then, her mind seems utterly to fail her. The most painful confusion of mind arises – in which she often makes the most painful mistakes & remarks.

This, which I am certain is much more common than people think, is surely worth attending to.

It is not the body walking about the room which is the mischief. It is the mind wandering about. It is the mind having the fidgets, which is the painful part – not the body being fidgetty. You might just as well give her a blow on the brain as talk to her while you are walking about – or encourage her to conversation while she is walking about.

I have observed it now so much as to be quite sure of it

Unsigned

Source: Wellcome

But the crisis of this decade had less to do with aging than with Nightingale's waning influence upon the government. She was unsympathetic to the cheese-paring policies of Gladstone, who became Prime Minister in 1868, and few of her friends were now in power. When Lord Mayo was assassinated in February 1872, Lord Northbrook succeeded him as Viceroy of India. A friend of the late Sidney Herbert, Northbrook did not pay her a visit before going to India. Feeling slighted, Nightingale wrote in a private note: '1872. This year I go out of office' (Woodham-Smith, p. 512). In retrospect, Nightingale's plea to Sir Harry Verney for help in filling out her 1871 census form foreshadows her changing status. Clearly her passion for accurate statistics had been aroused, but with tongue in cheek she wrote to her brother-in-law about a dilemma that was a figurative reflection of her life:

115. To Sir Harry Verney {31 Mar 1871}

My dear Sir Harry
    Could you advise me about filling up this *Census paper*, e.g.
1 (Col: 2) Am I the 'Head' of this 'Family'?
    There being no 'family,' there can be no 'head'.
But, I suppose, in Dr. Farr's language, I am the 'Head' (?)[1]
2. (Col: 6). As *every* body ought to have a defined 'Occupation', I wish to return mine.
    I ought, at least, to put 'War Hospital Matron, or Hospital Matron retired from active service thro' illness'. (?)
    [I asked a Government friend what I should return. And he said that, the object being to classify the industrial occupations, I ought to return: 'None. Gentlewoman'.
    In all three assertions I am quite sure he is wrong. By the Instructions, you are particularly desired to return 'Scientific' or 'Literary' or 'Professional' 'Occupations' – – you are particularly desired *not* to put 'Gentleman'. And if I were to return: '*no* "Occupation"' (for myself,) I should deserve to be fined 'for false information'
    not '£5' but £50.
But – *indeed* I could not.
    M. Mohl used to call me: 'Empress of Scavengers for India & the British Kingdom'.
    If I were to put 'Scavengeress for India & the United Kingdom', it would be near the truth. But – *what shall I do? what shall I return?*
    [In a return I had to make at the beginning of the year, the question was asked – Was *this* a 'House' or 'Office'? I put: 'House

and Office'. I think it most important to the truth that people, especially women, should describe really what they are] & make true returns.

3. (last Col:) If I were to put 'Imbecile & Blind', it would be right. And unless Mr. Cardwell, Lord Northbrook, & many others put 'Imbecile & Blind', they ought to be fined 'for false information'
     ever yours F.N.

Source: Wellcome

1. All questions marks are FN's.

Nightingale's exclusion from government circles did not mean that she stopped writing to officials. Her interest in Indian sanitation and irrigation never ceased, and until the end of her life she wrote letters of advice to the influential. The introduction of female nurses into the military was progressing, if rockily. Although Mrs Shaw Stewart had been a failure, the new superintendent, Mrs Deeble, got along well with the officers and seemed to be overcoming military opposition. Nightingale distrusted Mrs Deeble, however, and continued to fret over how few nurses served in the military hospitals.

In the 1870s Nightingale finally shifted her attention to the Nightingale School of Nursing. Her own illness, of course, exempted her from taking an active role in the drudgery and danger of nursing in a large urban hospital. When St Thomas' moved to its new site in Lambeth in 1871, it became possible to train more probationers. The educational and moral standards were thought to have deteriorated, however, and Nightingale intervened to improve them. The work involved close contact with women which she had not had since the Crimea.

Initially the greatest disappointment was the failure of educated women to come forward to take up the many matronships reforming hospital administrators asked Nightingale to fill. By the early 1870s, however, sufficient numbers were applying – and asking for special dispensation – so the Nightingale Fund Committee agreed to different types of admission. Probationers included the 'ordinaries', who received a salary of £10 per annum, the 'Free Specials' who had no salary, the 'Free Specials' who received a small salary, and the 'Specials' who paid £30 for room and board. All four types signed a contract agreeing to take whatever employment the Committee found for them for four years (after 1872, three years). A few

'Specials' paid £52 per year and did not sign a contract (Baly, p. 53). Nightingale, determined that her 'Specials' become leaders, was assiduous in forwarding their careers – and in monitoring their behaviour.

Frequent letters were exchanged with Henry Bonham Carter, her cousin who replaced Arthur Hugh Clough as the Secretary of the Nightingale Fund. She trusted him implicitly, and wrote candidly about the failings not only of Mrs Wardroper, but also of everyone else.

116. To Henry Bonham Carter   24 June 1871

Private

My dear Harry B.C.

I had a very long conversation with Miss Torrance[1] on Wednesday.

She is quite open, quite humble & generous in her opinions, quite, so far as I know, discreet. She has the talent which Agnes Jones had not only of insight into characters but of giving a well considered view of each in a few words which seem hasty but turn out to be correct. Altogether I had rather have her opinion upon our women than that of any woman now living.

She says that in our new St. Thomas the first thing we want is: better Sisters. She has a very low opinion of all our Sisters indeed – especially of 'Sister Extra'[2] – always excepting 'Sister Accident' (*Miss Pringle*) who, she says, would be a remarkable woman any where, remarkable for principle, religious feeling, ability, energy, work.

'Sister Extra', she says, is valuable to Mrs. Wardroper for some kinds of housekeeping work. But, she says, for stamp of character, is not a whit higher than Miss Crowdace – & you know what we think of her. She says 'Sister Extra' exercises but little influence over the Probationers – & what little is always bad.

that she makes favourites, does not understand their characters in the least, & generally patronizes the unworthy ones. [She gave me many little instances of this.]

She says: what we want there is a woman who w'd really exercise maternal influence & control over the Probationers – a woman whose superiority they w'd acknowledge – wh c'd give Bible classes to the well-disposed

writing classes to the ignorant

&c &c

[Do you know that Miss Horsford is doing all this at Highgate?]
She says (in which I concur)
that Probationers (& Nurses just as much)
    want a great deal more of this kind of thing to keep them up
than they do at home or in private families – & have a great deal
less. [I mean: of interesting Bible classes, religious conversation,
family prayers, something to keep them above the mere scramble
for a remunerative place.]
    She says: (in which I concur)
        that our Nurses are very conceited
I said: do you think our teaching makes women conceited?
No, she said, your *want* of teaching.
You put very ill-educated women under exactly the same
circumstances of training as educated women (what are called
'ladies') – you give them the temptation of boasting of sacrifices – –
which they *don't* make.
    And no opportunity whatever is supplied them of either
knowing or correcting their ignorance & want of education – not
even their bad spelling & writing – much less their want of higher
things, religious knowledge & principle.
    But, in all this, to have a good 'Sister Extra' over them is the very
first thing you should aim at. [The present woman encourages all
their faults & is not herself enough of a character to give them any
character.]
    2. She has a very low opinion of all our Ward 'Sisters' – always
excepting Miss Pringle – especially of Miss Duke, (of whom all that
I have ever heard tallies with what Miss Torrance says) fanciful,
capricious, ill-tempered, judging of Nurses & Probationers not by
what they do or are but by her own mood or temper of the
moment [She says Miss Duke is a real draw-back to a proper
training of women].
    I have remarked this in her Record book – indeed in almost all
the Record books.
    She says that 'Sister Edward' (Bull – the one Agnes Jones called
'steady but brainless Bull') is the only good one among them as a
woman – but that she is so 'excessively silly' that she is no use.
    On the other hand – she says Miss Pringle exercises a most
valuable & religious influence over her Nurses & Probationers –
w'd be quite capable of giving lessons & Bible classes – &c –
but has not time, could only do it for her own women, &
perhaps, if no one else did it, this w'd hardly do.
    She says that it *is* going into a *'cold bath'* going as Probationer to
St Thomas' now –
    the 'Sisters' doing so little to guide you – many of the Nurses

putting obstacles in the way of those they don't like – Mrs. Wardroper so occupied – no one to refer to.

Mrs. Deeble   *Private*

She spoke quite openly of Mrs. Deeble, who has been to see her at Highgate this year. And as Mrs. Deeble considers her a friend, which indeed she is, I thought it w'd be stupid of me not to speak quite openly too & enlist her influence with Mrs. D., whom she thinks of going to see for a day when she takes her holiday (a fortnight) in July.

Her view of Mrs. D.'s character is rather new to me but I believe the correct one.

It is this:

extreme changeableness

facility for being talked over to anything – then riding off upon some freak issue when she has passed from under that meridian & entirely forgetting that she ever was under it

absolute incapacity for ruling –

but c'd always be ruled by some one who was *always* with her –

kindheartedness

which might have kept her straight but might lead her wrong

wilful, ambitious, self-confident – but all by fits & starts –

conceited

believing herself all powerful with the War Office

Miss Torrance said:

she has been ruled all her life – while she thought she was ruling –

her mother, her husband managed everything for her, even the maids – she could not manage even a maid –

'how could you think she ever could rule'?

[I did not say: 'I never did'.]

Miss T. said:

'she is *very* kind-hearted – & that I hoped w'd have saved her –

'she began with wishing to be & really intending to be a mother to the Nurses/Sisters & "all that" –

'but she told me that "she had quite given up all that" – when I saw her 3 months ago – she "would have nothing more of that kind to do with the Sisters".

'My opinion is that she now does hardly anything, tries to do hardly anything for the Nurses (Sisters) – has little or no influence or control over them – sees *very* little of them.

'I think I can tell you exactly the time when her influence with them ceased – when she ceased even trying to be Sup't –

'it was when she nursed that Polish Dr. (5 or 6 weeks she was with him almost entirely – neglected the women almost entirely) – & then accepted presents from him.

'Now I ask you what influence you *can* expect her to have over them now.

'If a Sup't has not the Nurses *first, first* in all her thoughts, in all her habits of life, in all she does & says, even before the Patients – before the Institution – I need not say even before her own family – she will never really superintend or control.'

[Miss T. does not talk in this dogmatic way. But if I were to write down all the little incidents & reflections she gave me, as illustrations, it w'd take hours.]

'A woman ought to be a better woman for having her children. But she is worse.

Now – There is scarcely a question of the Nurses (Sisters) in her mind at all. It is all the children – individual Patients, like the Polish one – getting on. And —— she believes herself quite safe with the War Office.

'If you had given her a woman of Miss Pringle's stamp to be in Miss Wheldon's place, she would have governed her (Mrs. D.) entirely. She w'd have spoken out the truth to her – & Mrs. D. w'd have been kept quite straight.

'Miss Wheldon is a good woman – but timid, if not weak. Lennox & Kennedy very good women – but Lennox sentimental. And Kennedy w'd have made "a capital Sister under Mrs. Wardroper" – but not under Mrs. Deeble. Mrs. D. calls out all the "getting-on"-ness in her character – & absolutely nothing else, except kind-hearted-ness.

'I mean that Mrs. D. is absolutely incapable' (this again was modified by expressions & shades – so as not to seem so bald – & by answering my questions – F.N.) 'incapable of exercising any religious influence, of *teaching* any thing whatever – of holding any authority – she is too unstable herself.'

[I think Mrs. Deeble has told Miss Torrence that she 'never would have any Sisters from St. T.'s again' – that she 'could get plenty of others' – at the very time she was asking you & me for some. [The one she took (& who has left her,) Miss T. says came from Guy's.] But I did not enquire into this. Miss T. is not the least gossippy. And even if Mrs. D. did say so, it is a venial sin.

[Everybody seems to me to know of the 'Polish Count' & the 'presents'. I think if I did have any communication with Mrs. D. it w'd be almost affectation of me to ignore it. I sh'd treat it as a rumour I had heard but c'd not believe – & was anxious that she sh'd put it in my power to contradict if asked by the W.O.

Of Probationers Generally   June 24/71

Miss T. says:

it is often the best who are most discouraged – (not quite at first – but after the first is over.) who would go if not retained by the Matron's or Sup't's influence – or if they did not find that kind of influence which they look for, which they have a right to look for, & which it *is* the best (those whom to lose is the greatest loss) who do look for – i.e. in Bible classes, in some kind of religious sympathy or interest – something to keep them up to the mark – something to support them.

But, she says, this is nearly as true of Nurses & 'Sisters' – unless they are women, like Miss Pringle, of quite uncommon character – as of Probationers. [And I agree. F.N.]

She gave me many instances of this – in her Nurses – & in many of her own Ward Assistants, – who wanted to leave her soon after coming – & who are now most valuable.

Also – she says our Nurses on first going to her were most conceited, most insubordinate. But she has not lost one she was sorry to lose. All have come round in time – & are now excellent. Of her first batch of Nurses from us:

Mesher
Martin
Miller
& *Clark* (the 'best Nurse of them all')
are, above all, valuable.

But Miller (under whom Miss Torrance was, as our Probationer) was, as I have understood from other sources, insubordinate & troublesome to that degree, at first at Highgate, under Miss Torrance that no one but Miss Torrance would have kept her – & treated Miss T. as a slave, when Miss T. was under *her* – at St. T.'s.

[Miss T – brought her quite round by dint of steady authority & sympathy. And she is now one of Miss T.'s (4) most valuable Nurses.]

Cheeseman is a valuable woman – but an ingrained self-seeker & boasts of it. And this, Miss T. says, will always be our greatest danger, until we obtain more of a steady moral or spiritual influence over our women.

[Clark, she says, has become a really admirable male-Ward-Nurse – respected & beloved by her Patients. One day she was crying in her Ward, because one of her Patients had died – & she said aloud: 'I'm quite ridiculous', when one of the Patients said, (a most troublesome man): Would God, Nurse, that we were all as 'ridiculous' as you!

When the Patients won't go to Chapel, she insists on reading a Sermon to them –

& has real influence over them.]

Of her second batch of Nurses (10) from us:

Miss Cameron　　}
Miss Parkinson　　} who are all going as 'Sisters' to St.T.'s
Miss Starling　　}

are, she thinks, better women than any of our present 'Sisters' –
always excepting Miss Pringle.

But Miss Cameron she says, is by far the best at management –
better indeed at it than any one she has known at St. T.'s, excepting
Miss Pringle.

But, she says, Miss Cameron will not stay long with us, because
she wishes to have her mother *with her*. & w'd not stay
permanently in *any* situation where she c'd not have her
mother.

[Miss Torrance regrets very much that we did not let Miss
Cameron have the Matronship of *Poplar*.

She thinks *she* Miss Cameron w'd have done it at least *very*
much better than the woman who has got it – who is young,
pretty, dressy – from Colney Hatch – has never been in a Sick
Ward before – wholly unfitted for a 'Sick Asylum' Matron –
'wholly unfitted'. And, (Miss Torrance repeated twice), *'no one
will ever find this out. She will fail & no one will know it'*.

[Miss T. asked me whether I had had her letter suggesting Miss
Cameron for Poplar. I said, Yes: (without farther comment). And
Miss T. instantly dropped the subject – for she is quite discreet.] It
was the letter I sent you.

I asked her, whether Miss Cameron w'd be the sort of person for
a 'Sister Extra' or Mistress of Probationers. She shook her head
quite gently, but quite decidedly & said No: (nothing more.)

[She said, on another occasion: you can't teach a person to give
'Bible classes & all that' – as you can teach a person to be
Ward-Nurse.

She must have had previous experience as 'District Visitor', or in
holding 'Mothers' Meetings', or adult classes, or among poor
people. She must have a real love & experience of giving classes &c.
And that is the sort of woman you want for your 'Extra Sister']

Miss Parkinson, she says, is more fitted for a Nurse than a Sister
– & would *much* prefer it. What she is fitted for, what she likes,
what she does so well, is: taking charge of a few bad cases.

But she is a really good, religious woman.

So is Miss Starling, & has done excellently at Highgate. But she
too has not any great gift at Ward Management, as Miss Cameron
has.

But *none* of these women w'd do for our 'Sister Extra' or
Assistant, Miss T. says.

I feel certain, from many different circumstances, that Miss Torrance has improved all these women (of both batches) very much.

– that a large proportion of them, perhaps the majority, w'd have left or been exceedingly troublesome, under any other Matron or Sup't we have ever had, excepting Agnes Jones –

& that it is entirely due to Miss T.'s quiet steady influence that they have been not only kept together but have very much advanced both in training & higher things. Of the sheep we have given her she has only lost one – Fawkes (?)[3] who married & is *no* loss.

Miss Torrance does not think of always keeping Miss Horsford who, she hopes, will take a higher place somewhere else. [Her return to St. T.'s is quite out of the question.

– *not* that it has ever been spoken of.

Miss T. says that there c'd be no place in the world for training an Assistant-Matron (to serve somewhere else as Matron) so good as Highgate.

[oh shade of Mr. Rathbone, how it w'd jump if it were within hearing!]

– so much to do

– so much to do of *different* kinds

– of Poor Law books & accounts the Forms so good

– the way of filling them up so rigorously exacted

– much more of these various accomplishments required than at St. Thomas' –

– then, at Highgate, Steward being changed about every quarter, a great deal has come to devolve upon Matron & Assistant, (if Ass't can do it – now it is done by Miss Horsford)

To which Miss T. did *not* add, but *I* do, such a very capital Matron to be trained under.

[I think Miss T. feels, tho' she did not say the above at all a propos to Miss Cameron, that, if *she* had come in Miss Crowdace's place, she (Miss T.) c'd have trained her (Miss Cameron) in 6 months to take the Poplar Matronship.

And then all these disagreeables of Miss Cameron w'd not have come out.]

F.N.

P.S.   July 3/71

Miss Cameron's letter to Mrs. Wardroper was written the Saturday *after* the Wednesday I saw Miss Torrance –

I wish it had been the other way. For, tho' Miss Torrance has certainly not had cognizance of that letter, she w'd have been

321

able to tell us a good deal about what led to it (in Miss Cameron's mind).

Source: BL Add 47716: ff 202–09

1. Miss Torrance: Elizabeth Torrance Dowse, reforming matron of Highgate Infirmary (1869–72).
2. Sister Extra: Annette Martin. At St Thomas' head nurses were referred to according to the name of their wards (e.g. 'Sister Albert') or their responsibilities. Sister Extra, a favourite of Mrs Wardroper, was in charge of the nurses' Home – an ideal situation for an informant.
3. FN's question mark.

Nightingale acknowledged various male experts in the field of sanitary reform – doctors, engineers, dieticians and statisticians. In nursing she saw herself as the expert. But her Harley Street and Crimea experience had to serve a lifetime as touchstones of nursing. She never admitted that her absence from hospitals made a difference, even as her ideas became increasingly obsolete. Nursing reform went on apart from the Nightingale School of Nursing, but Nightingale rarely acknowledged the value of others' work (except that of her friend Mary Jones), nor did she have much tolerance for opinions that differed from hers in any area of nursing, ranging from probationers' training to nurses' registration.

Nightingale kept informed about what went on at St Thomas' and other hospitals through Bonham Carter, her matrons and the nursing students who were invited to tea. She was instrumental in designing the nursing programme and she read the diaries that the students were required to keep. There appear to have been few, if any, problems of which she was not aware.

117. To Henry Bonham Carter ⟨c. 24⟩ Nov 1871

'Sister' Butler

I think I ought to tell you about this (briefly) – tho' I feel rather disappointed that Mrs. Wardroper did *not*
                          'Sister' Butler's
A man died in her ward who left papers representing the amount of £700.
The family were sure he had these about him.
And a search was made for them in the Ward. But they could not be found.

Some little time afterwards (as it has *subsequently* appeared) Nurse Ann, the nurse of the ward, found them in the lining of a bag which had come, (I believe *not* nefariously) into her possession.

As it *subsequently* appeared, she & 'Sister' Butler kept this a dead secret between them, till they could turn it to their own profit – by Sister Butler having her holiday.

And as it happened this was the very thing which prevented their conspiracy from succeeding.

'Sister' Butler was (accordingly) out on her holiday – when Nurse Ann asked Mrs. Wardroper to give her 'a day out' – which was done.

As was *afterwards* discovered, these two women then took the papers to the family at Greenwich (?)[1] – & asked, more or less directly, for a reward.

The family stated that the papers were now of no use – as their Solicitor had put them in the way of claiming the £700 – which had now been paid to them.

But 'the family' paid these women's fares & expences – not, however, without telling the story to an Upholsterer, (?), who has served St. Thomas', & who, next time he came, told the whole story.

The women were examined & reprimanded separately by the Treasurer.

And Nurse Ann was removed to another ward.

Mrs. Wardroper says: 'it will do "Sister" Butler good'.

The fear of discovery may make her more cautious. But what real 'good' will this do to a woman like that?

What an influence to place our Probationers under! Because as above observed, ordinary women even those who call themselves ladies, sink to the inferior level. They do not rise to the higher.

We place *Honesty*, especially *that* honesty which consists in making no advantage, direct or indirect, out of the Patients – (the crying sin for which R. Catholics justly abused us –) in the fore-front of our Record book –

& *Trustworthiness* in our first column.

We print: that the first offence against *Honesty* ensures dismissal. And here is our Training Sister, the one who is to teach 'Trustworthiness', guilty of a lapse worse than any *I* have ever known – even in the Army.

[I have known a soldier summarily dismissed for a thing not 1/20th part so bad.]

The very Guardian of the Patients is the one who robs the dead.

Had it not been for the mere accident of the 'Upholsterer', all this might have been done without any soul of us knowing!

And now that it *is* found out, it is condoned with merely a reprimand in words.

What must the other women think of us?

Depend upon it that they all know much more than we do. – – – – And not only that, but that they think that *we* know much more than we do.

[They must think, as one of my Nurses once actually said to me: 'oh we thought you allowed – to do *anything*'.]

Butler & 'Sisters'

No wonder that Miss Torrance says

(who however does *not* know of *this* story, so far as I can make out) 'the first thing you must do is to get better Sisters –

your "Sisters", (except P. & B.,) are *not even good women*'.

Tho' struck by the emphatic manner in which she has said this, I did not even then suspect in the very slightest degree that there was a possibility of *these* kinds of things among our 'Trained Sisters', who are to be the Probationers' models.

But now, what is to be done?

I said as much as I could to Mrs. Wardroper. I had it on my lips to say: 'we cannot put our Probationers under such a "Sister" – it is impossible that our "Fund" can pay a woman to train (!) Probationers in this style of thing'.

But I did not.

I did not feel sure whether you would bear me out.

[Possibly, I thought, you knew of it already. And then I should be compromising you.]

Besides, it is such a very serious matter that I took time to think.

Of course, if we propose taking the Probationers away from Butler's ward, the 'Female Medical' (?) – Mrs. Wardroper will say: 'But their training will be incomplete then'.

Well, then, I am sure their training had better be incomplete than have them trained in such principles or no principles as these.

Selected Sisters

I think we must consider very seriously in regard to our new Establishment in St. Thomas'

1. whether we should not make a decided stand to have our Probationers *only under* 'Sisters' who are deliberately *approved*

> Female Medical
>   ,,   Surgical
> Male   Medical
>   ,,   Surgical (there are no accident Wards now)
>   Children's

possibly Magdalen[2]

these are the wards essential for our Training.

But we would only take those of each class under *approved Sisters*.

[And in time this would work a salutary reform in the Hospital].

[I understand that the 'Sister' of Children's Ward is a very good one, tho' young.]

2. Whether we should not come to some definite Rule which I thought existed (it exists at Netley)

that any taking of fees, or of any kind of present, direct or indirect, from Patients or the friends of Patients dead or alive ensures immediate dismissal

& some very stringent rule should be added (as it is in the Army) so as to put the *effects* of Patients – where there are such – in charge of one distinctly responsible person & to make it a misdemeanor for not delivering them up.

[I presume that Mrs. Wardroper would have instantly dismissed a Probationer who had been guilty of any breach of these essential rules.

A fortiori a 'Sister' should not be condoned].

25 Nov./71

'Obligation' at St. T's & 'Sisters' generally

3. [I feel quite ashamed of being yesterday so incompetent to form a judgment upon your point: as to whether persons should be admitted as Probationers 'without any obligation' or a 'further payment'.]

But I feel very strongly thus:

the question will be amazingly simplified for Mrs. Wardroper (& us) when she has a number of 'Sisters' say of the calibre of Miss Pringle.

– above all, when she has an Assistant of a superiority without question who will & can 'impose herself' on the Probationers.

I should not feel the least scruple then of taking Probationers on payment without an 'Obligation'.

– nor the least fear of the classes caballing against each other then.

As it is, I am rather inclined to marvel at what is done by Mrs. Wardroper – then at what is left undone.

When I hear the provoking requests of all kinds even from a woman like Miss Hill who ought to know better which come from Mrs. Wardroper & never ought to come to her at all –

– which she parries by a sort of ready, not over-spiritual *fence* – (the only way she could do it) –

when I see that Probationers' Home really without a head (Sister 'Extra' is worse than none)

I think it almost a miracle that, without 'better Sisters', &

without a competent Assistant – Mrs. Wardroper manages to keep things as good as they are.

As it is, whatever you decide (about 'paying' Probationers without an Obligation,) would it not be better to call them distinctly 'exceptions, sanctioned by the Committee' for the next year – not to have any finality – till Mrs. Wardroper has a proper Assistant at least – & till such women as Butler & Buckland are got rid of.

Note – I know Butler, quite independently of this pleasant story, & Buckland to be perfectly useless as Training Sisters – to us – 'if the blind lead the blind' etc. Duke was an incorrigible love-maker to the Students – but clever.

Unsigned

Source: BL Add 47717: ff 13–18

1. FN's question marks and exclamation marks throughout.
2. Magdelen: the ward for prostitutes with venereal disease.

While advances were being made in medicine, nursing and hospitals, certain experiences in the Crimea still proved valuable nearly two decades later.

118. To Dr John Sutherland   8 July 1872

Private

Pyaemia[1]   *St Thomas*

Mrs. Wardroper & I have as I believe discovered the cause.

All the refuse of the Hospital, of all the Officers' houses, had been ever since the occupation conveyed to a dust-hole between *No. 7* Block & the *Steward's* house – & only emptied twice a week.

The 8 (*first*) fatal cases of Pyaemia occurred in *No. 7 Block* – & in no other.

A few weeks ago the *Steward* (not liking the smell) transferred the dust-hole to the *basement under* No. 3 Block – & close under the windows of our Probationers' Home & of Mrs. Wardroper.

A fatal case of Pyaemia appeared immediately in *No. 3 Block* – & several cases of illness among the Prob'rs – & next Mrs. Wardroper had an attack of illness exactly as if she had been poisoned – but on going out of town for 2 days entirely recovered.

No case of Pyaemia has appeared in No. 7 Block since the dust-hole was removed from there.

All this time no one, neither Doctor nor Officer, made the least enquiry or remonstrance – tho' the smells have been appalling.

And it has remained for 2 women (one a sick woman in her bed 1/2 an hour's distance off)

> to make the enquiry
> to ascertain the nuisance
> to investigate the dates
> to make the remonstrance

The dust-hole is now to be removed to the ground beyond the Medical School.

It seems that neither Architect, Builder nor Treasurer ever thought of where the refuse (including poultices!) of between 500 & 600 sick & surgical & about 200 well people was to be put – & that it was left to an ignorant old Steward to appropriate *any Basement* he liked to the purpose!

In the whole course of my experience I never heard of such a case – beastly, barbarous wretches!

Floors

There is still a great difficulty.

No one to look after it but Mrs Wardr'r & me.

The bees-waxing ought to be renewed (this can only be done by men) every 3 weeks, Mrs W thinks.

It is often done not once in 3 months.

In the Infection block, it came off quite *black* upon the women's cloths – not having been renewed for 3 months.

The wet & dry rubbing is now done (this is done by the women) according to my instructions.

But – it takes off the polish – what polish there is – at once.

[N.B. The floors ought to be varnished.]

Please return me *this*

> with any comments.

FN

Source: BL Add 45756: ff 224–25

1. Pyaemia: Blood poisoning accompanied by fever; septicaemia.

In the 1870s Nightingale turned to close personal friends for sustenance, although she still preferred to live her emotional life through the intermediary of paper. She and the bachelor Jowett both found their correspondence emotionally sustaining without having to interrupt their work routine. Nightingale advised him on his Greek translations, urged him to cut back on his administrative obligations, and cautioned him about his health. He reminded her of her numerous political victories, encouraged her to remain true to her religious vision, and cajoled her into giving herself a little happiness. Yet the support he gave Nightingale did not always succeed in dispersing the bitter feelings that periodically assailed her.

119. To Benjamin Jowett

9 Aug 1872
(11 years)

I write as soon as it is possible.

You tell me to look back on the good that has been done.

I cannot.

It is not in me.

I am just as much stripped of my past life 'stand naked there' on the brink of the grave as if it had really been done in another life.

I have not the least idea what Addison meant by 'a good Conscience'.

I cannot remember, still less 'think of' my life in the Crimea or my 5 years' incessant work with S.H. or

my 9 years' Indian work – more than if it had been really the life of others –

indeed much less – for I am sure that I think much more of what Mr. Jowett has done than of what I have done. Rather is it absurd to say so. For I think every day of what he has done.

And I can't even remember at all my past. {I} never think of it.

I don't say whether this is right or wrong – but it is simply impossible.

I *am* so.

God has made me so – that when I try to force myself to look back & remember (as they say) the good that has been done, it is as if I were forcing my head to look over my heels.

It is like looking at the life of another person of whom I had never known anything.

It seems as if I had given away my deeds & could not get them back again – or remember to whom I had given them.

But I can remember quite & very well my evil deeds.

If I am forgotten it is not more than I have forgotten myself. If I am like a dead man out of mind, it is not more than a dead man is out of his own mind.

And F. N. is not less stripped out of anyone else's mind than she is out of her own.

I do not say that it would not be better otherwise.

Our past years are a scroll of prophecy

(prophecy for the future). Like the prophet {'}we must eat it'.

Only I cannot.

I cannot find it.

I have *none* but *many* friends. And I feel inclined to say And is this all? Can Friendship do {no} more – but ask me to write another letter? which won't be read either?

Such utter waste of time to finish this letter.

{Man}y things which are real become *unreal* by {b}eing told.

{'}hope' – to hope is for me like brandy. One feels all the weaker afterwards.

I cannot & do not wish 'to hope' for what I know will not come.

'Pray for time to finish your work'.

You are at the pinnacle of your power thank God

{You} only want time to *finish*.

{I} with an utterly shattered body have to begin all over again.

Now to be turned back into this petty stifling stagnant life – wh. has done to death so many of the best of those with whom I began life.

I should hate myself (I do hate my self but) I sh'd loathe myself & my God if I could *like* it, find 'rest' in it. Fortunately there is no rest in it but ever increasing anxieties.

Il faut que la oictieve soit mise en pièces.[1]

[Oh my God.   Aug 9/72

Had I no better hope than the one I have lost, I should become like – St.'s Antony.

       But I do trust in God –

       tho' not as I should.

Source: BL Add 45784: ff 96–99.   {edited copy}

1. Il faut que la oictieve {oitieve?} soit mise en pièces: The chord must be shattered {?}.

The Edinburgh Royal Infirmary governing board asked the Nightingale School of Nursing for trained nurses and a qualified matron. This request, from a large and medically distinguished institution, was irresistible. But St Thomas' was not training enough nurses to fulfil the demand. Only twelve could be sent to Edinburgh, which meant that the 'unreformed' nurses could not be wholly replaced. Nightingale feared that mixing the two groups would lead to moral contamination and failure. Fortunately Elizabeth Barclay appeared to be an excellent candidate to head the new experiment; she had had experience in the Franco–Prussian War and exuded self-confidence. Problems at St Thomas', however, made Nightingale anxious about the quality of the training 'her' nurses were receiving; if they were no better than those already in place at Edinburgh, she and the reformers might lose credibility. Mr Whitfield, who had been hired by the Nightingale Fund at £100 per annum to instruct the probationers, was neglecting his duties and quarrelling with Mrs Wardroper; the ward sisters were too busy and without teaching experience (Baly, pp. 152–59). All Nightingale's hopes rested on Elizabeth Torrance, who had agreed to leave the superintendency of Highgate Infirmary to become Mrs Wardroper's assistant.

120. To Henry Bonham Carter   35 South St 15 Oct 1872
Private & Confidential

My dear Harry B. C.

I have been waiting for time & strength to write to you one of my long pencil statements about St. T.'s all this past week.

Finding by your note just received that you are from home, I will postpone this: & merely write for your consideration the answers to your queries, as far as I can answer, with the 'remarks' (of the most immediate pressure) which constitute the reasons, as it is quite impossible to put all I have learnt during the last fortnight in ink.

I have seen Miss Barclay & the whole of her private notes, printed papers, & other papers which she brought back with her – made notes upon them – discussed each with Mrs. Ward'r – who took back the whole to Miss Barclay – whom I am now to see again – also Mrs. Ward'r – also Miss Torrance (about some women whom we *must* take from Highgate – if Miss B. is to go to Edinburgh.) Miss T. then goes to Lea Hurst. I have seen Miss T. & Mrs. Ward'r each several times. And I have had Miss Lees staying with me [you will see presently how this last applies.]

I merely mention this because my 'remarks' must necessarily look as if made ex cathedrâ. But they are really the result of days & nights of consideration & communication.

Edinburgh

'It *is* very unfortunate', as you say, 'that we have no ground-plan of the buildings'. I never can understand clearly without this. Still I

have picked up a *good* deal from Miss Barclay who is clear &
accurate, & am helped by my own recollections of the old building
(16 years ago, you will say) when I was invited to 'inspect' this
beastly den of thieves, for it is nothing else, by the authorities.

To answer your queries:

1. 'Shall she go?'

Yes: I think so –

tho' the difficulties are enormous – aggravated as you are aware by
Mrs. Ward'r not knowing one of the women from Abraham – Miss
Barclay not much more – & this undertaking coming before Miss
Torrance, who *can* tell a turnip from a sheep's head has gone in to
St. T.'s.

[I had quite made up my mind to ask you to undertake no more
Institutions till Miss T. had been at least 3 months at St. T.'s.

But now this has come upon us. I cannot think we should be
right to decline it. And they the Edinburgh Comm want Miss
Barclay to come in a fortnight!!!]

2. 'what stipulations shall we make *sine quâ non*?'

3. 'What recommend'?

That is just the difficulty – *that* we must discuss & are discussing
most closely with Miss B. But I do wish we had another head –
who knows the place & the men – in among ours – to knock out
sparks. That however we have not.

I like Miss B. exceedingly. She has simplicity, straight-
forwardness, uncompromising duty-ideas, strong will & courage
& I think sense [I doubt her knowledge of character – tho' greater
than Mrs. Wardroper's – which is in fact nil – is nothing to
compare with that

of Miss Torrance (alas!)

Agnes Jones

Florence Lees[1] –

But she is quite on the pedestal (Standpunkt) of these 3 – & *quite
above* every one of all the other 'ladies' we have yet had. [This sort
of thing Mrs. Ward'r never seems to see*.]

(*And we shall have to guard against this with Mrs. Ward'r as
long as she lives. How to do this: will always be our main question.
She is a real Hospital genius – manages St. T.'s better than any one
or than I could ever have done it. hardly ever makes a mistake. But
she does not know & never will know one woman from another.
E. g. She is always letting fly at Miss Lees to me & others & even to
Mr. Whitfield. Miss Lees has great faults. But she is of as different a
make from all our 'ladies' except 3 as a race-horse is from a cow.

E. g. again. Mrs. Ward'r says to me, in a patronizing tone: 'do
you know I think those notes of Miss Barclay's pretty fair?'

(putting her below the Deebles, Osburns, Kilverts, Kidds). The fact is: they are as far above anything Mrs. Ward'r can do herself, who, you must have observed, is quite incapable of giving you any reasonable outline of a scheme – or anything Agnes Jones even could give. (Miss Lees & Miss Torrance could do better –) as Mrs. Ward'r is above others in Hosp'l genius.)

But oh will her Miss Barclay's head stand it?

That is just what I don't know.

That is just what no one could tell us but Mr. Whitf'd, if he were a man – which is just what he is not.

[I must return to Mr. Whitfield by & bye – but will here mention that Mrs. Ward'r's inconceivable indiscretion in 'letting out' to Mr. Whitf'd even now every secret or delicate subject *fancied* by her or entrusted to her is at this moment one of our most serious draw-backs. I was obliged to ask Emily Verney about one of these things. (It concerned Miss Lees.) And she told me that there was not a shadow of truth in it – having been present at the time]

To return to 2.3.

In discussing these with Miss Barclay – I think that we must make such 'stipulations' *sine quâ non* as are easier for us to do for her than for her to do for herself, as e. g. that the Fever House, now to be converted into Nurses' House shall be limewashed so as almost to be turned into lime – floors thoroughly saturated with beeswax & turpentine or such mixture – drainage thoroughly seen to &c &c. But then this ought to be done at once – – also e. g. what furniture we should insist upon for Nurses' rooms

&c &c &c

I think she should make a sort of cat's paw of us.

3. I think there are some things which she will much better obtain by her own personal influence when *there* than in any other way.

E. g. the persuading the Doctors to evacuate the compartments appropriated to their use & their Clerks in nearly every ward – (a most horrible invention – how *can* you answer for Nurses' behaviour with such a trap *in* the ward?) or at least that each Doctor should only keep *one* – he having 4 – or 5 – or 6 wards – & we convert the others into Sculleries.

[We can scarcely convert them into Nurses' rooms. For it is hardly possible with any compartment short of a wall, or even then, to make a *corner* of a ward healthy or decent for a Nurse – the latter of course especially in a man's ward.]

These sorts of things I think should either be left to Miss Barclay entirely, to bring about when *there* or should be simply *'recommended'* by you.* (*We will enter with Miss B. upon *what* 'sorts of things' one by one)

There is a Nurse's room thus: to every Ward or cluster of Wards on Medical side & *two* (& better rooms –) to every Ward or cluster of Wards on Surgical side) I *understand* – but will enquire further of course.[2]

4. To return to your queries:

'Shall she take only a part at first?'

I think not.

I think she must undertake with our women (12) at first only

    1 Medical Ward   Female 3 Nurses
    1   „   „   Male 3 Nurses
    1 cluster of Surgical Wards
       5 or 4   Male & Female
                         1 Nurse 2 Assts Day
                         1 Nurse 1 Asst Night

And one Supernumerary

    These 12 from us.

[To this I will recur.]

I think she must take the Sup'cy of the whole at once with 4 Assistant Sup'ts from us, 2 by day & 2 by night.

I have gone very fully – into this part of the question particularly – with Miss B.

Could we have had a Division, either Male or Female, either Surgical or Medical, to ourselves in a tolerably distinct building, I should most certainly have recommended her beginning with this (as Agnes Jones took the Men's side at Liverpool first.) But the wards are intermixed in the strangest way – we cannot even have our own 3 Wards adjoining each other – & the having a distinct Division to ourselves is absolutely impossible.

This & the fact that she has been elected Sup't of the whole by the (Edin:) Committee – that she has accepted, subject to our & her own subsequent decision –

that no other proposal was entertained – by them –

that Mr. Fasson[3] (upon whom she must be more dependent than we like – but he has been very kind & wise) & nearly all the Drs. are warmly in favour of this –

that I have reason to believe that they will have her *thus* or not at all

that we do not know whether the willingness on the Edin: side would ever be renewed

these things, together with a multitude of reasons, such as the inevitable collisions, were she *not* to take the whole – make me think that, under the peculiar circumstances, she must take all or none.

She herself thinks so.

5. There *will* be 'great difficulties in maintaining any separation in Dormitory & meals between' our Nurses & the old ones.

I have suggested a plan – to be more fully discussed between Miss B & me tomorrow – by which she could apppropriate 2 Dormitories of 7 beds each in the Nurses' House – to our 12 Nurses – (thus admitting if any only 2 of the old Edin: lot –) & by breaking a door between 'Probationers' (her own) & Nurses' house – enable ours to have their meals in the Probationers' Dining-room. The worst of it is, till Prob'rs are not quite raw, our 11 Nurses cannot leave their wards at once – *some must dine at another hour. And this will make **4 sets of Dinners. Still the *'some' may dine with the Prob'rs making only **4

5.a. The difficulty about the abominable 'ward arrangements' I have already alluded to above

6. 'Mrs. Ward'r's going to Edin:'

I am not at all sure that Miss B. wishes it – nor that Mrs. Ward'r herself wishes it. I am sure that, if I were Miss B., *I* should not wish it. With all my immense admiration for Mrs. W.'s cleverness, for her noble qualities, I think her inconsiderate talky-talky has increased to such a degree, I think that her indiscretion, while always preaching 'tact' & 'conciliation', is so amazing – that, tho' I depend unreservedly on Mrs. W.s judgment about some things, & love her more & more, if I were Miss B., I would not have her with me at first.

I have however said nothing, & mean to say nothing of the kind.

I think Miss B. must decide. And I am sure she will tell me unreservedly what she thinks best.

N. B. I should just add that Miss B. who is a great & just admirer of Mrs. Ward'r's, told me (what Mr. Whitf'd told you I fear but too truly) that not a day elapses but 'Mrs. Ward'r says something so impulsive & aggravating to one or other of the Sisters that she repents it bitterly afterwards'. [*I* did not know that she even remembered enough to 'repent' what she said.]

I am sure that Mrs. Ward'r often does not know what she writes – oftener what she says.

E. g. she wrote to me a few days ago that 'Miss Torrance w'd now only stay with her (at St. T.'s) till *March'*

I, incorrigible, believed it.

It was a perfect bomb in the midst of my arrangements with my mother.

But I immediately decided to stay here till middle of November to instal Miss Torrance – then to go to my mother for 2 or 3 weeks only – & then to be here entirely till Miss Torrance goes, in order to learn from her (Mrs. Ward'r is incapable of learning) & be able to carry on the Home when she is gone – not to go to my mother in February at all.

[I mention this here, because my plans in this respect (modified) which I hope to carry out – will form the subject of a long communication with you.]

I actually wrote the foregoing to Embley – when, the next time I saw Mrs. Ward'r, I found that there was not a shadow of a fact in the '*March*' supposition – that she did not know she had said 'March', & could not think why she had said March 'except that March was the half year to September' !!! [I have since had a letter from Miss T. to the same effect]

I am afraid that Mrs. Ward'r's inaccuracies with the Sisters are so terrible (from her overworked state) that Miss Cameron is justified in what she has said.

And I do most sadly own that such are the contradictory statements which Mrs. Ward'r makes to me in the course of one conversation that, did I not know her so well, I sh'd say there was 'prevarication' (the word she applies to Miss Cameron) insincerity or concealment – but I am equally sure there are *none* of these faults – or – incipient brain-softening.

To this I shall have to recur, as I am quite sure we cannot conscientiously carry on the Training School without some plan which I am going to propose to you – for as it were perpetuating Miss Torrance's ways & rules.

Most Confidential

7. Mr. Whitfield

'Shall he go to Edinburgh?' Most emphatically: No. Most emphatically: we must have nothing whatever to do with him, in consultation or otherwise, till you rid us of him in name as well as in fact.

For 7 years he has been in habits of intoxication – as I now learn. I only knew before of 5.

For 5 years or more he has been in habits of intercourse with our women to the verge (& beyond) of impropriety – and – I say this in the strictest confidence – if I were to pursue the enquiry, I believe it would be found to the verge of immorality. [And – he is 'carrying on' at this moment with Butler.]

For 7 years he has done nothing – absolutely nothing – in instruction to our Probationers – nothing in the way of explaining even those models & diagrams we have – or in bandaging – or by the bed-side – or in Lectures – or in Examinations – nothing in short of all that he undertook to do.

The very (printed) Questions which he drew up himself he has left to the Probationers to answer by themselves. And (with the exception of a gifted person like Miss Lees) *the Probationers' constant habit* has been to *copy* the answers *out of Hoblyn's Dict'y*, or other books, *or from each other.*

[And Mrs. Ward'r knows it.]

For 7 years he has not even said one word to them to shew them *how to keep Cases.* The very entries in the Record-book are falsifications.

[Also: I must mention, but this is not his fault, that the entries about Sick Cookery are false. Our Prob'rs learn *no* Sick Cookery.]

For 7 years he has given them no assistance as to their Notes of Lectures –

nor in anything whatever. [He lost the key of our models & did not know it.]

neither in the explanation of stomach-pump or other appliances.

These are but a few of the facts – or rather of the no-facts now beyond all possibility of doubt – that I was going to write to you.

If he offers to go to Edinbro',[4] shall I tell Mrs. Ward'r that I shall tell our Comm'ee what I know? She knows that I have not done so already. She does not know whether I have told you, I leaving it purposely in doubt, because so many people, I find, know of his dishonourable conduct & 'wonder how we can keep him on' that I thought it less awkward for it not to be known exactly what you knew.

I shall myself have no further communication of any kind with Mr. Whitfield.

[And I have struck him out of my Will] It is silly, perhaps, to mention this. But I only want to express that I *can* have myself nothing more to do with him.

I happen to know, par parenthèse, that he scarcely knows most of our Probationers by sight – & that Miss Barclay is one of these. I believe she would refuse to go with *him* – but have had no talk with her about it.

I do trust that we shall begin with Mr. Croft[5] with the New Year. But this must form the subject of another letter.

I know from Mrs. Wardroper herself that he has done nothing whatever of any kind in the instruction of our Prob'rs since they came into the new building (a year). I think this fortunate – because if e. g. he had been very sedulous in instructing them for the last 3 months, it would have been then awkward for us to get rid of him at Christmas. But all the same it would have had to be done – for he has so disgraced himself in the eyes of all the Sisters & Nurses who know him that we could not without impropriety continue him as Instructor.

If I could tell you all I know against him, I am sure that you would feel this even more strongly than I do.

yrs

F. N.

Source: GLRO HI/ST/NC1/72/22

1. Florence Lees: (1841–1923), Nightingale lady nurse who served with the Prussians during the Franco–Prussian War; appointed Superintendent of the General, Metropolitan and National Association for district nursing (1875), she continued to play an active role in district nursing even after her marriage in 1879 to the Reverend Dacre Craven.

2. Nightingale drew an illustration of a ward and nurse's quarters to accompany this paragraph.

3. Mr Charles Hamilton Fasson: (1821–92), after serving as Deputy Surgeon-General at the Herbert [Military] Hospital, Woolwich, upon retirement became the first resident officer at the Edinburgh Royal Infirmary (1872–92).

4. Henry Bonham Carter wrote in the margin, 'He won't offer.'

5. Mr Croft: (1833–1905), Resident Surgeon at St Thomas', replaced Mr Whitfield in 1873 as the chief instructor of the nurses, serving until his retirement in 1891.

Just as the men serving on the sanitary commissions failed to live up to Nightingale's expectations, so too the nursing women one by one began to dash her hopes. Women with no great talent who committed wrongs were of little consequence, but the loss of those with promise was nothing less than tragic. Agnes Jones's death from fever made her a saint, but Elizabeth Torrance was the first to throw away a promising future deliberately by becoming engaged to Dr Dowse. Socializing with the medical doctors was a taboo that had to be enforced continuously; as late as 1893 Nightingale complained about the probationers to the Home Sister, Miss Crossland, 'They had much better see nothing of any Doctors consulting or Residential except in Hosp'l. One doesn't want them to be on visiting terms with the Doctors' (16 Aug 1893 BL Add 47741: f 458). Since a married woman could not be a hospital nurse, much less a matron, every woman who defected was a loss to the cause. Nightingale had sacrificed marriage; how could a new generation of trained and talented women do less?

121. To Henry Bonham Carter   21 Oct 1872

Most private. Please return
Miss Torrance

She is gone to Lea Hurst for a fortnight at least.
I have had, as you know, many conversations with her. She has

poured out the whole of her story with that wretched little Dowse.

She marries him merely to do him good.

In a moment of weakness, she engaged herself to him on account of his *threats!* (unmanly wretch) that he w'd 'go entirely to the bad' if she did not.

She says: that she wishes she could break it off
that she wishes he w'd fall in love with some body else
that she knows that it is God's call for her to come to us
that if I had but spoken to her a fortnight earlier
[yet I came up here at the very first hint she gave me]
She w'd not have engaged herself.

Over & over again, I have had it on my lips to say (as I believe she intended I should): 'Shall *I* break it off for you?'

But I hold that one must not do this for any but a girl in her teens.

I now pray for *her* sake even more than *our own*, for some way to get her out of this trap.

This is Strictly Confidential. All that is said to Mrs. Ward'r goes straight to Mr. Whitfield – & to half the Hospital besides.

Source: GLRO HI/ST/NC1/72/25

Several weeks later Nightingale and Bonham Carter discussed the matter via notes back and forth, with Nightingale in her bedroom and Henry Bonham Carter in the parlour. His scribbled responses confirm that little could be done, though he was willing to write Miss Torrance a letter she could show to Dr Dowse.

> *Miss Torrance*   9/11/72
> – one of the greatest misfortunes of our lives is that her rooms at St. T.'s were not ready for her as soon as she came back from Lea Hurst (I mean the 'Arsenic paper' room) she was *crying* to go in. Now that man has got hold of her.
> & see the letter she writes to me!
>
> If you knew the interview, all emotion on her part, all tenderness on mine, on which this followed, you would think it extraordinary. I suppose he dictated it. I need hardly tell you that *I* have never said or written a word to her about Dr. Dowse. *She* has poured out to *me* her misery.
>
> If you knew also that she has missed 4 appointments for which I had thrown up every thing to see her – & 2 of

these she did not send word till the day *after* that she would not come.

I am so unhappy – really unhappy
I have not answered this.
What *can* I say?
She told me with the deepest emotion that it was all 'worry' 'at home' – & she did not wish to be there but for one night.
What *shall* I do? (GLRO HI/ST/NC1/72/44)

Miss Torrance, in spite of Nightingale's pressure, became Mrs Dowse and was written off.

Over the years Nightingale changed her mind about the duties of 'special' probationers, the educated applicants who would become superintendents and matrons. She had originally maintained that they needed exactly the same training as the 'regulars', who were paid during their training, so that they would later be able to teach nursing fundamentals. But the exhaustion and subsequent loss of some of the best lady candidates caused her to shift her stance.

122. To Henry Bonham Carter   1 Feb 1873

St Thomas'

Lady Prob'rs have no means above the others to qualify themselves for the future course (of Superintend'ce & training others) wh: is that we ourselves hold out to them.

On the contrary the practical work, making beds &c – from the first day to the last of their being with us bears so heavily on their physical strength that they cannot even profit by the short intervals of leisure they have to write up their own cases, wh: they try to do of their own accord – or for some Medical Reading & Self-improvement.

Our present Probationers' Library too is so bad, so little up to the present day that it does not afford them the means of self-instruction. Some get books for themselves.

The want of Lectures & Classes is also severely felt by them. The need of better Training Sisters quite as much.

They have no one to help them in discerning symptoms, in discriminating the course of diseases. And many are placed on Sister's duty without ever having had their attention called or one hint given them as to how to observe Symptoms or answer the questions wh: the Doctors ask. But the intelligent ones then find that a week of Sister's duty improves them more than a year of Probationer's 'training' – because the Doctor's questions compel them to find out what to answer & how to observe.

This deficiency is still more felt in Medical than in Surgical wards. For in Surgical cases the Doctors see for themselves the course the injury is taking. But in Medical cases much must depend on the account the Sister is able to give.

It is all very well at first to put the Lady Prob'rs to exactly the same work as the others, viz. housemaid's work, making beds, dusting &c.

But after 6 months (say) surely they ought to be relieved of this – i.e. of all housemaid's work.

I w'd not relieve them of emptying slops & the like: for this is strictly Nurse's work.

But of the rest I would.

The more so because the less physically able who are by no means the less fit for Sisters like Miss Williams are actually tired before 9 in the morning for the day – & worn out before their year's training is over.

That the Lady Probationers must be relieved from the first of the afternoons from 2 – 6 p.m.

I am fully persuaded.

And this in spite of the jealousies of the other Probationers
1. to be exempted from housemaid's work[1]
2. to be free from 2–6 p. m.
sh'd be immediately granted.
And for those who are to become Sisters
(Training) at St Thomas'
it is of imperative necessity in order to prepare themselves for it.

We intend the Lady Probationers for a different course – we hold out to them a different future – from the others.

And yet we give them no means by wh: to prepare themselves for it.

To read *in* the Ward is physically impossible – even in the afternoon. They have, of course, to jump up at the least want of the Patients. Else they are unfit to be Nurses.

N.B. The Staff Nurses & the Nurse Probationers are so afraid of the Lady Prob'rs not taking their share of the work – the Sisters are so over-tasked & thereby compelled to over-task the ever-willing Lady Prob'rs that these actually get *more* of their share of the work – & of the most menial work.

Add to this that when they come into the Ward at 7 a.m. there is always a Chorus of Patients: help me this: help me that

And the Patients actually wait to ask for things – especially as regards slops – till the Lady P's come into the ward in the morning.

To relieve the Lady Pro'rs in the way indicated, there certainly needs to be 1 Extra Nurse to each Block.

Indeed unless we speedily fill up the 10 or 11 vacant Probationers places in the Home with good, hard-working women, there {they?} need & very urgently Extra Nurses *at this moment* – the Probationers, lady & other, are so over-worked.

The Lectures will do the Probationers little good, if they have no time to prepare for them – or to write afterwards: wh: is the case now.

Indeed they are so over-wearied that they are afraid of falling asleep at Mr. Croft's projected Classes at 8 pm.

N.B. They come off duty as a rule at 8.30 p.m –
    then prayers 8.40
    then supper 9
      too tired to do any thing.

I do very much wish that (at least) *for the Lady Prob'rs now near the close of their year)*
    those 2 rules

Unsigned

Source: BL Add 47717: ff 217–20

1. HBC asked in the margin, '? after 6 months' FN replied, 'yes, I only put it so, because I do want this permission to be granted *immediately* for those, like Miss *Leslie*, who are going soon'.

Nightingale's letters to men were either businesslike or with those she trusted, occasionally playful. Intellectual exchange, sometimes mixed with fantasy and inchoate misery, characterized her letters to such old friends as Hilary, Clarkey and Aunt Mai. But as she aged, Nightingale shaped her letters to attract the friendship of younger protégées and relatives. She 'adopted' several nurses whom she placed in leadership positions in reforming hospitals. Her warm letters to these favourites suggest that they were filling an emotional void that had blighted the years 'in office'.

Nightingale's letters to the stately 'goddess' Rachel Williams became as teasing as a lover, as scolding as a parent, as confiding as an adolescent girl; they hint of an older person's unconscious attempt to regain the lost pleasures of youth, glimpsed once again in the beauty and dreams of a young woman. She told the impetuous Rachel, for example: 'And now let us two pray – you in the vigour of your cruel, splendid youth – & I in the sadness of my much-tried age – that patience may have her perfect work in us: & above all that we may be gentle in our judgments of others . . .' (22 Oct 1873 GLRO HI/ST/NC3/SU 180/9). Her other favourite of this decade was Angélique Pringle, whom she nicknamed 'the Pearl' and 'Little Sister', contrasting her size with that of 'the Goddess'. Pringle came as close as anyone to embodying the virtues of the sainted Agnes Jones. Nightingale wrote to Williams: 'You are young, my Goddess: much younger than my Pearl: a thousand years younger than this old black beetle – And I have often a shuddering sort of maternal feeling in wishing you "blessings"' (30 Dec 1876 GLRO HI/ST/NC3/SU 180/23).

Nightingale looked after her favourites well. Not only were they given the best positions when they had completed their training; their nursing staffs and holidays also received her personal attention.

123. To Rachel Williams   35 South St 23 May 1873

My dear Miss Williams

I was indeed very glad to hear from you. (I had felt anxious about you –) this morning.

I hope that when you return to London – on Thursday, if it must be so – you will perform your promise of coming to stay 2 or 3 nights here – doing what you like in the day – going to St. Thomas' to see after your 'berth' – and – I only bargain for one hour a day for myself.

But – my dear soul – you must remember that all your Med'l advisers – including you yourself who are your own best Medical adviser – spoke of 'a month or 6 weeks' 'at the sea' – as the shortest time for your restoration.

Mr. Croft told me so with his own lips – & said that you had intended it.

You must do me the favour of allowing me to contribute £10 to this very laudable purpose. Or rather I will not speak in this formal way – you are all my children, & I only wish God gave me a mother's duties, as He has given me a mother's heart towards you – so, my dear child, I must really send my little mother's gift towards your expences, whether at Boulogne or at any other watering-place.

[The 7/s is for your cab, which my stupid Messenger, tho' strictly enjoined to pay, says he 'forgot', the day he brought you here from Peckham to see Miss Barclay.]

Any one at Boulogne will, I believe, change your Cheque – you must sign your name at the back.

I will not say a word about St. Thomas' now. You ought, like the babies, to divide your time between eating, sleeping & being out-of-doors.

I saw Miss Barclay after your interview. She went back to Edinburgh on Saturday by night-train.

But not a word about Edinbro' either now.

When I see you, you shall tell me your impressions upon the Hospital Augustinians. And I will tell you about those at Paris whom I once knew well.

Their standard is higher than ours. But their nursing of men, from false notions of delicacy, & their want of cleanliness, was lower. And they knew it.

You shall tell me whether the fees, so often given by Patients to Nurses but never to nuns, are possible at St. T.'s.

Excuse a brief note – from (tho' pressed by business & illness)
    yours ever tenderly

                                Florence Nightingale

God speed you.

Source: GLRO HI/ST/NC3/SU 180/3

Edwin Chadwick had introduced Nightingale to J. S. Mill. While she disagreed with his feminism, she greatly respected him as the foremost British philosopher of her age. Just as she frequently referred to herself in the masculine, she remembered Mill's kindness by personifying him as a goddess.

124. To Edwin Chadwick {Feb 1873}

Dear Mr. Chadwick

The loss we have in John Stuart Mill is irreparable – I think there must have been a Goddess called 'The Passion of Reason' in olden times: & *he* was that Goddess returned in the flesh to life. And he would not at all have considered the gender humiliating. For he was like neither man nor woman – but he was Wisdom 'thrilling' with emotion to his fingers 'ends' (which last was truly said of him) – impassioned Reason – or reasonable Passion – in the sense which one supposes the Greeks had in their mind when they made Wisdom a Woman. Or shall we call him Sancta Sophia?

There were none like him. And as he said himself with tears at Mr. Grote's funeral: Oh we might have kept him 10 years longer: so may we of him.

Well, he is gone to 'rejoice at the fidelity & smile at the Simplicity of his earthly toils' & to continue them gloriously.

Unsigned

Source: BL Add 45771: f 154

Nightingale never forgot the early support of Mary Jones, matron at King's College Hospital. Jones and her nurses had resigned from the hospital in 1867 because of a religious conflict, and soon thereafter the Nightingale Fund withdrew its support of the midwifery training programme (Baly, pp. 66–75). Jones, however, continued to be consulted by Nightingale; they both agreed that the lack of reliable, honest nurses was a major drawback to reform.

125. To Mary Jones 35 South St 9 May 1873

Dearest ever dearest friend

Your Easter letter did me no end of good, as it always does. Thanks 100.

A very dear friend of mine who went thro' the Crimea with me died at Bermondsey, after 4 weeks' struggle with Typhoid fever, at Easter tide. And tho' I could not wish her back, O no, yet 19 years of troublous recollections pass away for me with her. She was a nun.

I found a very nice maid for my mother, thank you, & took her down in that snowy weather at the end of February, settled her, & came back.

I have taken for the last 6 or 8 months to seeing a great deal more of our Matrons & Nurses – one or two every day – & to having those who come from a distance staying in the house. This not only compels me to give up a great deal of my Indian & War Office work, but takes out of me, I think, more than any thing did before. I have never been used to lead, except by leading in *work*. I am not good at talking & preaching & examining except on the spot.

But this seemed so clear a call of God that I could not refuse it. And of course it is a thing which, once embarked in, increases, & crowds upon & absorbs one more every day.

We have undertaken the wretched Edinburgh Infirmary – a 'beast' of a place – & a den of thieves – & have been in it since November. Miss Barclay, our Sup't there, is a woman after your own heart – a splendid leader of women – first in every thing – really a mother to our Nurses. She is staying with me now – (ran up by Night-train.) And – you will think I never write unless I want something – could you recommend me a *Night-Superintendent* for her?

– the advantage would be now that Miss Barclay could look at her for herself now or within the next week.

Miss Barclay has almost run us dry. We furnished her with 2 Night Sup'ts – the first really effected a reform in that lawless place among the drinking, profligate (old) Night Nurses – who are however being gradually weeded out – but Miss Barclay was obliged to give her an onerous charge of Wards which fell in unexpectedly – the next has fallen ill & is little likely ever to be strong enough again for such a place.

It should be, I need not say, a not young, but wiry woman – good on her legs, & in her head – absolutely trustworthy – & with something of the Missionary spirit – for nothing that I had ever known of War Hospitals surpassed the wickedness of this Edinburgh Infirmary when we first entered it.

Also: a London Hospital, the most busy in accidents & acute diseases, is really a slow place compared with this Edinburgh Inf'y, where, for & in consequence of the crowd of Med'l students, they get *in* & they *get out* acute & critical cases faster than in any place I ever heard of.

And the Night Sup't's wits are often called upon for Night Admissions.

The Night Sup't has £30 with 1/6 a week for washing – & uniform – tea, sugar & every thing found.

She superintends the night-nurses of the whole place – some 36 wards (many small) besides single rooms. Of these about 22 wards (number increases) are nursed by our own trained Nurses – besides Ophthalmic & Fever Wards – (which last in a separate building are *not* within the Night Sup't's domain.)

The place is rough – but Miss Barclay takes great pains that the food & accommodation shall be thoroughly healthy. And the advantage is being under such a woman as Miss Barclay who carries the women with her in every thing. The worst of it is: she is killing herself. She shares the Night Watch twice a fortnight.

[She was out in the War – & is aged about 37 – very wiry in many points.]

We get a great many Lady Probationers now at St. Thomas' – & very good ones. But how strange it is that no woman between 20 and 30 now has any constitution!

God speed & bless you. God guide us all.

How I wish I might think you pretty well.

ever my dearest friend's loving

F. Nightingale

(written amid so many interruptions)

Source: BL Add GLRO HI/ST/NC1/73/2

Unfortunately, Elizabeth Barclay had a fatal flaw. Either she began drinking under the pressures of work, or was already a confirmed drinker and opium taker. Nightingale had never professed unquestioned confidence, but Barclay had impressed her and she wanted the Edinburgh project to succeed. She could never bring herself to condemn Barclay as strongly as she had women guilty of far less. She wrote to Henry Bonham Carter, 'I do *not* think that *her* influence has been bad: it has been on those she has *imposed upon* very good: [her religious feelings (emotions rather than principles) are sincere . . . *none* so hardening & worldly, as Mrs. Deeble's & Miss Osburn's' (23 Nov 1873 BL Add 47718: f 261).

126. To Henry Bonham Carter

Lea Hurst, Matlock
1 Oct 1873

For your own eye alone   *Burn*

My dear Harry B C

I received your Telegram late on Friday night: & your letter, dated Sunday, this (Wedn'y) morning: just as Miss Barclay was driving off from the door.

[I believe that in those parts the Telegraph goes by post: & the Post on foot – However] you will see that she has been here. And I must give you the conclusions come to: reserving to another time the account of what has happened.

Mr. Fasson by a Telegram charged me with the responsibility of 'persuading her' as seemed 'best', after conversation.

It is essential, I need not say, not to lower her in her own eyes: nor speak of her lapses, as if known to the public.

I will not now give you an account of my 3 long conversations with her; [I was in such misery as to what she might do that I telegraphed to her to come here; & telegraphed to her friends that I had done so: *or* that I would come to London to receive her.]

I will simply tell you the conclusion, I will not say the best: but the only possible which we were able to come to.

She is gone back to Edinburgh to-day – to stay till November 1 – then to ask for '3 or 6 months' leave' – to 'recover her health': leaving her duties in charge of Miss Pringle, & perhaps of Miss Williams as Miss Pringle's Assist't.

She also put down on paper & left it with me: that she went to Edin'gh 'to strengthen Miss P.'s hands & give up to her my charge, & work'.

I earnestly hope it will not come to this.

But, as for the '6 months' leave', I never saw such a wreck of a woman, & am certain they are vitally necessary. And I could not have let her go without this promise.

She tendered me her resignation more than once: but I did not take it. God only knows whether I was right.

Unasked, she bound herself 'on honour' to take no Opiate, inside or out; no kind of Aether, or of Alcoholic stimulant – & to write to me if she even felt a 'hankering' –

– to resign at once, if she did. After thinking it over a night, I told her this w'd not do, without the other conditions: since to go back & fail w'd be: worst of all.

She was quite open with me: told me a racking history of her falls: & I perfectly plain with her: more so than I could have thought possible for either of us: tho' what the pain of those conversations was God only knows.

She will visit & travel in Germany & visit German Hospitals during her 'leave'. Some scheme of this sort is vitally essential for her.

I have written the principal part of this to Mr. Fasson: & she has written it to him too barring the confession. He will manage every thing with the Board without telling them the sad facts: & has already communicated to Mr. Hope: treating it simply as a matter of health.

Her confessions were heart-rending: and I never saw a face such a tragedy of woe. She seems heartbroken. But also I never heard such a history of yielding to indulgence, in an educated woman.

Now comes about the Nurses:

I have actually told her all I know about her (our) Nurses leaving if she returns: & about our (good) Prob'rs steadily declining to go to her. They want 6 by Nov 1.

I have written to Pringle an appeal ad misericordiam to the Nurses if they are true women not to leave her now. She is humbled to the dust.

About the P.s: it is difficult to ask them to go to her on the ground of going *not* to *her*.

But we must, if possible, send Miss Williams down, with 4 or 6 P.s, as soon as she is gone. O the pity of it, the pity of it!

She continues to find fault with Pringle's coming up to me.

She says: 'might she not have warned me when she saw me drifting into Sin?' It is too pathetic. But she knows Pringle's worth really: [that is the very reason why she is ashamed with *her* & not with Mesher.]

I spared her the humiliation of knowing that you knew it: & what you had telegraphed to me: but I should have given it her had it been necessary. For she cares very much for your opinion.

But she was only too much humiliated. And the only thing she would not accede to was: not going back to Edinburgh for a month. [I wanted her to have her things sent to her here]

We did not come to this all at once, as you may suppose. I told her she had out-generalled God in the August affair. [it seems that she had boasted when we had tried to get her away then of her success in evading us: she must have said *that* 'in her cups': for there was nothing but of right feeling: nothing even but of refinement here: there was even a certain dignity in her humiliation]

I said that she must not out-general Him now: that this might be a turning point in her life

&c &c &c She acceded to everything.

I was in such an agony the last week, lest she should slip thro' to Edin'gh, without seeing me, & pounce upon Pringle, & come to some open disgrace & shame (which was what her own friends expected) that at last I really *wished* her to arrive.

But when she drove up to the door, I felt as if all my senses were forsaking me: & I could not think what I had to say to her.

However I suppose God helped – – & spoke to her Himself.

I merely tell you this to give you an idea of the nature of the communications made to me: which she does not know.

Digression

[If you could make some note such as none but yourself can understand, of the pledges she has given: her memory & will do so fail: she forgets & misquotes almost like poor Mrs. Wardroper herself. – – – –]

and of the extremity of the case which *could* make me say that you are right in saying that it was better for *me* to do it than for the authorities.

I could speak to her as a woman to another woman's *higher self* in the presence of God: & not in the presence of authority: since I am only her chief by courtesy.

[The 'Poissarde'[1] scenes which have taken place at St. T.'s, Mrs Ward'r dragging Sisters before the Lord Petty Bay[2] for faults which compared with this are virtues – or fighting with them herself – have been such as to make *your* hair stand on end & to break *my* heart.]

Please if you approve forward the enclosed to Mrs. Wardroper (& with some word from yourself perhaps.) I want, if possible, to avoid *talking* over Miss Barclay with Mrs. Ward'r

You will think me strangely fanciful if I say that even after a fiery ordeal like this (which I would have gladly escaped by seeing 3 Bengal tigers get out of the Cab instead of Miss Barclay & come up-stairs to dine not with but *upon* me) I am more uneasy about Mrs. Ward'r & her work than about Miss Barclay & hers.

Oct 3

I have tried in vain for 2 days to tell you the much more I ought to tell you: please look at the last but one P.S. of mine to Mrs W'r, to see the reason why: besides which I have had of course to write long letters to Miss Barclay's friends who had written to me, to Mr. Fasson, & to Dr. J. Brown.

How vain is all this writing! what reams we have written about her these last 2 months.

The whole correspond'e might & ought to have been reduced by: 'Bet has been drunk 7 times this week'.

Now please look at my *last* P.S. to Mrs. Ward'r –

that has happened already: in the last 24 hours I have had 3 letters from Miss Barclay:

1. I go on Nov 1 on 6 months' leave
2. I go „   „   „   for ever
3. I do not go at all but stay at Edin'gh altogether.

This will probably happen every day this month.

Now please *don't* write to me: Mrs.— or Mr.— hears that Miss Barclay is quite fit to stay on – or Dr— says &c Believe what I have told you now: that *nothing could have justified me in letting her go from here* but the *condition* I have stated. And help me on Nov 1 to carry it out.

Dr Brown has abused the permission to be *weak*.

Of Mr. Fasson who has been *very* kind I must tell you another day.

He threw upon me what he ought not: but still what it is to be a gentleman! He is one: and our Petty Bay is not.

In greatest haste after trying in vain for 2 days to finish
ever yours

FN.

No one here has the least idea of the tragedy which was going on behind a little thin lath & plaster.

I have received one of poor Mrs. Ward'r's worst, most confused, forgetful letters: with a mistake of judgement or memory in every line.

I have many matters of minor importance to write to you about. One is: Miss Heathcote

Mrs. Ward'r says she won't keep *Miss Williams*.

FN.

Excuse scrawl   Burn

One more P.S. What I tell you about Prob'rs wanted for Edin'gh does *not* come *from Miss Barclay at all*.

She is perfectly incapable of making any calculation.

It all comes from Miss Pringle.

FN.

Source: BL Add 47718: ff 194–203

1. Poissarde: fishwife.
2. Lord Petty Bay: Nightingale's nickname for Richard Baggallay, Treasurer of St Thomas'.

The Barclay crisis was exacerbated by difficulties with Mrs Wardroper, who appeared to be buckling under the increased responsibilities (and fame) of the Nightingale School. On 18 May 1872 Nightingale wrote to Bonham Carter that Wardroper was 'degenerating into almost a Hospital scold' and 'governing like a virago' (GLRO HI/ST/NC1/72/2). Apparently she was unable to delegate responsibility, and instead developed a spy system so that 'every Nurse Prob'r's hand was against every Probr's & Sisters, & Sister's would have been against every Prob'rs . . .' (3 Oct 1873 BL Add 47718: f 216). Nightingale and Bonham Carter exchanged many letters over the years lamenting Mrs Wardroper's failings, but they never seriously attempted to have her removed. Instead Nightingale worked around her, appointing more reliable workers in subordinate positions. The letters indicate that she too had her spies, which must have placed Mrs Wardroper on the defensive (Baly, pp. 158–62).

Nightingale found Julius Mohl's letters 'so rich they are pasture for a month – which is more time than you let pass between one & another' (13 Sept 1871 BL Add 46385: f 15).

127. To Julius Mohl

35 South St 19 & 30 Dec 1873

Dear M. Mohl

I do think that I am the most unfortunate Tantalus in your hands I ever fell across. Nay: he was in heaven compared to me. What! you wrote to me on the very subject of all others I care most about, viz. the 'principle of morals' & your 'speculations'about it, & 'on its difference or agreement with the Stoics & others'. And you did not send it to me.

'Fiend! thou torment'st me ere I come to hell!' Send it me this minute.

Or I will shut you up in a country-house in Paradise for 3000 years with 3 Deans, 2 Bishops & 1 Archbishop.

Some time ago, you said you would send me your theory about the Gnostics, as embracing most forms of religion.

And you never did.

Send it me this minute. Or your term of 3000 years shall be lengthened to 30,000 and 3.

I want nothing so much as your inspiration.

If I have time & strength: but latterly I have been so broken up & broken down: nothing solaces me so much as to write upon the Laws of the Moral World: especially as exemplifying, if possible, the character of a Perfect God, in bringing us to perfection thro' them in eternity. Quetelet, who is an old friend of mine, sent me his new 'Physique Sociale' & 'Anthropométrie'.

These especially interested me: because in as far as the laws which register mankind's crime & other social movements *are* *Laws:* of course, all Legislature & Administration must be based upon them: instead of being just the reverse.

Latterly: I have been reading over again the 'Physique Sociale' with the view of writing as above. But of course there are weeks & months that I cannot write. And then it all has to be begun over again.

Now, give me a fillip, do.

Dec 30/73

Dear M. Mohl

All my misfortunes always culminate each year at Christmas. It's a way they have. So this letter has remained unfinished many days. But it shall go all the more & see what it can get out of you.

I am not like you. Because I have to ask a favour. You have to grant one.

And the more the letter won't go: the more I say, it shall.

About the Eucalyptus:

in our Sanitary Report on Algeria (we sent a Commission there) we alluded to its healthy properties.

They mainly show that Drainage is required.

In India we advised Bamboo for the same purpose. But Eucalyptus would do. Only neither one nor the other are substitutes for Drainage.

Indeed in India all tree vegetation is considered healthy in Epidemic times. But as Malaria exists notwithstanding trees, we must insist (not on Eucalyptus but) on Drainage works.

The Famine, instead of making us redouble our efforts to prevent such horrors seems likely to shrivel up all our small attempts, by Sanitary Engineering, draining & irrigation, to render such calamities less possible. Gulliver (Campbell of Bengal) is doing excellently well. So is Lord Northbrook, but he has as yet hardly realized the tremendous extent of the calamity which looms in the distance. And the Zemindars[1] & their foolish English advisers are still trying to mislead Gulliver by will' o' the wisps.

I am so hurried & bothered I can't say more: Nurses & Matrons & Superintendents besides hem me round.

Sometimes I ask myself, after all my 'Laws' & 'Moral Worlds': is there a good God after all?

You see I have the more need that you should write to me. And this goes for that purpose only. Do not disappoint it, poor beast!

ever yours

F. N.

Source: GLRO HI/ST/NC1/73/5

1. Zemindars: Bengali landlords who held their land on payment of certain revenue to the state; they were free to set the rate of taxation on their ryots or peasants. Their agents notoriously supplemented their income by extortion of the ryots.

The death of her father in January 1874 raised Florence's annual income to £2000, which was most welcome, as 'the expences arising from my work become every year greater' (To Sir Harry and Parthe, 15 Jan 1874 Wellcome). But amidst her grief she faced the complicated task of resettling her mother into a new home. She continued to claim both overwork and uncertain health for herself, but Parthe was also reluctant to take on the responsibility of the aged Fanny. In a letter to Parthe dated 25 June 1874 Florence, who always referred to their mother as 'my mother', wrote:

> *Of course*, personally, it would be such a task for me who
> ought to have some one to take charge of me to take
> charge of my dear mum at Lea Hurst that I should
> immediately decline it: I should not think of going there
> *for myself*: supposing poor Mother non-existent: the sole
> reason for going there would be that I believe it would be
> giving *her* the greatest pleasure that remains to her to be
> at what she calls 'home' once more for 2 months. In this I
> am sure you agree: that I ought to give her this pleasure if
> I can. (Wellcome)

The attention Florence lavished on her mother during these final
years of senility suggests an assuaging of guilt. But even then she
set limits. Fanny was now no threat to Florence, who seems to
have had better relations with women when she was in a dominant
position.

128. To Sir Harry & Lady Verney

35 South St
22 Aug 1874

My dear Sir Harry & Parthe
   I write this, tho' barely able to write, because Sir Harry told me
that he would have only 45 min: for his luncheon & me: & because
I know he will want something written to show Parthe.
   Feeling as I do so strongly about my Mother's plans, I need
scarcely even discuss the Telegram:
   but you dear Sir Harry said yesterday that my Mother would
come & be in a London house alone with her companion –
yourselves not in London – on the ground of 'seeing a great deal of
me F.N.': & of my taking charge of her. (for 3 months: Nov: Dec.
Jan.)
   I will not discuss what, when Parthe is in London, will be the
result of P.'s 'taking charge of her' in a different house from her
own although I think that it must be *far* less than P. anticipates:
that colds & other engagements will supervene, which will prevent
Parthe from seeing one half as much of her as she expects:
probably not even every day.
   But, about oneself, one *can* & ought to speak positively: & I do
most solemnly:
   what will my mother 'see of me?'
   She never does & never can go out before 3: at 4 it is dark: the
only time she can see me is then between 3 & 4: just the only time

when she ought to be taking her drive. [& Even that will be interrupted by rainy days]:

You do not expect or wish her to go out in the dark: (that is, after 4,) to see me.

As for my 'taking charge' of her; it is & must be the merest farce, as you see upon consideration.

I am a prisoner not only of my house but my floor.

I not only could not 'take charge': I must solemnly protest against her being in a house in London upon any such condition: as my being supposed to be able to undertake this: & I am sure that you, dear Sir Harry & Parthe, will see it at once.

This is really not a matter of discussion: it is a matter of fact.

I *can* be of no use to my mother, not only except I be in the same house with her, but except I be on the same floor.

Yrs affect'ly

F. Nightingale

Source: Wellcome

Family relations could hardly have improved when Florence sent a note in September informing Sir Harry and Parthe about Fanny's companion, a Miss Parish, 'Either she drinks: or she has a screw loose. In any case she is totally unfit to take charge of my mother alone. And I am totally unfit to take charge of Miss Parish' (21 Sept 1874 Wellcome).

After Elizabeth Barclay was eased out of the Edinburgh Royal Infirmary, Angélique Pringle was made Superintendent. Rachel Williams, her friend, was sent to help. Nightingale lavished praise upon her: 'No one but you could help our Pearl as you are doing. *That* has been a fire so terrible as nearly to have burnt up both her & me. And I thank God for having sent you to our help: in saving His work' (12 Dec 1873 GLRO HI/ST/NC3/SU 180/13). Williams, however, felt that she deserved a superintendency of her own and complained of her inferior position.

129. To Rachel Williams   35 South St 5 Dec 1874

My dear Goddess

I answer your imperious letter at once. I do not plead guilty to your heavy charge, for, if you had conferred with a certain little

Pearl not 300 miles off as I am – you would have found that she had not only 'written' to me 'a few days ago' but that she had had an answer in her pocket from me nearly a week.

But as I have observed all this year that there exist certain mysterious but insuperable obstacles to the Goddess & the Pearl in the same room communicating, and that they are obliged on certain topics to ascertain each other's meaning thro' an unfortunate hard-worked individual in another kingdom, I will say that the substance of this my letter was: that after much consideration my 'suggestion' was that you should remain 'another 6 months' (I said) in the same position: [but I will now say another few months more or less]: & this not because I had any idea of your remaining indefinitely on & on as you are, but because Edinburgh serves as a capital & indispensable preparation to what I had to 'suggest', had I seen you at Lea Hurst, but which is postponed (not by me): & will be more ready in another 6 months: or, if not that, something else.

Miss Pringle further told me that you were in no hurry to part: & indeed the wonder to me is rather how you can look forward to parting at all with any equanimity: & that you were too busy till Christmas to come to me with any convenience.

I now come to the only thing I have to add to what I said to Miss Pringle:

the Pearl says: 'I must go' –

the Goddess says: 'I must go' –

I agree with the Goddess: the Pearl had better stay. And it was this very thing for which I wished to see the Goddess *first*: to ascertain from her her own wishes & her friend's: as that sly little friend had very much misinterpreted her last February to me:

But all this is only an old woman's advice: which probably the Goddess will not much regard: & which is subject any way, of course, to hearing your own wishes, ideas & reasons for one course or another.

I cannot now see you before Xmas: for I have filled up my time far more than my strength will allow.

And I said 'February' to Pearl: but if there is such violent haste, telegraph to me any day, & come up by the next express or on the wires. And I will turn out India, my mother, & 'all the Queen's horses & all the Queen's men': together with one sixth of the human race: & lay my energies (not many left) at the Goddess' feet.

I cannot myself understand: but that is my stupidity: how there can be such a deficiency of employment for 3 in such a place as Edinburgh. And indeed it was an *unwillingness to disturb* such a place *at present* which made my Triumvirate, here, advocate another 6 months: quite independent of any other work. [I am sure too that my Goddess will regret *this* time when she has either left or is left at Edinburgh.]

N.B. Were it not that I conclude it was a brief & temporary revival of 'the baby' which provoked the word 'killing': I would suggest to my Goddess that, to one whose life has been *& is* like mine, the word savours rather of the Melodramatic: & that I wish I had ever had or was ever likely to have on this side the grave anything so little 'killing': as to be with such a friend in such a post.

And now, my dear & imperious friend:

seriously I must stop: seriously I have nothing more to give but this opinion, well weighed, tho' you may not think so.

But – as you say that 'little Sister' too 'does want & ask for an idea' &c &c:, & as this letter really contains but one 'idea' that mine to her did not, I have little hope but that I shall have by 3 successive posts: 'we do want & ask for' &c &c & it is 'killing' &c &c. [My Goddess will remember that in the week of my Father's death last January, after having written *3* times (to 'little Sister') & had *no* letter, I received a very imperial nod to the effect that I had *not* written the letters which I *had*: & that I had received the letters which I had *not*.]

And so seriously, dear soul, A Dieu & God bless you: & receive my warmest congratulations on your good work: *I give you joy*: Mercy & Truth be with you:

    & believe me ever yours aff'ly

F. Nightingale

I saw Mrs. Wardroper last night: looking so aged
You do not tell me Nurse Lyon's new address:

I would add: but this is expressly for the Pearl, (& your Goddess-ship can surely *penetrate* any *impenetrable* barrier to get at her): as well as for yourself: that, if your Serene Highness graciously accedes to another '6 months', there will probably be some correspondence anent between this miserable black beetle & Mr. Fasson: & then I think something might be said about two real grievances: Miss Forsyth: & the reporting Students.

F.N.

Source: GLRO HI/ST/NC3/SU 180/22

In 1865 Dr J. Pattison Walker had invited Nightingale to India, and she had replied: 'There is nothing, really nothing, on this side of the grave which I long for as much as a visit to India . . . I have studied the country so much, I seem to know so well what I want to do there, that it appears to me as if I would be going home . . . I shall never leave London, except for the grave' (3 Jan 1865 BL Add 45781: f 260). Nightingale's attachment to India found a new channel when in the seventies several severe droughts caused millions of deaths. She pressed for irrigation schemes that would serve as preventive measures from future suffering. Parthe and Jowett urged her to drop her involvement in India. The former questioned how she could possibly be well enough informed to be of any use; the latter had long urged her: 'Put not your trust in princes, or in princesses, or in the War Office, or in the India Office – all that sort of thing necessarily rest on a sandy foundation. I wonder that you have been able to carry on so long with them' (Quinn and Prest, p. 228). Yet the fact was that while she made some mistakes that were gleefully repeated the length and breadth of India, Nightingale was remarkably well informed. Few Englishmen who lived there understood this complex country as well as she did.

130. To Lord Salisbury   35 South St 5 Oct 1875

Irrigation Returns   *Private*
India

Dear Lord Salisbury,

In obedience to your most kind letter of May 10 I patiently waited for that Irrigation 'Account' or Returns which you said you were 'trying to make out for Parliament', 'to which' you could 'safely give official sanction'.

Not having seen it appear, I did not like to assault you the moment Parl't was over: nor do I now.

But your kindness and the extreme importance of the subject are compulsory.

Your willingness, some months ago, to take steps for securing accurate Irrigation Statistics from India: & your just complaints that there were none: seem to show you as thinking that there is ample scope for asking for enquiry: & make the prayer of me (who have been up to my neck in Indian 'Returns' for 16 years) less audacious.

You said that you could not be satisfied with the present position of the question. And the Irrigation matter is one which cannot drop. Therefore

1. Might I ask you, would you send me such *Irrigation Returns* as you have doubtless already procured & 'given official sanction' to, since May: I mean of course such as it would not be an impertinence to ask for?

2. And if you are not satisfied with what you have obtained am I too daring in suggesting that now would be the time to give effect to your desire *to make an enquiry* such as shall secure *results & returns* which *can* be laid before Parliament & the public with confidence?

May I venture to say that the 5 points or difficulties mentioned in your kind letter of May as standing in the way of obtaining accurate Returns suggest the following questions which are entirely based on your letter?

Pardon my troublesomeness & let me go on.

Irrigation Enquiry

Might not the enquiry be by a Commission,* if that is the shortest & best way of getting at authenticated *facts*? (*It has been suggested that the Commission might be of Sir Andrew Clarke:[1] & one good Civilian??)

bearing in mind that what is wanted is: *not theory nor opinions,* but *facts & the results of actual experience.*

that therefore no special or professional qualifications are required in the Inquirer, beyond those necessary to enable him to collect & present his facts (great qualifications indeed! perfect independence & impartiality & freedom from bias, *as to prevailing or fashionable theories* – with industry & promptitude, so that the inquiry may not, (as some of its predecessors have – have they not?) run on for years and official generations.

Might not the inquiry be easily made by means of *printed Questions & Tables*? (upon an *uniform* basis of course: so as to secure *uniform* data, which *can* be compared & tabulated: as you said, the great difficulty has been that hitherto Returns have not been comparable).

– *each local Governm't* & Administration* collecting the replies & returning them to the Commissioner. (*Note: that the information is wanted from practical & regular cultivators: not from wild tribes: so that as a rule the Superintendents of Hill & Forest Tracts need not be asked for returns – need they?)

Naturally, I suppose the Commission will summarize the results: especially as regards

      (1) extent of capital invested a by Government
                    b ,, Cultivators

B. Special Facts relating to great works which affect more than one village.

(Works which are *incomplete*:
should these either not be excluded? or special care taken to note extent & effects of incompleteness?
OLD WORKS repaired or extended:
should not these be so noted?)
1. State culturable acreage of area affected by each work:
2. Description of work as to locality, construction, extent of channels, main or subsidiary &c &c &c, date of construction & time occupied.
3. Cost of construction: showing separately *interest*, if any, has been charged for borrowed money
4. Cost of (a) maintenance
       (b) management
       (c) repairs
          actual or estimated
5. Returns distinguishing
       (d) direct, in form of water rate,
                         enhanced rents
                         tolls
                         forest rects
                         &c &c
   (e) indirect
6. Net Results according to local calculation of profit or loss.

Dear Lord Salisbury: I am sure that I need no apology with your kindness & genius & great interest (in a subject so vital to India that I should be impertinent if I were to doubt these). What I do need to make apology for is: not in asking for enquiry: but perhaps in the length of these notes meant to help to show the direction inquiry should take, if it is desired to have real results & returns.

But these notes can easily be set aside: the enquiry I am sure you will not set aside: since evidence is necessary to show *what is* the duty of the Gov't in promoting irrigation
   by great works?   by small?
   by wells & tanks?   by great & small Canals?
   by private Capital?   by great national grants & loans?
So many authorities are hopelessly at variance as to facts, or the basis of any theory of Gov't duty: (in writing this I am not simply writing as a parrot, if *parrots* write; – for I have laboured thro', & tried to tabulate, immense piles of (so called) Indian Statistics myself:)
that Secretaries of State have almost come to look upon the question perhaps hopelessly too as a mere worrying puzzle: & it seems left to Lord Salisbury's genius victoriously to solve it & arrive at real definite results which Governments can act upon.

Hope deferred makes my heart sick: what must the Indian Cultivator's heart be? – – & the famines? – – –
I will at least not take up your time with wordy apologies.
  but pray believe me dear Lord Salisbury
    ever your faithful serv't

Florence Nightingale

Source: BL Add 45779: ff 38–43   {copy}

1. General Sir Andrew Clark: (1824–1902), colonial officer, head of the Public Works Department in India (1877–80). In 1870 he had advocated the purchase of the Suez Canal by England.

Nightingale never ceased to recommend an improved irrigation system, but the great expense of large-scale water projects deterred the government. Building railways was more profitable and made it easier to deliver grain to the drought-stricken areas.

Cats had become a part of Florence's life when she set up her own home. Her favourites were pure-breds given to her by the Mohls, although she ruefully admitted: 'I take no end of pains to marry them well. But they won't have the husbands I choose, while they take up with low Toms, of recent extraction, out of the Mews . . . Not only have my Pupie's kits no long feathery tails but they have no long feathery ears – but ears like cropped bull dogs & tails like rats' (30 July 1864 BL Add 43397: ff 322–23). Her cats received meticulous care:

131. To Mrs Frost   35 South St 13 Dec 1875

Dear Mrs. Frost

Mrs. Wilson is so good as to invite me to write to you about my Angora Tom-cat (who answers to the name of *Mr. White*) – now hers.

1. Mr. White has never made a dirt in his life: but he has been brought up to go *to a pan*, with sand in it. You must have patience with him, please, till he has been taught to go out-of-doors for his wants.

2. He has always been shut up *at night*: (in a large pantry:) to prevent his being lost. And I believe he ought always to be shut up at night: for this reason. [I think you must keep him in the house

for two or three days till he knows his kind mistresses: & the place: for fear he should run away & try to get back to me.]

And perhaps if you could give him a pan with sand in it for the first night or two, it might be better.

3. He has always been used to have his meals by himself like a gentleman on a plate put upon a 'table-cloth' (on old newspaper) spread on the floor.

He is not greedy: has never stolen anything: & never drags his bones off his newspaper. But I am sorry to say he has always lived well: he has bones, & milk, in the morning: after 7 o'clock dinner he has any remains of fish not fish bones or chicken – or game-bones: which he eats like a gentleman off a plate in my room, as I have described: & never asks for more – then a little broken meat, & milk, when he is shut up at night:
& a large jar of fresh water (which he can't upset) always on the floor for him.

4. He is the most affectionate & intelligent cat I have ever had: is much fonder of the society of *Christians* than of cats: likes of all things to be above in a room with me: (but make acquaintance with the little dog of a baby friend of ours): & when his own little sister cat died, he refused food & almost broke his heart. He washes & dresses two little kits we have here (of his) himself. I never saw a Tom-cat do this before.

5. You will see Mr. White is very *black* now. But, when he is in the country, he is as white as the driven snow.

He is 10 months old.

I have written a long letter about him: but in short I recommend him to your kind care: & am

    yours faithfully

                    Florence Nightingale

Source: BUL N62: Box 1, Folder 5

Nightingale remained adamant in her opposition to women who attempted to enter 'male spheres'. The movement for medical women was a threat to her own plans to bring educated women into midwifery and nursing. Only in old age did she soften, and her last physician was a woman.

132. To Henry Acland, MD[1]   35 South St 19 April 1876

Women's Diplomas &c   (6:30 a.m.)
Private

My dear Sir
    I feel it such an immense question, the one you are so good as to ask me upon: & myself so unable to deal with it.
    I feel that I agree with you so entirely: as to 'Would we could induce the Women Doctors to take up *Midwifery & Nursing*': while *they* are moving heaven & earth 'to go in for the ordinary *men's examination*'.
    At the present moment when you are so earnestly & kindly striving to maintain the Netley Medical School *on the very ground* that this *'men's examination'* leaves, (upon the shewing of Annual Reports of Examiners &c) 'more than two thirds' of the men e. g. unable to use the Microscope, to apply practically any knowledge of Chemistry, to make even the most important analyses of food & drink, as are in daily requisition: & 'more than nine tenths', e.g. incompetent to perform the most trifling operation: I confess that, having always striven to induce the women to take up *Midwifery*, on this & other grounds, I feel then, if possible, more strongly than ever:
    But may I venture to say a few considerations before you?
    I. Can we force women to take up *Midwifery & Nursing* by legislation to prevent them from being *Doctors?* any more than we could force them to be *Midwives* by passing an Act to say that they shall not be *Officers of the Army?*
    Have we any right to shut women out? Give 'free trade' in Diplomas:
    & I have a lurking idea (in which I may be quite wrong) that, as in many other things, women will no longer be so very eager to toil for the 'fruit' which is no longer 'forbidden'.
    But, whether this idea be right or wrong, shall we not do more harm than good in shutting out the women?
    Let them try: Once we have 'free trade', supply & demand will, will they not?, adjust themselves: it will be seen, by the simple test of utility, of profit & loss, whether *women Doctors* can *get practice*, & *deserve practice.*
    Fortunately for them, they cannot make us legislate that the Public *shall* employ *women* Doctors: any more than we can legislate that the Public shall employ men-Doctors from what we think the best Schools.
    Give us free trade: *& let the Public decide.*

II. But may I venture to lay what seems to me the root of the whole matter before you:

is it not 'putting the cart before the horse' to say: 'we will legislate that *no woman shall practice as Midwife* before she has successfully passed an *Examination* of competence' –

& *not to provide such Training, such instruction, & such Institutions* as shall *enable her to pass such Examination*?

If the 'horse' were provided, i.e. if the State were to start a *Model School for Midwives*, would not this be much better than any *legislation for Midwives*? [might we not have had & might it not have saved us from the pressure of this legislation, now impending, to admit *women* to the *'ordinary men's examination'*? by this time a number of *fully qualified Midwives* (pointing the way to these aspiring Women Doctors, by the bye, who now will be satisfied with nothing but legislation to make them Women Doctors) these Midwives training others again in new *private Schools for Midwives*?

And we might then never want the 'cart': viz. legislation to tell us that no woman shall practise as Midwife but with &c &c. Because the public would itself have furnished the 'cart'.

[St. Petersburg *has* founded such a School for Midwives: a very admirable one: a 4 years' course: as you aware.]

Any how, if not the State: those who are interested in the subject: (attention of late years has been enough directed to it:) might have a *Model School for Midwives* started by a few rich men. And how much better it is, is it not?, to say to women: 'Show us what you can do': furnishing them *with the means of learning to do*: than all these fights & struggles about legislation?

[It seems to me a sort of lazy, unenterprising, in short, stupid thing, of the women to say: 'we will be *like men*': instead of trying to work the immense field, *Midwifery & Nursing*, which is theirs by right.

But, you see, Messrs Stansfeld, Cowper, Temple, Lord Houghton &c² 'aid & abet' them in this: & do nothing for the other.] As no School for Midwives is provided for them, they seem to have no invention to do anything but what men do.

Of course what will be answered to No. II is: 'that is a matter, like everything else in England, for *private* enterprise on a *self-supporting* basis, to supply: viz. *Schools for Midwives*'.

That is very true.

But it will be a *long time first*. And meanwhile a vast field for women's work is left untilled: & a vast amount of suffering among the poor (& rich too) is left unremedied.

A *Model School for Midwives* started *now by Gov't*: or by *a few* rich *individuals* with competent advice: would probably advance the matter by 100 years.

[Almost every thing of this kind of work in England has been done in this way: a wise philanthropy has started it: the public has taken it up, when it has found the benefits in its own body or mind: & joint-stock & commercial enterprise has then placed it on a *self-supporting* footing.]

I am afraid of overpassing all sensible & reasonable limits of language: & certainly all proper bounds to this letter: if I were to say – what, if I am right, you will know far better than I – of what *vital importance* it seems that a *Model School for Midwives*, in which the *course of practical & scientific instruction* should command the confidence of the public, should be started with as little delay as possible (instead of all these discussions about legislation:)

Nothing but this will show *women* panting for a *Medical career* where their *true field* is to be found.

No one but you would so command the confidence of the public if it were known that you were the promoter of such a start.

There is, I believe, but little doubt that women, so trained, would command half the ordinary Midwifery practice in England: perhaps even *we* should live to see it.

[It does not appear to me that *Midwifery* is in the same category as *Medicine & Surgery*: or that legislation, (or anything else) concerning it, should necessarily follow in the same lines: if only for this reason that Child-bearing is *not* a disease or an accident: it is *naturally* a *natural process* of health: which would happen naturally, I suppose, with every properly constituted couple.

This is not to say that *Midwifery* should not be *thoroughly* taught: The Midwife should have a sound Medical as well as general Education: which should comprise Diseases of Women & children: & above all *Hygiene of Women & children*: & comprise everything Obstetric.]

You are kind enough to wish to see me & 'ask' my 'opinion' on this subject: (otherwise no apology would suffice for this letter:) & would 'come up to London' 'almost any day' 'to see' me 'at 4.30'. Possibly this letter may, as I wish it, save you this trouble at present: probably you will cry 'enough & too much'.

But if at any time you *are* in London (*not* to come 'on purpose') & would let me know *the day beforehand*: & fix any hour in the afternoon: there is scarcely any engagement I would not put off: if you think me of the least service.

Pray believe me   my dear Sir
    Most faithfully yours

Florence Nightingale

Source: GLRO HI/ST/NC1/76/1

1. Henry Acland, MD: (1815–1900), Regius Professor of Medicine at Oxford (1854–94), honorary physician to the Prince of Wales; published widely on sanitation and medical education.

2. Stansfeld, Cowper, Temple, Lord Houghton: reforming MPs; Sir James Stansfeld (1820–98), Unitarian Radical who worked for the repeal of the Contagious Diseases Acts and served as President of the Poor Law Board; Hon. Henry Frederick Cowper (1836–87), Liberal MP for Hertfordshire; Rt Hon. William F. Cowper-Temple (1811–88), Liberal for Hertford and later Hampshire; Lord Houghton, the former Richard Monckton Milnes.

When Dr Parkes, Chair for Hygiene of the Army Medical School, died in March 1876, the school was again threatened. The difficulty of recruiting good doctors for the army had been a problem from the beginning.

133. To Colonel Stanley, MP[1]   26 Sept 1876

Private   *Army Medical School*
& Confidential   *Netley*

Sir

Very meekly Florence Nightingale comes before you, trusting only to Lord Derby[2] to 'speak for' me: & principally as to the share I had in Sidney Herbert's 'Royal Commission on the Sanitary State of the Army' in 1857; & again in the R. Commission on that of India in 1859–63, over which Lord Derby himself presided; [Sidney Herbert died in 1861.]

In carrying out the conclusions of that first Commission, Sidney Herbert was the founder of the Army Medical School, grafted first on Fort Pitt Hospital at Chatham, which was the practical Training-place for Army Medical Officers then. When Netley Hospital was finished, the School was transferred to Netley, which is an Invalid Establishment, and the only Hospital in England where the effects of tropical disease on soldiers can be studied to any good purpose.

The Warrant of 1859 was also Sidney Herbert's solution of another problem of that R. Commission – and it was a successful one – to frame a Warrant & conditions which would enable the Army & Navy to offer inducements to the class of men they want, better than those offered in Civil life.

[The R. Commission of 1857 was well aware of the difficulties of getting suitable men, & of the need of improving both their education & status. If I might, I would refer you to the letter of

Sidney Herbert prefixed to the Army Medical Regulations, & to the Warrant at the end.

If I might, I would appeal from the present constant changes in small details to the great principles contained in these documents, which, if adhered to, could scarcely fail to fill up the ranks of Medical Officers with men suitable to consort with their brother Officers of any grade.

Forgive me: there is scarcely any one but I left to speak for Sidney Herbert's 'ghost'.]

The consequences of the departure from that Warrant of 1859 have been, increasing difficulty in obtaining the best men for Army Medical Service. And since then the Army Medical Department has undergone repeated alterations which have more & more departed from the intentions of the R. Commission of 1857 & the Warrant of 1859, so that subsequent proceedings have more & more borne the impress of want of acquaintance with the necessities of the case – almost of a breach of faith with the public – while the great advance in Civil Medical education & status, in consequence of recent Medical legislation, has given to men entering the Civil profession a very different estimate of their position than they formerly had:

2. As Government has to draw its supplies of Officers from this source, it need hardly be said that such men cannot be attracted into Her Majesty's service by small arrangements altering Departmental details, such as abolishing the entrance examination, or weakening the Netley School – or sending Candidates to Aldershot to learn Hospital work proper, Hospital discipline proper & riding; which Aldershot training might very well be entered on *after* the present Netley School course of 4 months – all too short for the work – but not *substituted* for it.

Even in 1857 this was the case: Is not what the Government has to do to compete with the Civil profession by offering such inducements in the way of rank, status, pay & privileges as will induce young men to forego the advantages in money & position of Civil practice & enter Her Majesty's Service?

Will petty changes make any difference in the present state of matters – bring one good man to the poll – or prevent the Department from having to content itself with the worst leavings of the Civil Medical practice?

3. Is there any real road out of the present difficulties arising from littleness of candidates (in both senses of *littleness*), except in the direction of the Royal Warrant of 1859 with such additional inducements as the changed position of the Civil profession renders necessary? [And on this subject Government has an official

adviser at hand in Dr. Acland & the General Medical Council:] – and then to issue such a Warrant as will bring in the required supplies: and to keep to it:

What is wanted are the men:

4. After a Warrant is once issued, the public look upon it, I suppose, as of the nature of contract: which ought not to be departed from at least in the case of those who have entered the public service under it: due notice of any contemplated change to be given in order to keep faith with the public.

At present there is no continuity in the Service: is there?

5. If I might, I should venture to ask that there should be no interference with the Warrant on the Organization of the Army Medical School &c without those who remain of the framers of that Warrant – – or without the Professors of the Army Medical School who have been for years carrying out its provisions – – being formally consulted on the subject.

Ought not the British Medical Council also to be one of the advisers of the Government on such an important matter?

6. Other matters absolutely necessary to the efficiency of the Department may be put as follows: namely

– the strictly technical teaching of the School –

– its observation of young men during their School course: with its power to cast out the unfit *as now*, subject of course to the confirming sanction of the S. of S. for War – the teaching to be thus in the same hands as the discipline *as now*:

– and the final Examination.

These things appear to be the very root of the School's usefulness.

I will not make this too long letter longer with words of apology: but pray believe that I am (with many apologies)

ever your faithful servant

Florence Nightingale

Source: GLRO HI/ST/NC1/78/4

1. Colonel Stanley, MP: Frederick Arthur Stanley (1841–1908), son of Lord Derby, appointed financial secretary to the War Office in 1874; moved to the Treasury in 1877.
2. Lord Derby: as Lord Stanley he had succeeded Herbert as chair of the Indian Sanitary Commission.

Rachel Williams finally became Superintendent of St Mary's Hospital, London, on Nightingale's recommendation. Although the hospital was not as prestigious or as large as Williams had hoped for, it was the best Nightingale could do.

134. To Rachel Williams[1]   1 Jan 1878

My very dear Miss Williams & my Goddess:

I have done your behest: tho' not very sure I quite understand your meaning. If I have failed, put it all in the fire, I need not say.

I was so very glad to hear from my cousin Shore that he thought that tremendous Engine could & would be moved. Pray tell me: And tell me how you are:

Over & over again I wish you the highest New Year's happiness – a thousand and one New Years. And a thousand and one times I pray that my Goddess may walk worthy of her high calling.

Our Nurses are such a source of irritation & vexation to my Goddess, as I mourn to think, that, grievous as it would be to me, I cannot but ask: had she not better get rid of them?

Shall I send you any good (untrained) Nurses I hear of for you to see?

I heard of one lately from a Doctor, a brother in law of Miss Irby's Miss Johnston, who wished for a 'permanent' place – [I suppose her a private Nurse]

Would you like to hear more of her?

Good work is being done. Thank God for it! When the Engine is gone, my Goddess will be herself again.

Fare you very well, my dear Goddess: wear a few clothes: this world is too cold to go about in your shift. And don't look too tall down upon your worshippers.

& believe me ever your faithful serv't

(whatever you may think) & loving old friend

F. Nightingale

Am I to expect Nurses Whagman, Mason & Tearoe?

Source: GLRO HI/ST/NC3/SU/66

1. The letter was hand delivered. On envelope: With 3 pots tulips 2 pots cyclamons & a packet.

The Indian famine of 1877 preoccupied Nightingale for much of the following year. Her article 'The People of India', published in August 1878 in *Nineteenth Century*, began:

> We do not care for the people of India. This is a heavy indictment: but how else account for the facts about to

be given? Do we even care enough about their daily lives of lingering death from causes which we could well remove? We have taken their lands and their rule and their rulers into our charge for State reasons of our own. (4 [1878], 194)

The famine in the Madras Presidency, which had fifty-five thousand villages and a population of thirty-five million, killed between 21 and 27 per cent of the people. While the India Office had estimated the number of deaths to be a million and a quarter, Sir James Caird, the English representative of the Famine Commission, placed the figure above four million. The latter's figures silenced those who had called Nightingale's early estimate of between five and six million in Mysore, Bombay and Madras 'a shriek'. She appears to have been the most accurate, although it would be impossible to give exact statistics (Cook, II, 292).

The problem of peasant indebtedness was formidable. The English created the zemindar, ' "a collector of revenues on behalf of Government" by Lord Cornwallis' Permanent Settlement of 1793' ('The People of India', p. 201). Through a system of 'Takavi' money was advanced by the government at seed time to be repaid at harvest time, but the peasants would not take government loans. They borrowed from the zemindar who, at exorbitant rates of interest that could run from 36 to 90 per cent, was also the village shopkeeper, general dealer and banker. Nightingale contended that England ought to reconquer India by enabling the ryotwari, or peasant, to redeem his land and pay off his debts at 7 or 10 per cent (3.5 to 10 per cent was common in England at the time), by introducing factories, co-operative stores, opening cheap village courts, and so on. Hindu law forbade interest from exceeding the principal, but money lenders circumvented the law by obliging their debtors to sign fresh bonds, the sums of which made up the former principal plus the interest. Debts were payable from generation to generation. Rack-renting was common.

135. To Sir Louis Mallet[1]   {35 South St Feb 1878}

Dear Sir Louis Mallet

I dare say that you would be almost amused if you knew how your little note of Sept 25 stirred me.

And I was only prevented from answering it by your saying that you had 'no time to write', & by my fearing that you would think I wished to claim your time.

It grieves me beyond measure that you think this great Madras calamity – so much greater than our Governm't at all allows – will be a pretext for the postponement to another generation of the real duties of England to India.

But you are too good an Englishman ever to know you were beaten – & that is the surest element of victory

To be before or ahead of one's Government is the most uphill game:

but then it is the greatest reward that our work should be so complete that the next generation should forget us & call our work an obsolete truism which our own generation called a visionary fanaticism.

But it was not to moralize that I venture now to write to you.

It is about the Indian Ryot:

[to ask some questions, I should say, but that I have no hope you have time to answer them.]

the Indian Ryot – so incomprehensible to us: the poorest in the world: & it is said getting poorer & poorer every year: the most industrious in the world: the most heroic, the most secretive & false:

the Irrigation, so vitally, so mortally needed:

the indebtedness to money-lenders, so that a full crop, if he has one, merely means so much in the money-lender's pocket:

the slavery (in Bengal) to Zemindars, worse than any Bulgarian slavery to Turks[2]

These are the subjects, heart-stirring enough in themselves, which in your hands might stir all England:

1. *Water*: if we had given them water, we should not now have had to be giving them bread: & not only this but to have seen millions (take all the Famines in this century) perishing for the want of it, in spite of all the Governm't has done:

i.e. Irrigation by strengthening, repairing & keeping up the old Tanks:

by storage & regulation of water: where possible, for keeping the old Tanks always supplied.

I see appeals from 'influential' & numerous natives, notably from Arcot & Trichinopoly, for this: by wells: & accounts of success from Scinde & Bombay: in other Irrigation means:

Irrigation by every attainable means: canals, tanks, storage, wells:

and

Cheap Water Transit, including

Steam   Navigation   Canals.

I see appeals from Mr. Leslie & other Railway Engineers for Cheap

Water Navigation *by the side* of Railways: notably from Goalundo. Indeed it seems to me that all (Royal) Indian Engineers are for it, wherever practicable. Was not Lord G. Hamilton's speech, ('Times' of Oct 5.,) appalling, saying that 'Rails pay & Water does not'?

But who is to expose it?

Also: L'd Salisbury's speech at Bradford, ('Times' of Oct 12): 'water can't run up hill' & therefore we can't have Irrigation. He does not know the facts when he says this: perhaps he does not know what he means.

Above all, showing the English people that Irrigation pays: Mr. Thornton, of the India Office, has done this, & I understand is to do it again in a Lecture. And the last official 'Progress Report' gives the financial result of Godavery & Cauvery at 81 per cent.

2. The giving the Ryot in Bengal every legal help against the Zemindar, his landlord, pampered by us under the Permanent settlement, so that all his, the Zemindar's, dues have been more than paid him: [good Zemindars to Maharanu in Burdwar] none of his duties under that Settlement required of him – to require of him as a landlord some at least of those duties under the form of Water Cesses, Road & Education Cesses, &c &c.

Otherwise give the Ryot water, & the profit will all go into the pocket of the Zemindar: who has had all the rights without any of the duties of landlords given him:

Some high authorities say:
'give the people of India, as you at last gave the people of Ireland, a poor law: make the Zemindar insure the lives of the people on the land against death by starvation – & they will take care that the ryots are duly instructed in the uses of irrigation: & in religious dogmas, affecting life & property also'. 'Where the State is the Landlord, it must accept the duties as well as the rents, say in Madras'.

However it may be about this question of a Poor Law, at least one thing seems proved by the Madras Famine relief: that the people are the farthest from pauperization that can possibly be, often preferring death to relief: Indeed all over India there is less pauperism & less mendicancy, other than religious, than in any country we know of.

The extraordinary self-control shown by the Madras farmer in almost every village in keeping the secret of his hoarded pits of grain, hoarded for seed-corn but also for another year of famine – a secret which must have been known to many in each village – & not selling at the time of highest prices – reveals to us a thrift, a self-denial, a Political Economy, but one the very reverse of our Policial Economy, unknown to any Western nation.

3. The giving the Ryots, especially in Southern India, every legal help against the Money-lender, into whose hands the ancestral lands seem to be passing: & the Ryot becoming not metaphorically but in some cases literally & legally the Money lender's slave

instead of as we do now giving the Money lender every legal help to possess himself of the lands of India & to make the Ryot his slave

Otherwise, give the Ryot water, & the profit will all go into the pocket of the Money-lender

Is it not strange that under a nation probably the justest in the world & the Abolisher of the Slave Trade, a poverty, an impecuniosity, an *im*property-ness, leading to virtual slavery should be growing up, actually the *consequence* of our own laws, which outstrips in its miserable results, because it enslaves & renders destitute a land-possessing peasantry, anything except the worst Slave-*Trades*. And in some respects we are worse than the tax farming Turks.

One thing has been most urged by my Madras correspondents: a system of small loans from Government at moderate interest to the country ryot (which is now carried out to a very small extent) to be extended to meet the need & supported by British capital:

But the ryots, it is said, won't take them.

Is it true that a rate of 36, 40, 50 or even 60 per cent is a not more uncommon rate of interest in the (country) interior of India as exacted from country ryots by money lenders than a rate of 3 1/2, 4, 5 or 6 per cent is in England?

If so, the fear must be not of the conquest of India by the Russian but the conquest of India by the money-lender?

Is it possible that England would reconquer India by enabling the indebted country ryot to redeem his lands & pay off his debts, lending him money at 7 or even 10 per cent?

What a glorious conquest that would be!

Was it the old rule: that more than twice the principal could not be exacted? It was said that Sir Arthur Hobhouse[3] was going to re-introduce this into Bengal.

It is said that '*Thrift*' is what must save the Indian ryot. This is what the S. of S. for India says.

We have heard of the horse being made to live (or die) on a straw a day: but I don't know that we ever heard before that the horse ought to exercise 'thrift' & save his one straw a day.

Yet this is what it appears the country ryot has actually done. [He justified Lord Salisbury & died.]

There is so little danger of pauperization that for one who threw himself without need on the Relief measures, ten died in silence almost unknown to our Masters: (*not* like the wolf, 'biting hard'.)

There is such an element of endurance & heroism that quite unknown to our Masters, during the greatest starvation & the highest prices the hoarded pits of grain have remained buried in the earth

[none betrayed the secret:]
put by not to sell again at the highest Famine prices but for seed-corn against another failure of crop. And not till the present crops were safe have they appeared: What thrift, what endurance have we Westerns compared with this?

And we in the West preach thrift to them. The horse literally 'saved' his one straw a day for his children's sowing.

And they call these people not thrifty. It is the very heroism of thrift.

Compare the people of Liverpool with their drunkenness, their vice & brutal crime, their reckless waste, & unthrift, with the people of India.

Which is highest, even in the scale of civilization?

But there is no comparison.

4. The first Irrigation question to be asked is: in cases where ryots are said to be unwilling to accept the water for Irrigation purposes, why are ryots unwilling to accept the water?

Because it puts them in the power of the minor officials, all natives, the Tehsildars &c? Bribery, oppression, corruption, bullying, is said to be the rule, the universal rule with these. They have unlimited power to make themselves disagreeable, & must be bought off with a bribe.

Does the official network of petty administration require improving?

The second question refers to the point already alluded to: viz. that the indebted ryot, indebted tho', except at his children's marriages, he is the most frugal of mankind – & the usurious money-lender are pretty much the same all over India.

Government is the first mortgagor on the land: It has all the machinery ready for lending: it would lend at less than 7 per cent. But this is taken advantage of by the ryot in an almost infinitesimal degree: perhaps in all India only a quarter of a million is out at interest in this way.

The question is:
Why is the indebted ryot unwilling to accept the Gov't loan at less than 7 per cent & prefers going to his own money-lender at 5 or 7 or even 8 times that rate of interest?

Is he afraid of putting himself in the power of minor officials of Government?

Is he afraid of offending his banker?

Is it quite true that the land is passing into the hands of the money-lenders?

that the ryot's crops are not his own but the money lender's?

that all over India land is changing hands?

that the money-lender sells the ryot up & gets his land for a tenth or less of its value?

that the ryot is absolutely in the money-lender's power?

It is said on Government authority, in the last India Office Progress Report, that 'even when, after floods at Ahmedabad, Government sanctioned the advance of £1000 to poor cultivators *without any interest at all*, no one availed himself of the offer' – – – –

And it is added: 'There are few ryots in a position to offend their bankers. The great object of the money-lenders is to evade repayment – if the season is good he lets the debt run on from year to year at 36 per cent interest: & this system is preferred by the cultivator to the tedious formalities & rigid terms of repayment attached to Government advances'

It is Government which says this:

Is there no procedure to obviate it?

The same Progress Report speaks of 'their (the "money lenders") heartless & unscrupulous action towards their debtors'. & adds: it is the Government who say this:

'it is hoped that some amelioration may be effected in the position of the ryots by a modification of the present system of civil procedure'.

One echoes the hope that the Government will make good their hope.

The same Report says: it is the 'Financial Commissioner' who speaks: 'That sales & mortgages take place to a large extent' is not to be doubted. It is 'desirable that the landholders should, if possible, retain their lands & should prosper'.

Probably.

It is in relation to the flourishing Punjab that this remark occurs.

5. Improved agriculture: Another thing urged by my Madras correspondent is:

that the orphans & destitute children lately forming the main population of Relief Camps should be taught the useful trades instead of being sent back to swell the already too large agricultural hosts:

But should not rather better agriculture be taught?

Can nothing be done for these Deccan people?

To show them how to raise better & more produce & to give them a market for their produce:

the first by irrigation & better methods of agriculture fodder crops &c

Could there not be a model farm under a Mr. Robertson at Poona?

the second by cheap Water communication & roads.

'The common people who find it hard to live when bread is cheap feel themselves about to die when it becomes dear'.

Unsigned

Source: BL Add 45779: ff 148–55 {draft}

1. Sir Louis Mallet: (1823–90), Permanent Under-Secretary for India, with whom FN corresponded 1874–79; he did not always agree with her, but was sympathetic with her aims.

2. Bulgarian slavery to Turks: A Bulgarian nationalist uprising in 1875–76 was brutally suppressed by the Turks, leading Gladstone to attack Prime Minister Disraeli for his indifference. The issue became a Liberal cause.

3. Sir Arthur Hobhouse: (1819–1904), law member of the Council General of the Governor-General of India, 1872–77. He was responsible for the Specific Relief Act (1877), in response to the famine.

In July Sir John Lawrence died. Lawrence and India held the drama and the promise of which dreams are made. Compared to the magic of India, nurses' training – while it filled her days – must have seemed mundane. Her sanitary mission extended beyond hospital walls, and in India the opportunities for improvement appeared limitless.

136. To Sir Harry Verney {?} 10 South St 1 July 1879

O what a loss. O the pity of it – the pity of it. to all India as to me. I received a letter from him, the day *after* his death, dictated, but signed by himself: sending me Indian Reports he had read & wished me to read, all marked, & the page turned down where he had left off.

precious remembrances, tho' as remembrances not needed, but precious as what he wished one to do. God & he had not forgotten one.

O that I could do something for India which he saved & for which he lived & died.

I am glad you have offered to go to the funeral: tho' I hope it will not overdo you. I am glad it is to be at Westminster Abbey. That all may see & be inspired by his greatness – the greatest man of our age.

'unselfishness & firmness' an Indian official said to me 'that could not be surpassed'. & his voice broke down with tears.

I am in great trouble. Diphtheria in the house: Doctor 4 times a day: trained Nurse. I forbid every one coming to the house.

It is my little cook.

Last night he came prepared to perform Tracheotomy. But it was not needed.

I had to put off Miss Crossland & Miss Machin.

I am very sorry for this continued rain. It is a real misfortune.

I have a terrible letter from Ida (Mohl) Schmidt, to whom I recommended Mme Werckner, about her. from Vienna.

ever yrs aff'ly

F.N.

I have an Article in *to-day's* 'Good Words' on Bombay Famine.

Source: Wellcome

And so the seventies ended. England would become involved in the first Boer War the next year and Fanny died in February 1880. Death – public and private – formed the thread of continuing loss. For Florence, who had anticipated death from an early age, life now must have seemed like marking time, however busy a marking it was.

6

Old Age: 1880–1910

Fanny Nightingale was nearly ninety-three when she died on 2 February 1880. Florence and Parthe drew closer now, and Claydon became Nightingale's home outside London. But old quarrels flared anew; even the official notice of Fanny's death could yield a testy letter:

137. To Parthenope, Lady Verney   11 Feb 1880

I withdraw my Mother's age, my dear P., tho' it greatly loses in pathos thereby: but my Father's age must in that case be also withdrawn.

But the *place* of death is *always* put: & in this case the circumstances are so remarkable that it is quite impossible to omit it: the antithesis of the house in London & 'the house not made with hands' is not pain but half the pathos: (so in the verse so popular leaving 'the cottage on earth To dwell in a palace in heaven'.)

The poor people would not think it the right card without.

I send several that you may patch them as you like.

[I put on my wreath about joining our Heavenly & earthly Father.]

I *think* I like No. 4 the best – but am not particular: only I feel it *quite* impossible to leave out that she died with Shore: don't you?

your

F.

If Sir H. likes the black instead of the gold line, *please* let him have it. But I explained to him that what we did was: gold edged card in *black* edged *envelope*. And I thought he concurred.

F.

Source: Wellcome

The cast of familiar characters was steadily dwindling. Dr Farr, Nightingale's collaborator in statistics, died in 1882, while Sir John

McNeill, her wise counsellor from the Crimean days, died the following year. Clarkey, or Madame Mohl, who had encouraged her ambitions so many years ago, died in 1883. Sir Bartle Frere, a favourite India expert, died in 1884, and Lord Houghton, who had waited nine years in the hope that Florence would marry him, followed in 1885. General C. G. Gordon, whom she admired for his loyalty and sense of duty, was killed at Khartoum in 1885. Florence and Aunt Mai were reconciled following Uncle Sam's death, which was eight years before Aunt Mai's in 1889 at the age of ninety-one. The bitterness and self-pity that had followed Sidney Herbert's death was absent as Florence, now in her sixties, had begun to mellow.

The Prime Minister's office shifted back and forth between Gladstone and Lord Salisbury during the decade. Nightingale's hopes for reform again soared when Lord Ripon, formerly Lord de Grey, a reformer firmly in her sanitary camp, was appointed Viceroy of India in 1880. Under Sidney Herbert, he had served as Under-Secretary for War, and subsequently as first Secretary for War before becoming Indian Secretary. But Lord Ripon resigned before his term was up in the face of an unyielding opposition that considered his policies too liberal. His successor, Lord Dufferin, however, undertook several reforms that had been begun by Lords Mayo and Ripon, including the development of irrigation. During the eighties, female nurses were finally introduced into military hospitals in India. Nurses at home became involved in the Egyptian War in 1884. Mrs Wardroper retired in 1887, to be succeeded by Nightingale's favourite protégée, Angélique Pringle.

Another important retirement was that of Dr Sutherland in 1888. He was eighty and in poor health. There was danger that his position – the only paid member of the permanent Army Sanitary Committee – would not be filled after his retirement. But Nightingale still had people ready to collaborate with her to prevent the loss of whatever remained of the work of the Army Sanitary Commissions. With Sir Douglas Galton's help, she succeeded in getting Dr J. Marston appointed Sutherland's successor.

While Nightingale's prominence had diminished, her fame and expertise enabled her to remain involved in Indian questions and she continued to play an active role in nurses' training. Newly appointed viceroys still went – or sent a delegate – to her for instructions regarding Indian sanitation. Reports sent to her were digested with her usual thoroughness. And Sir Harry Verney continued to ask her questions about public health, a field in which she had clearly fallen behind the times.

138. To Sir Harry Verney 10 South St 18 Mar 1880

My dear Sir Harry

In answer to your question about 'compulsory vaccination', the facts, considered well & briefly put, are as follows:

While Sanitary measures give a perfect immunity from Small pox, Vaccination does not:

& while '*compulsory*' vaccination really means, *for the poor*, the Public Vaccinator taking the matter from *any poor child* he can get, probably out of the *Workhouse*, Vaccination, to be safe from carrying anything wrong into the system of the Vaccinated child, must be performed *from arm* to arm: & you must know the child from whom the Vaccine is taken, to be a perfectly healthy country child, & not only know this but know the family for its two previous generations.

Or the Vaccine must be taken from the *calf*. [I believe the best, ever the oldest Physicians are coming over to this opinion.]

If there is to be any 'compulsion', it should be as to the *source* from which the Vaccine is taken.

[In England a Public Vaccinator would be scouted, if he were to ask questions as to the parents or grandparents of the child from whom the Vaccine lymph is taken: yet, we know that disease may be propagated down thro' two generations]

I have given the facts generally, as well as I can. But I must say I think it unfair to press you with such a question (*non*-political) & unnecessary for you to answer it, unless you have a decided opinion of your own one way or other.

Vaccination, tho' it does not protect from Smallpox, as Sanitary measures do, appears to protect in a measure from *Death* by smallpox.

And I confess, if I were asked: 'Would you abolish compulsory Vaccination? Yes or No?' – without being allowed to enter into the facts as I have given them here, I should be at a loss to answer: much as I have gone into the subject.

The anti-Vaccinators' liberty of-the-subject cry against compulsory Vacc'n is absurd. I only wish there were more that was *compulsory* – such as house-to-house visitation of sinks &c &c. But, if there is a State machinery for Vaccination, it is *worse than* absurd *not* to have a State *organization* for *providing (compulsorily) good lymph* but to leave the choice of this lymph to a parcel of Village apothecaries throughout the land. Austria has her *Calf* Vaccination State organization.

Thank you for your 2nd song: very charming that & the working men's feeling & love & activity.

379

We pray daily in our family prayer that God will send us a good Ho: of C.

(I like Garibaldi, cannot pass the Ho. of C. without tears) & we pray for all those who are working for a Ho. of C. that shall serve Him.

God speed: I hope the leg continues better.

ever yours & P.'s

F.N.

Source: Wellcome

One way in which Nightingale kept intimately involved with the training of nurses was inspecting the probationers' diaries, in which they recorded their ward experiences. It is unclear how many of her daunting comments were passed on by the Home Sister.

139. To Mary Crossland   {Aug 1881}

to Mary Crossland, H.S.[1]   '1880 Diaries October'

The object of reading these Diaries from month to month is of course to see how each Probationer improves in keeping her 'sheet' from month to month.

This is satisfactory as to progress – but not so satisfactory as it should be.

I quote almost at random
take the sheet of 1st day of month in several months: as this is never by same probationer my remarks are quite general:

Sometimes it says that *as* this was the first day in a new Ward, she learnt nothing. One would think it would be just the contrary. She ought at least to be shown how to do the Lavatory. Another says, 1st day in a new Ward she learnt the names of the cases. (that is right) but she does not tell us what any of them were. She might at least have given us the more interesting cases.

Another remark I would make almost universally. No one gives you the *progress* of the *cases*. One cannot make out from any one's Diary whether the case is going well or ill. Surely for one interested in her cases, this is of the first interest.

This cannot apply of course to first day in Ward.

There is an immense deal of Zinc rubbing but I have not met

with a single observation as to whether there was danger of bed sore.

Miss Bird, a 9 or 10 months Prob'r, writing a very full Diary, is rather disappointing. She makes '14 beds' 'in the usual way' – but 'three of the Patients' are 'helpless'. Had the beds to be made with the Patients *in* them? She does not describe the process.

She washes a Patient 'all over' in bed – but does not describe this process.

She 'uncovers *a little*' an Enteric case 'in a profuse perspiration' to wash him. O why, Sister George, let her 'uncover' him at all? why let her say:, 'I uncovered him *"only a little at a time"*.'

In 'taking the temperatures', she does not tell us *what* they are. Surely in taking the temperatures at least of such Critical cases as 2 Enteric Fevers & one Acute Rheumatism, she might have told us. Also no giving the '12 o'clock medicines' to such cases *what they are*.

She does tell us in one case – the one she 'uncovered *a little*' – his temperature & medicine. *Not one word* as to how these Enteric cases are going on, on the *25th* of the month.

These are unsatisfactory
where *test* details are omitted which they too often are.

It is nothing for instance to tell us that she has 'taken the temperatures'.

She should at least give us those 'temperatures' which are abnormally high.

This would be equally, good for herself & for us.

There is rarely or never any notice given by which one can tell whether any critical disease is doing well or ill. This is a capital fault.

Notices of cleaning Lavatories &c are right but it should be said whether they were done to the satisfaction of the Sister or not.

FN

Source: BL Add 47738: ff 210–12

1. H. S.: Home Sister, the Warden of the Nurses' Home and in charge of the care and education of the probationers. As second-in-command to Mrs Wardroper, the position was often extremely difficult. Mary Crossland held it from 1875 to 1896 (see Baly, pp. 155–59).

During his term as Viceroy Lord Ripon sought two highly controversial legal changes. The Ilbert Bill proposed that some Englishmen in India could be tried by Indian judges; Lord Ripon was forced to compromise by agreeing that a European tried by an Indian judge would have a right to a jury; in this form, it passed in January 1884. The second proposed reform concerned Land Tenure Bills which would give the ryots or peasants security from oppression, but this was not passed until Lord Ripon's successor, Lord Dufferin, was in office. Nightingale continued to agitate for improved conditions for her soldiers, and most especially for better hospitals.

140. To Lord Ripon   10 South St 14 Apr 1881

Private & Confidential

Dear Lord Ripon

May I venture to recall to your kind remembrance one Florence Nightingale & to ask you a favour for auld lang syne connected with old times, at the War Office?

I have heard with delight of your measure, which was so very much needed, viz. the creation of a native Army Hospital Corps.

The wants of the present system, or no-system, of Hospital attendance in India were so enormous: the name even of Nursing was such a farce: the ward coolies, who are the Nurses at 4 rupees a month & are not even enlisted – any day they may desert – seem there merely to be 'kicked' by the European soldier, who says then, & truly, he didn't know who the Coolie was for no uniform, & cannot be recognized in the Bazaar if they abscond, which they are always doing. Then there is the Mehter, or sweeper, who is of a yet lower caste, & does indeed all the most necessary work about the sick soldier. Alike they are of course utterly untrained.

There is absolutely no supervision of these Nurses: When the Medical Officer is not there the Indian Hospital is deserted. You hear, Coolie! Coolie! Coolie! called but no Coolie is there. The Ward Coolie who washes & nurses the Patients is worse paid than the 'Shop' Coolie who washes the bottles. The better paid ranks, the 'Compounders' & the 'dressers', so-called, are in the Dispensary & none in the Wards.

But when *in* the Wards the Coolie Nurse seems to be there only to be gentle & to be 'kicked'.

This is the real state of things in a Military Hospital in India in time of peace. It is not known to inspection, because when the Hospital is inspected, of course it is not *there*. Then every thing is in order, & prepared to be inspected. But the very best Medical Officers are those who will tell you most of it, & who most anxiously longed for a remedy.

A Regimental comrade is sent for to nurse a man dangerously ill.

The old system of taking an untrained comrade from the ranks to nurse the worst cases which Sidney Herbert condemned at home 20 years ago & far more prejudicial in India, there is this aggravation that the Reg'l comrade, not knowing the language, nurses the Patient by beating the coolie. This is the state of things in ordinary times, with this crowd of untrained men.

In times of Cholera & Epidemics what the Hospitals become in point of attendance, nursing can neither be conceived or described: tho' these poor natives are devoted in Cholera wards. The Medical Officer has to do everything, if it is to be done at all:

In time of War it is yet worse, especially in the recent campaign. [last Affghan War.] Then Hospital servants, one can't call them nurses are not to be had at all. And the Medical Officer has had to 'scramble' his Dooly-bearers into Nurses to improvise attendance on the sick when there is not a moment to do it. And the Medical Officers then die of it.

These Ward Coolies or Nurses may be children of 10, old men of 80, cripples, blind: in short any one who will come for 4 rupees a month. No other inducement is given: no promotion: no reward: no good conduct pay: no increase of pay for long service: no camp equipage. The Nurses lie for shelter under the walls of the Hospital tents during the bitter cold nights: In a cholera camp in the monsoon they are sometimes roasted & sometimes drowned. Having no uniform, they may any day be stopped or seized for entering their own lines.

But it would be too indiscreet to enlarge to *you* on what happened during the last Affghan War.

In a word, there is no *training* of native Hospital servants, no *ranking*, no uniform, no *supervision*, no responsibility, no *organization*, & very little pay: of course, no esprit de corps. There cannot be. There is nothing constituted, nothing that is not hap-hazard in the most critical & essential of all current duties. And no steps had been taken to attach the new representatives of the old Regimental Orderly, viz. the Army Hospital Corps men, to Indian Regiments.* (*There is of course the difficulty of the language here.)

The Nursing is *the worst Nursing* in *any* existing Army. & threatens often to become no Nursing at all. The cooking is as bad.

But all this will now be altered by your beneficent arrangements measure. And might I ask the favour I am going to ask you to be so very good as to send me the further arrangements & particulars of your new Army Hospital Corps

– I mean the details of the system

– perhaps a copy of the Regulations:

but especially

what is the proposed system of *Ward training*? What the organization. What the supervision if I may be so daring as this to trouble you.

May I remind you of the Recommendations 26, 27, 28: of the R. Commission on the Sanitary State of the Army in India, of which Sidney Herbert first & Lord Stanley (Lord Derby) next was the head & which reported in 1863:

That *trained* Hospital attendants be introduced into all Hospitals in India

female Nurses at large Station Hospitals

European Hospital Orderlies 'to provide personal attendance for the sick'

26. – – – Hospitals to be supplied with properly *trained* cooks

It seems like a God-send that you should have taken up this mean though large & important & difficult question: to work out: difficult in India preeminently because of caste. But many things may be said for the poor Mehters: they are invariably sober: they are physically strong: they & the Chumars, from whom the Ward coolies are taken are gentle & tender: they are devoted in time of Cholera, the material is good: but there has been no organization, no training. And material without these is like bricks without a building – indeed, like bricks without burning.

May God speed your great, your immense work in India, with 200 millions of our fellow creatures. May its difficulty be your opportunity. I cannot say what I feel about this.

Pray believe me dear Lord Ripon
ever your faithful serv't

Source: BL Add 45778: ff 75–81   {draft}

A series of letters followed with further suggestions, including the necessity of sending some trained English orderlies, because 'all the well paid people give orders' in the Indian hospitals, so the bulk of the work by necessity fell on the untrained coolies.

Nightingale regularly wrote inspirational addresses for nursing schools throughout the world. Although often formulaic, these give a clear statement of what a nurse – and a true lady – ought to be, according to her standards. The strenuous calls to duty and obedience also imply a less than perfect workforce. Her annual addresses to the Nightingale School of Nursing, usually read by Sir Harry to the assembled women, were distributed widely. Her 1881 address, for example, was later sent to Hobart, Tasmania, to inspire the nurses.

141. To the Nurses and Probationers of St Thomas' Hospital   London 6 May 1881

My very dear friends

Now once more 'God speed' to you all; my very best greetings & thanks to you all, all: to our beginners good courage, to our dear old workers peace, fresh courage too, perseverance: for to persevere to the end is as difficult & needs a yet better energy than to begin new work.

To be a good Nurse one must be a good woman: here we shall all agree. It is the old, old story. But some of us are new to the start.

What is it to be 'like a woman'? 'Like a woman' – 'a very woman' is sometimes said as a word of contempt: sometimes as a word of tender admiration.

What makes a good woman is the better or higher or holier nature: quietness – gentleness – patience endurance – forbearance – forbearance with her patients – her fellow workers – her superiors – her equals. We need to remember that we come to learn, to be taught. Hence we come to obey. No one ever was able to govern who was not able to obey. No one ever was able to teach who was not able to learn. The best scholars make the best teachers – those who obey best the best rulers. We all have to obey as well as to command all our lives.

Who does it best?

As a mark of contempt for a woman is it not said, she can't obey? She will have her own way? As a mark of respect – She always knows how to obey? How to give up her own way: You are here to be trained for *Nurses* – *attendants* on the wants of the sick – *helpers*, in carrying out Doctors' orders (not Medical students) Though theory is very useful when carried out by practice, Theory without practice is ruinous to Nurses.

Then a good woman should be *thorough* thoroughness in a Nurse is a matter of life & death to the Patient. Or, rather, without it she is no Nurse. Especially thoroughness in the *unseen* work. Do that well & the other will be done well too. Be as careful in the cleaning of the used poultice basin as in your attendance at an antiseptic dressing. Don't care most about what meets the eye & gains attention.

'How do you know you have grace?' said a Minister to a housemaid. 'Because I clean under the mats': was the excellent reply. If a housemaid said that, how much more should a Nurse, all whose vessels mean Patients.

Now what does 'like a woman' mean when it is said in contempt? Does it not mean what is petty, little selfishnesses, small meannesses: envy: jealousy: foolish talking: unkind gossip: love of praise. Now, while we try to be 'like women' in the noble sense of the word, let us fight as bravely against all such 'womanly weaknesses'. Let us be anxious to do well, not for selfish praise but to honour & advance the cause, the work we have taken up. Let us value our training not as it makes us cleverer or superior to others, but inasmuch as it enables us to be more useful & helpful to our fellow creatures, the sick, who most want our help. Let it be our ambition to be thorough good women, good Nurses. And never let us be ashamed of the name of 'Nurse'.

This to our beginners, I had almost said. But those who have finished their year's training will be the first to tell us they are only beginners; they have just learnt how to learn & how to teach. When they are put into the responsibility of Nurse or 'Sister', then they know how to learn & how to teach something every day, & year, which, *without* their thorough training, they would not know. This is what they tell me.

Then their battle-cry is: 'Be not weary in well-doing'. – 'we will not forget that once we were ignorant tiresome Probationers – we will not laugh at the mistakes of beginners – but it shall be our pride to help all who come under our influence to be better women, more thorough Nurses.' What is influence? – the most mighty, the most unseen engine we know. The influence of one a year or two in the work over one a month or two in the work is more mighty, altho' narrow, than the influence of statesmen or sovereigns. The influence of a good woman & thorough Nurse with all the raw Probationers who come under her care is untold. This it is, which either raises or lowers the tone of a Hospital.

We all see how much easier it is to sink to the level of the low, than to rise to the level of the high: but dear friends all, we know how soldiers were taught to fight in the old times against desperate odds: standing shoulder to shoulder & back to back. Let us each & all, realizing the importance of our influence on others – stand shoulder to shoulder – & not alone, in the good cause. But let us be quiet. What is it that is said about the leaven? Women's influence ever has been ever should be quiet & gentle in its working like the leaven – never noisy or self asserting.

Let us seek all of us rather to be good than clever nurses.

Now I am sure we will all give a grateful cheer to our Matron & to our Home Sister & our Medical Instructors.

God bless you all, my dear, dear friends. And I hope to see you all, one by one – this year

Florence Nightingale

Source: GLRO HI/ST/NTS/C43/1881. See also 6 May 1884 Florence Nightingale Society, Hobart, to Sister Alexandra and Nurses; Mitchell Library B501.

Once a woman was trained at the Nightingale School of Nursing, she was expected to accept whatever post was found for her. Nightingale was not particularly sympathetic with the wishes of nurses when they conflicted with what she perceived as the appropriate position for them. Good trained nurses remained a scarce resource, to be controlled as much as possible by those in authority.

142. To Rachel Williams   10 South St 1 Aug 1881

My very dear Miss Williams

I have not waited for your letter to ask Mrs. Wardroper (upon a hint from 'Little Sister') whether she could not give up Miss Hogg for your post of Night Sup't, describing to 'Matron' what it was.

From a series of untoward circumstances Matron is in such need of Miss Hogg for a Sister that I fear she cannot give her up. You would have been touched as I was at Matron's relief when she heard that Miss Hogg who has been changing her mind *was* coming to her.

[When I spoke to Miss Hogg about it – I was then trying to persuade her that her duty lay with Miss Pringle. She told me that she wished very much for a *Sistership* at St. Thomas'.]

More grievous it is to me than I can say that your Miss Byam is going to leave you. To my poor mind it is as unintelligible that Miss Byam should have a 'call' to Rome as that Miss Machin should have a 'call' to S. Africa. It seems like leaving good solid much wanted work in God's cause for an 'adventure'.

Miss Hogg, tho' sadly wanted at St. Thomas', cannot come there till September.

I feel like a mother, all whose children are crying for food, & she is agonized at having little or none to give them.

I am terrified at your prospect of having 'only a week's holiday' this autumn. I was in hopes that you & Miss Pringle were going abroad for at least a month. How do you think she is? And will she not take a good long holiday? & where?

I cannot help hoping that Miss Byam may yet stay with you where she is happy & useful.

You do not know of a lady 'Nightingale trained' who will suit for Mr. Rathbone's post of Lady Sup't to the Liverpool Royal Infirmary & Nurses' Training School & Home, with its Hospital, Private & District Nurses, do you? She will have two Assistants.

We are beset with applications & the demand is far greater than the supply. Cannot you send us some good *Lady* Probationers?

May every blessing attend your work, my dear friend, as you must feel it has already. May you not be overworked: & may your Hospital grow big. If I could but cut myself up to help you, I would do it tomorrow: alas! I am useless.

but ever yours

F. Nightingale

Source: GLRO HI/ST/NC3/SU 180/90

Nightingale tried to stand by her early moral standards, but the number of women applying for training did not meet the demand.

143. To Henry Bonham Carter   24 Aug 1881

Miss Turner Addenbrooke

My dear Harry
You know I have no *woman* to apply to in these matters. And therefore I must apply to you & trouble you. After Mrs. Wardroper has accepted Miss Carroll, whose husband might have claimed her at any moment, not only as a Prob'r but as a 'Sister', I cannot see that it is legitimate to refuse a woman who is divorced on account of *her husband's* conduct. But – she bears a maiden

name 'Miss'. Is she to put on her papers single, widow or divorced? She *must*, of course, tell her history to Matron. Yet, if she does, it will be known all over the Hospital.

What do you advice?

yrs

F.N.

Source: BL Add 47720: f 162

If standards were hard to maintain at a reputable hospital such as St Thomas', how much more difficult it could be at an army hospital, where men might be ambulatory but still not fit to return to their regiment for months.

144. To Dr Thomas Crawford[1]   10 South St 29 June 1882

Private

My dear Sir

I have been turning over in my mind what you were so good as to ask me, viz. about a proposal to allow one or two Night 'Sisters' for special cases at the Herbert Hospital. And I cannot forbear troubling you with these few remarks or rather questions.

I think I understood you that there are very few serious cases in the Herbert Hosp'l. And most of them, I suppose, are among Artillery 'Invalids'. But taken as a whole you would perhaps say that the great building is rather a sick barrack than a Hospital.

Its pavilions are so separated that a Nurse cannot have more than 64 sick on one floor. And she might have only 32 (or even 20) on a floor.

Would it be possible so to arrange the cases that the one or two or three bad cases requiring (occasionally) night Nursing should be in the same ward or floor?

Systematic Night Nursing, I understood you to say, was not at all required. [And indeed I know that, at Netley, where there are so many more 'Invalid' bed-ridden cases, the Night 'Sister' has often nothing to do all night: the Patients are 'all asleep'.]

What you propose is simply to detach a Nurse for special duty, as the Medical Officer should judge needful.

The 'partitioned room' for the Nat. Aid Soc'y's Nurses is no doubt in the Nurses' block, which is too far away for effective

389

work. I hardly see how you can have night supervision from there. But a telephone to Miss Caulfield's room would bring her at once.

In each Pavilion there is a Nurse's room & scullery in line; Could one of these rooms be given up to the Night Nurse?

If you detached two Nurses for the night work, could one of them be on duty & the other at hand in this room?

What occurred to me after thinking over what you had said to submit to you & to ask you was this:

would it be possible to have the bad cases on one floor of the same Pavilion?

If so, could the Night Nurses have one of the Ward rooms *for the time*? (with a telephone to the Sup't's room)?

But if the bad cases were in different Pavilions, might it not be necessary to have a similar arrangement for each?

In the great difficulty of having one woman alone at night in that great building with perhaps two bad cases requiring her care in different Pavilions – & in the great unwillingness to leave those bad cases without trained female Night Nursing, *if it is desired*, pardon me if I have submitted these things *for your consideration*; merely.

And thanking you for your most kind visit which I trust will not be the last.

pray believe me ever your faithful serv't

Florence Nightingale

Source: GLRO HI/ST/NC1/82/4

1. Dr Thomas Crawford: (1824–95), Director-General, Army Medical Department, from May 1882. FN probably knew of him through his work as Principal Medical Officer in India (1880–82), when he introduced the Station hospital system.

Nightingale had built strong connections with several of her younger relatives. Frederick Verney, Sir Harry's son who had become a deacon and did social work in London, kept in close contact with her. He read her papers at scientific and political meetings. Two favourites were Margaret Lady Verney, wife of Sir Harry's oldest son, and Rosalind Shore Smith, the daughter of Shore. Florence continued to treat Parthe with hectoring affection even after a serious illness in 1883 which left her crippled.

145. To Sir Harry Verney
10 South St 5 Feb 1883

My dear Sir Harry

I give you joy on your Jubilee. It was completely successful.

Not so of your windows in South St. I go out every day that is fine to see whether Parthe's windows are open. They are *always* shut: & the blinds are generally down. And the drawing room windows also always shut. When we think how many weeks Parthe's room was necessarily kept shut, we must see that the windows ought now to be *always* open: open at the top (as far as they will go) every fine day – and a chink open at the top every bad day & all night. the blinds *always* ought to be up. drawing room windows open as much as possible.

It will take weeks of summer air to do away with the moulderiness & mustiness which the woman has been preparing for Parthe's return.

[I have been on the point of sending in many times: but I thought *she* might send to tell my maids to *shut my* windows.]

Will you write your orders to her? You may add that you authorize me to throw stones & break the upper panes every time I see the windows shut – but as the Bill will be a large one, *she* must pay it. It breaks one's heart to see all sun & air excluded from Parthe's rooms.

Miss Pringle of Edinburgh is now at Bournemouth. I believe she will come to me on Friday the 9th. Would you like to ask her to Claydon? She is *such* a Nurse & such good company.

I have had constant accounts from one & another of Parthe.

Whose & yours I am ever

F.N.

I trust we may think that as much progress has been made as could be.

I hope that Mrs. G. Verney & her little girl are with you.

Pray give my kind regards to Mr Greene.

I think of our dear Parthe by the Cedar-room fire with sun shining in.

Source: Wellcome

Nightingale always wanted to control the placement of doctors active in army sanitary reform. Surgeon-Major G. J. H. Ewatt, who had provided her with information about the reorganization of the Army Medical Corps in India and had served at the Royal

Military Academy, was too important to lose to civilian life. When he wrote to her that he planned to work for an Irish prison, she responded:

> We have heard of 'The Hour & the Man'. You are the 'man'. This is the 'hour' . . . And would you leave this, your life's work, for another work to which you are not directly called!? . . . And Mrs. Ewatt, I am sure, wishes for her husband's true glory. True glory is in the highest usefulness, as I know she thinks. There is no one else to do the kind of work you do . . . in writing and publishing, as well as in teaching – training &c &c &c . . . If you leave the Army . . . it is all lost. You are lost to your paper work. (26 Sept 1884 BUL Dr Ewatt)

Nightingale came to be a lukewarm supporter of women's franchise, without anticipating marked progress for women. She wrote to Parthe on 20 March 1884, soliciting her signature on a petition, 'And certainly it is now ludicrous not to give them the franchise, when "agricultural labourers" too have it. Only let women *look to what they want to be "represented in"*' (20 Mar 1884 Wellcome). In contrast, she was remarkably sanguine about extending the vote to the working class and quite enjoyed the massive rally that passed near her windows on its way to Hyde Park that summer.

146. To Sir Harry and Lady Verney

10 South St
22 July 1884

My dear Sir Harry & Parthe
 Yesterday was the Franchise v. Lords 'Demonstration'. And of course we saw the whole passing up from Hyde Pk Corner to Marble Arch – about 30,000 of them, besides people at large, perhaps 100,000 more.
 It is always a touching inspiring sight, to see men walking in serried ranks, shoulder to shoulder, in silent, steady strength, possessed with their object – & gives one more the idea of strength than a Battery of Artillary.
 From this point of view, the Procession was a sorry sight. I was quite mortified. If it was to be done at all, it should have been done well. I don't like the Lords to make a mock of us.
 There was no formation at all – at least not in the Park – the men did not march at all – scurried & stopped – great gaps – then a rush

– no walking abreast – nothing impressive – quite as many dirty little boys in the Procession, if Procession it could be called, & even women with smart babies, and men in dirty shirt-sleeves, as proper men.

I was in hopes that the proper men had turned aside to their respective Platforms – but am told this was not the case – they looked like weary tramps.

The Bands would have disgraced a child's penny trumpeting. One big drum kept time – & round it a few men did march:

The Procession was just an hour passing this house, with a good deal of running.

The flags & banners would have been impressive floating above the dark green foliage, had there been the least order kept. But they might just as well have been in donkey carts. There were a good many open vans, drawn by one skeleton of a horse. As a Procession indeed, it was beneath contempt. But now comes the pathetic and admirable part of it. Not a policeman was in sight: not a policeman was wanted. Tho' the people poured in & spoilt the so-called March, if ever March there was, there was not a bit of horse-play, or even of pushing – babies walked about unmolested, in pink frocks, on their black pins. There was the most extreme order in disorder – the utmost good humour throughout this long, weary afternoon of crowds – & no drink.

The head of the Procession did not *enter* the Park till the hour mentioned for the speaking to begin (5) – the tail of the Procession had not entered when the hour struck for the speaking to close – (6)

There was not a struggle or a push during the whole Demonstration.

They did 'demonstrate': but it was their own good humour – & though there was strong language used against the Peers on the platforms, a Peer would have been as safe as a baby among the 130000 we saw.

Some of the emblems of the Trades were good, and the Compositors, as they went by, were printing off the Resolutions in their van & throwing them among the people, as the march passed.

One thing was conspicuous – is the standard of English height lowered? The Procession was of the most undersized men I ever saw. Conspicuous by its *absence* was order on the other side – the streets – opposite your public-house was drunken singing & dancing the whole afternoon – the drinking was simply disgusting, the row, the uproar. Then a mock sermon was delivered by one of them & applauded to the echo.

This went on for hours. The police did not interfere. Perhaps they were right. I was glad you were not at home, for I certainly should have asked you to inform against the Public house.

I wondered the gentle-folks could keep quiet. Indeed I often wonder.

But at last the drinkers moved off, *where* I know not – *not* to the Park. Nothing of drinking was visible or audible just across the Lane (Park Lane) in the Park.

It was as if the Park & the Demonstration were sacred to the highest feelings.

I scrambled out of bed upstairs to see all I could.

All the maids were on the Drawing-room balcony. All the leads cats ran shrieking into your garden [That was the effect of the (cat-call) bands]

Only one little bull-dog pup with a tail curled so tight as to lift him off his legs stood his ground manfully on the leads. My cats disappeared under the bed – whether from dislike of the Demonstration, or the Lords, or because they disapprove of household suffrage I don't know. We had hardly a drop of rain. Do you remember 19 or 18 years ago the pulling down the Park railings? This is the march of Education tho' it was not the march of Demonstration.

ever dear people yrs affly

F.N.

Source: Wellcome

Nightingale prided herself on the careful training of her servants, but she could be demanding and imperious, once writing: 'Let us remember that as Mrs. Nield is to me, so I to God' (Woodham-Smith, p. 578). While visiting Claydon in autumn 1884, she wrote to young Frances Groundsell at South Street:

> I have raised your wages to £15 {per annum}, tho' I had cause, as you know, to suffer from your want of skill. But I hope to be able to raise them to £16. And if I find when I come home that you have put something in the Savings' Bank & that you have done well in your now somewhat responsible post, I hope to be able to add to what nest-egg you have in the Sav'gs Bank. (25 Sept 1884 GLRO HI/ST/NC1/84/3)

Frances, however, felt that she deserved more, and wrote to Nightingale demanding additional wages.

147. To Frances Groundsell   Claydon 1 Oct 1884

Dear Frances

I expect to be home in about 10 days: but it will depend upon Lady Verney who is very ill. I am no better: & little able to write.

Most people would pass off your letter to me with: You silly child. But I am anxious, as you have good sense, to show you why you are a silly child.

You say you are 'disappointed': do you think *I* am not disappointed? You did what in the whole course of my Nursing life I have never known done but twice, & never by the same person more than once. You did it twice in ten days.

If you had done it to any one else rather than *me*, I should have parted with you at the end of your month. Any one else would.

You say: I did not say that if you did 'anything wrong' I should 'not raise your wages'. No: people don't say so: they part with you. *I* did not. And I raised your wages to £15.

Now think what you would have had, if I had raised them to '£16' after the 2nd month. *Just 2/6 more.*

Now think what you *have had* more.

10/10 to put in the Savings Bank.

And the change of £1 to pay your journey home. (tho' it is quite unusual for a mistress to grant a holiday to a maid a very few weeks old) – that is to say you have had 8 or 9 times the half-crown you are moaning & mourning over. And you have had a promise of more for the Savings Bank now. Do not make *me* wrong in keeping you.

My dear child, I would gladly have suffered the very serious loss of my small strength & health if it had done *you* good.

Now I can write no more.

May God bless you. And no one shall look in *your* face when I come home to see if you are not ashamed of yourself. I am sure you will never be so silly again, dear Frances: F. Nightingale

One would have thought that, merely out of self-interest you would have known better than to write such a letter. But I hope you don't think only of interest.

F.N.

Source: GLRO HI/ST/NC1/84/6

Rachel Williams, a short-tempered woman, had had continual difficulties with the doctors and her governing board at St Mary's Hospital (Baly, pp.166–67). After an awkward fight over her salary, Nightingale had written sympathetically: 'I am so very sorry for your sore Medical woes. But why should my Goddess be disturbed by them? Goddesses are never disturbed by the sorest worries' (5 Jan 1884 GLRO HI/ST/NC3/SU 180/106). But when Williams seemed to be throwing away a good post on a technical point, Nightingale drew on her own experience:

> About the resignation I can only judge as for myself. Everything, I believe I may say *every*thing was done that could be done either on earth or under the earth to make me resign during the Crimean War. But I never felt a moment's doubt on the question:
> I would not resign.
> I might be driven from my post
> I would not run away. (2 Dec 1884 GLRO HI/ST/ NC3/SU 180/125)

Williams did resign. She was immediately invited to lead a group of nurses in the Egyptian campaign. Although Nightingale initially disapproved of this decision, she still worked behind the scenes to give her every possible assistance. Ironically, she had earlier considered Williams unfit to superintend a military hospital 'because she would fight with every trained woman in the place and she has such a tongue with the medical men' (Baly, p. 119).

148. To Rachel Williams 10 South St 18 Feb 1885

Dearest Miss Williams
   God guide us.
   I scarcely see how you *can* go in the teeth of such a remonstrance from dear 'Little Sister' – or, what is much more, the bringing her over here, as you see she is determined to do – & perhaps finding you gone. For it is quite *possible* that the summons might come this week.
   This might kill her.
   I do see great danger in your going – the hot weather will be on you directly – the destination probably Souakim – the troops themselves you see are not to fight between say end of March & August but to lay up.
   To my mind, as you know, it seemed thus: I was *aghast* at your going – – risk to you not worth running, Edinburgh & Little Sister

not worth giving up, if it was only for a transient rush to nurse the Wounded – *almost* any risk worth running if it were to lead to your occupying the post of a reformer in Military Nursing or any Nursing.

Your losing your calling & wasting your great powers, (which one word in your dear note makes me fear you contemplate) is, *unless* deliberately done & with your whole heart, to me appalling. Dearest – I seem to write coolly – but I feel the decision almost more weighty & more anxious than even you or Little Sister, as you see.

If your idea was merely to go to nurse a few men, I am afraid Little Sister's letters must make one feel it almost more important to nurse *her*. God bless you & her a thousand times with all his blessings.

> ever yours
>
> > F.N.

If your going led to the reform, nay the creation of Military Nursing by your hands, then your leaving St. Mary's would have been a 'reasonable, holy & lively sacrifice' to God.

But if not then Little Sister is probably right.

May God bless you ever.

Source: GLRO HI/ST/NC3/SU 180/135

149. To Thomas Crawford, MD

10 South St
21 Feb 1885

Private

My dear Sir

Pray let me thank you with all my heart for your great kindness to Miss Williams whom you have appointed to be Superintendent of Nurses at the Hospital for Wounded at Suez – & for approving of a Miss Byam on Miss Williams' recommendation for one of her Nursing Staff. We understand that she has sent in for approval a second name.

This permission to her is a true kindness.

Will you think me too encroaching if I ask – not with Miss Williams' knowledge – would you not think it desirable to allow her to recommend to you the names of the remaining two Nurses to complete the Staff of four?

You probably think as we do that it is important that

Superintend'ts should have Nurses with whose character &
qualifications they are acquainted.

 Pray believe me my dear Sir
 ever your faithful & grateful serv't

Florence Nightingale

Source: GLRO HI/ST/NC1/85/2

Nightingale followed the Egyptian campaign carefully in *The
Times*, and wrote encouraging notes to Rachel Williams: 'We are
still, of course, without direct tiding of you which we yearn for.
The terrible hand to hand fighting which is now going on every
day at Souakim but which, one trusts, will be over before this
reaches you, makes us suppose that there will soon be wounded
under your careful & devoted hands' (27 Mar 1885 GLRO
HI/ST/NC3/SU 180/150). Soon after a brief period of military
service, Williams married Daniel Norris and left hospital nursing.
Once again Nightingale's fears had materialized; after this desertion, their correspondence virtually ceased.

 Parthe had often entertained the Nightingale nurses at Claydon
before her illness; Florence now wrote to keep her in touch with
the careers of the more interesting.

150. To Parthenope, Lady Verney

10 South St
25 Sept 1885

My dearest Pop

 I was going to answer the enclosed from Mrs. Hawthorn by
saying that it was really impossible for you to write the 'Life of
Gordon' as she entreats – that you had done all in it that you could
do &c &c &c &c.

 But I thought perhaps you would just like to see her letter. And
then, if you return me the Envelope with 'Blow me if I do' or any
other graceful literary refusal, I shall write as I said, & know what
to do as you say.

 She has sent me a large illustrated cahier published by Vizetelly,
price 1/ called 'Gordon & the Mahdi'. I mean to get a good many
to give away. But I will not send you a copy unless you wish it.

 Many thanks for your letter.

 I trust your canvass is prospering.

398

Besides Miss Williams, I have had a very interesting Miss Lennox who came over from Belfast to see me, staying. You may possibly remember her. She was with Livingstone & Bp Mackenzie in C. Africa. Sir James Clark sent her to us to be trained – & now she has kept an appointment we gave her to the Belfast Children's Hospital for 12 years. She makes it truly a life work – a calling. She was drest in her uniform here – a good deal quieter than any of my maids. She was full of all her Patients – a boy, aged 12, had had his leg amputated (with her) – his parents & 4 brothers & Sisters lived on 6/ a week. When he went home, money was given him to buy (when his stump was ready) an artificial leg. With this money he bought a baby pig – the pig grew up – & with the proceeds he bought two. All, you understand, for his parents & family.

She disapproves of the great Training Ship with 300 boys & no mothers – as against God's laws. The Patients who come to her from it die – so depressed. She got a lady to go & live in this hold for 3 months to nurse them up a bit. To one of the boys who seemed terribly depressed she the lady said, 'Come: I don't think there's much the matter with you' & gave him a pat. She was passing out when a boy moaned up: 'Oh Ma'm if you would but gie me one pat like his'n.' This was not a Patient – a rough (cabin boy –) Miss Lennox says: 'don't let the Gordon Schools have no mothers: the boys don't grow up good men.'

Ask Margaret to 'gie me a pat' in the form of news of you & Ellin & all of you. And with best love to all – & especially I hope my god-daughter will prosper,

ever, dear Pop, your loving

F.

In the outside sheet of the 'Times' one day, there was a letter signed 'A Liberal and a Landlord' which had some of your ideas. But it said: in '*this* county of Surrey'. I was rather glad it was not yours, because it is so very important to unite the Liberal Landlords & the Liberal Manufacturers – not to sound a note of defiance against the latter – is it not?

Source: Wellcome

After her husband's appointment as Viceroy, Lady Dufferin became actively involved in promoting sanitary education among Indian women, and Nightingale corresponded frequently with her. In 1888 the government of India finally established a Sanitary Board with independent and executive authority in every province. As Nightingale was well aware, however, progress depended to a large extent upon the education of the native population. She recommended beginning with the village as a unit. Health missionaries were to work with the village women rather than lecture them. How to finance sanitary projects remained an issue. Nightingale, never loath to express her views, claimed:

> what the Gov't of India & the I.O. deprecate is *not* 'the expenditure of Imperial funds' but the *local* taxation of natives. And this, Mr. Cunningham never offers anything to meet. The way to meet it, is, as in Bombay, to take the natives into your confidence – not because you are afraid of them but from a hearty sympathy & desire for their co-operation without which indeed all your 'Acts' fall useless.
>
> No one (in Bombay at least) is more willing to be taxed than a native, especially for *water-supply* & education, when he has been made to understand them.
>
> But of this Mr. Cunningham does not appear to think – tho' Bengal is far more easily led than Bombay.
>
> What he says about (see end) 'unpopularity' is the same. It is not from the 'worst Press', but from all educated natives that we incur 'unpopularity', & inevitably so, if we will never take the trouble to explain ourselves. But a native will come half way to meet you, far more than *any* Englishman, if you do. And then you gain *popularity*, instead of 'unpopularity', for your measures & your rule. (17 July 1887 BL Add 45766: f 23)

151. To Dr John Sutherland   10 South St 27 Nov 1885

Dear Dr. Sutherland

1. I have received the proof as usual from Mr. Hill of the I.O. Sanitary Blue Book, with the *usual request for criticism* &c &c.

Now is the time if you want anything strengthened or corrected.

Please tell me what.

I do trust that you are very much better. There is a blessed change in the weather today. But I also hope that you use common prudence.

Sanitary Tracts for India

I am very much obliged for the parcels I have received from the Ladies' Sanitary. 2. but also I should be very much obliged *for a List marked by yourself & Mrs. Sutherland* of those which *you* think might possibly do, adapted, for India. I am also grateful for the caution conveyed in Miss Adams' letter about translation or adaptation, which I will carefully transmit to Lady Dufferin.

But I could very much have wished that nothing had been said to Miss Adams or Jarrold about leave to translate or adapt till we had decided whether we should have even *one* book or tract to recommend to Ly D. for translation or adaptation. At present I have not one. And I had made up my mind to tell her so. *Now*, if she puts that 'Cleanliness is necessary to health', Jarrold will say it is 'adapted' from him. I have other books to send to Lady Dufferin which I have just ordered from my Bookseller, but without any intention of asking for leave to translate or adapt till we know whether we want it.

I have got together such a mass of information & advice for Lady Dufferin that I hardly know how to arrange it for her – from Dr. Hewlett,[1] from Mr. & Mrs. *Man* Mohun Ghose,[2] (*she* is like a highly educated English lady) – from Mrs. Hume Lothers.

3. Dr. Hewlett recommends that in each province should be selected *an Indian native* to write, *under the superintend'e of the Sanitary Commissioner* of that province, *a Sanitary home manual for women & girls.*

But *what Sanitary Commissioner* is there besides *himself & Dr. Bellew*, of the Punjab, who is fit for the task?

No one knows so well as you. *Please tell me.*

[The *Madras* San'y Comm'r is nobody. Dr. Cuningham's successor with the Gov't of India is much worse than no one.]

3. Could you kindly *send me a List of the present Sanitary Commissioners* whom *you* would consider fit for *supervising* the writing a *home Manual for women* – each for his own Province?

I shall take care to include in my letter to Lady Dufferin (when it *gets* written) your excellent suggestion for teaching home Sanitary practice in any proposed Ladies Med'l College, that the Lady Doctors may lecture to the women – one of the principal suggestions of Mr. Man Mohun Ghose, (a very superior brother of Lal Mohun's).

Every one of my advisers has considered adaptation or re-translation from any English books as useless, except that, as you say, hygienic *principles* are the same everywhere; but we need not ask Jarrold for these.

According to Dr. Hewlett, it is also useless to send these kinds of things to 'Parsees', whose women's habits & superstitions are unknown to English people.

God bless you both: & with great love to Mrs. Sutherland, believe me ever yours faithfully

F. Nightingale

We are 'cast down but not destroyed' about the Elections.

Source: BL Add 45758: ff 195–96

1. Dr Thomas Gillham Hewlett: (1831–89), Deputy Surgeon-General of the Bombay Presidency and author of *Sanitary State of Bombay* (1869) and *Village Sanitation in India* (1891).
2. Man Mohun Ghose: (1844–96), first Indian advocate of the Calcutta High Court; he drafted the Ilbert Bill for Lord Ripon.

Nightingale was unflagging in her role as overseer of the many petty problems of the Nightingale School of Nursing.

152. To John Croft   10 South St 7 May 1887

Private
Probationers' *food* 'Complaints'

My dear Sir
You kindly ask me: what 'complaints', if any, 'that the food & cooking for the Probationers was constantly below what it ought to have been?' The 'complaints' latterly made, not to me, were from two persons, a dismissed Probationer, & another who was constantly troublesome in the Home, was for a time a Sister, & then left.

Both these sources were tainted sources.

But as you are good enough to ask me the question, & as after all it is not the 'complaints' that we want to discredit, but to find out what is the real state of the case. I am glad of the opportunity of laying before you what I gather, & what my impressions are –
　　　want of variety
　　　want of sufficient *supper*
　　　want of milk

They are very tired of the cold mutton; they would like cold ham (a thirsty thing, methinks) & (more) eggs for breakfast.

They would like at *every* meal, but especially at the 'little lunch', about 10:30 a.m. & at supper, sufficient pure milk to be placed *on the table*, for everybody to have a glassful, if she likes it.

[This is done at poorer London Hospitals than ours.]
'Complaints' have not often been made about the *'cooking'* –
except as regards *supper* where the cooking or rather the no-
cooking was a grievance – especially to those who came late.
Supper is often an essential meal, tho' it should not be a heavy
meal, to hard-worked women – not cold mutton but hot stews or
hashes or &c &c – pudding which there sometimes was but
ill-cooked. This is the most definite complaint about 'cooking'. On
the other hand, the great difference *for the worse* when they go
from the Home into the Hospital is often commented upon.

All there was at supper for those who wanted it but not milk.

'Want of variety', tho' not much complained of, is I think a real
grievance.

I am reminded that there can be no possibility of 'making'
anything, which has been imputed, by stinginess.

The Hospital provides –

The N.F. pays a fixed sum.

It is for the Hosp'l Officers to supply the things good.

It is for the N.F. to see that they are good.

It is now in the hands of the House Committee, as you know, to
enquire.

Mrs. Wardroper has already raised the price of the meat by 1d
the lb. & has already arranged, I believe, that boiling water shall be
supplied to the Prob'rs for breakfast. [It was a complaint that they
had to make their own tea & boil the water]* (*Also, I understand
that the milk has been found to contain 25 p. c. of water.)

You have been so good as to obtain the Dietary for the last
week.

Would you mind showing it me?

I am sure that *you will not let it be known* that you & I are in
communication.

If you are good enough to send me the Dietary (*with this*) I may
have some more to tell you.

Pray excuse pencil & believe me ever sincerely yours

F. Nightingale

Source: BL Add 47742: ff 295–98

Nightingale's interest in the poor and destitute had never
wavered from the day when she had undertaken the education of a
poor girl in Rome, but she was never in favour of England losing
its respectable working class through emigration. Colonization,
she felt, should be restricted to orphans and paupers.

153. To Angélique Pringle 10 South St 1 Mar 1888

My dearest Miss Pringle

I have written & enclose a letter to the Secretary of the York Road Lying-in Hospital (whom I only know by a slight correspondence) for Miss Formby, if you like to send it, according to your request. [I send her £2.2., to conciliate her for you]

But for ourselves, we always insisted, as perhaps you know, in the Midwifery School we kept for 6 1/2 years for Nurses, & have always stoutly stood by it since, on 6 months' training (2 months in large *out-door* practice) & *then* would only certify not as Midwife but as Midwifery *Nurse*. In most, if not all of the places where these 6 months' women afterwards served, the Doctor was not '9' but 2 miles off – he might even be in the next street.

[N. B. All *abnormal* as well as normal cases were under the skilled Midwife at the head of the School]

Would it not be better probably, in order to obtain admittance to the York Road Lying-in Hospital, for Miss Formby to apply to some of the St. Thomas' Medical Officers, Dr. Gervis or Dr. Cory?

And should not Mr. Arnold White take this matter in hand – we having done what we can to ascertain the best place to go to for his purposes?

[I should deprecate 'Endell St.', but if York Road fails, will talk farther about it]

I want to clear up my own ideas about Miss Formby's 'high enterprise' by a little confab with your superior practical knowledge:

We are not sent, are we?, except to the lost sheep of the house of – – Britain.

Is it not a higher 'enterprise' to be District Nurse to '25' poor Holborn 'families' than to '25 agricultural families' in E. Africa? or even to be a trained Sister in a Hospital Ward?

If of those wretched boys who rioted for 3 weeks in Hyde Park & were driven about by the Police, a number could be trained & organised by competent men for some Colony into a Mettray, a Rauhe Haus, or a 'Dutch settlement' (I do not say it is possible) *that* would be a 'high enterprise': and one would say even to a trained Sister: Go, if you have a calling to look after their health & morals.

If of those poor seamstresses & London workwomen – often on the verge of prostitution but not prostitutes – a number could be trained & taken out to Colonies by competent ladies (I do not say it is possible) as domestic servants, perhaps as working women, in out-lying farms, at last as good wives far from the towns, that would indeed be a 'high enterprise' – & a high calling even for a trained Lady Nurse to 'mother' them out.

But to take 25 'sober, industrious', healthy 'agricultural Hampshire families', out to the Colonies, is an interesting thing as benefiting & raising the individuals, but could almost be done by a devoted landlord in England.

[And is there much more to be done for 25 good labourers' families in East Africa, (possibly less) than in Hampshire in influencing & looking after them. Only no one thinks of giving a lady at £200 a year to look after them in Hampshire?]

Seems it not the present plan rather a step *not* to the *de*pauperization but to the pauperization of England – not to reformation but the reverse – taking away the 'sober & industrious' & leaving the idle, drunken & destitute.

It is not those who are doing well here, or anywhere, but those who are doing ill or going to ruin – our lost sheep, that one wants to save. Does one want to take the best of labourers & workmen out of England, or the worst, & save *them*?

[The best, the young & sober stone-masons near Lea Hurst are emigrating to Ohio – leaving the idle drunkards behind. Is this a movement one longs to help?]

Everything about Emigration is interesting – everything about the reward & prosperity of good labourers.

But it might almost be said that it is another step to filling the Gaols & workhouses here to take away the best & leave those boys & girls who populate prisons & Unions – but whom no one thinks of giving a lady to help & reform.

In short, the plan may be a good thing as benefiting individuals who deserve it – but is it a great work – a 'high enterprise', a saving of our lost sheep, a depauperization & reformation? I don't know.

Does not the work of a trained Hospital Sister, certainly of a trained London District Lady Nurse partake much more of all these things?

Why do not people seriously think of taking & reforming a wretched London court of '25 families'? [Miss O. Hill did.[1]]

All the while I am enthusiastic about Emigration – but for the lost sheep, as far as *we* are concerned.

ever, dearest Miss Pringle, most affectionately yours,

F. Nightingale

Source: GLRO HI/ST/NC1/88/4

1. Miss Octavia Hill: (1838–1912), pioneer in providing model housing for the poor that combined 'fair rents' with careful overseeing of the tenants.

154. To Miss Annie Whyte[1]   10 South St 1 Mar 1888

Send circular
Miss A. Whyte

Madam

I have never thanked you for allowing a Midwife's attendance to a poor Charwoman of mine, Mrs. Wilks, with her first child, last year. Will you allow me now to enclose a small contribution, £2.2?

And might I ask you whether it would be possible for you to admit *immediately* for *3 months'* teaching & training, in Midwifery, from our Nightingale Training School for Nurses at St. Thomas' Hospital, a trained Lady Nurse of ours, Miss Formby, who is engaged to go out to East Africa to look after 25 agricultural families, emigrants, in *3 months'* time. There is therefore not a day to be lost. Miss Formby's age is 30; she has had 3 months' experience in the Obstetrical Ward of St. Thomas'.

I believe Miss Formby has applied to you – & was told that there was no room at present for her.

Might I ask if it would be possible *under the circumstances* to make an exception in her favour, without displacing any one else?

May we take for granted that, at your Institution which has such claims to our admiration, the pupils live *in* the Institution to be ready for cases at night – that they have also *out-door* practice – that they have constant clinical instruction as well as lectures – & that after a successful 3 months' training, they are certificated, *not* as Midwives but as Midwifery *Nurses* only? What *abnormal* cases have they the chance of attending under a skilled Midwife? And do the skilled Midwives of the Institution deliver all abnormal, as well as normal cases?

Pray believe me Madam faithfully yours

Florence Nightingale

Would you kindly send me 2 copies of the little square book of 'Hints', the best I know?

F.N.

Source: GLRO HI/ST/GLI/A36/1

1. Miss Annie Whyte: Secretary, General Lying-in Hospital, York Road, Lambeth SE.

Miss Formby did receive the necessary training, and a second letter of thanks gives insight into contemporary health care.

155. To Miss Atkinson, Matron or Miss Annie Whyte, Secretary

10 South St 24 May 1888

Dear Madam

First, allow me to thank you very much for the excellent training & great advantages which Miss Formby has enjoyed during her 3 months' stay with you, & practice both on in-door and out-of-door Lying-in cases. And tho' I must always deplore that your 3 months' term of training is not at least 6 months', so as to give the pupil-Midwives more practice, & a better chance of seeing abnormal cases, yet I most gratefully acknowledge the Superiority of training, practical, Sanitary and theoretical, for the infants as well as the mothers, which you give your pupils.

I could wish indeed that a supplement to your excellent little book, (for which I beg to enclose 3/, 2 copies, which you kindly sent me) were published, containing those lessons on the care and feeding of Infants, which I understand Miss Atkinson so wisely gives to the Nurses.

[The very child, a first child, of Mrs. Wilkes, for whom you kindly sent a Midwife, Mrs. Martin, at my request all year, a beautiful little boy, I believe – died of '*Nursery Biscuits*', which you so justly denounce.

This was no fault of the Midwife. The child was several months old.

But if your Midwives could be taught to put a little sense into the poor mothers, when attending them in their Lyings-in, perhaps there would be a chance of the poor mothers leaving off the practising the blunders of their predecessors – fatal blunders indeed.

2. I am now going to ask you to be so good as to send Mrs. Martin, of Medway St. Westminster, to the same Mrs. Wilkes (whose marriage lines I enclose – & beg you to return to me), for a second confinement. She is expecting her lying in, I understand, in about a month. So she has not left much time to lose. [The child was born, I believe, *before* the Midwife arrived, in her first confinement.]

Again thanking you for your great care & kindness, by which Miss Formby has, I trust, so largely profited, believe me to remain,

Most faithfully yours,

Florence Nightingale

Source: GLRO HI/GLI/A36/2

Unable to travel herself, Nightingale kept up a steady correspondence with women throughout the Empire, many of whom carried her health tenets to the most unlikely situations.

156. To Miss Munro   10 South St 21 May 1888

My Dear Miss Munro,

I think so much of your Egyptian Expedition. You must not, please, say, 'I may fail, & then I shall come back in a year.' But screw your courage to the sticking point, And you'll not fail.

Would you like to have the *Scriptures in Arabic* to *take with you* – for your own use, I mean? Or perhaps you have a copy already? Please say.

2. It is such a momentous thing to go among the Mahometans – *not* in order to convert them, but that they may 'see Christ' in us.

In India the natives say: 'there are the Hindoos, & they know their religion & practise it – there are the Mahomedans & they know their religion & practise it, there are the Christians, & *we* know their religion & they *don't* practise it.'

And this is the great bar in the way of conversion.

A Governor of India said this to me.

We know they will not have to say it for you.

The natives who are as sharp as needles have lynx-eyes upon us now.

But so have our own East-Enders – patients in Hospital – 'infidel workmen', as they are called, upon us.

3. I feel very anxious about your outfit. But you have more recent counsellors than I. I think the gauze flannel worn in India the best (inside) wear. And I always observe that natives themselves, who ought to know best, of hot climates do *not* clothe lightly.

A flannel stomach-belt I think a great protection.

But whatever else there may be difference of opinion upon, there can be none on one point: To clothe *loosely*, to have *nothing tight* about one, is a sine qua non in a hot climate.

You know the '*Sirene Stays*' (to be had at any Indian out-fitters) made of a cross stitch material like canvass? These are *so* recommended by those who wear them, as combining the utmost comfort with the necessity of having good stays for Nursing in.

I am sure you will agree with me that half the soul & health are squeezed out of a woman who wears tight stays. In a hot climate it is destructive, simply.

High heeled shoes/boots are the same. But I suppose nobody wears those now. Holland, 40 South Audley St., I am told makes good half inch heels (boots). But you will know all these things.

4. You feel yourself called to this Egyptian work – a great work it is. This is the accepted time when God will send his spirit. I pray for you hourly that He, full of grace & truth, will grant it abundantly.

Do you know that in the most ancient Egyptian hieroglyphics, we found those words, 'God,' 'full of grace & truth.'?

They are in some of the Thebes Tombs – & in some of the Nubian temples.

There is as it were a foretaste of the Christian religion.

5. Not neglecting the temporal,

I trust that you will find you are able to put by almost the whole of your 'free salary', as we call it. The arrangements are quite as liberal as, if not more so than those for the Sisters recently sent out to the Military Hospitals in India by Gov't. of India – for which we struggled so.

Commend me to Miss Hughes. I rejoice that you have such a spirited companion. I shall be so anxious to hear from you.

I do not press more advice, for it must be tiresome. And you know it all, I have no doubt.

6. Only,

Please have a very loose dressing-gown to throw on at night, if you *should* have to get up.

All blessings attend you. ever yours hopefully

F. Nightingale

Source: BL Add 45808: ff 83–85   {copy}

The greatest crisis of this decade was Angélique Pringle's decision to become a Roman Catholic, which meant that she had to resign as matron of St Thomas' Hospital. After Mrs Wardroper's retirement, Nightingale had hoped that Pringle would be able to make sweeping changes. Now, in one blow she lost both a favourite and a more promising school. Although Pringle continued to be in contact with Nightingale for the rest of her life, her conversion caused profound pain and disappointment.

157. To Angélique Pringle

1 Dec {1888}
8 a.m.

Dearest ever dearest

Your letter received last night. I cannot look upon it as final. You are in a more dangerous state than if you were 'ill'. If you were 'ill', you would be in bed with a Doctor attending you, under treatment. And he would most certainly order you to rest & country air for a much longer time than a week, *in order* to enable you to do 'the accounts' uniform time & all your other yet more important affairs.

But you are in a far more dangerous state – that most dangerous of all – suffering from nervous exhaustion, even more than you know yourself. There is *no chance* of your being able to go thro' the next two months beginning to-day unless you rest. You will make a gallant, almost violent struggle – you will become more & more exhausted & depressed. You will break down – possibly have an illness – which possibly might save you – if not, you will become so that you must resign, probably before the two months are up. Would you recommend such a course to any one else?

In order for you to be capable of doing the essential duties you enumerate it is that this week for rest was proposed – 4th to 11th – because it was supposed you could not get away before the 4th. I *fully* enter into the difficulty of getting away. But, my dear, have you considered that God may take altogether out of your power the health of body & mind to stay?

The 11th was supposed to give you a fortnight before Xmas. But if Miss Woolfrey does not return till Tuesday – would you go on Thursday afternoon – there is a 5 o'clock p.m. train which gets you in I think before 7 – till Monday morning or afternoon – there is a morning train 8 – something which gets you back soon after 10.30. I don't advocate this. It would do you 5 times the good to go from Tuesday to Tuesday – & coming in to a hard day's work after the little fatigue of the morning departure is not good. But I am suggesting reasonable alternatives. Is the alternative of giving it all up reasonable? Miss Buchanan will stay easily & willingly – & she is well in for the Xmas preparations

I have telephoned to Claydon not to take your answer as final. Forgive me.

But if I *must* use stronger arguments, dearest, since I saw you so depressed on Thursday week till the moment you came last Th. I could say little to God but O God receive the agony of my heart – but always adding meaning it I hope. But what signifies my agony? It is she who signifies. Would you not do this little week for my sake?

If I said anything on the first Thursday to run counter to you, I ask your forgiveness on the knees of my heart.

I can say no more – but May God guide & bless you

ever yours

F Nightingale

Shall I come to St. T.'s & carry you off?

I never leave Claydon without thinking I shall never go there again. Sir H.'s life may be numbered by days. My sister w'd then leave C. Will you not go there once before he dies? Something should be arranged by & bye to give you time to think & to plan, as you once said.

Source: BL Add 47735: ff 161–64

158. To Angélique Pringle {2 Dec 1888}

Dearest, ever dearest

Thanks for your kind letter. But first let me say what I am sure you will believe without asseveration or explanation on my part or wonder what expression in my letter *could* have given rise to it.

that my thoughts about Claydon &c were simply & wholly about your health, & that the ghost of an idea about 'madness' was about as far from my mind as murder or the North Pole – i.e It could not be further.

You will recollect, my darling that you said to me *that* Thursday 22nd that you felt as if you 'should go out of your senses'. But that was about Claydon you kindly ask me to 'decide'. I cannot 'decide' in the least. You transfer it to another ground that Upon the basis you now put it – not I – of making a 'difference in the current of your thoughts' – & as regards 'occupation of mind', you say that 'work' may do more than 'the quiet of Claydon'. At all events as you will see *I* cannot judge for you now.

[I had a note from Sir Harry yesterday evening written by the earliest morning post, when he received yours, asking me 'to persuade you to come'. I merely give his message. That I cannot do.

Do not read what follows till another moment unless you wish it. Could I continue that 'I' acting

To you the great sacrifice, the going 'to Him without the camp bearing the reproach of superstition & foolishness', has a charm.

But have you ever thought of the 'reproach of foolishness' you bring upon others? That seems to me quite a secondary use.

However there is a much more important question in comparison with this to another having regard to the circumstances under which you were appointed to St. Thomas', & to the duties you have to carry out – do you not think that you are bound to go on with it at least for another year?

A person has

You have generously accepted a heavy responsibility

sticking to the work before her *is* a duty

And we can't be certain of the 'call'

One is what is good for herself.

The other is a certainty – as to the good she is doing to other people.

You kindly ask me not to grieve for you. Am I not to grieve for this?

Advent Sunday

About your being separated by 'only one generation' from your 'Catholic ancestry', it would seem as if the Puritans & others were not separated even by 'one generation' from their Catholic ancestry.

I too am 'grieved' that I told you about my prayer. But you forbade our having any 'talk' about the subject uppermost in both our minds & hearts. And I obeyed you so implicitly that it seemed we were both like were actresses/acting that second Thursday. Could I continue that acting? I could scarcely, Could I? write keep up that strange farce between us in writing.

But I am sorry. Consider it with drawn

Today is Advent Sunday

Xt is coming to us –

May He not come in the guise I have just tried to express?

Unsigned

Source: BL Add 47735: ff 168–71   {draft}

The Pringle crisis carried over into the new year. On 12 June 1889 Nightingale wrote to Sir Harry that Pringle had proposed saying nothing to the treasurer until her views had 'stood the *test* of a little time'.

> The tone of her letter *is* a little altered from her previous ones. She *is* 'pausing' *before* taking *the final step* – she *is* aware that her 'affections lean to Rome, & that this may have influenced her judgment'. She *is* going 'to strive with all her might against partiality'.

Then comes the usual strain; And then next she thinks that the 'personal bereavement' to me of herself is what influences me, as if I *could* have the unutterable baseness (in what I feel – I hope I exaggerate – shakes our work almost to the foundations) of thinking of *my* loss!! (12 June 1889 BL Add 47721: f 224)

Clearly Nightingale's personal emotions were not as detached as she claimed. Both leading characters were buying time before the inevitable occurred. Pringle was undoubtedly sincere in her desire to continue as matron of St Thomas', even should she convert. Nightingale, however, believed that a leading Protestant voluntary hospital would never accept a Roman Catholic as its matron, whatever her own feelings.

Nightingale's interest in old family responsibilities must have served as a welcome diversion from the Pringle problem. She corresponded with the master of the school her family had started at Lea Hurst, where she paid the fees for several of the children, including Selina Gregory.

159. To Mr J. P. Burton   10 South St, Park Lane 5 July 1889

Dear Mr. Burton,

I am very much obliged to you for your letter, and for its very satisfactory enclosures. And I was very much pleased to see (what you did not tell me) that you had kindly offered prizes at the Village Horticultural Show for the best Collection of Leaves from Trees, with the names appended, by the schoolchildren. That is the way to make them observe.

And – I should very much like to know whether you have found any opportunity of teaching the children the ways the leaves grow, and the ways the flowers are made; instead of the common way of teaching them classification and Latin names, usually called Botany.

And have you been able to make use of the collection of fossils and spars and specimens to teach them the simplest geology which all Derbyshire Children should know? I forget whether I mentioned to you that the man who supplied the small collection I sent you, and who is, I believe, a Fellow of the Geological Society, offered me, for a few shillings more, to make that collection complete, and such as would be used in the Kensington Museum and Society of Arts. Would you like this to be done? I should be so very glad. I was so pleased with what you told me of your taking down the boys into the mines (at Burton on Trent I think you said) and shewing them the fossils and the strata. It is worth anything to make the children observe. To teach and to train *themselves* when they leave school – that is the real meaning of schooling. I have sometimes thought that the real test of a schoolmaster or mistress would be whether the children go on after they have left school liking to inform themselves, liking to observe, liking to read up a thing: or whether they forget all they have been taught, never to open a book, and even forget how to read or write correctly. worse still, forget religion & morality.

I had a good deal of talk on Saturday with a General who is my Sister's nephew, and who cares for his men so much that I learn from him a great deal, and perhaps he learns a little from me. He was amazed to tell me, and I was amazed to hear that out of 350 recruits for the Guards, whom he was going to inspect and to talk to, 60 could not read or write. [You know perhaps that in the Guards they are obliged to be particularly careful that every man should read and write well, because the men of the Guards have to do so much mounting guard at important buildings in London and at the Palaces. They have their written orders, often very important ones; given them every night, which they must be able to read correctly.] My General was going to see every one of these 60 men each by himself, to ask them where they had been to school, to get them to wish to go to school now to the Regimental Schoolmaster, (because there is no *compulsory* schooling allowed now in the army) and to get into their confidence. I told him that it would be most important for Civilians as well as for the Army that we should have this information, because it tells us really what are the results of elementary education. Soldiers are almost all recruited from the country; they are almost all in their teens, 18 or 19; and therefore hardly any of them can have left school more than 5 years. There are, I imagine, either Lending-Libraries, or Night-Schools, or Institutes of some kind or other – (only I fear they don't all admit boys as early as 14) almost everywhere, and therefore the boys can scarcely lack all opportunity of continuing their own education. I am sure that the boys and girls who have completed their education with you, would not have forgotten how to read and write in 5 years.

2// I was very glad to see the successful report on the religious instruction of the children, and especially on the '*tone*' of the School. And I have no doubt that the religious teaching is really impressed into the Children's hearts and practical lives by you and Mrs. Burton, and does not remain as a mere book of History and Geography to them.

It very often happens to me to have to do with girls from 15 to 20, chiefly when they have gone into domestic service. I will tell you one recent experience. It is that of a very nice girl of 15 from the country – a particularly good and intelligent girl. She had been ten consecutive years, from 4 to 14 at a national school. I had occasion to take her through, and make her re-capitulate each of her Confirmation Classes as they went on for she was just going to be confirmed. She could not bring back one single idea from any of her Classes, and she was unable to write a single sentence. I had to write down for her answers to every one of the printed questions, and even then, she could not fit them on to the questions. As for discovering the moral, she was quite incapable; tho' to my great joy, I found that, after I had given her some of them in a sort of familiar way, she had repeated it all to one of her fellow-servants. But the most curious part remains to be told. Tho' she had had Scriptural instruction every day for 10 years, I found she was apparently quite ignorant of the Gospels. I therefore told her, without allowing her to look at the Testament or looking at it myself, the principal events and parables of our Saviour's Life, and especially of the last week of His Life, and she was evidently very much interested; but – she did not recognize one of them. I attribute this to her having been in a School where the Children only read verses in rotation, when of course they can only be thinking of their own verse, and not of the story; and where the master gives no *oral* Religious Instruction. But I am sure this would never be the case with your children.

3// Among all the country girls still in their teens, whom I have known or taught, and who had been probably for 8 years at elementary schools, I have never known one who knew, or wished to know, the names of trees or of flowers, or plants, not even of the commonest wildflowers [they might know a Rose] nor of the common birds when they saw them, nor of what made it possible for birds to fly, nor of any of those common things which they had been seeing every day of their lives. I am almost afraid of asking you whether your boys and girls know, (as well as the English names and ways and habits of common plants), English names and ways and habits of common birds – because the boys are only too ready to throw stones at birds, and to rob their nests. But do they know that bird's bones are hollow, and like lungs, and the way which enables them to fly?

Do you know any good book which teaches this? The Rev'd T. G. Woods' Readers were the best – but even these are not satisfactory, I think. I don't think they give a clear account of how the bird flies. Bishop Stanley did, but his book is not for children.

4// A niece-in-law of mine, the one who wrote that leaflet on the Elements of Botany I gave you, visited this year many of the best Board Schools in London for her own instruction. She thought them greatly improved from those of 10 years ago. But she found no teaching of History. She suggested to one excellent School Master the teaching of the History of *London*. Why not, she said, label the places which they pass every day with their genuine history – the place where the Great Fire of London began or stopped – that of the Great Plague ditto – the most picturesque incidents of the Tower of London – the execution of Lady Jane Grey – and so on – and so on – the familiar history of London.

5// She was very much pleased with the teaching by the School Mistresses – of Health – of the Value of Foods, e.g. of Milk to children – of Domestic Economy.

How does your teaching of Domestic Economy fare? I hope well: & that you are satisfied with the children. I hear on all hands of their great improvement – in discipline & progress.

And how goes the Girls' Needlework?

My kind regards to Mrs. Burton, who has also brought about such great improvement.

I thought it might be interesting to you to hear the above experiences.

I should be very glad to know how Selina Gregory does at the Mill. There are many temptations to girls there: whether she forgets her education. I hope not.

I should like to send her some little present, such as a book, if you would kindly tell me what.

And I should like some day to hear how my other children are doing at School.

I am very, very sorry that Mr. Wildgoose is moving to Matlock – even that small distance.

Your holiday to Cornwall was a success. I am so glad.

> God bless you
> sincerely yours & Mrs. Burton's

Florence Nightingale

Source: BUL N62: Box 1, Folder 9　　　　　　　　　　　　{partially dictated}

During the final years of her life Nightingale's major nursing battle was not against obtuse politicians and bureaucrats, but rather a new generation of zealous nursing leaders who wished to professionalize what she had defined as a vocation. She steadfastly opposed, as she always had, public examinations and state regist-ration of nurses.

160. To Angélique Pringle   10 South St 12 July 1889

Memorial (B.N.A.)[1]

Ever dearest 'Little Sister'

With regard to signing this Memorial, we think that, believing as we do that you not only see no objection to it, but that you share, and to a vivid degree, the conviction of the objections to the course of the B.N. Assoc'n, & of the mischief that course is doing to the steady quiet progress of Nurse-training & Nurse-life, it is highly important that you should sign. The blank the absence of your name would leave would be so serious that those who are taking the course we think so unhappy for Nurses would of course take advantage of it to represent you as being on their side.

It is not as if you or we had been forward to appear in the 'fray' – for fray it is. On the contrary we have, as you are aware, done everything we could to avoid it – perhaps more than we ought to have done, judging by the result – which is that, unhappily, party-spirit, which ought of all places to be banished from a Nurse's life is raging furiously.

The opposition to the B. N. A. Registration scheme has by no means originated with us. – & other considerable Hospitals & Training Schools are even more convinced of its evils than we are.

To take a public part in the matter as experience & judgment dictate has been *forced* upon St. Thomas' – do you not think so? & upon *you*:

We also think that Miss Crossland should sign, as being in charge, under you, of the daily instruction & 'home' of the Training School – that is, if you see no objection.

Sir Harry Verney has signed the Memorial, as Chairman, which I now return.

I think Mr. Bonham Carter's signature, which is in Sir Wm Bowman's possession, should be obtained, as his name has been prominent.

ever yours

F. Nightingale[2]

Source: GLRO HI/ST/NC1/89/8   {incomplete letter}

1. BNA: The British Nurses' Association, founded by Mrs Bedford Fenwick with the

aim of state registration of nurses after three years' training.

2. On envelope: The sheets enclosed dated July 12th, July 17th & Friday, are for the Council of the Nightingale Fund. One sheet marked Private I destroyed. A. L. P.

Nightingale had always depended upon Sir Douglas Galton to assist in her public and personal affairs, but in retirement he became more evasive.

161. To Sir Douglas Galton   {10 South St 3 Dec 1889}

Dear Sir Douglas

I must take your leavings, as beggars must not be choosers.

Yes, please, your dog will see you to morrow (Wed'y) on your way from Euston for as long as you can stop – but *also* on Thursday at one.

Will you consider the points of, if Cornish is to do the Indian, who is to do the Home business – & other points for that interview?

Your dog

F.N.

Source: BL Add 45766: f 305

162. To Sir Douglas Galton   {10 South St 16 Dec 1889}

Dear Sir Douglas,

I am an egg full of meat, and you might have come and cracked me if you had made an appointment. Other people rejoice that their correspondence is compromising. Therefore, I can only tell you by word of mouth what you would know. Shall you be in London this week?

As for revising my Article for Dr. Quain,[1] before Xmas, the type is so diabolical, the mornings are so dark, and my eyes are so bad, that if he must have it before Xmas, I think I must return it to him as it is. But if he chooses to let me have a little time before Xmas, and if so, how much? I will try to do it.

I think the only thing that wants adding is the remarkable development and improvement of District Nursing (instead of Almsgiving.) during the last 10 or 12 years. But I don't know whether Dr. Quain wishes me to add to it or only to revise it. Could you kindly tell me.

And are you doing your article on Construction &c of Hospitals?

You said I was to send you something about the differences between these & Poor Law Infirmaries.

Sir Henry Yule[2] is dying.

ever more truly yours

F. Nightingale

Source: BL Add 45766: ff 306–07

1. Dr Richard Quain: (1816–98), editor, *Dictionary of Medicine* (1882), which sold 30,000 copies. The second edition finally appeared in 1894.

2. Sir Henry Yule: (1829–89), worked on the irrigation system in the Northwest Provinces in India. He served on the India Council 1875–89.

At seventy Nightingale's interest in various issues had not waned, though her extraordinary capacity for work had clearly declined.

163. To Unknown correspondent   4 July 1890

Please return this to F.N.

You ask *me* upon one of the most difficult subjects of the present day, namely: 'To the rule inexorable by which families where an unmarried daughter has had what they call a "misfortune" should be turned themselves (with her) out of their cottages?' *I* should rather ask of *you*. In these days the subject is so much more complicated. Besides, the sin is *not* in having an illegitimate baby, but in the sin which precedes it. And the new doctrine about the connection of the Sexes is now, I am told, so widespread among the lower classes, that it is quite an open secret. Thus, the great danger is that man & woman do learn how to commit the sin without the consequence. A public schoolmaster, of gentle boys, I mean, who has particularly studied the subject, & has succeeded in maintaining purity among his boys, to a degree, I believe that no other Public School does, though many do a great deal, has obtained the most varied information from ministers, Anglican & Dissenting & from Roman Catholic Priests, who

419

commonly know more about this than any other ministers, and he declares that this open secret is more and more extensively practised among the poor. (You probably know that quite respectable socialists have printed this – and, on one occasion, a very superior bookseller was prosecuted for publishing a book of this kind, and condemned.) This appears to me greatly to alter the whole question.

2. The danger of increasing child murder is so obvious, that it is scarcely necessary to mention it.

3. Again, it makes the case so different if the woman marries the man. We may charitably suppose that they intended to follow God's Law of one woman to one man, and it is quite different if a woman has had 2 or 3 children by different men. And it is so dangerous if a woman for her first offence is condemned to disgrace.

(In all institutions now, a difference is made between primiparae and women who have fallen 2 or 3 times. Indeed there are institutions, as I think so wisely, which take in only primiparae, and then help the woman to service and to maintain her child herself instead of sending it to the workhouse. Otherwise its usual fate. These women are generally recovered. One of our cousins is actually a prime mover in a division of one of our vast London Workhouses for this object.)

4. I need scarcely allude to the nonsense which is talked among the very poor, about the honour of being married at sixteen; which I know leads almost un-consciously on the young woman's part to sin with this purpose. But this is very different from the coarse brutish sensuality which leads men & women to behave like animals.

You know that very superior upper servants even, will talk this sort of jingo among themselves. 'I think it is time for Miss (mentioning one of their Mistresses friends) to "go off".' This means to be married, of course you know. All this sort of thing, like the publications of perfectly respectable socialists, leads to mischief, without the poor young thing knowing it is mischief. And now, when so many know that the mischief can be done without the consequences, this is a very serious consideration.

I am far from thinking that these considerations are final. I know how much may be said about maintaining a high standard of morality, by the Londoner in his villages; but I think, that considering the almost promiscuous mixing up of young men & women in the Cottage bedroom, & the London one room, this sin is almost inevitable, and I think the chief hope, which it will take 2 or 3 generations to fulfil, is in the better moral education which we may hope to see, and which will prevent fathers & mothers from

jesting openly before their young children on the most delicate &
sacred subjects in the rooms of the poor.

5. The man is not punished, & the more villainous the man, the
more he escapes.

Unsigned

Source: BL Add 45809: ff 248–51   {dictated}

After suffering for seven years from crippling arthritis, Parthe
died on Florence's birthday, 12 May 1890. The two sisters had
established the habit of seeing each other on Sundays; 4 May was
their last meeting. Following Parthe's death, Florence went to
Claydon for several months for Sir Harry relied heavily upon her.
Dr Sutherland, after a short retirement, died in 1891. Jowett, who
had been her counsellor for so long, died on 1 October 1893. In
February 1894, Sir Harry Verney died at the age of ninety-three.
Shore Nightingale, Aunt Mai's son who had become the heir to the
Nightingale property, died in August 1894. Two years later,
Embley was sold. Sir Robert Rawlinson, the only surviving
Sanitary Commissioner for the Crimean War, died in 1898. In 1899
Sir Douglas Galton died. Nightingale, who had expected to die
early, had outlived them all. She had for some time ceased talking
about her pending death, but she continued to complain about her
infirmities. All the people connected with her youth, with the
Crimea, and with sanitary reform were gone, but Nightingale was
not alone. Younger friends, family members and supporters had
been added through the years. Although their correspondence had
dropped off after Rachel Williams's marriage, Nightingale was
anxious not to lose touch.

164. To Rachel Williams Norris   6 July 1891

Dearest Mrs. Norris

I was so glad to see your handwriting & address. I have been
thinking & feeling, feeling & thinking with you – & longing to see
you again & hearing more from you.

I saw an old pupil of yours, 'Baroness von ? Rosen',[1] but she did
not know where you had moved to.

I was longing to know what your plans were – whether the
Riviera or Edinburgh – & how you were.

Besides this, I have a question to ask your kindness:

Gen'l Symonds, brother of the Capt. Symonds (who is dead) who gave me all that Cocoatina in 1885 for the Egyptian Military Hosp'ls wants me to give him a Certificate as to the usefulness & goodness of this Cocoatina (the manufacture of which – pure – is their family's subsistence).

I refer back to a letter of mine, dated April 23/85, telling Capt. Symonds, without of course giving your name, when you arrived from Souakim what you told me, viz. that to make the Cocoatina acceptable, it should be combined with *milk* & that the only Cocoa they (the men) liked was the cocoa & *milk* – supplied in small quantities by the N. A. Soc'y.

They the Symonds' have sent me however copy of a Telegram (without date) which I sent Capt. Symonds: 'Just heard from Egypt. Cocoatina highly appreciated – more greatly desired if sent at once'.

I am greatly puzzled what to do. I do not like to refuse these poor Symonds. Yet, if I give them a 'Testimonial', I shall be deluged with similar requests.

They want me to date my Testimonial from the date of the War – 1885.

Might I ask *what your impression is now* of your kindness of the *good* or *no-good* his (Capt. Symonds) Cocoatina did in that War? [I have given away in the last few years large quantities of Cocoatina to poor people in England. And it was uniformly liked.

They Savory & Moore make now at Verney Junction!! *peptonized* Cocoa *and Milk* which is excellent but expensive.]

I am interrupted, & I seem to have told you nothing, dear friend, of what I feel with you: nor thanked you for your excellent book. But let me say God bless you & believe me ever yours faithfully & sorrowfully

F. Nightingale

Source: GLRO HI/ST/NC3/SU 180/181

1. FN's question mark.

When Shore's daughter Rosalind became engaged to the journalist Vaughan Nash, Florence was unfeignedly delighted.

165. To Rosalind Smith   10 South St 8 Feb 1892

Dearest, very dearest,

My heart *is* full of you; but, immersed in very sour business, I find nothing to *say* worthy of your sweetness. I do give you joy for having found a man whom you can so thoroughly love & esteem & work with. And I, of course, give him joy at having found you. And I give us all joy.

But please look to the shillings. We cannot live on sweets. And we must live in order to work together. I know you think me very worldly. But, you see, unfortunately, we live in the world. It is a great bore.

But then you heroically set to mending the world. So I pray you to live.

This does not at all say what my heart is full of, dearest child. But I hope soon to hear from yourself what your heart is full of – that is, when your nursing of dear mother & father is finished. I am afraid both still want it. My love. And may I send a message to Mr. Nash?

God bless you both ever your loving

Aunt Florence

Source: BL Add 45795: f 179

166. To Margaret Verney {?}   20 April 1892

Yesterday was Parthe's birth-day; and I celebrate it by thinking of all you have done by bringing out the books during *his* lifetime, for which she was so anxious, for her.[1]

And I celebrated it too by having Rosalind Shore Smith before her unique, singular marriage with absolutely no *certain* provision. They were going to live in a cottage at the East Pole of London, separated from us by 5 millions of people, but not from the Easterns among whom they are going to labour.

They are called by respective relations
    the Naughties
    the Babes in the Wood
    the Early Christians
I have not told Sir Harry because if he were to write to the parents, recommending a house in Grosvenor St., he would send them stark staring mad, the one from indignation that it should be thought desirable – the other from regret that he is too poor to give it her.

Verily the world is full of the strangest & saddest contradictions.
But if you like to communicate this note to Sir Harry, please do.
ever your loving

Aunt Florence

Source: Wellcome

1. Before her death Parthe had edited, but not published, the first two volumes of
*Memoirs of the Verney Family during the Civil War, compiled from letters, and illustrated
by the portraits at Claydon House* (London: Longmans, 1892). Sir Harry's daughter-in-law,
Margaret Verney, edited volumes 3 and 4, which were published in 1899.

District nursing, with its focus upon prevention and sanitation,
had become one of Nightingale's prime interests. She helped to
underwrite the costs of a lecture series on 'Health at Home', given
by Dr De'ath in the towns near Claydon. She was, however, most
anxious that local women take up the cause after he had left.

167. To George H. De'ath, Esq., MD   10 South St
20 May 1892

My dear Sir
    Most heartily do I give you joy on the success of your 'Health at
Home' Education Mission – the enthusiastic attendance on your
Lectures of rural educated women from all over the County
allowed to attend for their own profit – your sifting & re-sifting till
you obtained a Class of 12, who appeared willing & able to become
instructresses or missioners of Health to the uneducated rural
women at their own homes – the object of the whole course being
the new one not simply to give Sanitary information but to teach
how to teach – the examination by an independent well-known
Sanitary authority – both in writing & by word of mouth (to test
their power of speaking to the uneducated) And six of them
passing the Exam'n with the utmost success three indeed above
what had been expected.
    the main object of the Exam'n being to see not only if their book
knowledge or theory were competent but if they could give in the
most *practical* & *plainest*, in the most lively & dramatic manner –
their knowledge to uneducated women in their own houses –
translate in fact the object-lessons they had received from your
skill & kindness in the worst houses of the worst villages – into the
cottage life with their own hands & tongue.

Your object was to teach practical work to the class – just as we teach practical Ward work at the bed side to the Nurse Probationers in Hospital – the object-lesson of the former being the Ward & the Patient – the object-lesson of the latter being the Cottager's home & its inmates – the rural domestic life.

Just as the District Nurse goes into the cottage to nurse & to teach the Patient by the family with her own head & hands – so would the Health Nurse (Missioner) teach what to do in the cottage for health with her own head & hands.

It remains to be seen how it is to be worked out – say a meeting in a willing cottage – visits to each cottage – and when she is in touch with the cottager's wife, sent for by the wife–mother herself.

Of course it will take a *long* time before prejudice & ignorance are overcome.

> ever yours sincerely
>
> Florence Nightingale

Source: Wellcome   {original letter}

In 1889 the British Nurses' Association decided to apply for a Charter in order to enable the nurses listed therein to claim to be 'registered'. Nightingale, as head of the anti-registrationists, was furious when the Privy Council granted the Charter in 1892, even though the names entered were narrowly defined as for 'the maintenance of a list of persons who may have applied to have their names entered therein as nurses . . .' (Cook, II, 364). Nightingale continued to insist that the best form of registration was the lists each nursing school kept – with up-to-date evaluations – of its students.

168. To Sir Henry Acland, MD   10 South St 18 Jan 1893

Dear Sir Henry Acland

Yes, please, on Monday. Will 5–15 suit you?

Are the Certificates which you are kindly going to present to Nurses at St. George's in the East?

Of course everything in 'what is to be said' at a particular place depends on what the *training* is, what the *length of service*, what &c &c certified.

[Certificates are given after 6 months service at Hospitals of the

Metropol: Asylums Board where there is no pretence at training!!!]

Now for the larger question

– the essential question – more essential 'now' than ever – viz. the character, the moral discipline of the Nurse as a woman. It is not technical training only which makes a woman into a Nurse.

And 2. what is the moral & technical discipline which she will receive when armed with her certificate, of which the public does not know the value, she leaves her Inf'y or Hosp'l.

We are glad to think that the Med'l Profession are in some degree awakening to this.

Is there to be nothing between the 'Profession' that is, the Army & the individual?

People would think this disastrous, ridiculous in the Army. *There* there is the company, the Regiment, the Corps, the 'Tommy Atkins' &c &c &c. No one thinks that the soldier is *vouched for* by belonging to the Army, the 'Profession'. It is 1000 times more necessary where the Private Nurse after she has left her Hosp'l, but is still in her 'Profession', becomes an 'irresponsible' normal [People little know what the conversation of these Nurses is]

But the Med'l Profession is beginning to know. 'Take a Nurse who has been 6 months away from her School or Hosp'l? No thank you, she has deteriorated from her Certificate,' said one the other day.

One Hospital Sister is as unlike another, tho' with the same 'qualifications', as can be. The tone of the one influences our Students to all that is right – of the other to much that is wrong or *not at all* says another.

I could multiply these instances ad inf.

As you ask me, I venture to think that the one thing to call Nurses' attention to 'now' is

1. the need of what no Cert'e can certify, no Exam'n can touch *and* 2. the necessity of attaching herself to some Home with motherly & trained supervision, so that she *may* have some 'esprit de corps' to guide & support her. This applies of course to Private Nurses especially.

We venture to think that there is little real analogy between the Medical (or 'Pharmacy') Profession & the 'Nursing Profession'.

We venture to think that Nursing in the Social (or 'State') sense is not a Profession at all, but a calling, as you are aware.

A Physician of the Hosp'l which has put itself most forward about 'Registration' & 'Profession' expressed his opinion forcibly when he said that it could end in nothing but an 'inferior class of Med'l Practitioners' especially in the country.

As to '*India*' to turn a *class* of Nurses up-country without other supervision but the Doctor's takes one's breath away. [In one branch of this matter the consequences already have been disastrous.]

Lastly, how much has been purely 'doctrinaire' in all these Registration & Certificate advocacies. The advocates have not themselves believed in it.

Your kindness to Sir Harry & the younger Harry is beyond thanks.

Unsigned

Source: BL Add 45786: ff 114–17

Nightingale was dismayed to find, after years of trying to encourage more ladies to become nurses, that the occupation had become fashionable. She wrote to the Matron of the Edinburgh Royal Infirmary:

169. To Frances Elizabeth Spencer[1]

10 South St
16 Aug 1893

My dear friend – dearest Miss Spencer

It is such a joy to me to hear from you, & to hear of your Nurses & your work – & that you are 'well' & 'strong' tho' I don't quite believe your account of yourself, except about the 'work'. I hope you don't do *too* much.

I know your difficulties – & yet it always seems to me as if Edinburgh R.I. were a bit of Jacob's ladder

'let down from heaven to earth'

Thanks be to God.

Thank you very much for your two beautiful photographs – beautiful as to Wards, beautiful as to execution. I should like to know the name of the good Head Nurse of Ward 25.

Every good Matron & Lady Sup't of experience of years makes but too truly I am afraid the same complaint about the difficulty of getting the right people for training. We find that few or none have any life purpose & many are not purpose-like at all. And there are many more changes from want of vigour of body or mind to endure more than a few weeks or months. There is a want of *staying* power even among *young Matrons*. There is *fashion* now in

Nursing. We have fallen now I will not say upon evil times but upon *modern* times. And these while taken into account – not ignored – must be steadily neutralized as it were. The *modern* tendencies seem to be to let out Nurses like Plumbers – for so many hours a day to the Wards – Sisters or Head Nurses included – & then to let them live for the remaining hours quite apart from the Hospital – wanting the motherly element altogether – essential to a Nurse who is not a Plumber – but has the care of soul & body in her Patients, & in her Assistant Nurses to certify them as Plumbers.

2 to substitute the literary Nurse for the practical Nurse who is to be raised by the moral side quite as much as by the technical side – to have a spirit put into her quite as much as a hand.

E.g. I was aghast – & I am sure you & yours were with your unfailing good sense at the Glasgow R.I. plan – 1st putting the candidates to live in lodgings, as I understand, in the City at the very beginning of things when the moral discipline of a 'Home' is most wanted.

then giving lectures *first* & *last*, practice – which is putting the cart before the horse – or teaching Greek before English.[2]

But I am quite as sensible as you are to the truth that we crowd too much into the 1st year's probation – & we are trying to think how we can obviate this – & further to give more advanced lectures & classes in the 2nd year. & the 3rd

And I should be truly grateful to you if you would be so very kind as to let me have your 'plan' *when* you *can* for 'relieving the Prob'rs of so much study during the first 6 months of their training' – which is the time when they ought to be as free as possible body & mind for the practical Ward work.

Strictly Private

I hope that you find help & not hindrance in your Med'l Sup't – I *do* hope.

I am so glad that Miss Canning answers so well in the 'Home'.

Private

As you ask, may it not be I think that a good deal of what we have to deplore in the Modern Tendency is due to the R.B.N.A. & the Pr.[3]

Nursing has become a fashion, an amusement, a talk, or a literature – a dress.

E.g. at the recent Oxford meeting with the Pr. as President, some ladies were quite shocked at the Nurses – noisy untidy, exclaiming 'worth while to belong to the R.B.N.A. for the pretty badge' – & this tone pervading everything. There was not one, they

said, like a Nurse of the (not modern) Schools. This is grievous –
the public will take them for the crème de la crème – & they are not
even the skim milk.

But it is a supreme impertinence to be anxious even about the
truth, as if God could not take care of that.

Unsigned

Source: BL Add 47751: ff 106–09

1. Frances Elizabeth Spencer: Replaced Pringle as Lady Superintendent of Nurses at the Edinburgh Royal Infirmary in 1887; retired in 1907.
2. Mrs Rebecca Strong, matron of the Glasgow Royal Infirmary, started the first preliminary training course in 1893. Before entering the hospital, students took classes for three months; they had to find their own rooms and lodging.
3. The British Nurses' Association had been granted a Royal Charter on 6 June 1893; Princess Christian Helena, third daughter of Queen Victoria, had earlier agreed to be their president.

Nightingale had always turned to authorities whose expertise
she respected when she received a request for advice that she felt
she could not answer. After the death of all her experts, she asked
her favourite nieces and nephews.

170. To Rosalind Smith Nash   10 South St 12 Jan 1893

Dearest Rosalind

I am requested to take the learned Counsel's opinion on the
following:

The Women's Trades Unions have held a meeting & are going to
send a Deputation to Mr. Asquith *on Jan 24* to request *Women*
Inspectors for the Sanitary arrangements for Women in
Workshops & Factories. Frederick Verney accompanies the
Deputation.

Mr. Asquith is supposed to be favourable 'if they will be
reasonable'.

The question I am to ask the two learned Counsels
    Mrs Nash
    & Mrs. Rosalind
is:

how do you recommend the women Inspectors to be selected?

What do you propose instead of examination? i. e. how get over
the difficulties of examination? What should be the substitute?

how you would select & how dismiss?

Ought these Women Inspectors to work under Men Officials?
If so in what position they should be?
and whether they could work in factories or workshops where
both men & women are employed?
[N. B. I come in as the 'Devil's Advocate'. I fear the Women
Trades' Unions are much too much inclined to ask for all the
Women Inspectors to be factory workers –
& entirely to overlook various dangers, one of which in that
such women would be open to pressure – not to say corruption –
and where are you to find the educated Sanitarian among them,
when you cannot find her even among Lady Doctors?]

ever yours

F. Nightingale

Source: BL Add 45795: ff 187–88

Rosalind remained a favourite until Nightingale's death, and
numerous letters testify to a tenderness that she had been unable to
express in earlier years. The birth of Rosalind and Vaughan Nash's
first son was a source of infinite pleasure.

171. To Rosalind Smith Nash   10 South St 14 June 1895

Dearest Rosalind
    How are you? I am afraid you were very tired yesterday. And I
tired you – especially by my crusade about milk for the poor
people – about the extraordinary superstitions as to food of poor
mothers.
    But I don't think you need apply these to the Prince-let. Just do
what the doctor at Hampstead whom you like says – & take Sam
who will be seeing the Prince-let into your counsels. I have great
faith in Sam.
    As to the facts we were talking of about the harm to the infants
of their mothers' dieting, just see the difference between their
cooking & yours – between the meat they get & yours – & see how
little it applies to the Prince-let. The frying pan is the only cooking
they know. Or they do every thing in one saucepan. Or the
children drink out of the kettle. But I will not go on for fear Mr.
Vaughan should call our poor 'pigs'.
    A Derbyshire working man once said to me: 'We live on

beefsteaks & mutton-chops' (they eat or used to eat much more meat than we do) 'not because we like it nor because we don't know that it's extravagant, but because our wives don't know how to do anything else.'

Now the Prince-let is an exceedingly sensible young man. And in his name I say: 'the moral of all this & a great deal more is: don't be so uneasy about me'.

[They used to say of Sam at St. Bartholomew's: that he was the only man or woman who knew how to wash a baby.

I have great faith in the scoundrel of my heart, Sam, tho' he *will* say (all at once) something to the effect that the world is made to be ill & had much better die off at once. But you – get him to Hampstead, don't be at him, but use him.

God bless you both & the Prince-let.

ever your loving

Aunt Florence

I will send Hodgkin tomorrow with many thanks

Source: BL Add 45795: ff 215–16

When Mrs Charles Roundell asked Nightingale to check her address to workhouse nurses on the life of Agnes Jones, she responded warmly, perhaps because she sensed that the values Jones represented – and Nightingale had celebrated in her nursing addresses year after year – were out of fashion. She drafted two separate letters to Mrs Roundell.

172. To Julia Ann Elizabeth Roundell[1]

South St
4 Aug 1896

Agnes Jones   *Mrs Roundell*

This is a delightful account of dear Agnes Jones, & carries me back to the days when I used to say to myself: (in '68): How could I ever be unhappy while *she* lived? [P. 18 is especially admirable]

But there is a whole side of Agnes Jones' character which is not touched on here: & which it is very important for Workh. Inf'y Nurses to understand.

She felt it a *privilege, not a sacrifice* – to attend the sick. Every Nurse must do so. Or she is not worth her salt.

You don't know how to be nursing the Patients is all in all. the 'Wine of the entertainment', as the best Nurse we ever had said to me.

I pity the people who have all the organization, all the writing, all the speaking to do, but who never see the Patients – they do so much for Agnes' life was not gloomy.

2. It is a great truth that we love those we make happy, whether loveable or not

3. So much more can be done for the Workh. Inf'y than for Hospital Patients, who change so fast, & where there is such a continual drive.

The Workh. Patients are like those who were brought in to the King's supper from the 'highways' & hedges – especially the children. They are not at all impervious to 'Good Words' – many an one has said: 'it is the first Good Word we have ever heard'. And a child was heard praying behind its crib when it had to leave the Infirmary that it might not forget the 'good words'.

But remember it must be the best of good nursing – & ever better & better than best – that opens the way to the 'good word'.

One year's training is only enough to show one how to train oneself. It takes 5 years to make a Ward Nurse. How I wish I had time to tell the facts I know about the 'highways' & hedges responding. One woman, left a widow at 23, with a family of step-children to bring them up did bring them up & at 40 had to go into the W.I. from consumption & said it was 'like heaven'.

4. I cannot depreciate Workh: Nursing, nor training. There is so much to be done for Workh: Patients. Nurses always dread the Infirm Wards, where the old Patients have to be 'changed' 5 or 6 times in a night. But a good & clever Nurse will, after nursing them like children, treat them like reasonable beings.

'Ah you were an orange woman – weren't you? How much did you charge for an orange? A penny? And perhaps you *gave* the penniless boy an orange. Bad for trade – but very good for the penniless boys'. And the old woman is so delighted. She says 'O you know all about me'. And 'perhaps', she thinks, 'it is all known to the Queen'.

Treat them like your fellow-creatures, however tiresome they are. Or rather each of us wishes to know, 'the love of Christ to me'. – treat them like those to whom comes the love of Christ.

While you are in it, look at it as your life's work. That is what Agnes Jones did.

One of our very best Nurses said to me once: while you have a Ward, it must be your *home* – & the inmates your children. Don't be like water turned on from a cock – & turned off again.

Returning to the old women: one of our Nurses, now a Matron, said: 'They *must* be those *tiresome old women* or those *dear old things* to you'.

432

Now that is real philosophy & real Christianity.
She is now promoted to an important post.

Unsigned

Source: BL Add 45813: ff 215–18

1. Julia Ann Elizabeth Roundell: author of *Cowdray: the History of a Great English House* (1884) and similar books, as well as *Agnes Jones; or She Hath Done What She Could* (London: Bickers & Sons, 1896). A portion of an address FN had given to workhouse nurses is reprinted as a supplement.

173. To Julia Ann Elizabeth Roundell   4 Aug 1896

Private

Dear Madam

You cannot think what pleasure your 'Letter to "the W. I. Nurses"' about the dear heroic Saint, Agnes Jones, gave me. I only want every side of her many-sided character to be understood

1. her intense pleasure in Nursing. She, like many others, wanted the worst, not the best Hospital to be given up to her.

2. *Kaiserswerth* The Nursing was nil. The Hygiene horrible. But the tone was excellent admirable. And Pastor Fliedner's addresses to the Pupil *School Mistresses* the very best I ever heard. And the Penitentiary outdoor work & Vegetable gardening under a very capable Sister excellently adapted to the case. And Pastor Fliedner's solemn & reverential teaching to us of the sad secrets of Hospital life what I had never heard given in England. But the Hospital was certainly the worst part of Kaiserswerth Institution.

3. What I am going to say would not be worth saying if it did not bear on the question of training, p. 13.

I took all the training that was to be had – there was none to be had in *England*. So far from Kaiserswerth having trained me, after having seen some of the best Hospitals on the Continent, I went to Paris, saw the Augustinian Sisters there, who were not so good as the best trained English Nurses are now but like Saints to savages then. I lived in a Miséricorde, (there was one to every Municipality in Paris then). The Miséricorde under the Soeurs de S. Vincent de Paul, did all the 'petite chiourgie'[1] of outdoor Patients, like our District Nurses, but more than they – & all the dispensing. They were, besides, the Relieving Officers – & *we* have nothing like it – they and they alone *knew* the poor –

they distributed all the 'bons' of the Municipality for meat, firing &c –

they were also allowed to distribute private charity – for the French only understand or understood then the combination of public & private charity –

they had besides boarding schools for poor adult girls – into which I will not enter now.

After that, I became Matron of a small Hospital in London, where I remained till summoned to Scutari in the Crimean War.

I have 'retired' into work ever since.

All this is of no consequence except for the purpose indicated.

There was no training. Therefore it pleased God thus to establish training in England.

4. It is a pity that so much of Agnes Jones' depression written under physical exhaustion & at night – so little of her divine unconquerable courage should have been preserved.

More than I have lamented the publication of the 'Memorials' They give no real picture of her.

5. It is a pity she had so much of *stores* to do. But she would never accept an Assistant.

6. The cause of Her death seems to us a deplorable mistake. But God made her an example.

But the most deplorable mistake was: the trying to make paupers into Nurses by Mr R² & her. The failure of this was what depressed her, when it might have been foreseen from the beginning.

You who have done & are doing so much: don't depreciate Workhouse Inf'y Nursing nor training.

7. Her ever increasing deafness made her superintendence not a *dead* letter but a *deaf* letter *latterly*.

8. It is perhaps but little known that in more than one London Poor Law Infirmaries long years after her death, there was throwing of tin cups & tin plates across the ward by the Patients at each other, each then giving the other in charge to the Police.

All this disappears when there are educated women as Matrons & Ward Nurses. All really trained women are educated women.

But another danger appears now: the Doctors say: 'those women know as many words as we do – but they don't know how to make a Patient comfortable'.

This was not a danger in the time of the dear Pioneer of Workho: Inf'y Nursing.

Agnes Jones

To the Nurses

It is a noble calling, the calling of Nurses but it depends on you Nurses to make it noble.

F. N.

Source: BL Add 45813: ff 219–24

1. petite chiourgie {*sic*}: small surgery or medical office.
2. Mr. R.: FN crossed out the full name: Rathbone.

The deaths of young probationers affected Nightingale profoundly. Her notes on Nurse Harvey reflect both her lifelong habit of recording medical details and her deep compassion for the sufferings of someone who had dedicated her life to helping others become well.

174. To Henry Bonham Carter {?}   20 Nov 1896

Notes on *Nurse Harvey's death from Scarlet Fever*
Confidential

Florence Ward Male Medical
Nurse Harvey had seemed run down for some two months before. While Sister Florence was away on her holiday, Sister/She had instructed the Nurse who supplied her place to let Harvey who was one of the 3 Prob'rs sit down whenever one was to sit down.

Cold with severe sore throat – possibly *beginning of Scarlet* Probationers take one side one week & next week the other of the Ward. For the week previous to her being taken ill she was on Dr. Theodora Acland's side. *Night & morning she had to wash a boy with Carbolic & water – his back & everything. That boy had Scarlet Fever, Sore Throat –* rash (not then come out). *Here* lies the whole story.

On Saturday evening she was sent down to Home Sister with head ache. She got up on Sunday as usual & was put into a room with a fire. But *no Doctor was sent for till Monday* when Dr. Sharkey was summoned; & said at once that it was a very 'slight' case of Scarlet Fever – & ordered her into Block 8 – but by some mistake a room could not be prepared for her or she carried in till the evening. After that the case made but too rapid progress towards death – and on the Friday she died.

435

During these days her throat was in the 'most frightful' state. She had the utmost difficulty in swallowing, ending in not being able to swallow at all. Every means was tried, but in vain.

As for the Ice baths, she implored that they should not be continued – but till the case became utterly hopeless, they were thought necessary.

As long as she could speak at all, she kept saying: 'Do you think Matron will let me go to my work tomorrow?' She was the best of Probationers – quiet, thoughtful, most kind to the Patients, most forgetful of Self – receiving every new piece of instruction such as sub-cutaneous Injections, as if it was a 'handsome present'.

She was at her work in *Florence Ward* Male Medical on one Saturday – and on the next Saturday she was in her coffin.
[A boy who came in from the country (with some lameness) after Nurse Harvey's death, contracted Scarlet Fever *in the Ward*, was sent to Block 8, but was allowed to die undisturbed, as the Ice baths had been such a useless aggravation of Nurse Harvey's sufferings.

Nurse Harvey had discharge of pus from nose & ears – haemorrhage under the skin, blood poisoning. She was purple from head to foot when she died. She had suppression of urine. She was ordered Brandy Champagne, & something of meat Juice, but after some very short time (2 days) it was found impossible to get them down.

Dr. Toller said he had never seen such a case. In fact she was dying before they hardly knew she was in danger (4 days).

The Probationers are exceedingly shocked & distressed at her death. *Note* F.N. is not discussing the Medical treatment at all. That is not her business. The *whole kernal of the case lies in p. 2*.

as p. 2 & p. 6

After two such as p. 2 & p. 6 frightful cases, might it have been a question whether *the Ward* should not have been *purified*?

F.N. has not mooted this.

Unsigned

Source: BL Add 47727: ff 243–45

For the celebration of Queen Victoria's Diamond Jubilee in 1897 a display devoted to nursing, with relics of the Crimean War, was planned. Nightingale, who had always shunned publicity, wanted the organizers to publicize the achievements of Herbert's Royal Commissions. Only after Lady Wantage appealed to her personally did she concede and donate personal mementoes.

175. To Edmund Verney   10 South St 10 Mar 1897

My dear Edmund

Thank you for your kind letter. You know how delighted I am
at your success in getting the Claydons under the Public Libraries
Act. I wish *we* could get out 3 *Private* Libraries at Lea Hurst under
the Public Libraries Act. But it is said that the small rate-payers, of
whom there is a large body there, are unwilling – & we have no one
to canvass them properly. However, I hope we shall come to it at
last.

Bust given me by the soldiers

I About the *bust* of me by Steeli of Edinburgh, which is the one,
I believe, at Claydon: it is after this wise:

it was given me by the soldiers after the Crimean War; and I sate
for it –

it is left in my Will back to the soldiers, if it were not given back
to them during my life – and enquiries have already been made
where soldiers would like it best to be, whether at Aldershot, or
where.

I do not know who told Lady Wantage of this bust – it was not I
– tho' she had previously written to me on behalf of Lady George
Hamilton. When she, Lady Wantage, came to me, she knew about
it. And it was impossible for me to decline *lending* it to them for
the Earl's Court Exhibition. [I have such a respect for Lady
Wantage. She sometimes just reminds me a little of Margaret] So I
did promise it her.

: You perhaps know that I had previously refused all
solicitations to give them 'relics' of 'me & the Crimean War', on
the ground that the real 'relics' were:

1. *Sidney Herbert's* R. Commission & 4 Sub-Commissions
which laid the imperishable seed of the great improvements in the
soldier's daily life – direct & indirect

2. the *training* of *Nurses* both in character & technical skill &
knowledge. The untrained Nurses sent out to the Crimean War
were – well, it is unspeakable what they were

3. the *Hygiene* & *Sanitation* the want of which in the Military &
Medical authorities caused Lord Raglan's death & that of
thousands of our men from disease.

That frightful lesson really, thanks to Dr. Sutherland, Sir
Douglas Galton, Sir Robert Rawlinson & others, began &
continued the enormous strides which have since been made in
(Civil & Military) science of Life & Death.

Excuse this long story. I only wanted to be assured that the

437

bust of me at Claydon was the original one which the soldiers started.

III *Revision of Old & New Testaments* – I like to hear of it. It has always seemed that some of the alterations in the *New* are unpardonable e.g. in the Lord's Prayer 'But deliver us from *evil*' is (or was) altered to the '*evil one*'. We always want to shift everything on to the Devil. That was a wise child who said to his little sister: 'The Devil wasn't thinking of you'.

Also: in St. Paul's Conversion: they have omitted those memorable words, which have saved so many.

'Lord, what wilt Thou have me to do?' how short the prayers in the N.T. are: how heart felt.

Excuse again this long story. I did not have your letter till late last night, because I had a lady with me, & the servants were all at 'Aladdin'. But I hope this letter will be in time.

A good journey to you & blessed Marg't. I am so glad she is 'well' – & love to all.

yours sincerely

F. Nightingale

Source: Wellcome

By the turn of the century Nightingale could read and write only with great difficulty. A companion was employed in 1902. She received visitors for a few years more, but was coached beforehand to recall the relevant facts. Her sight, memory and intellectual capacities failed her during the last decade of her life. She was given the Order of Merit by King Edward in 1907, the first woman to receive such an honour; on 16 March 1908 she was granted the Freedom of the City of London, the second woman to receive this award. But she probably understood the significance of neither honour. Nightingale was now recognized worldwide for her pioneering work in public sanitation. Honours and good wishes poured in from around the world on her ninetieth birthday, three months before her death.

The final curtain sank on 13 August 1910 when Nightingale fell into a sleep from which she did not waken. She had made and remade her will numerous times, but finally she decided to leave her monumental collection of letters and papers to her heirs to dispose of as they saw fit. To the end she tried to avoid publicity. Only two bearers were to accompany her coffin to the family grave at East Wellow. Instead, sergeants from several regiments of the

Guards carried her coffin, and the churchyard was filled with a large crowd of people paying homage to this woman who had broken the code of upper-class Victorian womanhood to do service to humankind. But the inscription on the memorial followed Nightingale's directions; a small cross bore only the words 'F.N. Born 1820. Died 1910'.

Abbreviated Family Trees of Florence Nightingale's Parents

William Smith (1756–1835) m. Frances Coape (1759–1840):

- Martha Frances (1782–1870) (Aunt Patty)

- Benjamin (1783–1860) common-law m. Anne Longden
  - Barbara Bodichon

- Anne (1785–1854) m. George Nicholson (1787–1852)
  - Marianne m. Douglas Galton
  - George Henry (d. 1851)
  - Lothian (1827–93)
  - Laura (Lolli) m. Jack Bonham Carter

- Frances (1788–1880) m. William Edward Nightingale
  - Parthenope (1819–90) m. Sir Harry Verney
  - Florence (1820–1910)

- William Adams (1789–1870)

- Joanna Marie (1791–1884) m. John Bonham Carter (1788–1838)
  - Jack (1817–84) m. Laura Nicholson/Hon. Mary Baring
  - Joanna Hilary (1821–65)
  - Frances Marie (Fan-Fan)
  - Henry (1827–1921) m. Sibella Norman (11 sons/1 dau)

- Samuel (1794–1880) m. Mary Shore (Aunt Mai) (1798–1889)
  - See below for children

- Octavius (1796–1871) (Uncle Oc) m. Jane Cooke

- Frederick (1798–1882) m. Mary Yates

- Julia (1799–1883) (Aunt Ju)

George Evans of Cromford m. Anne Nightingale:

- Mary (d. 1853) m. William Shore (1752–1822)
  - William Edward Shore Nightingale (1794–1874) m. Frances Smith
  - Mary Shore m. Samuel Smith
    - Blanche (d. 1904) m. A. H. Clough
    - William Shore (1834–94) m. Louisa Hutchins (2 sons, 2 daus inc. Rosalind
    - Bertha
    - Beatrice

- Elizabeth (Aunt Evans)

Chronology of Florence Nightingale's Life

12 May 1820	Born Florence, Italy.
Sept 1837–Apr 1839	Extended European tour; Nightingales meet Mary Clarke.
1847–48	Travels with Bracebridges to Italy. Meets Herberts, Mary Stanley, the Rev. Henry Manning.
1849–50	Travels to Egypt, Greece, Germany with Bracebridges. Two weeks at Kaiserswerth.
July–Sept 1851	Trains at Kaiserswerth while Parthe and Fanny visit Carlsbad spa.
1852	Begins *Suggestions for Thought,* a religious treatise. Studies government reports.
1853	Visits hospitals in Paris.
Aug 1853–Oct 1854	Superintendent of Harley Street Hospital for Gentlewomen.
Oct 1854–July 1856	Superintendent of Nurses of the English Hospitals in the East during the Crimean War.
Aug 1856–May 1857	Works behind the scenes for a Royal Commission on the Health of the Army.
1857	Testifies before Royal Commission; helps Sidney Herbert write Commission report.
Mar 1858	Selects committee to oversee the Nightingale Fund.
1858	*Notes on Matters Affecting the Health, Efficiency, and Hospital Administration of the British Army*
1859	*Notes on Hospitals*
31 May 1859	Royal Commission on the Sanitary State of the Army in India begins work.
24 June 1860	Nightingale School of Nursing opens.
Summer 1860	Writes paper on the importance of hospital statistics; read for her at International Statistical Congress.
1860	*Notes on Nursing* *Suggestions for Thought* privately printed.
1861	Deaths of Dr Alexander, Sidney Herbert, Arthur Hugh Clough, Prince Albert.
1862	Publishes articles on Contagious Diseases Acts.

1863	*Observations on the Evidence Contained in the Stational Reports submitted to her by the Royal Commission on the Sanitary State of the Army in India* (Summary of Royal Commission Report). *How People May Live and Not Die in India.* First read at the National Association for the Promotion of Social Science Congress, October 1863.
1864–68	Works with War Office on Indian sanitary reform; with William Rathbone on workhouse nursing.
1867	*Suggestions on the Subject of Providing, Training, and Organizing Nurses for the Sick Poor in Workhouse Infirmaries*
Feb 1868	Death of Agnes Jones.
July–Oct 1868	Returns to Lea Hurst to care for Fanny; first visit home since 1858.
1870	Consulted by both sides in regard to military nurses during Franco-Prussian War.
1871	*Introductory Notes on Lying-in Institutions*
1874	Her father, W. E. N., dies.
1880	Her mother, Fanny, dies.
1887	Eyesight begins to fail.
1890	Her sister, Parthenope, Lady Verney, dies.
1894	Her brother-in-law, Sir Harry Verney, dies; Shore Smith, heir to Nightingale estate, dies.
1895	Memory begins to fail.
1907	Receives Order of Merit.
1908	Granted Freedom of the City of London.
13 Aug 1910	Dies in her sleep.

Glossary of Florence Nightingale's Major Correspondents

Henry Bonham Carter: (1827–1921), secretary of the Nightingale Fund (1861–99); continued on the Council until 1914. He received an honorarium of £50 per annum for his work, while continuing as full-time managing director of the Guardian Assurance Co.

Hilary Bonham Carter: (1821–65), first cousin and confidante to the young FN. Spent 1849–50 living with the Mohls in Paris studying art, but devoted herself to her family rather than her art. Spent 1860–62 with FN after Aunt Mai returned home.

Lady Charlotte Canning: (1817–61), in 1835 married Earl Canning, a distinguished Peelite who became the first Viceroy of India (1856–62). She shared with Elizabeth Herbert and Lady Laura Cranworth the interviewing and hiring of nurses sent to the Crimea.

Sir Edwin Chadwick: (1800–90), sanitary reformer, head of the New Poor Law Commission (1834–46). Supported FN's lobbying for an Indian sanitary commission. They were firm allies against the germ theory of contagion.

Sir William Farr: (1803–83), pioneering statistician. Became Assistant Commissioner of census returns in 1851 and 1861; Commissioner in 1871. Worked closely with FN in the development of statistics on the causes of mortality.

Sir Douglas Galton: (1822–99), Captain in the Royal Engineers, member of the Royal Commission on the Sanitary Condition of the Barracks and Hospitals. Appointed Permanent Under-Secretary of State for War in 1862. Member of the barrack and hospital improvement sub-committee; served on the Army Sanitary Committee (1865). Transferred in 1869 to Director of Public Works until his retirement. Married Marianne Nicholson August 1851.

Sidney Herbert [Lord Herbert of Lea]: (1810–61), Secretary-at-War under Aberdeen. Honorary Secretary of the Nightingale Fund, Chair of the Royal Commission on the Health of the Army, the Indian Sanitary Commission, and of the four sub-commissions on army sanitary matters. Asked his friend FN to lead a group of nurses to serve officially in army hospitals in the Crimea. Died of Bright's disease. His wife, Elizabeth Herbert, converted to Roman Catholicism soon after.

Mary Jones: Superintendent of St John's House, which sent six sisters to the Crimea under FN. The Nightingale Fund supported a midwifery training course and ward under her supervision until she resigned from King's College Hospital, London. When her sole authority to hire and dismiss nurses was questioned, she left to form a religious order in Hastings to nurse long-term convalescent patients.

Benjamin Jowett: (1817–93), Regius Professor of Greek (1855) at Oxford University; Master of Balliol College (1870). Held tutorship at Balliol from 1842; was a major reforming force in the college and university. Served as Vice-Chancellor 1882–86. A diffident and poor conversationalist, except with very close friends, he felt more at ease as a correspondent. Met FN through Arthur Hugh Clough.

Sir John Lawrence: (1811–79), first went to India in 1847; distinguished himself in the Indian Mutiny and in various battles in the Northwest Provinces. During his term as Viceroy of India (1863–69) he encouraged military and municipal sanitation, irrigation and the building of railways. FN's favourite viceroy, despite the limited achievements of his term.

Henry, Cardinal Manning: (1808–92), a leader in the High Church movement until his conversion to Roman Catholicism in 1851. Archbishop (1865) and then Cardinal (1877) of Westminster. He was popular among the educated considering conversion, but felt his own mission was to expand parochial school education. Known as an authoritarian, ultramontane leader.

Harriet Martineau: (1802–76), journalist and popularizer of Benthamite political economy. A non-believer from a well-known Unitarian family. Her sister taught Hilary Bonham Carter. Supporter of wider employment for women and improved sanitation.

Sir John McNeill: (1795–1883), diplomat and doctor. In 1855 sent to the Crimea with Col. Alexander Tulloch to report on the management of the commissariat and its methods of keeping accounts and delays in distribution. All his children but one daughter (Margaret Ferooza) died in childhood. Second wife died 1868.

Julius Mohl: (1800–76), German who became a French citizen. Leading Orientalist of his day, who translated many oriental classics into a European language for the first time. President of the French Asiatic Society and the Académie des Inscriptions. Married Mary Clarke August 1847.

Mary Clarke Mohl: (1793–1883). After a peripatetic childhood and adolescence, 'Clarkey' settled in Paris on a small income and organized one of the most brilliant intellectual salons of the day.

Was especially close to Hilary Bonham Carter, the novelist Elizabeth Gaskell, and FN.

Rachel Williams Norris: (1840–1908), trained as a 'Free Special' at St Thomas' 1871–72. Served under Angélique Pringle at the Edinburgh Royal Infirmary until she became matron of St Mary's Hospital, London. Served in the Egyptian Campaign (1876), where she met and then married Daniel Norris. Called 'the Goddess' because of her height and imperious personality.

Angélique Pringle: (1846–1920), trained at St Thomas' Hospital in 1868. Appointed Lady Superintendent of Nurses at the Edinburgh Royal Infirmary (1873–87). Replaced Mrs Wardroper after her retirement at St Thomas' Hospital, but served only two years (1887–89) because of her conversion to Roman Catholicism. Called 'a pearl of great price' and 'little sister' by FN; she was FN's favourite, even after her resignation as matron.

Lord Ripon: George Frederick Robinson (1827–1909), held joint title of Lord de Grey after the death of his uncle in 1859. Under-Secretary for War under Sidney Herbert (1859), became Secretary for War in 1863 and Secretary for India in 1866. Served as a reforming Viceroy for India 1880–84. Became a Roman Catholic in 1874. A faithful supporter of FN's policies, he ensured that the army sanitary committee survived against the War Office bureaucrats.

Dr John Sutherland: (1808–91), had had a long career in public health when he was appointed chair of the commission sent to the Crimea to investigate the sanitary conditions of the English troops. Played an active part in the Royal Commission on the Health of the Army and again on the Royal Commission on the State of the Army in India. Served as the only paid member of the permanent Army Sanitary Commission until his retirement in 1888. FN's chief adviser and secretary.

Lord Derby: Edward Henry Stanley (1826–93), served under his father's Conservative Party leadership, but was always known for his liberal stand on civil liberties. Long interest in sanitary reform. Served primarily in the Foreign Office; resigned as Foreign Secretary over the Bulgarian affair.

Sir Harry Verney: (1801–94), had seven children by his first marriage, including his heir, Edmund Hope, whose wife, Margaret, was much admired by FN. Frederick William, a barrister, and Emily, who was interested in nursing, were FN's favourites. Emily died in 1872 of fever contracted in Malta. Sir Harry was active in promoting FN's health and sanitary measures both in his native county of Buckinghamshire and in Parliament. Married Parthenope Nightingale in 1858.

Selected Bibliography

Place of publication is London unless otherwise indicated

Works by Florence Nightingale

'Cassandra', in Strachey, Ray, *The Cause*. G. Bell & Sons, 1928. pp. 395–418

A Contribution to the Sanitary History of the British Army During the Late War With Russia. John W. Parker, 1859

Florence Nightingale's Indian Letters, ed. Priyaranjan Sen. Calcutta: Mihir Kumar Sen, 1937

Florence Nightingale to her Nurses: A Selection of Miss Nightingale's Addresses to Probationers and Nurses of the Nightingale School at St. Thomas' Hospital. Macmillan, 1914

How People May Live and Not Die in India. Emily Faithfull, 1863

'I have Done My Duty': Florence Nightingale in the Crimean War, 1854–56, ed. Sue M. Goldie. Manchester: Manchester University Press, 1987

Introductory Notes on Lying-in Institutions. Longmans, Green, 1871

The Institution of Kaiserswerth on the Rhine for the Practical Training of Deaconesses. Ragged Colonial Training School, 1851

Letters from Egypt: A Journey on the Nile, 1849–1850, selected and introduced by Anthony Sattin. Weidenfeld & Nicolson, 1987

Notes on Hospitals, 3rd edn. Longman, Green, Longman, Roberts & Green, 1863

Notes on Matters Affecting the Health, Efficiency, and Hospital Administration of the British Army, founded chiefly on Experience of the Last War. Harrison & Sons, 1858

Notes on Nursing: What It Is and What It is Not. Harrison, [1860]

Observations on the Evidence Contained in the Stational Reports Submitted to her by the Royal Commission on the Sanitary State of the Army in India. Edmund Stanford, 1863

'The People of India', *Nineteenth Century*, 4 (1878), 193–221

446

Selected Writings of Florence Nightingale, ed. Lucy Ridgely Seymer. New York: Macmillan, 1954

Suggestions for Thought to the Searchers After Truth Among the Artizans of England. 3 vols. Eyre & Spottiswoode, 1860 [privately printed]

Sugggestions for a System of Nursing for Hospitals in India. Eyre & Spottiswoode, 1865

Secondary Works

Anderson, Olive, *A Liberal State at War: The Crimea*. Macmillan, 1967

Abbott, Evelyn and Campbell, Lewis, *The Life and Letters of Benjamin Jowett, M. A. Master of Balliol College, Oxford*. 2 vols. John Murray, 1897

Baly, Monica, *Florence Nightingale and the Nursing Legacy*. Croom Helm, 1986

Bishop, W. J. and Goldie, Sue, comp. *A Bio-bibliography of Florence Nightingale*. Dawsons, 1962

Bonham Carter, Henry, *Suggestions for Improving the Management of the Nursing Departments in Large Hospitals*. Blades, East, Blades, 1862

Bonham Carter, Victor, *In a Liberal Tradition: A Social Biography*. Constable, 1960

Chorley, Catherine, *Arthur Hugh Clough: The Uncommitted Mind*. Oxford: Clarendon, 1962

Cook, Sir Edward, *The Life of Florence Nightingale*. 2 vols. Macmillan, 1913

Cope, Zachary, *Florence Nightingale and the Doctors*. Museum, 1958

Cope, Zachery, *Six Disciples of Florence Nightingale*. Pitman, 1961

[Davis, Elizabeth] *The Autobiography of Elizabeth Davis, A Balaclava Nurse*, ed. Jane Williams. 2 vols. Hurst & Blackett, 1857

Douglas, Sir George and Ramsey, Sir George, *The Panmure Papers*. 2 vols. Hodder & Stoughton, 1908

Ffrench, R.L.V. Blake, *The Crimean War*. Leo Cooper, 1971

Filder, Commissariat-General, *The Commissariat in the Crimea: being remarks on those parts of the Report of the Commission of Inquiry into the Supplies of the British Army in the Crimea which relate to the duties of the Commissariat*. W. Clowes, 1856

Garrett, Elizabeth, 'Hospital Nursing', *Transactions* of the

National Association for the Promotion of Social Science, X (1866) 472–78. Longmans, Green, Reader & Dyer, 1867

Garrett, Elizabeth, 'Voluntary Hospital Nursing', *Macmillan's* 15 (April 1867), 494–99

Goldie, Sue, *A Calendar of the Letters of Florence Nightingale*. Oxford: Oxford Microform, 1983

Greenleaf, W. H., 'Biography and the "Amateur" Historian: Mrs. Woodham-Smith's *Florence Nightingale*', *Victorian Studies*, 2 (1959), 190–202

Hall, Herbert Byng, *Sayah; or the Courier to the East*. Chapman & Hall, 1856

Hibbert, Christopher, *The Destruction of Lord Raglan: A Tragedy of the Crimean War, 1854–55*. Longmans, Green, 1961

Huxley, Elspeth, *Florence Nightingale*. Weidenfeld & Nicolson, 1975

Kinglake, A. W., *Invasion of the Crimea: Its Origin & An account of Its Progress Down to the Death of Lord Raglan*. 8 vols. Blackwood, 1863–67

Leslie, Sir J. R. Shane, *Henry Edward Manning: His Life and Labours*. Burns, Oates, 1921

Lesser, Margaret, *Clarkey: A Portrait in Letters of Mary Clarke Mohl (1793–1883)*. Oxford: University Press, 1984

[Macalister, Florence Stewart] *Memoir of the Right Hon. Sir John McNeill, G. C. B. and of his second wife, Elizabeth Wilson*. By their granddaughter. John Murray, 1910

Martineau, Harriet, *England and Her Soldiers*. Smith, Elder, 1859

Martineau, John, *The Life and Correspondence of Sir Bartle Frere*. 2 vols. John Murray, 1895

Mathur, L. P., *Lord Ripon's Administration in India, 1880–84*. New Delhi: S. Chand, 1972

Memorials of Agnes Elizabeth Jones. By her sisters. James Nisbet, n. d.

Mitra, S. M., *The Life and Letters of Sir John Hall*. 2 vols. Longmans, 1911

The Nightingale Fund, *Report of Proceedings at a Public Meeting held in London on Tuesday, November 29th 1855*. London: Office of the Nightingale Fund, 1855

O'Malley, I. B., *Florence Nightingale 1820–1856: A Study of Her Life Down to the End of the Crimean War*. Thornton Butterworth, 1931

O'Meara, Kathleen, *Madame Mohl: Her Salon and Friends*. Bentley, 1885

Osborne, Sidney Godolphin, *Scutari and Its Hospitals*. Dickinson, 1855

Parsons, Frederick, *The History of St. Thomas' Hospital*. 3 vols. Methuen, 1932

Pickering, George, *Creative Malady*. Allen & Unwin, 1974

Pincoffs, Peter, *Experiences of a Civilian in Eastern Hospitals*. Williams & Norgate, 1857

Quinn, Vincent and Prest, John, *Dear Miss Nightingale: A Selection of Benjamin Jowett's Letters to Florence Nightingale, 1860–1893*. Oxford: Clarendon, 1987

Rathbone, Eleanor, *William Rathbone: A Memoir*. Macmillan, 1908

Reid, Sir T. Wemyss, *The Life, Letters and Friendships of Richard Monckton Milnes, First Lord Houghton*. Cassell, 1890

Rich, Norman, *Why the Crimean War? A Cautionary Tale*. Hanover, NH: University of New England Press, 1985

Ridley, Jasper, *Lord Palmerston*. Macmillan, 1970

Saint John's House: A Brief Record of Sixty Years' Work, 1848–1908. St John's House, 1909

Rosenberg, Charles E., 'Florence Nightingale on Contagion: The Hospital as Moral Universe', in *Healing and History: Essays for George Rosen*, ed. Charles E. Rosenberg. New York: Science History Publications, 1979. pp. 116–36

Simpson, M. C. M., *Letters & Recollections of Julius & Mary Mohl*. Routledge & Kegan Paul, 1887

Smith, F. B., *Florence Nightingale: Reputation and Power*. Croom Helm, 1982

Stanmore, Lord, *Sidney Herbert, Lord Herbert of Lea*. 2 vols. John Murray, 1906

Strachey, Lytton, *Eminent Victorians*. Chatto & Windus, 1918

Summers, Anne, *Angels and Citizens: British Women as Military Nurses, 1854–1914*. Routledge & Kegan Paul, 1988

Summers, Anne, 'Pride and Prejudice: Ladies and Nurses in the Crimean War', *History Workshop*, 16 (Autumn 1983), 33–56

[Taylor, Fanny] *Eastern Hospitals and English Nurses*. By a Lady Volunteer. Hurst & Blackett, 1856

Thompson, John D. and Goldin, Grace, *The Hospital: A Social and Architectural History*. New Haven: Yale University Press, 1975

Tulloch, Alexander, *The Crimean Commission and the Chelsea Board*. Harrison, 1857

Woodham-Smith, Cecil, *Florence Nightingale*. Edinburgh: Constable, 1950

Official Parliamentary Publications

Report upon the State of the Hospitals of the British Army in the Crimea and Scutari. vol. XXXIII (1854–55)

Report of the Royal Commission into the Supplies of the British Army in the Crimea. vol. XX (1856) [McNeill and Tulloch Commission]

Report of the Commissioners Appointed to Enquire into the Regulations affecting the Sanitary Condition of the Army, the Organization of Military Hospitals, and the Treatment of the Sick and Wounded. vol. XVIII (1857–58)

Report of the Proceedings of the Sanitary Commissioners dispatched to the seat of war in the East, 1855–56. vol. IX (1857)

Report of the Royal Commission on the Sanitary State of the Army in India. vol. XIX (1863)

Index

Unsworth, Rev., 152

venereal disease, 4
ventilation, 195, 200
Verney, Edmund, *letter from FN on the Crimean War*, 437–8
Verney, Frederick, 390
Verney, Sir Harry (Parthe's husband), 7, 239, 253, 378; death of, 421; *letters from FN on: census form*, 313–14; *death of Sir John Lawrence*, 375–6; *deaths of FN's 'just men'*, 235; *Fanny*, 353–4; *franchise demonstration*, 392–4; *India Army Sanitary Commission*, 242–4; *Miss Pringle's conversion*, 412–13; *Parthe's illness*, 391; *vaccination*, 379–80; *women doctors*, 277–82
Verney, Lady Margaret, 390; *letter from FN on editing Parthe's books*, 423–4
Verney, Lady Parthenope see Nightingale, Parthenope
Verney, Sir Ralph, 11
Victoria, Queen, 19, 159, 160, 161, 232, 237, 301; commands FN to write a précis, 168; Diamond Jubilee, 436; gifts, 130; money for soldiers' comforts, 122
Villiers, Charles, 260, 261
Vivian, Sir R., 204
von Rosen, Baroness, 421

Walcheren, 170
Walford, Mrs, 124
Walker, Dr J. Pattison, 356; *letter from FN on climate and sanitation*, 266–8; *on sanitation in India*, 251–3
Wantage, Lady, 436, 437
War Department, 143, 165
War Office, 121, 136, 145, 146, 195, 217, 225, 241, 245, 256, 263–4, 302, 304; loses Sanitary Works [India] Report, 251
War Office Instructions, 99
Wardroper, Mrs, 7, 10, 206, 315, 317, 321, 323, 325, 326, 327, 330, 331, 332, 334, 335, 338, 349, 350, 356, 409; retires, 378
washing, 88, 115
water, 370; navigation, 370; supply, 193, 195; water supply in India, 400
Watson, Mrs, 240
Watson, Sir Thomas, 216
Weare, Miss, 113, 132

Wellcome Institute, 11
Wheatstone, Mrs, 140
Wheldon, Miss, 318
White, Arnold, 404
Whitehead, Mrs, 124
Whitfield, Mr, 85, 206, 330, 331, 332, 335–6, 338
Whyte, Miss Annie, *letters from FN on: training for Miss Formby*, 406; *thanking for training Miss Formby*, 407
Wilbraham, Col. Richard, 250, 297, 298
Wilkes, Mrs, 406, 407
Williams, Capt., 294
Williams, Charles James Blasius, 215
Williams, Mr, 265
Williams, Rachel, 340, 341, 346, 349, 395, 397, 421; appointed Superintendent of St Mary's, 367; *letters from FN on: advice to stay in Edinburgh*, 354–6; *Cocoatina*, 421–2; *Egyptian campaign*, 398; *holiday*, 342–3; *leaving for Egypt*, 396–7; *sending nurses to St Mary's*, 368; *training nurses*, 387–8; marriage of, 421; resigns from St Mary's, 396; sent to help Miss Pringle, 354
Wilson, Sir Thomas, 213
Wiseman, Cardinal Nicholas P.S., 147
Wollatt, Rev., 142
women, 210, 300–2; doctors, 276, 361–4; having no sympathy, 229–33; in official life, 163–4; Medical Colleges, 277; Missions, 258; rights, 166; suffrage, 287–9, 392; thoughts on, 30; trade unions, 429–30
Wood, Sir Charles, 251
Woodham–Smith, Cecil, 12
Woodward, Nurse, 165
Woolfrey, Miss, 410
Woolwich Hospital, 213
Workhouse Infirmaries, 4, 246–7, 257, 260, 270–74, 432
Wreford, Mr, Purveyor-General, 88, 101, 103
Wyse, Miss, 128

York Road Lying-in Hospital, 404
Yule, Sir Henry, 419

zemindar, 369, 371